This book is dedicated to the memory of Bill Speirs, former general secretary of the Scottish Trades Union Congress. Bill was a good friend and work colleague who died in 2009 after a long battle with illness. I attended many conferences at home and abroad with Bill and his company was always scintillating. It was during a conference of the Russian Federation of Trade Unions in Moscow in the late 1990s that the idea for this book came about. There were a number of overseas visitors with name badges indicating Scottish ancestry. I suggested to Bill it was about time someone wrote a history about the contribution the Scots made to trade unionism internationally. He thought this was an excellent idea and, true to form, suggested I write it.

Bill's exceptional ability made him one of the giants of his generation. He could have chosen a parliamentary career but his passion was the trade union movement and he worked tirelessly on behalf of Scottish workers. His contribution to the movement for a Scottish Parliament and his renowned internationalism made him particularly keen on this book -or Kelly's project, as he called it. I'm sorry it took me so long to complete it that he did not get a chance to read it, but dedicating it to his memory is, I hope, the next best thing.

Contents

Acknowledgements

I have many people to thank for assistance with this book. I am particularly indebted to Professor Steve Babson of Wayne State University, Detroit for the information about the United Auto Workers in Chapter 3. Likewise Prof David Frank's book entitled *J B McLachlan: a Biography* provided many of the details for Chapter 4. Dr John Shields, professor and associate Dean of the University of Sydney Business School offered me encouragement and supplied me with the database he is compiling of Australian labour movement activists. Dave and Bev Jones from Blossburg, Pennsylvannia gave me invaluable assistance with my research for Chapter 1, as well as photographs and memorabilia. Dave is a descendant of William B Wilson and both he and Bev created and maintain the website 'We're Blossburg Proud'. Dr James Quigel and Dr Paul Clark from Penn State University gave me their time, support and hospitality when I visited their university. Pat and John Webster from Auckland have given me lots of help searching for contacts, photos and information on New Zealand Scots. Sadly John has since passed away and I'm sorry I will be unable to discuss the completed book with him.

I was given valuable advice and encouragement from authors Stuart McHardy, Ian Scott and Professor Gregor Gall. For help with typing, filing and administration I would like to thank my former work colleagues at PCS, Mary Wilkie and Norma Webster, as well as Karen Doran of the Labour Party who transcribed some of my interviews. Grahame Smith and Ann Henderson at the Scottish Trades Union Congress helped with advice and contacts; my former colleague on the STUC General Council, Annie White, did an excellent job proof-reading the text.

I have received enormous assistance with photographs and there are a number of people I wish to mention. Ian Waugh designed the front cover and took my portrait photograph for the back. Christian Cassidy from Winnipeg, who writes a blog entitled 'This Day in Manitoba', volunteered to take and send me the photo of the R B Russell Vocational High School. Prof Ken Osbourne of the University of Manitoba and author of a school booklet on R B Russell, gave me some of the photos in Chapter 5. Betty Smith, International Publishers, New York gave me permission to use photos of John Williamson and Bill McKie. My neighbour Jim Malcolm tidied up one of the old photos using his photoshop skills.

There are a number of union officials who gave up their time to locate photos and I am grateful for the support of the following; Ghislaine

Prince, Canadian Labour Congress; Tim Chapman, AMWU, Sydney; Ann Digiuseppe, AMWU, Perth; Dan Murphy, CFMEU, Victoria Branch; Bob Burchell, Canada representative of the United Mine Workers of America; Victor Billet, Maritime Union of New Zealand; Ged O'Connell, Energy and Mining section of the EPMU, New Zealand; Julia London, New Zealand Council of Trade Unions; Aalya Ahmed, Canadian Union of Postal Workers. I am especially grateful to Peter Whitaker, a retired official of the Canadian Union Postal Workers and now their unofficial archivist.

Thanks also go to those working in libraries, museums and research foundations who have sent photos. Doug Massey, Douglas-Coldwell Foundation, Ottawa, Canada; Peter Murphy and Dennis Docherty from the Search Foundation, Australia; Paul Maunder, Blackball Museum of Working Class History, New Zealand; Tom Miller, Director, Cape Breton Museum, Nova Scotia; Anne Marie McNeil, archival researcher, Beaton Institute, Cape Breton University; Elizabeth Clements, archivist Reuther Library, Wayne State University; Barry Kernfeld, archivist Penn State University.

Lastly, the book would not have been possible without the loving support of Jane Lindsay and my children Kirsty, Roisin, Liam and Niamh. Thank you all.

Pat Kelly
Edinburgh
August 2011

Foreword

I recently attended an event in Glasgow at which the former Republican Mayor of New York, Rudy Giuliani, thanked Scotland for 'gifting' capitalism to the world. The form of this 'gift', whether in the works of philosophers or economists such as Adam Smith or David Hume, or in the deeds of industrialist such as Andrew Carnegie or Robert Gilmore, he didn't say.

I am sure some regarded his gratitude as undeserved or received it with a misplaced sense of pride. For others, however, it provoked a sobering thought. Should Scotland in some way be held responsible for a system sustained by human exploitation and inequality; a system which encourages the sort of greed and irresponsibility that so recently caused a banking crisis and a global recession, of a scale not witnessed since the great depression, which brought the misery of unemployment and poverty to millions of working people across the world?

Fortunately, those Scots who gained international renown as industrial pioneers or whose ideas are claimed by free marketeers are not Scotland's only 'gift' to the world. There is another side of the story that is little known but arguably more important: the contribution made by Scots to countering the inevitable excesses of capitalism through their leadership of the trade union and labour movement across the globe.

Scotland's Radical Exports goes a long way towards shining a light on this lesser known aspect of the Scottish diaspora.

The STUC has a proud tradition of internationalism and it is appropriate that one of its former Presidents is the author of this book. I have known Pat Kelly since I was appointed to the STUC staff and he was a member of the General Council. He was a forthright speaker on international issues, often leading the debates on behalf of the General Council at our annual Congress. Pat was also a fierce advocate of Scotland's national identity and meetings of the 'Campaign for a Scottish Parliament' met in Pat's office in Edinburgh. He represented the STUC in what became known as the 'Claim of Right Committee' which, although almost unknown, had a profound impact on the shape of Scotland's future. It produced the blueprint for the establishment of the Scottish Constitutional Convention, which of course galvanised opinion on the Scottish Parliament until it became the settled will of the Scottish people.

Pat's well-written and highly entertaining book tells us not just about Scottish emigrants and their lives, but about the history of the labour movements in main countries of the Scottish diaspora. Some of the key political figures, such as Andrew Fisher, Peter Fraser and Tommy Douglas, have been the subjects of biographies. Others names are familiar in their own countries, but unknown in Scotland. Most, however, are people who are unheard of outside their own small circles of trade union and political activists.

As we would expect a large number were coal miners. William Wilson, from Blantyre, was the first Secretary of Labor in the USA; Prime Minister Andrew Fisher, an Ayrshire miner, led the Australian Labor Party to three general election victories; Philip Murray, another Blantyre miner became President of the American Congress of Industrial Organisations; and many other Scottish miners led their unions in New Zealand, Canada, Australia and throughout the coalfields of the USA.

The contributions of people from other industries were equally impressive. The leader of the giant US Autoworkers Union in the 1980s was a Glaswegian. The man dubbed the 'father of the Australian trade union movement' was born in the Shetland Islands, and the most recent leader of the Australian Manufacturing Workers Union – the biggest union in Australia – is a former fitter from Bellshill. Scots led the trade union federations in all four countries at different times and in New Zealand one of the country's most successful Labour Prime Ministers was a joiner from the Highlands.

All of the accounts in the book are well worth reading. Perhaps in future when the question of what has Scotland given the world is asked, great trade union leaders will feature on the list together with some of the more predictable candidates!

Grahame Smith,
Generary Secretary,
Scottish Trades Union Congress

List of Illustrations

Glossary

Abbreviations

ACTU	Australian Council of Trade Unions
AFL	American Federation of Labor
AFL-CIO	American Federation of Labor-Congress of Industrial Organizations
AMWU	Amalgamated Metal Workers Union (until 1995), afterwards Australian Manufacturing Workers Union
ASE	Amalgamated Society of Engineers
ASU	Amalgamated Shearers Union
CCF	Cooperative Commonwealth Federation
CCL	Canadian Congress of Labour
CFMEU	Construction, Forestry, Mining and Energy Union.
CIO	Congress of Industrial Organizations
CLC	Canadian Labour Congress
Commintern	Communist International
CTU	Council of Trade Unions
FOL	Federation of Labour
GM	General Motors
IAM	International Association of Machinists
IWW	International Workers of the World
KOL	Knights of Labor
NDP	New Democratic Party
OBU	One Big Union
PSA	Public Services Association
PWA	Provincial Workmen's Association
SDP	Social Democratic Party
STELCO	Steel Corporation of Canada
TLC	Trades and Labour Congress (Canada)
UAW	United Auto Workers
UCS	Upper Clyde Shipbuilders
UFA	United Farmers of Alberta
UFL	United Federation of Labour
UMWA	United Mineworkers of America
USWA	United Steelworkers of America
Wobblies	Industrial Workers of the World
WUL	Workers Unity League

Notes

1. American spelling of proper names is used in the first three chapters. Although Australian spelling is normally the same as British, in 1912 the Australian Labor Party adopted the American spelling for its name. Some Trades and Labor Councils still use the British spelling, but for convenience 'labor' has been used throughout the chapters on Australia.

2. There are a number of terms used to describe the basic unit of a national trade union, whether it is workplace, craft or geographically structured. The most commonly used in the UK is 'branch', although the mining unions in Scotland used 'lodge', and in the printing industry it was 'chapel'. In North America the main term is 'local', short for local union. In New Zealand the terminology is similar to the UK, but in Australia a branch normally refers to a state organization of a national union, (Victoria, Queensland etc).

3. Some US unions have locals in Canada and therefore call themselves *International* unions. The highest body of these unions is the International Board, usually known as the National Executive elsewhere.

4. The AMWU was originally the acronym for the Amalgamated Metal Workers Union (Australia). In 1995 it merged with unions in the printing and car industries to become the Australian Manufacturing Workers Union, keeping the same acronym.

5. The acronym 'CIO' originally referred to the Committee of Industrial Organizations that was later re-named the Congress of Industrial Organizations.

Introduction

Emigration is a key aspect of Scottish history and has had a significant influence on the development of Scotland's national identity. During the nineteenth and twentieth century, a higher proportion of Scotland's population left home than most European countries, despite Scotland having a well-established manufacturing base. This was in contrast to the agricultural economies of other countries with high emigration rates. As a result, most of Scotland's emigrants came from urban centres and arrived in their host countries with experience of industrial conditions, discipline, trade union organisation and collective action. Fifty per cent of the emigrants were skilled workers, a section of the workforce where trade unionism was strongest.

The bulk of these emigrants settled in England, although a sizable number went abroad, particularly when economic instability in Scotland coincided with periods of economic growth in North America and Australasia. They belonged to a small minority whose skills were in great demand, which accounts for the relative success of many Scots. They firmly stamped their mark on various aspects of colonial life and exerted an influence that was disproportionate to their numbers.

However, the recorded history of the Scots abroad is dominated by the successes of the entrepreneurial minority, and scant consideration has been given to the vast majority who worked at their trade. In particular, insufficient attention has been paid to those Scots who made their contribution to their host countries through representing their fellow workers in trade unions and in the political parties of the working class.

This book highlights the unheralded achievements of Scottish immigrants, concentrating on the labour movements of the USA, Canada, Australia and New Zealand. I have chosen not to explore the stories of emigrants who left Scotland for England and Wales, as the trade unions and political organisations straddled the border. South Africa is a unique case, and although Scots were involved in the country's trade unions and political parties, it needs more specialist analysis and therefore doesn't feature here. The same goes for the contribution of Edinburgh's James Connolly to building the Irish Transport and General Workers Union and his leadership of the Easter Rising, although I do cover the period when he was organising unions and working for the American Socialist Party in the United States.

In this book the history of the founding and development of working-class organisations is chronicled through the biographies of Scottish-born activists. It records the determination and sacrifices of people who passionately believed in the causes for which they fought. Their experience in trade union and political activity made Scottish emigrants especially suited to leadership roles. Those who had not been particularly active in Scotland quickly learned from their colleagues, and others who had left Scotland as children became involved through the influence of their parents or others in the expatriate Scottish community.

North America was the first part of the world to experience Scottish trade union influence. The introduction of steamships and the development of railways from the mid-nineteenth century led to a transatlantic labour market. Some workers, such as the Aberdeen granite cutters, travelled to the eastern states of the USA on a seasonal basis. In addition, unions used emigration as a means of controlling labour supply to their industries, and hence, wage rates. Special emigration funds were set up to encourage workers to move to North America during downturns in the economic cycle.

Alexander MacDonald, the Scottish miners' leader from the mid 1850s to the end of the 1870s, was a great enthusiast for emigration. The miners' union acted as an agent for North American coal companies for the supply of miners to the east-coast coalfields in Maryland, Virginia, Nova Scotia and Pennsylvania. Priority was given to union members who had been victimised by the Scottish coal owners, resulting in a higher than average proportion of union activists making the trip across the Atlantic. Many of them moved on and settled in the 'Wild West' mining towns of West Virginia, Illinois and Kansas. They set up miners' unions wherever they went and were prominent in the establishment of the United Mine Workers of America. This union became the largest in the country and is still one of the most powerful today.

Scottish emigration to the colonies of Australia and New Zealand was not on the same scale as North America, the sailing time and the price being the inhibiting factors. Nonetheless, the discovery of gold in Victoria, coupled with government subsidies for travel, enticed thousands of Scots to make the journey. Taking advantage of the labour shortage caused by the rush to the goldfields, Scottish building workers, engineers and miners in Victoria and New South Wales set up unions and secured some of the best working conditions in the world, including the eight-hour day.

When Socialist ideas found fertile ground in Scotland, many of Keir Hardie's disciples emigrated and became leaders of the early Socialist organisations abroad. Scots were in the vanguard of the attempts to establish labour parties, and they succeeded in Australia and New Zealand. Scottish-born prime ministers and key cabinet members in both countries had been prominent in the early organisation and development of the labour parties. Although Scottish miners unsuccessfully tried to develop an American Labor Party, Scottish endeavours in Canada were rewarded when Social Democratic parties were set up and won popular support in some provinces. According to a poll conducted by the Canadian Broadcasting Corporation in 2004, the most popular Canadian of all time was Tommy Douglas, the Scottish leader of the New Democratic Party from 1961 until 1971. This was largely a result of his introduction of a national health service when he was premier of Saskatchewan, a model later adopted throughout Canada.

In the decade that followed the devastating collapse of the British economy after the First World War, almost 400,000 people left Scotland, many of them highly skilled workers. Most of the exodus settled in England, but more than sixty thousand moved overseas. The Scots were brought up with trade unionism, some explaining metaphorically to their colleagues how they sucked it with their mother's milk or were fed it with a knife and fork. It came as a great surprise to them to find non-union factories in North America in the 1920s, in contrast to Scotland, where you could not get a job unless you belonged to a union. Their American-born colleagues had tried and failed in the past, and told them that the owners of great industries like steel and auto were so anti-union that it was impossible to organise them. But the Scots rejected this notion and not only believed that it could be done, but could not understand why it had not been done before.

Marxism had a profound impact on leading Scottish union activists. John McLean, who was regarded as Britain's greatest revolutionary leader of his time, taught Marxist economics to an entire generation of shop stewards, with four hundred attending his Glasgow classes at the start of the First World War. Along with other lecturers, he gave classes every Sunday from 1906 and later formed the Scottish Labour College, extending his classes to Edinburgh and the mining areas. His students later provided some of the key leaders of the Communist Party in Britain and abroad. In Canada the first general secretary of the Communist Party came from Falkirk. In New Zealand, a young Scottish miner was general secretary a few years after the Communist Party was established. In Australia there were so many Scots involved in the Communist Party leadership that people joked that Australian Communism was a Caledonian conspiracy.

Scotland's class-conscious workers left their home country with a formidable combination of trade union conviction and Socialist understanding. Many were veterans of the anti-war campaigns, the shop stewards' strike for a forty-hour week, and the 1926 general strike. They often organised political education classes or shop stewards' training courses, using Scottish events for practical examples of struggle. They shared a deep commitment to their cause and a willingness to challenge authority. American trade unionists noticed that the Scots were among the first to volunteer for picket duty and to stand up to the police. Such courage and dedication enabled them to gain the trust of other nationalities.

There were a number of other reasons why the Scots rose to the leading positions. The unique British apprenticeship system provided opportunities for journeymen to induct young workers in the values of their union. For those who showed particular enthusiasm, encouragement was given to progress through the union structure, often starting with the apprentices' committees. A similar system of mentoring existed in some of the miners' union districts. Part of their induction was the importance of union rules, the proper conduct of meetings, and the role of office bearers. In contrast, their workplace colleagues, most of whom had come from agricultural backgrounds, were totally bewildered by the procedures and some did not even understand the concept of a trade union. A key aspect of trade union training was the art of public speaking, an essential skill for a trade union leader. Speakers found that a Scottish accent was highly effective when addressing audiences, and for added impact, they sometimes made the burr more pronounced. It was fortunate for the Scots that union business was conducted in English, which in the United States in particular left other European immigrants at a disadvantage.

Although Marxist and revolutionary Socialist principles influenced a high proportion of Scottish union activists, others were guided by their religion or other beliefs. It has been said that Methodism played a more important role in the British Labour Party than Marxism, and that was certainly true of many of the Scots who helped build the Canadian Social Democratic parties. Tommy Douglas and William Irvine from Shetland had been church ministers before entering parliament, and their convictions came from the 'social gospel'. Philip Murray, the

Blantyre-born president of both the United Steelworkers of America and the Congress of Industrial Organizations, was a devout Catholic. His views on the relationship between labour and capital were based on Papal encyclicals that lay on his desk as a constant reminder of his obligations. A high number of Scots were members of the Masonic Lodge and placed their loyalties accordingly.

The conflicting ideological views of the Scots often found them in opposing camps in the internecine warfare that commonly affects labour movement organisations. Sometimes this reflected a change of the old guard for the new, which was the case in the late nineteenth century. In the splits between those who believed in craft unions and those who believed in industrial unions, the Scots were divided. The twentieth-century ideological disputes between left and right, particularly between pro-and anti-Communists, heralded some of the most bitter divisions. It advanced the careers of some Scots and spelled the end for others. And for a few leading Communists in the United States, it ended with their deportation back to Scotland.

The ideological views of individuals often changed during their lifetime, usually from left to right. In New Zealand, Peter Fraser, who was born in the Highlands, and Angus McLagan from West Lothian, were revolutionary Socialists when they emigrated. Fraser, who became prime minister in 1940, was arrested for opposing conscription during the First World War. After the Labour Party took power, he started to drift to the right, becoming so anti-Communist that he introduced compulsory military service at the start of the Cold War, splitting the Labour Party in the process. McLagan was a former general secretary of the New Zealand Communist Party and president of the New Zealand Federation of Labour. However, he became a union-busting minister of labour when left-wing unions took strike action that threatened his government. A similar metamorphosis occurred in others mentioned in this book.

Some of the important personalities left Scotland as children, but were influenced by their families and by experienced members of the Scottish community. William Spence, who is regarded as the 'father' of the Australian labour movement, left Shetland as a child of six in 1852, but grew up in a Scottish mining community in Victoria. William Wilson, the USA's first secretary of labor, had his first experience of fighting injustice when the bailiffs came to evict his father during a strike. Forced to flee Lanarkshire, the family moved to America in 1870, where father and son worked together in the same pit when Wilson was only nine. Doug Fraser, who led the auto-workers' union, came to the USA with his parents. His father took him to union and political meetings in Scotland and America, and both of them took part in the sit-down strikes in Detroit when Fraser was twenty.

Scottish emigration to the United States tailed off after the 1930s, and there has been no significant input to the US labour movement since Doug Fraser. Canada, Australia and New Zealand remain popular destinations for Scottish emigration, and many Scots continue to volunteer at every level in their unions and political parties. Some are already in leadership positions and other up-and-coming labour movement activists will, I hope, have their contributions recorded in future publications.

Chapter 1

William Wilson, the US miners and the Department of Labor

In 1917 the United States had just joined the First World War and William B. Wilson, the Secretary of State for Labor, was called to the White House. He returned with an allocation of $60m for the biggest housing project ever conceived in US history. Accommodation was needed for workers near to the country's shipyards and armaments factories and Wilson's department was responsible for ensuring its success. The budget for the housing development was the equivalent of $1bn at 2011 values.

As he considered the opportunities for building decent housing for industrial workers, Wilson reflected on his own past, when he'd been evicted by landlords and left homeless a number of times. The first such incident occurred when he was a six-year-old child living in a row of miner's cottages in Lanarkshire. His father had been involved in a strike and the coal company sent the bailiffs to remove his family from their company-owned property. He stood beside his mother and father, armed with a kitchen knife, determined to resist any enforced eviction. It was his first confrontation with authority and the first of several occasions during his life when he found himself homeless due to trade union activity.

Wilson was born in the Lanarkshire mining town of Blantyre in 1862. Originally a quiet and rural village, Blantyre's population of around five hundred increased dramatically during the Industrial Revolution. Several cotton mills were built and the community expanded further when large coal deposits were discovered in the surrounding area. The miners became unionised and successfully maintained high wages in the early part of the nineteenth century by controlling the output of coal. Each collier was allowed to mine a darg (quota) by the union and this was varied according to demand for coal. At a time when there were a large number of small-scale coal operations, this collective discipline proved highly effective, especially when supplemented by control of numbers in the industry.

The Miners' National Association of Great Britain was formed the year after Wilson was born and it was led by Alexander MacDonald, the country's most inspirational trade union figure. Born near Airdrie in 1821, MacDonald left school at the age of eight to work down the mines beside his father. In his twenties he took evening classes in Latin and Greek, and saved up enough money to enrol as a student at Glasgow University. When he graduated he was appointed to a management position, but he later left the industry to become a schoolteacher. However, he remained close to the mining community and maintained a keen interest in the welfare of the miners. He had been one of the leaders of a strike in 1842 and was highly respected by the miners. After listening to the pleas of his friends, he agreed to try to organise a union for the miners. In 1855 he was instrumental in forming a Scottish union of coal and ironstone miners and soon became recognised as the pre-eminent Scottish trade union leader. When the Miners National Association was formed in 1863, uniting all of Britain's miners, MacDonald was elected president. His credentials were further underlined when he won a parliamentary seat for the Liberals in 1874, becoming one of the first working-class members of the British House of Commons

MacDonald's trade union philosophy was based on the collaboration of miners and mine owners. He believed that there should be an equal partnership between both and a shared responsibility for the running of the industry. When profits were high he supported maximising colliers' wages, but was willing to accept wage reductions when the price of coal dropped. From this perspective, he argued, mine owners should be willing to negotiate with the union about output and numbers in the industry, and be prepared to submit any differences to arbitration. This approach to pay bargaining was relatively successful and was the predominant view within the Miners National Association until the late 1870s. MacDonald's philosophy was exported to the United States of America by his many disciples who emigrated to the expanding US coalfields in Maryland, Pennsylvania, Illinois and West Virginia.

Like union leaders in other industries such as textiles and printing, MacDonald believed emigration was a useful means of controlling labour supply. It is uncertain to what extent this enhanced the bargaining position of the unions, but they set up special emigration funds and encouraged their use during economic downturns in Britain. The catalyst for the policy was a request in 1864 to MacDonald from a coal company in Maryland to supply fifty colliers. Soon other US coal companies followed suit and within a year almost six hundred Scottish miners left for the United States, supported by the union's emigration fund. Priority was given to union activists who had been blacklisted by Scottish coal companies.

Eviction and emigration

Adam Wilson, father of the future US Secretary of State for Labor, had been one of the leaders of a strike in Blantyre in 1868. He was sacked and evicted from his home in the middle of winter. Along with other strikers' families, the Wilsons found shelter in the stables of the village tollhouse, where they stayed for several weeks. Most of them knew they would be placed on the employer's blacklist, leading to discussions about emigration to America. Two of Wilson's children had died from the effects of poverty when only a few years old and he was determined this would not happen to the others. He made up his mind to leave Scotland, and the following year he took up the offer of a job in northern Pennsylvania. The rest of the family joined him in the autumn of 1870.

Although only eight when he left home, William Wilson's emotional attachment to Scotland never diminished throughout his life. He had a wide knowledge of Scottish history and later in life the sound of a Scottish song brought a tear to his eye. No doubt his father jogged his memory, but he retained vivid recollections of his home and the Clyde Valley. Later he began to write poetry and some of his most poignant verses were laments about Scotland. In 'My Father's Day Dream', Wilson describes the beauty of his native land and the heartache of leaving 'Old Scotia'.

The Wilson family's new home was in the mining village of Arnot in Tioga County, northern Pennsylvania. The village consisted of rows of flimsy wooden huts along four narrow streets. There was a Presbyterian church, a railway station, a general store, and various bars – all owned by the coal company. The miners' shacks were built of cheap wood and left unpainted, so in time they became blackened by coal dust and weather-beaten by storms. There were no toilets, the water supply was inadequate and conditions unsanitary. Later, a school and other churches were built, reflecting the diversity of cultures and identities of the miners who made up the township. Episcopalian, Swedish Evangelical, Irish and Polish Catholic churches were added as the population of the village expanded to 3500.

The mines were ten minutes' walk from the centre of the village, which was named after John Arnot, a New York businessman born in Doune, Perthshire in 1793. He had emigrated with his working-class parents when he was ten years old, and started a merchant business when he was in his twenties. The company prospered and he expanded his interests into manufacturing and banking, becoming president of the biggest banking institution in the state of New York.

William Wilson was enrolled at the local school and although he had only managed a year of schooling at St John's Primary in Hamilton, he soon raced ahead of the rest of the class. He absorbed everything he read and bought a second-hand copy of an encyclopaedia with pocket money he earned from running errands for neighbours. Every evening he read an extract to his illiterate father, which they then discussed until late. However, after several attacks of lumbago, his father was finding work in the mine more arduous and needed help to load the coal he had cut. With a heavy heart, he was forced to take his eldest son out of school to assist him in the pit. Waving goodbye to his childhood, William was soon working a ten-hour day down a mine. He wrote about giving up the fun and the untroubled life of a child to start life as a miner in another poem, 'The Coal Miner'.

For the first few months all he wanted to do after work was go home, have supper and sleep. Then he was involved in an accident in the mine. He was almost killed when a prop gave way and he was buried under a shower of rock and coal. Other miners rushed to his rescue when they heard the screams of his panic-stricken father. William was fortunate to escape serious injury, as other children suffered worse fates in mining accidents: some were caught in machinery and badly mangled or slipped into the centre of the chute and were suffocated. Despite this ominous beginning to his life as a miner, William Wilson worked beside his father for the next seven years, learning all aspects of mining, and continued in the industry for the next twenty-seven years.

The cobbler's shop was Adam Wilson's favourite place in the village. Every evening lively debates took place on international affairs, philosophy, economics and, of course, trade unionism. He took William along with him, and the boy revelled in the discussions. He was a bright, cheerful lad with keen blue eyes, and his infectious personality made him friends easily. Although he was extremely courteous to adults, he was not overawed in their company. There was a reading room and library in the back of the cobbler's shop, and before long William had devoured every book. His favourite authors were Walter Scott and Charles Dickens, and the poets Burns, Shelley, Wordsworth and Tennyson. He read Adam Smith's *Wealth of Nations* to his father, another cause of late-night discussions.

Depression, wage cuts and strikes

The relative peace and prosperity was shattered in 1873 when mine owners throughout the country cut wages drastically in the wake of a major depression. The Arnot miners' union called a strike and for the second time in five years the Wilsons were evicted from their coal-company home. Throughout the winter, the miners found shelter in the nearby town of Blossburg, where a co-operative was formed with the farmers who provided them with food. The coal company then tried to use immigrants newly arrived from Sweden. However, when the Swedes found out they were being used to break a strike, they refused to work. Somehow the people of Blossburg sheltered and fed the Swedes as well as the sacked miners. After six months the strike was settled with the former wage rate restored, but it had been a long, gruelling struggle.

By his fourteenth birthday William Wilson was a strong, strapping lad, able to load as many cars as his father could cut coal to fill. He started a debating society for the boys in the village, and had joined the union. But after the strike very few miners seemed prepared to raise their heads above the parapet. This reluctance to participate in union activities was not restricted to Arnot, and seemed to be the case throughout the American coalfields. But Wilson was confident enough to take on the role of secretary of the local union and this immediately brought him into contact with union leaders throughout the country. By the time he was eighteen, he was identified by the coal companies as a potential troublemaker and was blacklisted throughout Pennsylvania. Even though he was forced to leave home to look for work in other states, this merely strengthened his resolve to fight for justice. His contribution to trade unionism in the United States had only just begun, and during the next decade he would emerge as one of the national leaders of the country's miners.

Just before the 1873 strike, the Miners National Association of the US was formed, modelled on Alexander MacDonald's British union, and even taking the same name. Previous attempts at building a national organisation of miners had failed, but there was a great desire to succeed this time. MacDonald took a keen interest and was a frequent visitor to the United States during this period. His close friend John James was elected general secretary of the new union. James was born in the Nitshill area of Glasgow in 1829 and left school at ten to go down the pit. The family moved to Johnstone, where he became involved in petitioning for a mine inspection bill that Alexander MacDonald was advocating. Like many union activists, he was blacklisted, and moved around the

Scottish coalfields, working in Renfrewshire, Ayrshire and Lanarkshire, changing his name frequently to conceal his identity. With MacDonald's encouragement he emigrated to America, along with twenty-eight miners from Lanarkshire.

MacDonald had an agreement with an agent that the men would be working for a coal company in Maryland. But when they arrived, the agent told them there were no longer any jobs and offered an alternative employer in West Virginia. When James and his party arrived at their destination they realised they were to be used as strike-breakers. Refusing to work, they were offered board and lodgings by the strikers, and local farmers gave them some casual employment. The group then made their way to the coalfields in western Pennsylvania, where they found jobs for a few months, before eventually settling in the town of Braidwood, Illinois. From the time they arrived in America they had travelled over a thousand miles, taking them through seven states before reaching their final destination.

Substantial coal deposits had been discovered in Braidwood, a town named after James Braidwood from Glasgow. He was an engineer who had sunk the first mineshaft in the area and had been a close friend of Alexander MacDonald. The rich vein of coal was 3½ feet thick at a depth of only 80 feet. The town was built around the mines in open prairie land, 53 miles from Chicago. The initial population of two thousand quickly grew to over eight thousand in a few years, made up of a combination of ethnic groups from America and Europe. The original Scottish pioneers who came in the 1860s were followed throughout the 1870s and 1880s by other shiploads of Scottish colliers, many of them experienced union activists who went on to play an important role in the development of trade unionism in the USA.

The buildings in the town were made of wood, as any brick-built structure ran the risk of subsidence or collapse due to the shallow mine workings. Initially the population was almost all men, some of whom were married and had left their families behind until they could earn enough to send for them. With a pub on nearly every street corner, the town had a reputation for violence, and was said by some to have been the roughest and toughest in the west. There was a readiness to settle disputes with guns and it was estimated there were over five hundred hand revolvers in use. Although a law was passed in 1871 forbidding the carrying of firearms, it was largely ignored. The immigrants brought with them the customs, organisations, and sometimes the ancient hatreds from their old countries. In one example, a riot between Irish Catholics and Scottish Protestants broke out on election day in 1876, as the two groups battled for political office. But despite its 'wild west' notoriety, the standard of living was much higher in Braidwood than other coalfields in America, and miners could buy cheap plots of land for houses and smallholdings.

Dan McLaughlin from Glasgow was another of MacDonald's followers who came to Braidwood a few years after the Lanarkshire miners arrived. The son of an Irish stonecutter, he started work at the age of nine down a coalmine in Maryhill, Glasgow in 1840. He took part in his first strike when he was eleven and became secretary of the Maryhill miners union when he was sixteen. For the next twenty years he worked alongside Alex MacDonald in the union and gained national prominence as a fiery speaker and excellent organiser. However, his reputation condemned him among employers, and he found it increasingly difficult to find work. In 1869 he left Scotland and joined John James and the others in Braidwood.

Attempts to form a national union

The Scottish miners set up a local union and extended it to most of the Illinois coal towns. They were also in communication with unions in other mining states and tried to form a national union. The first effort failed, but another attempt was made in 1873 when delegates from five states attended a convention in Youngstown, Ohio and formed the Miners National Association. John James drafted the constitution of the new organisation following MacDonald's principles of arbitration, conciliation and co-operation. James had been blacklisted from the Illinois mines after leading a strike in 1868 and had invested his savings in a general store in Braidwood. When he became general secretary of the Miners National Association, he sold the store and moved to the union headquarters in Cleveland, Ohio on a salary of $100 a month.

Although the constitution of the new union included the strike weapon, the rules gave authority for calling of strikes to the national executive alone, with the objective of reducing them to a minimum. However, in the atmosphere of the 1873 depression, there was no basis for agreements with mine owners. They were determined to cut wages to stay in business as the demand for coal fell by 50 per cent. The officers of the Miners National Association travelled throughout the country, meeting with the coal-company owners in an attempt to establish friendly relations. They promised to do all in their power to prevent strikes, but

John James, general secretary of the Miners National Association of America, was born in Glasgow and was a close friend of Alexander MacDonald. In 1873 he was instrumental in forming the American union, which he modelled the on its British equivalent. But divisions amongst the members led to his resignation three years later.

with one exception the companies emphatically dismissed the overtures and declined to deal with the union.

Despite this rejection, union organisers tried to explain to the rank and file miners that the depression was having a devastating effect on industry throughout the United States and the time was not right for strike action. This came as a great disappointment to those who had welcomed the new union and expected to be led into battle to defend their conditions. Some miners, like those in Arnot, ignored their warnings and took action anyway. However, when the second convention of the union met the following year, a membership of 22,000 was reported, and delegates were optimistic that once the economic situation in the country improved, there would be higher pay, better conditions and further increases in members.

But the depression continued for several years and a number of strikes broke out against further cuts in pay. John James and the advocates of class harmony found their ideas increasingly difficult to defend and local activists looked for other sources of inspiration. By 1876, just three years after it was formed, the Miners National Association was on the verge of collapse. But James refused to alter his position and was eventually ostracised by the younger, more militant miners. Disillusioned at the growing class divisions between mine owner and miner, he resigned as general secretary and left Cleveland to become a mine manager in New Mexico. In Scotland, Alexander MacDonald had also come in for fierce criticism from the growing number of socialists, led by Keir Hardie. A similar recession in Britain had damaged his collaborationist ideals and the miners eventually ditched his philosophy.

Dan McLaughlin had originally shared the same fundamental beliefs as MacDonald and James, but he had become radicalised during the depression. As president of the Illinois miners, he led a strike in 1874 and another longer, violent, and very bitter dispute in 1877. Just before the 1877 strike, McLaughlin was voted mayor of Braidwood. When the dispute started, the coal companies refused to pay the miners the last two weeks' wages they were due. They brought in strike-breakers who were attacked by the miners and chased out of Braidwood. As the dispute dragged on into its third month, the miners became more desperate to feed their families. They started stealing chickens, horses and cattle and some shops were looted.

Under pressure from the coal owners, the county sheriff told Mayor McLaughlin that if he could not maintain law and order in Braidwood, then he and his deputies would do the job for him. It is alleged that

McLaughlin threatened to kill the sheriff if he attempted to come near the town. Not taking any chances, the sheriff called in the state militia. Arriving by train along with representatives of the coal companies and the sheriff, the militia were met by crowds of jeering protesters. The general leading the militia – who had been informed that the miners were armed and prepared to resist – ordered McLaughlin to disperse the demonstrators and demanded that they surrender all weapons. McLaughlin refused the request and the crowd stood their ground. The general knew there would be a riot if he tried to arrest McLaughlin, and decided to retreat. But the town was placed under martial law and the strike eventually ended without success. However, McLaughlin's support was undiminished and he was re-elected mayor in 1881. He was also successful in elections to the Illinois State Assembly in 1886 and 1888.

David Ross from Edinburgh was another miner who was elected to the Illinois State Assembly in 1888. He had emigrated in 1868 and was a prominent figure at union conventions. Such was his status amongst the miners that he was frequently urged to stand for state or national president of the union. He had started work in the mines at the age of nine and received very little education, but he studied law and passed the exams with flying colours. As a member of the State Assembly, he was instrumental in the passage of a number of laws relating to mining. After practising as a solicitor for a number of years, he was appointed Secretary of the Illinois Bureau of Labor in 1897.

Various attempts were made to resuscitate a national union and the National Progressive Miners Union was formed in 1888. But Dan McLaughlin was involved in another union that was making inroads throughout the United States. The Knights of Labor (KOL) was originally established in 1869 as a secret organisation. Members joined local assemblies, which were either single-trade bodies, such as miners, or mixed groups of workers. The KOL projected a society based on co-operative industrial and agricultural enterprises owned and operated by the workers. The vision of the KOL was the creation of a just and moral 'co-operative commonwealth'. Its key policies were the introduction of an eight-hour working day, prohibition of employment of children under fourteen, and equal opportunities and wages for women. The KOL was a unique experiment in class-wide solidarity, open to all workers, regardless of trade, creed or race, and was the leading general organisation of working men and women during the 1880s. It grew rapidly during the depression of the 1870s, when it advocated militant action and played an important part in the coal strike of 1877. The miners had their own section of the Knights, which was headed by John Rae, an experienced trade unionist and a lay preacher, who emigrated from Scotland in 1875 at the age of forty. He had worked in the mines since he was a boy and soon after joining the Knights he became prominent in the assemblies in Pennsylvania, where he settled. When the miners' section was formed, Rae became leader and was given the title of Master Workman. Dan McLaughlin was elected to the general executive board.

The KOL abandoned its secret nature in 1881 and became a powerful force with over 1500 local assemblies. By 1886 it had over 700,000 members but it gradually adopted less radical measures and transferred the bulk of its funds towards producer co-operatives and a much lesser sum towards support for strikes. This caused a split between the local assemblies and the trade unions, which eventually resulted in the formation of the American Federation of Labor (AFL) in 1886. McLaughlin led a section of miners out of the KOL and was elected first vice-president of the AFL in 1887. But, similar to John James over a decade before, he became disillusioned with the political disputes in the union, and in 1890 he left Illinois to become a mine manager in Colorado.

This was the same year as the formation of the United Mine Workers of America (UMWA), one of the most important landmarks in American labour history. Despite its tiny initial membership of just 17,000, it stood the test of time and became the largest and most powerful American trade union for over forty years. And like its British counterpart, the Miners Federation of Great Britain, formed a year earlier, it played a key role in the development of the rest of the trade union movement. It was established when the National Progressive Miners Union merged with the Knights of Labor. At its inaugural conference in Columbus, Ohio, John Rae was elected president. Some felt that Rae looked and sounded more like a Presbyterian church minister than a union leader, but he was seen as a vital unifying force amongst the different factions of miners. A veteran of many mining disputes at home, Rae was a cautious man who never took a step forward unless he was sure of his ground. One of the first major decisions of the executive board of the UMWA was to launch an eight-hour-day campaign. But with no money in the treasury coffers, Rae did not think the union was ready for the battle for shorter hours, and tendered his resignation in 1892, despite attempts to persuade him to continue.

Shortly after its formation, Patrick McBryde became the UMWA's secretary/treasurer. Born in Ireland and raised in Scotland, he attracted

John Rae, first president of the United Mine Workers of America, was a veteran of many mining disputes in Scotland. He became leader of the miners' section of the Knights of Labor in America and was elected president of the UMWA at its inaugural conference in 1890. (Courtesy of Historical Collections and Labor Archives, Special Collections Library, The Pennsylvania State University).

the attention of Alexander MacDonald when he worked in mines near Glasgow. He had initially emigrated to the United States in the 1870s, but the depression forced him, and many others, back to the Scottish mines. But he returned to the United States in 1884 and settled in Pittsburgh, where he became active in the union. By the time the UMWA was established, McBryde was recognised as one of its senior figures, and held the position of secretary/treasurer until 1896.

Persecution of Wilson

William Wilson's name was never far from people's lips whenever leadership positions were discussed, and he was elected to the UMWA's national executive board at its inaugural conference. He played a key role in the formation of the union, having drafted the constitution, which specifically barred discrimination based on race, religion or national origin. The ten years that had elapsed from his enforced departure from Arnot had been eventful. At first he went from mine to mine outside Pennsylvania until the owners found out he was on the blacklist. He drifted west to Ohio, Illinois and Iowa, working in lumber yards, digging ditches, shovelling coal on a locomotive, and many other jobs. He went back to Arnot from time to time and even found work as a typesetter in the local paper in Blossburg. In 1883, at the age of twenty-one, he married Agnes Williamson, who lived in Arnot, but had been born within a few miles of his home in Lanarkshire. He was devoted to his wife throughout his life and their marriage produced eleven children. Never a man who showed his emotions openly, he turned to poetry to express his deep feelings. His poem 'Blue Eyes' was dedicated to his love for Agnes, and the pain of leaving his wife and children to find work is expressed in 'Lines on Leaving Home When Blacklisted'.

The persecution of Wilson intensified when a nationwide strike was called in 1894. In an economic depression known as 'the panic of 1893' the mining industry was badly affected. Wages were slashed two years running and the UMWA responded by calling a nationwide strike. Although they had only 13,000 paid-up members, over 180,000 miners responded to the strike call. Some mine owners agreed to make slight adjustments, but the vast majority would not even discuss the issue. Violence erupted in the coalfields and some state governors called in the militia. Battles raged between National Guardsmen, sometimes supported by sheriff's deputies, and the striking miners. In Pennsylvania the fighting was fierce. Five miners were killed by troops in Uniontown, and the whole militia

The Wilson Family. William B. Wilson married Agnes Williamson, who had been born within a few miles of his home in Lanarkshire. She came from a mining family and moved to Arnot in Pennsylvania with her parents. Wilson was devoted to his wife and their marriage produced eleven children, one of whom died.

of the district surrounded a miners' camp in Frostburg, where William Wilson was leading the strikers. They waited for an excuse to arrest Wilson, but left disappointed.

Labelled a dangerous agitator, Wilson was a wanted man throughout the strike. He was arrested, but mass demonstrations outside the courthouse forced his acquittal. A week later he was arrested again and bundled out of Pennsylvania by company agents working with the police. Without disclosing his arrest to his friends or family, he was taken across the state border to Maryland where he was jailed. However, after just two days he was located, $500 was raised for his bail, and the case against him was subsequently dropped. He was arrested for a third time in West Virginia and was served with an injunction to stop union organising. Wilson's response was, 'I will treat it as I would an order of the court to stop breathing.'

The 1894 strike ended in defeat and led to the eviction of his family from their home, the third occasion Wilson had suffered this indignity. Afterwards he vowed never to let it happen again, and in 1896 he initially rented, then purchased a small farm about three miles from Arnot. The farm offered Wilson and his family the security of their own home and also provided the opportunity to earn a living during the periods when he would inevitably be forced out of work. The owner agreed that the rental for the farmhouse and the land could be paid out of the shared profits of the farm. Only a few acres were suitable for tillage but, assisted by his wife and children, Wilson managed to make it pay. He later took out a mortgage and bought the farm for $1500, naming it Ferniegair, after a small town near his birthplace in Lanarkshire. He sometimes found work at the mines as a check-weighman, appointed by the miners to verify the weight of each miner's load of coal. But he continued as a member of the national executive board of the UMWA.

A successful strike and the Interstate Joint Agreement

The failure of the 1894 strike left the miners in a weak position when the country recovered from 'the panic of 1893'. Wage rates varied considerably throughout the country and in some coalfields pay was being driven down by an abundance of immigrant labour from southern Europe. The downward pressure on pay was in sharp contrast to the higher profits the coal companies were now making. By 1897 the UMWA was down to only 10,000 members and looked as though it was about to become yet another failed experiment. There was not even enough money in the kitty to call a meeting of the national executive board. Almost in desperation, Michael Ratchford, the newly appointed president, called an immediate national strike. To the astonishment of the coal companies and the union leadership alike, over 150,000 miners stopped work in the central coalmining states.

Previous strikes had always been called in April or May, so that wage changes could be included in prices set by the operators. But no one expected a strike in July, and the coal operators were caught on the hop. Since no notice had been given, there was no time for the owners to build up reserves of coal or to import strike-breakers. This bold strategy resulted in the first successful strike since the union had been organised. The employers were forced round the negotiating table and a deal was reached, known as the Interstate Joint Agreement. It gave a significant wage increase, the deduction of union dues from pay, and the introduction of an eight-hour day. Membership of the UMWA rocketed to 93,000, and hundreds of new locals were formed, lapsed districts revived and new districts created. The agreement was seen as a model for industrial relations in the US, and shaped the philosophy of a number of leading trade union officials. The American President, William McKinley, was delighted at the prospect of harmonious relations in the mining industry and was impressed by the UMWA officials. The following year he established an Industrial Commission to deal with labour issues, and appointed Michael Ratchford to the board. This created a vacancy for the UMWA presidency.

Patrick Dolan, president of the Pittsburgh district of the union, the biggest in the UMWA, was the favourite to take over the top position. Born in Coatbridge, Dolan started work in the mines at the age of nine and became involved in the Lanarkshire Miners Union when he was a teenager. In 1886 he emigrated to the United States and settled in the mining village of Macdonald in Pennsylvania. A prominent figure at the annual conventions of the UMWA, he had always been seen as a future national president. The convention to decide the next president was due to be held in his stronghold of Pittsburgh. Had the convention been held a year or so earlier he would have been a shoo-in for the position, as his leadership style and militant approach were in keeping with the majority of activists. But there had been a change in union outlook after the success of the strike and the agreement reached with the coal companies. Some senior figures now felt that the union needed a leader who promoted harmony and co-operation. They believed that the time was right for someone with an ability to persuade the rank and file to accept compromise rather than arouse them to fight. Dolan was seen as one of the 'old school' of inspirational union leaders in the forefront of militant activity. Convention delegates decided that a safer pair of hands was needed to lead the union. Instead of Dolan they opted for John Mitchell from Illinois, a twenty-eight-year-old pragmatist who had learned his trade union philosophy from his mentor, Dan McLaughlin.

Mitchell had lost both parents when he was only six years old. His father was an Irishman who had moved to Scotland to work in the mines. He then emigrated to Braidwood, where he became good friends with McLaughlin. When he and his wife died within months of each other, McLaughlin took young Mitchell under his wing. He later explained his philosophy of labour-capital relations, and in particular his belief in the need for harmony between employers and employees. The Interstate Joint Agreement was to a large extent the fruition of McLaughlin's dreams, and for Mitchell it was the blueprint for all future contracts in the mining industry. With trade improving and resurgence in the demand for coal, there were high expectations that this would herald a new era of labour peace, high wages for miners and higher profits for operators. For these reasons, John Mitchell, and not Patrick Dolan, was deemed to be the man to lead the miners during this period. But there was a sting in the tail of the Interstate Joint Agreement. It contained a formula that allowed the coal companies to reduce wages when the price of coal fell.

William Wilson was one of Mitchell's closest associates and was elected president of the central Pennsylvania district in 1899. Almost immediately he was involved in a dispute in his home area of Tioga County, where a new mine manager had decided not to implement the Joint Agreement. Wilson took charge of the union campaign and tried to find an accommodation, but when this failed there was no alternative to a strike. It lasted eight months and was the longest ever strike in Tioga County, before political pressure forced the mine owners to negotiate a resolution. Mitchell admired Wilson's ability and recognised his vast experience. When the strike ended he pleaded with him to stand for secretary/treasurer of the union. Wilson agreed, and in 1900 won the election and took over the second most powerful position in the UMWA.

The Interstate Joint Agreement reached in 1898 only covered workers in the bituminous coalfields, where the coal mined was used in the power industry and in the manufacture of iron and steel. The agreement did not apply to miners in the anthracite fields, most of which were in

United Mine Workers of America badge.

Lunchtime down an Illinois coalmine, 1903 (Courtesy Library of Congress)

Before mechanisation, coal was cut with a pick axe and loaded by hand on to carts before being weighed for payment, circa 1900 (Courtesy UMWA archives)

northeastern Pennsylvania. The anthracite mines were generally deeper than the bituminous mines, and working conditions were different. There was also a greater ethnic mix, with a high proportion of eastern and southern Europeans, who had little tradition of union organisation. The hard coal was used mainly in the domestic heating market or for steam locomotives, and the railroad companies owned many of the mines. The powerful railroad corporations viewed unions with hostility and refused to meet with the UMWA. The stage was set for a confrontation and the UMWA were all too aware of the ruthlessness of the companies.

The Lattimer Massacre and its aftermath

In the same year as the victorious pay campaign that kick-started the UMWA, a strike by anthracite miners in northeastern Pennsylvania was met with a brutal reaction. Peaceful marches by thousands of miners were held in various towns, and as the numbers on strike swelled, around four hundred Polish and other eastern European strikers marched towards a colliery in the village of Lattimer to persuade them to join the strike. The sheriff and a posse of sixty armed deputies stopped them and ordered them to disperse. But they ignored the order and carried on towards the colliery to picket the miners. When they reached the mine, amidst the jostling and confusion, deputies opened fire indiscriminately on the unarmed marchers. At the end of the carnage, nineteen miners lay dead and fifty more were wounded. When news of the incident spread, the American public were outraged. But although the sheriff and his deputies were arrested and tried, no one was found guilty of the murders. However, in the backlash to what became known as the Lattimer Massacre, laws were passed against the use of deputies in labour disputes.

The Lattimer Massacre also added 15,000 anthracite miners to the UMWA. Those 15,000 were about the sum total of the membership in the anthracite coalfields. With only 10 per cent of the miners in membership, the UMWA executive nevertheless decided to call a strike in 1900. A substantial number responded and the strike lasted six weeks, achieving some success. A 10 per cent increase in pay was won, but no joint agreement on future relations was reached. However, the members learned a great deal about strike discipline and the number of union members in the anthracite coalfields jumped to 53,000. The limited success of the 1900 strike was used to plan the next battle in 1902, a more prolonged affair, but one of the most celebrated victories in US labour history. It put John Mitchell and William Wilson in the national limelight, and gave them a place among the great trade union leaders in the USA. The five-month-long strike was said to have been the best-managed industrial action that ever occurred in the US.

The UMWA submitted a claim for a 20 per cent wage increase, a reduction in hours from ten to eight per day, and union recognition. The employers refused to meet them to discuss the claim. Appeals by the union for arbitration by a neutral third party fell on deaf ears. A call for an investigation by a commission of eminent clergymen was brushed aside by the employers. So, at the beginning of May 1902, over 100,000 miners and maintenance engineers started their strike. Before long, battles broke out between strikers and strike-breakers. The Pennsylvania National Guard, local police and hired detectives waded in to support the scabs. Months passed and no negotiations took place. The miners' families relied on union relief and donations from the public, which were irregular and often insufficient. As a result, hunger and suffering was widespread, especially amongst the children. But the miners grew more determined. With winter approaching and the need for anthracite at its greatest, the strike threatened to shut down the fuel supply to all major cities and close down the rail network. US President Theodore Roosevelt, worried about the political implications, decided to intervene, and for the first time ever, the federal government mediated in a labour dispute. He then set up a commission to take evidence from both sides and the union agreed to suspend the strike, twenty-three weeks after it had begun.

Mitchell and Wilson appeared in front of the commission and both performed superbly. The commission proposed a wage rise of 10 per cent and a reduction in working hours from ten to nine. The coal operators were also required to accept a six-man arbitration board with the power to settle disputes, made up of equal numbers of union and management representatives. Much of the credit for the victory went to John Mitchell, but Wilson was responsible for the organisation of the strike and the superb publicity that won the support of the public. The leadership of Mitchell and Wilson seemed unassailable and during a period of prosperity for the coal industry the National Joint Agreement operated satisfactorily.

But an economic slump was inevitable at some point, and it duly arrived in 1904. The price of coal fell and the coal operators sought wage reductions based on the agreed formula. Tied to the agreement and bound by public pledges to uphold labour peace in the industry, the leadership felt they had no choice other than to accept the wage reductions. But activists put them under heavy pressure to reject the pay cuts and tear up the agreements.

Miners' camp during a strike in West Virginia, 1922 (Courtesy Library of Congress)

Miners' families being evicted from their homes at the start of a strike. The coal companies owned the miner's homes and eviction was used as a deterrent to strike action. (Courtesy UMWA archives)

As delegates travelled to the national convention in 1904 they were in a distinctly militant mood and were prepared to vote for strike action. However, before the convention got under way, Mitchell and Wilson announced there would be a ballot of the membership on the pay proposals. They won the vote and were showered with praise from the government and the press. But many delegates left the convention feeling aggrieved and a growing number of activists became disillusioned by the leadership and critical of their collaborationist policies. Much of the condemnation was directed at Mitchell because of his underhand ways of operating and his track record of subterfuge against Patrick Dolan and others on the left.

When the deal was due for renewal two years later, the employers were divided on what to offer the miners. Some wanted to reinstate the pay levels of two years before, but the majority of coal owners were against any wage increase whatsoever. However, instead of calling a national strike, the leadership sought separate agreements with the minority of coal operators who were prepared to reinstate the wage scales. Strike action was only sanctioned against those employers who refused to pay the increase, in the misguided belief that they would quickly cave in. But the strikes dragged on for months and the settlements were different for each company and in each coalfield. This completely undermined the principle of national agreements, and shifted power from the national executive to the districts.

Wilson's move into politics

By 1908, Mitchell's authority was fatally undermined, forcing his resignation at the age of thirty-eight. William Wilson was still a highly respected figure in the union, and was untainted by Mitchell's autocratic style and anti-democratic methods. With Mitchell's support he stood for the presidency, but was challenged by a leading critic of the leadership and lost by a narrow margin. Wilson had stood at Mitchell's side during most of his years in the presidency, and he took his share of the responsibility for the catastrophic mistakes. He resigned as secretary/treasurer, although no one forced him out of the position. During his stewardship, annual turnover had risen from $16,000 to over $1m, and membership had grown to over 300,000. He left the union with good grace to continue a political career, which had already begun in 1906 with a victory in the Congressional elections.

Despite his bitter experiences as a trade union activist, Wilson refused to analyse society in class terms. Coal companies had evicted him on three

1908 UMWA Scranton convention delegate pin.

Congressman William B Wilson, 1906–12. Wilson's political career began in 1906 with a victory in the Congressional elections while still Secretary/Treasurer of the UMWA. He was appointed Chairman of the Labor Committee when the Democrats won control of the Congress in 1910.

occasions and his campaigning activity frequently led to imprisonment. Yet he professed never to have felt bitterness against the capitalist system. His father was a member of the Socialist Party but Wilson opted for the Democratic Party, and while still secretary/treasurer of the UMWA, he won the nomination for Congress in the district of northern Pennsylvania. His Republican opponent, who had served three terms in Congress, was a wealthy businessman who owned lumberyards, a bank and several newspapers in the district. However, Wilson was now highly respected throughout Pennsylvania, and not just in the mining areas. With a campaign budget of a fraction of his opponent, he won the seat by a narrow margin and was re-elected in 1908, tripling his majority. His vote increased again in 1910, despite being absent for three weeks during the campaign while he attended the British Trades Union Congress.

In his third term, the Democrats took over control of the House from the Republicans and Wilson was appointed chairman of the Labor Committee. He pioneered mining legislation, particularly in relation to health and safety. Apart from his own brush with death in the mine, he had witnessed a number of fatal accidents, including that of a man who was trapped after an avalanche: Wilson led the attempted rescue. He was also well qualified to pursue legislation on child labour. An eight-hour day was granted for government employees and greater protection was given for workers during disputes. Merchant seamen had cause to be grateful when he steered a Bill through Congress improving their conditions, which became known as 'Wilson's Seamen's Bill'.

Meanwhile, in the mining industry, a more aggressive employer stance changed the attitude of the miners. Compromise and co-operation with the mine owners was replaced with militancy and confrontation. District coalfield bargaining had changed the power base of the union. The Midwest coalfields were developing fast and Illinois was becoming the most powerful district in the UMWA. Its president, John Walker, was born in Binniehill, a small mining village near Slamannan in Stirlingshire. He came to Braidwood in 1881 with his parents when he was nine, and started work in the mines soon afterwards. Encouraged by the inimitable Dan McLaughlin, he became active in the union and was sent to organise miners in southern Illinois and West Virginia. He became president of District 12 (Illinois) in 1905 and for the next thirty years was one of the most powerful figures in US trade union and political circles. Narrowly failing when he stood for national president of the union in 1909, he was unsuccessful in further attempts in 1916 and 1918, mainly due to shady political manoeuvres by his opponents.

Hopes for an American Labor Party

Walker was a member of the American Socialist Party, which was founded in 1900. It attracted the support of some leading trade unionists, including Duncan McDonald, another Scotsman who was secretary/treasurer of District 12. Although it scored a number of electoral victories in the mining towns of Illinois, it was unable to widen its electoral appeal. Many trade unionists believed it was time to establish a broad coalition similar to the British Labour Party, but the leadership of the Socialist Party rejected any attempts to follow this approach. Walker was eventually expelled when he endorsed a pro-labour Democratic Party candidate in an election, and he then turned his attention to forming an American Labor Party.

The concentration of large numbers of miners in coalfield constituencies gave them tremendous influence in determining the outcome of elections. In Britain, the transfer of allegiance of the miners from the Liberal to the Labour Party was largely responsible for Labour's parliamentary breakthrough. But in the USA miners were traditionally encouraged by the union to vote for the candidate with the best pro-labour record, irrespective of party. Often their recommendation was based on securing protective legislation for miners on issues such as mine safety and training. Although the Democratic Party was later seen as the more pro-labour of the two main parties, the first generation of Scottish colliers tended to support the pre-civil war Republican Party, based on its philosophy of 'free soil, free labor, free men'. Another reason for the non-partisan approach was that the American Federation of Labor (AFL) insisted on an unaligned political position for all its affiliates. These were some of the barriers Walker had to overcome if he was to have any success in forming a Labor Party.

However, Walker was in a very powerful position. Not only was he leader of District 12, but he was also elected president of the Illinois Federation of Labor, which was the biggest in the United States. It gave him an influential role in state politics, access to leading industrialists, and a prominent position in national AFL affairs. In 1920 he and Duncan McDonald made their move to form a new party, which was based on an alliance between the industrial workers and the farmers. The National Farmer-Labor Party was established, with Walker as national chairman and McDonald becoming leader in Illinois. There were high hopes for its success, but it depended on trade union affiliation and financial support. The key union was their own District 12 of the UMWA and the pair were confident that the miners would back the party. But they suffered a humiliating defeat when delegates at the District 12 convention voted by a narrow majority against committing union funds. Failure to break the traditional non-partisan policy of the Illinois miners was a fatal blow to their plans. Later in 1920, Walker stood for Governor of Illinois on a Farmer-Labor ticket, but was heavily defeated. Although he won support in the mining areas, Chicago's huge working class shunned the new party.

A dispirited Walker gave up the idea of challenging the two main parties. Without funding from the unions, a Labor Party could never get off the ground. It has been speculated that had the Illinois miners followed their Scottish counterparts in endorsing and funding a Labor Party, the face of American politics may have changed. A few years later, when the British Labour Party formed its first government, the National Farmer-Labor Party was defunct.

During John Walker's attempts to establish an American Labor Party, William Wilson's star was rising. However, he had suffered a setback in 1912 when he lost his seat in Congress. The Republican candidate won by a few hundred votes, with a Socialist candidate taking over two thousand. Although there was a strong lobby for him to stand for Governor of Pennsylvania, Wilson thought he was finished with politics. But Woodrow Wilson, who became President of the US in 1913, had other plans for his namesake. He offered him the newly created cabinet post of Secretary of Labor, responsible for running the Department of Labor. Its purpose was to foster, promote and develop the welfare of wage earners. It also had authority to mediate in labour disputes.

The Department of Labor

However, a few months into the new job, a miner's dispute in Colorado exposed the limits of the Labor Department's powers. In August 1913 a strike was called by the UMWA against the Colorado Fuel and Iron Corporation, which was owned by the Rockefeller family. It ended in one of the most brutal attacks on organised labour in American history. The union sought a 10 per cent rise, compliance with health and safety legislation and union recognition. When the strike started, eight thousand miners and their families, most of whom were southern and eastern European immigrants, were evicted from their homes. The UMWA were well prepared and set up tent colonies on land rented outside the coal company's property. Union organisers helped arrange the social life of the tent community, as well as picketing and guard duty. The corporation brought in strike-breakers and over the next few months, sporadic violence occurred. After several deaths caused by fights between miners and scabs, the National Guard were called in to maintain order. As the strike dragged on through the harsh Colorado winter, the miners were kept alive by supplies from the UMWA and donations of food from trade unionists throughout America.

In March 1914, after the death of a strike-breaker, the Governor of Colorado ordered the destruction of the colonies. The following month militiamen, accompanied by armed company guards, surrounded the settlement. Each night after dark they attacked sections of the colonies, ripping down tents in an effort to terrorise the miners and their families. Then, on 20 April, nine months after the strike started, National Guard troops opened fire on the Ludlow tent colony, where over a thousand men, women and children lived. In a frenzied assault, they pumped rifle shots directly into the tents from nine o'clock in the morning until dusk. They then entered the colony, looting and burning the tents as they went. When the attack was over, seven men, two women and eleven children lay dead. The enraged miners swore revenge against the militia. They collected every weapon available and for ten days southern Colorado was gripped in an armed rebellion. The American establishment was taken aback by what was described as the nearest approach to a worker's revolution seen in the country. President Woodrow Wilson ordered the US Army into the coalfield to take control.

Public anger was expressed at the brutality of the militia but none of the National Guard faced punishment for the murders. Instead, the strike leaders were arrested and hundreds of others were victimised by the company. Throughout the dispute, the company owner, John D. Rockefeller, refused William Wilson's attempts at mediation. When the dust settled, it was Rockefeller's obstinacy that was blamed for the dispute and its outcome. A monument was erected in Ludlow by the UMWA in memory of those who lost their lives, and in December 2008 the US Government designated the Ludlow site as a national historic landmark.

The Ludlow Massacre led to a deterioration in relations between unions and employers. Requests to arbitrate in disputes inundated the Labor Department and the civil servants found it difficult to cope with the volume. When the US entered the First World War in 1917, labour shortages put the unions in a strong bargaining position and the number of disputes increased. As employment issues assumed paramount importance, the Secretary of Labor's role became more significant.

In return for a no-strike pledge from the AFL, William Wilson guaranteed the right to collective bargaining, an eight-hour day, curbs on war profiteering, and the establishment of grievance procedures. A National War Labor Board was established, composed of equal numbers from industry and unions to adjudicate in disputes not resolved by the conciliation service. To ensure an adequate labour pool around factories and shipyards, a huge housing development was started at a cost of $60m. Union membership soared from two million in 1916 to 3.2 million in 1919. William Wilson was the toast of the AFL.

Howat v. Lewis, a battle for the soul of the union

The UMWA remained the strongest union in the AFL, but a bitter power struggle started when John L. Lewis was elected president in 1919. The charismatic but highly autocratic Lewis was the son of a Welsh miner. He held office for the next thirty years, his lengthy reign due as much to his ruthless suppression of dissent as to his ability. Lewis saw the centralisation of power as essential for a strong, disciplined union and he was set on a collision course with powerful district leaders like John Walker, who fought to retain their autonomy.

The first district to feel the full effect of Lewis' authoritarian methods was Kansas (District 14), where the president was Alex Howat. Born in Glasgow in 1876, Howat emigrated with his parents to New York and then to Braidwood where he grew up alongside John Walker and John Mitchell. In 1889 the family moved to Kansas, where Howat attended school before going down the mines. At twenty-two he decided to go back to Scotland and worked his passage on a cattle boat. He stayed for a year working in the mines and learning about union organisation and class politics from some of the veterans of the Lanarkshire miners' campaigns. He returned to Kansas inspired by socialist philosophy and a firm understanding of how to lead the state's miners. By the time he was thirty he was president of District 14 and turned it into one of the most militant and left wing in the country. The Kansas miners began to revere a leader who managed to unite the diverse ethnic groups in the industry and turn the union into a powerful economic and political force.

District 14 became renowned for defying national union instructions in relation to strike action. Howat, who was a member of the anti-war Socialist Party, had led strikes during and after the First World War that broke the no-strike pledge given to the Government. In response, a law was introduced in Kansas in 1921 that essentially took away the

Alex Howat, president of District 14 (Kansas) of the UMWA, was born in Glasgow.
He was elected President of District 14, turning it into one of the most militant and
left wing in the country. A vigorous opponent of John L Lewis he became President
of the short-lived Reorganised UMWA before being expelled from the UMWA.
(Courtesy Bain Collection, Library of Congress)

right to strike and made all disputes a matter for compulsory arbitration. However, when a miners' strike started a few months later, Howat refused to accept the new legal impositions, and was jailed. Lewis had waited for his opportunity to bring the most dissident district into line, and saw his chance to sack Howat and his allies. Lewis then installed his own supporters as officials in a new Kansas district office and ordered the miners back to work. Many of them stayed out on strike, but Lewis helped recruit miners from neighbouring coalfields, while federal officers raided and harassed strikers' camps.

Howat continued organising in the western mining states, where he was well known for his lengthy speeches, which often lasted for several hours. At every UMWA convention he rallied his troops in battle against Lewis, sometimes resulting in punch-ups at the rostrum. In 1924 he was almost successful in destroying Lewis's machine when he narrowly failed to have all full-time officials elected by the membership instead of appointed by Lewis. Towards the end of the 1920s the national convention restored some of the autonomy to the districts, and Howat was re-elected to lead the Kansas miners.

But the internecine war was costing the union dearly. By the end of the 1920s UMWA membership had plummeted but Lewis's attacks on his perceived enemies continued. He even attempted to suspend John Walker and the officials of the powerful District 12. However when Lewis's placemen arrived at District 12's HQ to take control, they were met by armed resistance and were forced to back off. A split in the union seemed inevitable, and in 1930 miners' representatives from Ohio, Pennsylvania and West Virginia joined their Illinois colleagues at a convention to launch a new union. It was named the Reorganised UMWA with Alex Howat elected president and John Walker as secretary/treasurer.

However, Lewis out-manoeuvred his opponents. Using his senior AFL connections, he had the Reorganised UMWA branded as an outlaw organisation. The two unions fought it out in the coalfields, with physical attacks on organisers of both sides. As UMWA chronicler McAlister Coleman described it, 'guns began to pop, brother shot it out with brother, father with son. Through twisting alleyways of the small towns, out along the new hard roads, union man hunted union man.' The superior resources of the UMWA won in the end, and within a year the rebels were defeated. Lewis was now in complete control of the UMWA and surrounded himself with loyal supporters. At the top were Thomas Kennedy, secretary/treasurer, and Philip Murray, a Scotsman, who was vice-president. (see Chapter 2)

William B Wilson, Secretary of Labor. Wilson was the first Secretary of Labor in the USA when he was appointed in 1913, and held the cabinet office for eight years. (Courtesy Library of Congress)

The futile attempt at setting up an alternative miners' union allowed Lewis to finish off his most implacable enemies. Walker was forced to resign from the presidency of the Illinois State Federation by the AFL. In 1933 Lewis removed him from the presidency of District 12. Alex Howat refused to appear before the executive of the UMWA and was expelled. He ended up editing a labour newspaper and working for the Kansas City council.

William Wilson's lasting legacy

William Wilson was in charge of the Department of Labor from 1913 until 1921. Afterwards, he returned to his farm from where he continued to play an active part in public life and in 1926 made an unsuccessful bid for the US Senate. Of his eleven children, his daughter, Agnes, was the most political, but sadly she died of a heart attack while campaigning for a Senate seat in 1928. Wilson died in 1934 and the American Legion now owns his farm. In front of the building there is a memorial statue to Wilson and inside the memorabilia includes a tapestry given to him by the Seamen's Union in appreciation for the Maritime Act that Wilson steered through Congress.

In the Department of Labor building in Washington, Wilson's portrait has pride of place as the first of over twenty Secretaries of Labor. In 1989 the Department of Labor established the Labor Hall of Fame, which posthumously honours those whose distinctive contributions have enhanced the quality of life of Americans. Each year an individual is chosen, and in 2007 William B. Wilson was inducted. His great-grandson proudly accepted the award from the President of the UMWA and the Secretary of Labor.

Chapter 2

Philip Murray, the US steelworkers and the CIO

At the 1920 convention of the United Mine Workers of America, the newly elected President, John L. Lewis, waited nervously for the result of the vice-presidential election. The contest was between two Scotsmen, only one of whom he could possibly work with. The result was close: Philip Murray had defeated Alex Howat by a margin of 11,000 out of almost 400,000 votes. Lewis breathed a sign of relief and congratulated his new partner at the head of the union. Murray had been one of Lewis's main supporters in his bid for the presidency, and the two remained close colleagues for the next twenty years. Indeed, Murray served his enigmatic president with unswerving loyalty, even when he disagreed with his policies. They worked well together. Lewis was the inspired orator, the flamboyant leader. Murray was the cool, calm, reasonable man who eventually hammered out the final agreements with the mine owners.

Their partnership was crucial to the formation of another major union led by Murray – the United Steelworkers of America. But arguably the most important legacy the duo left the US labour movement was the organisation of unskilled workers into a new trade union centre, the Congress of Industrial Organizations. However, their special relationship came to an abrupt conclusion over a difference of opinion about US involvement in the Second World War, with Lewis declaring, 'It was nice to have known you, Phil.' In the end the break with Lewis was a relief for Murray, who was then able to pursue his own policies without having to seek approval from the domineering UMWA president.

Philip Murray was born in Blantyre, Lanarkshire, not far from William Wilson's birthplace. His Irish parents came to Scotland to escape the ravages of poverty, joining tens of thousands of compatriots in the mines, mills, factories and steelworks of the central belt of Scotland. His mother was a weaver at a cotton mill and his father was a miner. Philip's mother died when he was only two years old, and his father was left to bring him up along with his four-year-old sister. Known to his colleagues as 'the intellectual', his father was president of the local miners' union. He remarried and had eight more children.

Blantyre's population had continued to grow as its coal and steel production increased to meet the demands of the shipbuilding and heavy engineering industries in nearby Glasgow. But some of the families of the town paid a heavy price for the rapid industrial expansion. On 22 October 1877 a massive gas explosion ripped through one of the local collieries. In Scotland's worst mining disaster 218 men and boys lost their lives. The blast was heard for miles around and a column of dense black smoke filled the sky above the village as streams of men, women and children ran from their cottages towards the pit. Volunteers worked day and night to retrieve the bodies and it took over a week before all the dead were recovered. An enquiry was conducted to establish the cause of the explosion but the mine continued in production. Two years later, another explosion at a nearby pit owned by the same company claimed twenty-eight lives.

Memories of these disasters were still fresh in the minds of the villagers when Philip Murray was born in 1886. His father wanted an education for his children and a future away from the mines, but with the number of mouths to feed increasing, he reluctantly concluded that Philip would have to leave St Joseph's primary school and start work. In common with most Blantyre boys, Philip joined his father down the pit at the age of ten, but even with two of the family working there was often insufficient food on the table. There seemed little prospect for improvement except emigration. Philip's uncle had moved to Pennsylvania several years before and sent glowing accounts about the standard of living in America. After family discussions, it was decided to give America a try.

The rise of Philip Murray

Sixteen-year-old Philip and his father left the rest of the family behind and sailed to New York carrying international union transfer cards issued by the Lanarkshire Miners Union. Arriving on Christmas Day 1902, they cleared immigration at the new centre on Ellis Island and boarded a train for the western Pennsylvanian coalfields. Trudging through a snowstorm for the last four miles of their journey, they finally arrived at the uncle's home in Maddiston, Westmoreland County. With no time to waste, they started work a couple of days later to earn enough to pay for the fares of the rest of the family. Within a year they were reunited and housed in coal-company accommodation.

Murray started a correspondence course in maths and science designed for coalminers seeking promotion to supervisory positions. He completed the eighteen-month course in six months and looked forward to a career in management until he was involved in a confrontation that proved to be a turning point in his life.

Miners were paid by the weight of coal they produced, and at the mine where Murray worked the men were convinced they were being cheated by a dishonest weighman. Murray, who had attended union meetings in Blantyre with his father since he was a child, agreed to lodge a protest on behalf of the men. He suggested to the manager that the miners should be allowed to appoint their own man to check the weights, which was common practice in Scotland. The manager rejected the proposal out of hand and denounced him as a foreign agitator. For the first and only time in a labour dispute, Murray lost his temper, and with one blow from his fist he knocked out the manager. The next morning he was fired. Immediately the five hundred men at the pit stopped work, demanding his reinstatement. Company police arrested Murray and held him prisoner for the duration of the strike. Meanwhile his family and the striking miners were evicted from their homes and forced to live in tents. The strike collapsed after three weeks and Murray was escorted by deputies out of Westmoreland County and warned never to return. The pain of leaving his family fuelled his anger about the way a reasonable request was dealt with. From that moment, Murray resolved to devote his efforts to building a miners' union strong enough to prevent such injustice.

Murray headed for Pittsburgh, joining a sea of immigrants who flooded into the city to work in its burgeoning coal and steel industries. Described as 'hell with the lid off', Pittsburgh's steelworks, smelters, coke ovens, chemical and metallurgical factories belched out smoke and flames twenty-four hours a day. Housing, often flimsy wooden tenements, was inadequate, and health and sanitary laws were not enforced. The buildings were blackened by soot, industrial waste piled the streets and smoke spread everywhere. Work was literally sweated out of people, with hours of work unlimited and child labour common. But with vast deposits of coal and iron ore, Pittsburgh was a natural place for manufacturing and had become a focus of unrestrained American capitalism.

Finding work in Hazelkirk on the outskirts of the city, Murray became president of the local union at the age of nineteen. He quickly impressed officials in the UMWA with his knowledge of union affairs, and his affable personality assisted in his rise through the ranks. In 1912, ten years after he arrived in the United States, he was elected to the international board, the new name for the national executive of the UMWA. Three years later, while still in his twenties, the soft-spoken, skilful young negotiator became president of District 5, western Pennsylvania. Murray's astute organisational ability and his capacity for inspiring and winning trust propelled him to the vice-presidency of the union in 1920.

Elizabeth and Philip Murray. The couple were married in 1910 and remained devoted to each other until Murray's death forty two years later. Murray, from Blantyre in Lanarkshire, became America's best known trade union leader. Elizabeth, who came from a mining family, had lost both parents when she was very young. (Courtesy, Murray papers, box 5 folder 21, Historical Collections and Labor Archives, Special Collections Library, Penn State University)

In Hazelkirk Murray also met a young woman whom he married after a whirlwind romance. Elizabeth Lavery had eight sisters but she was only three when her father was killed in an gas explosion at his pit. Not long afterwards, her mother died, and the burden of raising the family fell on her eldest sister Jane. During her childhood Elizabeth had suffered hardship and poverty, but was cheerful and optimistic about the future. The couple were married in 1910 and remained devoted to each other throughout their lives.

At the age of thirty-three, Murray was now one of the three top men in the largest union in North America. He was assisted in his successful early career by backing the winning side in the internal union battles. Such was the overpowering nature of the UMWA president, John L. Lewis that few people could have served as his lieutenant. But the Lewis–Murray relationship was based on mutual respect and an understanding of the different strengths each of them brought to the union. Sometimes they played good cop, bad cop with employers. Lewis stirred up the storm and Murray came in at the right moment and calmed the waters to achieve the settlement. Internal disputes and disagreements with other unions were dealt with in a similar way. Lewis played the devil's advocate and then Murray came in and offered the compromise they had both agreed beforehand.

Their personalities and outlooks were also quite different. Lewis had few loyalties, whereas Murray was a man who believed in commitments. He was extremely loyal to friends, union associates and political allies. Unlike the regal lifestyle of Lewis and other union leaders, Murray lived modestly in a working-class neighbourhood of Pittsburgh. He married a coalminer's daughter and continued living in the same house after he attained high office. He was from the union ranks and never drifted far from them in his style and behaviour – a classic case of the union leader who never forgot his roots.

The authority of the pair within the union was consolidated after the UMWA secured excellent long-term contracts with employers in the early period of their leadership. Their relationship grew closer and their hold on power stronger in 1924, when the secretary/treasurer William Green, with much encouragement from Lewis, left to become president of the American Federation of Labor (AFL). Green did not have a clear run, however, and Lewis's influence within the AFL was used to secure him the position. His challenger was a Scotsman, James Duncan, president of the Granite Cutters Union, who was born in Kincardineshire. Duncan

James Duncan, president of the Granite Cutters Union and first vice-president of the American Federation of Labor. Duncan, who came from Aberdeen, was a close friend of Samuel Gompers, the AFL President. When Gompers died, Duncan stood for the AFL Presidency, but was defeated by William Green and the UMWA election machine. (Courtesy Bain Collection Library of Congress)

served an apprenticeship as a granite cutter in Aberdeen before going to the United States in 1880 at the age of twenty-three. Thousands of granite cutters and quarriers from the Aberdeen area worked in the USA, many of them staying for a few months each summer season, and then returning to Aberdeen for the winter.

Duncan originally came to New York before moving to Baltimore. He became secretary of the Baltimore local union and was elected national president of the Granite Cutters Union in 1885. Shortly afterwards he led a successful strike for an eight-hour day. Duncan had attended the inaugural convention of the AFL, and his participation in AFL affairs grew when he was elected to the AFL executive and became one of its vice-presidents. Five years later he was promoted to first vice-president and developed a close personal friendship with Samuel Gompers, the AFL president. He became the AFL emissary to international trade union centres, attending the British Trades Union Congesss in 1898, the AFL delegate to the International Trade Union Conference in Budapest in 1911, a special envoy to Russia in 1917, and a member of the US mission at the Paris Peace Conference in 1919. When Gompers died, Duncan received the support of a wide cross-section of unions for the AFL presidency, but was defeated by William Green and the UMWA election machine.

Green had been secretary/treasurer of the UMWA for several years before Lewis and Murray rose to the top, and was not one of their trusted clique. With him safely ensconced in the AFL, they not only got rid of a potential problem, but also had a UMWA stalwart leading the AFL. Everything seemed to be going well for the duo until the mine owners began to break agreements during the latter part of the 1920s. Some employers stopped recognising the UMWA and membership began to fall. Attempts to recruit members were met with injunctions from employers. Disillusioned by the inability of the union to influence the coal companies and exasperated by ongoing internal union conflicts, miners left the union in droves (see Chapter 1, page 38). The autocratic methods used to purge the dissident activists meant that very few were prepared to come forward to take their place. The once powerful western Pennsylvania district, where Murray was formerly president, was down to its last two unionised mines, with a paltry 250 members. The UMWA leaders gradually found themselves rulers of an empire fast becoming bankrupt. The onset of the Great Depression deepened the problems of the UMWA and most of the American labour movement.

Philip Murray (left) and John L Lewis. Murray was vice-president of the UMWA and Lewis was president. They were close colleagues for twenty years until they clashed over US involvement in the Second World War.

Roosevelt and the unions

Lewis and Murray, who were both registered Republicans, tried to persuade the ruling Republican government to introduce favourable employment legislation. When these attempts failed, they then turned their attention to the Democratic Party, a move that was to have profound consequences for the future of the American trade union movement. In 1932 a delegation headed by Murray met with Franklin D. Roosevelt, the Democratic Party nominee for president. Roosevelt discussed his vision of a 'New Deal', part of which would strengthen the legal position of trade unions. These proposals were similar to William Wilson's wartime policies that gave unions a legitimacy they had not known before. The 'New Deal' proposals guaranteed a right to collective bargaining and recognition if a majority of workers in a company voted for it. From that point on Philip Murray pledged his absolute support and steadfast allegiance to the Democratic Party, establishing a lifelong friendship with Roosevelt. This relationship later drove a wedge between Lewis and Murray.

Roosevelt kept his word when he was elected in 1932. His legislation shifted the balance in industrial relations in favour of trade unions and the UMWA made full use of the new provisions. An initial union recruitment drive in the central coalfields met with enormous success, surprising even the leadership. Soon the entire country was reporting miners joining in their tens of thousands. In the Pennsylvania coalfields alone, 128,000 new members joined within a few months. Contracts were signed with coal operators, covering 90 per cent of the bituminous coal mined in the United States. And not only was the UMWA resurrected where it had once been strong, but it also succeeded in penetrating anti-union bastions. By 1934 the UMWA was again the largest and most influential trade union in the United States.

The upsurge in trade union activity was not confined to the mines. Unskilled workers in the mass-production industries were taking strike action and attempting to organise themselves into industrial trade unions. In the auto, steel, rubber and electrical goods industries, hundreds of thousands were looking to the American Federation of Labor to organise unions, but many of the craft unions doubted the feasibility of establishing permanent unions for the mass-production industries. Instead, they wanted the workers distributed amongst the existing craft unions. The UMWA, itself an industrial union of mainly unskilled workers, sought to encourage the growth of new independent industrial unions and this difference of approach led to a major split in the trade union movement.

At the AFL Conference in 1935 the UMWA called for the establishment of industrial unions. The proposal lost by a two-to-one majority. But the disgruntled minority formed the Committee of Industrial Organizations, with the aim of encouraging industrial trade unionism. The following year this group was expelled from the AFL, leading to the biggest ever rift in the trade union movement in the USA. The CIO was renamed the Congress of Industrial Organizations, and set up as an alternative trade union centre to the AFL. Lewis became president, with Murray one of two vice-presidents.

The UMWA had a particular interest in unionising the steel industry. The major steel companies mined much of their own coal and did not recognise the UMWA or any other union. The CIO set up a Steel Workers Organising Committee, and put Philip Murray in charge. But he knew that the steel industry was going to be a hard nut to crack. There was a history of bitter battles with the steel barons and memories of crushing defeats were still fresh in the minds of the workers.

Skilled steelworkers had at one stage been organised in a craft union that had been relatively strong. The Amalgamated Association of Iron and Steel Workers was formed in 1876 and for over a decade was recognised by all the main steel producers. William Martin, who came from Calderbank in Lanarkshire, was general secretary from its foundation until 1890. Martin served his apprenticeship at the Monklands Iron Company and emigrated to the United States in 1868, working in Pittsburgh and various towns in Ohio. Martin, who was also a vice-president of the AFL, was a first-class negotiator and an expert on differentials between the plethora of trades in the iron and steel industry.

The biggest employer was the dominant Carnegie Steel Company based in Pittsburgh and owned by fellow Scot, Andrew Carnegie. Carnegie initially encouraged his managers to deal with the unions because he believed in the right of workers to organise. He also knew that standardised pay agreements throughout the industry ensured others would not undercut his company. Carnegie was impressed by William Martin's ability, and offered him a senior management role in his company in charge of labour relations. Carnegie often promoted union activists, sometimes for ulterior motives, but at the age of forty-five, Martin accepted the offer in good faith and looked forward to a new career. But Carnegie became obsessed with cutting costs and his views on unions started to change. Unions were now obstacles to profits, and he was determined to drive them out of his companies. William Martin's new career came to a rapid halt two years after it started, following the company's union-busting at the Homestead steel mill.

Andrew Carnegie and the Pinkerton union-busters

Carnegie's history is well documented elsewhere, but his role in the Homestead lockout has been overlooked in many accounts of his life. The son of a weaver who led the radical Chartist movement in Fife, Carnegie was influenced by his father's belief in universal suffrage. The Chartists led a number of strikes in Britain, but were suppressed by an anxious ruling class determined to preserve their power and privileges. Carnegie's uncle, Tom Morrison, was jailed along with other leading Chartists and, as a result of the persecution, Carnegie's father decided to emigrate to America. The family settled in Pittsburgh, Pennsylvania and thirteen-year-old Carnegie started work as a bobbin boy in a cotton mill. When he was eighteen he was employed by the Pennsylvania Railroad Company as a telegraph operator before being promoted to more senior positions. Through his connections in this employment he was given insider information regarding investments. He borrowed money to buy shares in railroad related industries and this became the foundation for his later success. Gradually he acquired a controlling interest in iron and steel companies, eventually building an empire producing 25 per cent of US iron and steel.

Homestead was the company's flagship plant and employed almost four thousand workers. The skilled workers belonged to William Martin's union and the Knights of Labor had a foothold amongst the unskilled. Carnegie gave instructions to his lieutenant, Henry Frick, to reduce the wages of the Homestead workers and to derecognise the union. He then left for a shooting holiday in Scotland. Frick was a well-known anti-union dictator and he prepared the steel plant for a lockout of the workforce. To protect the steelworks, he contacted Pinkerton Detective Agency, a union-busting security firm.

The Pinkerton Agency was established in 1850 by Alan Pinkerton, an immigrant from Glasgow. A cooper by trade, he was also active in the Chartist movement and was seen by the establishment as a dangerous radical. Wanted by the police for subversive action, he was forced to leave Scotland the day after his wedding in 1842 and spent his honeymoon aboard a sailing ship heading for the United States. He initially found a job at his trade in the town of Dundee, 40 miles from Chicago, where he was elected deputy sheriff. Chicago was growing rapidly but had no

Alan Pinkerton, from Glasgow, was active in the chartist movement and was forced to leave Scotland on his wedding day. He set up the Pinkerton Detective Agency in Chicago that later became famous for its union-busting assignments. (Courtesy Library of Congress)

Homestead Strike, 1892. Armed Pinkerton agents sailed up the Monongahela River in barges in the middle of the night. But union guards spotted them, raised the alarm, and within thirty minutes thousands of strikers were attacking the barges. (Courtesy Library of Congress)

professional police force. Pinkerton saw a niche in the market and set up his detective agency. The origin of the term 'private eye' stems from the logo of his company: a large black and white open eye with the phrase 'we never sleep' beneath it. Initially the work involved preventing train robberies and checking the honesty of railway employees. Then, during the Civil War in the 1860s, the agency was asked to work for the Union army, including protecting President Abraham Lincoln. An assassination attempt at his inauguration was thwarted and the agency recorded a number of other notable successes.

Pinkerton, true to his radical roots, initially refused to accept any work connected with labour disputes. However, he broke his pledge when he was asked to assist in dealing with the Molly Maguires, a secret organisation of Irish–American coalminers. He had strong ideological disagreements with the Mollys, who were accused of acts of sabotage and assassination of coal-company bosses. A number of Pinkerton's staff infiltrated the organisation and identified its leaders, who were subsequently executed. A precedent had been set, and after Pinkerton died in 1884, his sons had no inhibitions about accepting union-busting assignments.

In July 1892, at the request of Henry Frick, the agency despatched three hundred of its battle-hardened union-busting men – known as Pinkertons – to Homestead. They were armed with Winchester rifles and revolvers, and were given instructions to secure the steel mill. However, the Homestead community had appointed a strike advisory committee, which was well prepared for a fight and had posted a round-the-clock guard against intruders. The Pinkertons sailed up the Monongahela River in barges in the middle of the night from Pittsburgh, expecting to take the strikers by surprise. But the union guards spotted them and sounded the alarm. Within half an hour thousands of steelworkers had risen from their beds and headed towards the river.

Union leaders warned the Pinkertons not to step off the barges, but were ignored. As they set foot on land, a gun battle started. The strikers rolled a flaming freight-train carriage at the lead barge and threw dynamite onto the others. Oil was pumped into the water and set alight. After fourteen hours the Pinkertons hoisted a white flag, by which time three detectives and seven steelworkers had been killed.

News of the gun battle spread quickly and support for the strikers flooded in from trade unionists all over the country. But the establishment were appalled and Carnegie became even more determined to crush the union. He gave orders from Scotland to refuse to negotiate and called on support from politicians. The full force of the state apparatus was then used against the workers. A week later, the Governor of Pennsylvania sent eight thousand National Guardsmen armed with high-powered weapons to take over the plant. The strike leaders, John McLuckie, Hugh O'Donnell, and Hugh Ross were charged with murder, organising a riot, conspiracy and treason. Other members of the strike advisory committee were later charged with lesser offences. Legal proceedings began in September 1892 and lasted two months. All the accused were acquitted, as no jury in the county could be found to convict them.

Although the company was defeated in court, the trial took its toll on the individuals and the union. While the leadership was tied up in court proceedings that lasted months, the company gradually began to draft in strike-breakers. As winter approached there was no sign of any attempt by the company to negotiate. Donations of food had become sporadic, union funds had dried up and the families faced the prospect of starvation over the winter months. As the strikers' morale fell lower, some began to return to work, and after five months they voted to end the dispute and return on company terms.

From the company's perspective the dispute successfully swept trade unionism from Homestead and the rest of the Carnegie mills. Wages were reduced substantially, a twelve-hour day was reinstated, and many rights and conditions were lost. But the tragedy of Homestead tainted Carnegie's reputation as a philanthropist and he was roundly criticised by the public, the church and the press. There were calls in Pittsburgh to reject grants he had given for the city's public libraries, and he was blamed by the Republican Party for the loss of the election in the same year. His radical friends in Britain snubbed him, and Keir Hardie, who had received £100 in election expenses from Carnegie, forwarded the money instead to the people of Homestead. The Glasgow Trades Council denounced him and even the conservative Cleveland Chamber of Commerce stripped Carnegie of his honorary membership. Over the years Carnegie tried to disassociate himself from the decisions before and during the strike, implying he would have done things differently had he been in the US. But throughout the dispute he was giving clear instructions by cable from his holiday base in Scotland.

Over 1,200 of the original Homestead workforce did not get their jobs back and were left destitute and homeless. The reverberations of the dispute were felt throughout the steel industry. The steel union was reduced to a negligible role in other companies as Carnegie's competitors followed suit and derecognised the union, with little resistance from the steelworkers. Henry Frick was shot by an anarchist during the dispute, but survived and continued as Carnegie's chief lieutenant. William Martin, bitter and disheartened at being duped by Carnegie, watched the union he had led reduced to a rump. He left the Carnegie Steel Company and started working on engineering innovation. He made a name for himself for a number of inventions, including a streetcar fender, a window lock and an emergency brake.

Murray rebuilds the union

The vulnerable steelworkers were virtually reduced to slavery. They worked a twelve-hour day with one day off every two weeks and no holiday apart from two public holidays a year, on 4 July and Christmas Day. In 1912, an investigation was carried out into conditions in the industry, and one steelworker was quoted as saying, 'Home is just a place where I eat and sleep. I live in the mills.' In 1919 an attempt to organise a union for the industry was made by the Industrial Workers of the World. They called a strike for an eight-hour day, better wages and improved conditions. Over 300,000 walked out, but the steel companies brought in strike-breakers and company police broke up union meetings. Hungry and dejected, the men drifted back to work and after fifteen weeks the strike was called off. Once again the steel companies had plenty of allies in other businesses, abundant supplies of cash and loyal support from national and state governments. This was the foe that Philip Murray now faced!

Murray realised that these demoralising defeats against an obdurate enemy made it difficult to persuade steelworkers to join a union. He explained later, 'Our first problem was to banish fear from the workers' minds.' The UMWA committed $500,000 for an organisation and recruitment drive and employed two hundred full-time staff for the task. There was little glamour attached to the job. Men had to be approached one at a time as the first step in establishing a core of secret union members. They were visited in their homes, usually after dark, so that neighbours would not get suspicious. Conscientious organisers worked day and night and Murray deliberately sought out communists for the task, as he believed they were the most dedicated. The staff on the union payroll were assisted by thousands of unpaid volunteers, who were mostly members of the Communist Party and other left-wing organisations.

But some spoke openly about trade unionism and were fearless in their attacks on the steel companies. Bert Hough was well known in

Bert Hough, President Pennsylvania steelworkers, addressing the Congress Labor Committee, 1939. Hough, from Glasgow, was well known in steel towns in Pennsylvania during the organizing years of the 1930s. He became President of the Pennsylvania District of the United Steelworkers. (Courtesy Library of Congress)

Pittsburgh and other steel towns in Pennsylvania for his fiery speeches at street-corner meetings. His pronounced Scottish burr was heard by thousands of steelworkers during the organising years of the 1930s. Hough had fought in the First World War and was badly wounded in action. After his demob he returned to his home in Glasgow but could not find a job. In the early 1920s he moved to the United States and found work in the steel town of Midland, near Pittsburgh. He became immersed in the campaign to build a union for steelworkers, and was one of Murray's most trusted organisers. He was a key witness in Washington at the House of Congress Labor Committee's hearings on workers' conditions in the steel industry. He explained to the Committee how he had often worked continuous seventy-two hour shifts in his steel plant. Hough became president of the Pennsylvania District of the United Steelworkers when it was founded in 1941 and continued in that position until he died in 1960, aged sixty-three.

The sceptical steelworkers were assured by union organisers that they would not be engaged in strike action until they were properly organised. Instead, Murray advocated co-operation with the steel companies. He used his high-level contacts in government and traded on the growing reputation of the UMWA to secure agreements. Membership began to rise to over 125,000, although a large proportion was exempt from paying dues for an initial period. A breakthrough came in 1937 when a recognition agreement, brokered by John Lewis, was reached with the country's biggest steel manufacturer, the US Steel Corporation. The agreement gave steelworkers a 10 per cent rise, a forty-hour week, time and a half for overtime and longer holidays.

Within three months of this breakthrough, 140 companies, representing 75 per cent of steel-making capacity, signed contracts recognising the union. Membership surged to 250,000 and dues began to be collected from all members. However a group of smaller steel companies, which employed over 186,000 workers between them, refused to follow suit and chose to resist union recognition. Their leaders were entrepreneurs with strong anti-union attitudes. Known collectively as 'Little Steel', they prepared for a strike, stockpiling arms and ammunition for the inevitable battles. Confident of political support from President Roosevelt and the New Deal Democrats, Murray gambled on a short traditional strike with mass picketing. Three of the companies were targeted and 78,000 workers were called out. Miscalculating the depth of political assistance, the union was ill prepared for the reaction.

Tapping Slag at Blast Furnace, Pittsburgh, PA 1938 (Courtesy Library of Congress)

Two days after the strike started, a peaceful demonstration of several thousand marched to the Republic Steel Company's South Chicago plant. For no apparent reason, police suddenly opened fire on the marchers. When the crowd dispersed, ten strikers were found dead and fifty-eight wounded, most of them shot in the back. On the same day in Ohio the Democratic Governor used the National Guard and state police to break local strikes. In Johnstone, Pennsylvania, martial law was declared and steel plants forcibly reopened. A further six strikers were killed in these and other demonstrations. Ironically, the atrocities happened on Memorial Day, an anniversary commemorating Americans who were killed in battle. The 'Memorial Day Massacre' as it was named, devastated the union. An attempt by President Roosevelt to end the strike proved fruitless, and in the end the union was forced to concede defeat. This was a severe blow to Murray, who was blamed for not properly preparing for the strike. The inability of Roosevelt to end the strike was a source of further problems that affected Murray's relationship with John Lewis.

However, outside the steel industry the push to form unions came from the rank and file, who were restless to organise. In the rubber and auto industries the workforces were fearless. Even in the depths of the Depression, they secured breakthrough agreements at Goodyear Tyres and General Motors after momentous strikes. These victories resonated with ten of thousands of other workers. Assisted by the CIO, unions were established for workers in the packing houses, the wharves, the textile mills, the shipyards and factories throughout the country.

Unions among the shipbuilders

In the shipbuilding industry, where a high proportion of Scottish tradesmen worked, unions had flourished until the end of the First World War. But when military orders from the government fell sharply, there were massive lay-offs and employers used the economic conditions to impose an 'open shop' policy, driving unions from the yards. After the New Deal, the shipyard workers fought back. Even before the CIO was formed, the 3,300 workforce at the Camden shipyard in New York set up a union. Following a successful strike they won recognition and a pay increase.

A number of Scots worked at the yard, including their charismatic leader, John Green from Clydebank, a highly experienced union official who was famous for his rousing oratory. Green served his apprenticeship as a plater with Barclay, Curle and Co., Glasgow and was a member of the Boilermakers Union. He was arrested and charged with conspiracy

John Green, president of the Industrial Union of Marine and Shipbuilding Workers, addresses the union's Convention in 1942. Proceedings were transmitted to UK via short length radio. Green, from Clydebank, who was famous for his rousing oratory, was also a vice-President of the CIO. (Courtesy Library of Congress)

during the First World War for leading an apprentices' strike in 1915. Unemployed after the War, Green emigrated to New York in 1923, and started work at the Camden yard. A year later his wife and four children joined him. At the start of the Depression he was forced to move to Philadelphia, where he found a job with William Cramp Shipbuilders. He joined the Socialist Party and became active in the Philadelphia branch. Various groups of workers in the city were involved in strike action during this period, and Green assisted them with publicity and organisation. Returning to Camden in 1933, he led a number of committed activists in forming a union and organising the strike. After the success of the strike, other workers along the East coast achieved union recognition. Within a year six locals met in Quincy, Massachusetts, to form the Industrial Union of Marine and Shipbuilding Workers. Green was elected president, and in 1937 became a vice-president of the CIO when the union affiliated.

Across on the West coast, Ben Carwardine from Renfrew started another shipbuilding union. Born in 1885, Carwardine served an apprenticeship as a moulder with William Simons and Co., a dredge-building company in Renfrew. He was one of the leaders of a progressive group in the Iron Moulders Union. Active in the Independent Labour Party, he set up a local branch and was elected to the Scottish Divisional Council. A scholarship for Ruskin College, Oxford enabled him to study economics and politics for two years. Founded in 1899, Ruskin College provided university-standard education for the working class. Its students came from trade unions, political parties and co-operative societies, and were expected to go back to work in these communities.

Post-war unemployment on Clydeside forced Carwardine to look elsewhere, and he emigrated to San Francisco in 1921, working as a shipwright for the Bethlehem Shipbuilding Company. The company was a subsidiary of Bethlehem Steel, one of the Little Steel companies, and notoriously anti-union, as the steelworkers found out in 1937. In 1934 Carwardine was sacked for trying to organise a union. But he continued to campaign in Oakland and Seattle, recruiting enough workers to establish the Independent Shipworkers Union, and leading two successful strikes. The East and West coast unions merged in 1937, with Green and Carwardine elected president and vice-president respectively.

Despite the growth of the CIO, its finances were in a mess and there were constant personal and political squabbles. One of its most important affiliates, the Ladies Garment Workers Union, with 250,000 dues-paying members, left and returned to the AFL. An internal political conflict in the

United Auto Workers threatened its existence, and only the intervention of Philip Murray saved it from a major split. Disputes between pro-and anti-Communists were taking place in almost every union, attracting bad publicity and frightening away members. In addition, John Lewis, despite his uncanny ability to pull off agreements with company bosses, was behaving in an unstable and politically insensitive manner.

Lewis had been appreciative of the opportunities that Roosevelt's New Deal had offered trade unions, but was angry that the President did not do more to control the Little Steel companies. Lewis also denounced the Chicago Democrats for calling in the police at the Republic Steel plant on Memorial Day. Lewis believed that trade unions had been responsible for delivering millions of votes for the Democrats, but they were now getting little in return. Consequently, when Roosevelt announced his decision to stand for a third term, Lewis declared his opposition. Against the overwhelming sentiment within trade union circles, Lewis openly supported the Republican candidate in the 1940 presidential election and threw the weight of the United Mineworkers of America behind him. Such was the vehemence of Lewis's opposition to the Democratic Party that he announced he would resign as leader of the CIO if Roosevelt won. Following Roosevelt's victory, true to his word, Lewis stepped down, and at the next CIO convention, Philip Murray was the only nominee for president.

As a devout Catholic, Murray's trade union ideology was inspired by his Church's teaching. He placed great emphasis on Papal encyclicals relating to the rights of the working class and the relationship between labour and capital. These lay on his desk and served as a constant reminder of his obligation to the Church and his union members. He attended mass regularly, sometimes daily, in whichever city he was in, and drew strength from the Church's view of social Christianity. Politically, Murray believed that capitalists were exploiters of labour and class struggle was necessary, but he rejected Marxism. In Scotland, he had been close to the Fabians and he never lost his early Social Democratic beliefs. As a progressive liberal who supported Catholic reformism, he understood and generally tolerated left-wing activity in the unions.

Murray takes over the helm

Murray accepted the CIO presidency with some reluctance. His salaried position was still vice-president of the UMWA and he was unpaid as leader of the Steel Workers Organising Committee. Lewis was his boss and, having played second fiddle to him for almost twenty

Philip Murray at the Senate Civil Liberties Committee, 1938. Murray was keenly aware of the importance of political support for the unions. In 1940 he took over as president of the CIO and two years later became president of the United Steelworkers of America. (Courtesy Library of Congress)

years, Murray doubted that he would be allowed to be his own man. He was uncomfortable in this dual role, especially as he and Lewis had such opposing views on President Roosevelt and the Democratic Party. However, other CIO union leaders were confident that Murray would prove an able leader and were more comfortable with him than they were with Lewis. Their faith in him proved justified during 1941, after Murray shaped the CIO into a more coherent organisation with proper financial governance and a more appropriate structure.

However, the following year Lewis and Murray had a bust-up over American involvement in the Second World War, which eventually ended their relationship. Roosevelt wanted America to join the Allies and needed union support for his wartime economic policy that required no-strike agreements. Murray believed that Fascism posed a major threat and supported Roosevelt's request. Lewis was against it and maintained that organised labour should take advantage of the wartime industrial boom to aggressively pursue trade union demands. The question of America's neutrality in the Second World War was a topic that divided the nation. Lewis had hoped to get CIO support for his position and Murray knew it was about to open a rift between them. Unable to contain his frustration at Murray's defiance, Lewis's last words to Murray were, 'It was nice knowing you, Phil.' Murray knew that it was only a matter of time before he was sacked from his UMWA job.

Initially it looked as though Lewis would win the argument. On his side were the Communists and their allies, who played major roles in building the CIO affiliates and made up around one third of the delegates at the CIO convention. The Soviet Union and Germany had signed a non-aggression pact and the US Communist Party was opposed to American involvement in the war. However, this position changed when Germany invaded the Soviet Union in June 1941. Communist activists now supported the war effort and denounced Lewis for leading strikes by miners. The argument over American involvement in the war was settled by the bombing of Pearl Harbor by the Japanese in December 1941, and all union leaders signed no-strike pledges for the duration of the war.

However, relations between Lewis and Murray, who had both suffered heart attacks in 1941, now degenerated. Lewis hatched a plan to reunite the American Labor movement and remove Murray from leadership, but this backfired. Then Murray's position was strengthened when a rank-and-file-inspired strike at the Little Steel companies ended in a victory for the union. With wartime contracts up for grabs, the Little

Steel companies reached recognition agreements and by 1942 practically the entire steel industry, including office staff, was unionised. The Steel Workers Organising Committee, which had been set up as a temporary organisation, was replaced by a permanent union, the United Steelworkers of America (USWA). There was never any doubt that the president would be Philip Murray and, when he accepted the $20,000 per annum salaried position, Lewis expelled him from the UMWA. Lewis later withdrew the UMWA's 600,000 miners from the CIO.

Although he resented his expulsion, Murray was now free of the constant dilemma between his leadership of the CIO and his allegiance to the miners. But as president of the United Steelworkers he was in a position to rival Lewis as the all-powerful leader of a union that now had more members than the UMWA. The other CIO unions also developed and matured, making Murray, according to public opinion polls, the best known and most popular labour leader in America. For the duration of the Second World War, he was constantly in the public eye and had to balance the need for maximum production with the defence of union members' interests. His loyalty to Roosevelt was often in conflict with the needs of his members, who faced restrictions on wages as prices soared. However, workers often ignored the no-strike pledges and even his own steelworkers took action, with Murray turning a blind eye.

But expanding wartime production boosted manufacturing, and membership of the industrial unions soared. The CIO grew from 1.8 million before the war to almost four million in 1944, despite the loss of 600,000 miners. The auto workers increased from 165,000 to over a million members, and the United Electrical Workers went from 50,000 to 432,000. With the boom in shipbuilding, John Green's Marine and Shipbuilding Workers Union expanded throughout the US and at its peak represented a quarter of a million members. The steelworkers reached the 700,000 mark before the war ended.

Post-war strikes

At the end of the wartime no-strike pledge, a wave of industrial disputes affected just about every industry. Workers attempted to make up for the drop in earnings due to wartime inflation. Massive walkouts in steel, auto, electrical goods, coal and the railroads took place. A national steel strike lasted a month and was the biggest walk-out in US labour history. Authorised by a vote of five-to-one, more than 500,000 workers took part. It was entirely peaceful and was so strongly supported that no attempt was made by the steel companies to break it. The settlement was almost exactly the amount the union had demanded. It is hardly surprising that at CIO's first post-war convention in 1946, Philip Murray glowed with pride about the steel settlement and about the strength of the CIO.

However, the extent and success of the post-war strike action provoked a reaction from the newly elected Republican administration in Congress. The additional wage costs for companies were recovered by hiking up prices. The large corporations deliberately announced price increases immediately after wage settlements, directing public anger at the unions. It was not long before public resentment of strikes allowed right-wing politicians to seize the opportunity to introduce anti-union laws. Some state legislatures passed laws banning strikes in key service sectors and outlawed solidarity action. Congress passed the notorious union-busting Taft-Hartley Act in 1947. It gave employers and the government powers to raise injunctions against unions, banned solidarity action, allowed employers to interfere in union recruitment, outlawed mass picketing and curbed the political and economic activities of unions. But the most divisive clause in the new law required all union officials to sign an affidavit stating they were not Communists!

A man prone to use religious metaphors, Murray depicted the Taft-Hartley Act as the work of the devil. At the 1947 CIO convention he declared that the Act was 'a sinful piece of legislation, and its promoters were diabolical men who, seething with hatred, contrived this ugly measure for the purpose of imposing their wrath on millions of workers'. Six months later, at the United Steelworkers' convention, he recalled some of his early involvement in disputes 'when company police, deputy sheriffs, county and federal courts were put to use to bludgeon, to murder, to imprison, to incarcerate and beat up the workers engaged in strike action … along comes the Taft-Hartley Act with all its repressions and all of its oppressions … the courts are now being used in almost every instance, the strong, mighty arm of the Federal Government, to repress labor'.

The Communist contribution

Having previously been partly responsible for the purge of Communists and Socialists in the UMWA, Murray had seen his union almost collapse as a result of the loss of some of its most enthusiastic and committed activists. Learning from this lesson, both Murray and Lewis agreed to employ scores of Communists and left-wing activists when the CIO was established because they were among the most dedicated and fearless organisers in the labour movement. The major role Communists had played in building the CIO affiliates was reflected in the election of Communists to senior positions in most unions. Communists also led fourteen unions, accounting for around 1.4 million of the CIO's four million members.

Charlie Doyle, vice-president of the Gas, Fuel and Chemical Workers Union , was a well-known Communist. Born in Coatbridge, Lanarkshire, he attended All Saints school before starting work at Stewart and Lloyd's steel mill. In 1923, at eighteen years of age, he emigrated to Buffalo, an industrial city in New York State with a number of huge steelworks, car plants and chemical factories. There were thousands of other Scottish workers there and he had little difficulty finding a job as a crane driver in a steel plant. He had been a member of the Communist Party of Great Britain and joined the American Communist Party as soon as he arrived. The Buffalo Communists met at the Labor Institute and Doyle was the branch secretary. When the CIO started the push to organise in Buffalo, the first person they contacted was Doyle.

With a nucleus of Communist steelworkers in the giant Bethlehem Lackawanna plant, the biggest steel-making complex in the world, Doyle already had a start. Initially, meetings were held in private, but when the first open meeting took place, only sixty people turned up out of 20,000 steelworkers. Of those, forty were already union members and company spies made up a large proportion of the remainder. Doyle was beaten up after one meeting by company heavies, but he persisted and slowly the number of union members increased. When there were enough members in a section of the steelworks, union-badge-wearing days were held, and strikes lasting a few hours were organised.

At the Republic Steel Plant in Buffalo, other Scottish steelworkers were active in the union recruitment and organisation drive. Led by David Sneddon from Motherwell, they met in Ryan's Bar in South Buffalo to plan the campaign. With only 5 per cent of the workforce in membership, and no dues-collecting system in force, they went ahead and set up a local with Sneddon as president. Across the city at the Bliss and Laughlin Steel Company, James Millar was the main union contact. Born in Motherwell, he started work at David Colville's steel plant when he was fourteen. His sister had settled in Buffalo and Millar decided to join her in 1929, just as the Depression was about to grip the country. His experience as a crane operator at Colville's was invaluable in securing work during difficult times and his involvement in the Iron and Steel

Trades Confederation in Motherwell led to him becoming President of the Bliss and Laughlin local. It took several years of campaigning before unions were recognised in all the Buffalo plants, but Scottish steelworkers played a major part in the success.

Doyle's efforts led to one of the landmark victories in the US steel industry. He was one of the leaders of the rank-and-file-inspired strike previously referred to which brought the Little Steel companies to the negotiating table. It started in the Lackawanna plant in 1941 when the whole workforce walked out after disciplinary action was taken against union supporters. An all-day battle was fought with police, in which strikers gave as good as they got. By the next morning Bethlehem's chairman, who had resisted unionisation until then, agreed to negotiate. Within weeks other Bethlehem plants followed suit and a company-wide deal was agreed. The other Little Steel firms soon fell into line, completing the unionisation of nearly the whole of the US steel industry.

Philip Murray respected the work done by Communists like Doyle to build the United Steelworkers. Once the Taft-Hartley Act was passed, the survival of Communists depended to a great extent on Murray's support. Failure to sign the 'non-Communist' affidavit would result in a union being decertified. It would be denied access to the National Labor Relations Board, the government agency responsible for implementing employment law. The union would also be exposed to raids on its members by other registered unions. The left wanted a militant campaign against the proposals, and encouraged locals throughout the country to take strike action in protest. But Murray and the CIO leadership thought this would make matters worse and concentrated on political lobbying. Murray, John Lewis of the miners, and some key CIO and AFL affiliates made defiant statements declaring they would refuse to sign the affidavit on principle. But in the end the CIO decided to leave it to individual unions to choose whether or not their officials should sign.

The establishment v. the Communists

As Cold War hysteria grew to fever pitch in the prelude to the McCarthy era, the pressure on Murray to ditch the left intensified. Then the Communist Party announced their support for Henry Wallace for US President in 1948. A former vice-president to Roosevelt, Wallace had broken from the Democratic Party and helped set up the left-wing Progressive Party. Communists were instructed to push his candidacy in trade unions, and this caused a bitter division in the CIO. Wallace risked splitting the Democratic vote and letting the Republicans through. Accused of being conciliatory towards the communists by the AFL, Murray came under severe criticism in the media. And in his own steelworkers union he was surrounded by vociferous anti-Communists who demanded he took action.

In the end, Wallace only received 2.4 per cent of the vote and had no effect on the outcome, which was a victory for the Democratic Party candidate Harry Truman. But after the election a witch-hunt was launched against anyone in the CIO who had supported the Wallace candidacy. Communists were sacked from CIO staff positions and attacks on the Communist Party appeared in the CIO press. At the 1949 Convention scores were settled with the unions that had supported Wallace. This was then extended to any support for Communist Party positions on a series of political issues starting from the German–Soviet pact of 1939. Eleven left-wing unions with a total of almost one million members were expelled, opening them to raiding by CIO affiliates as well as the AFL unions. Most unions signed the affidavit regarding Communist Party membership, and many used it as a means to defeat the left in their own unions.

Charlie Doyle observed these events from a prison cell. After his success with the steelworkers he was transferred to organise the chemical workers in the Buffalo area. The Gas, Fuel and Chemical Workers Union was formed with a membership of 50,000, and Doyle was elected national Vice-President. But in 1948 he was arrested and imprisoned for his Communist activity along with another Scot, John Williamson, the National Labor Secretary of the Communist Party.

Williamson was born in Partick, Glasgow. His father, a ship's engineer, had died after an accident at work in 1911. Struggling to raise a child on her own, his mother dreamed of a better life in America. She arranged to work as a housekeeper in Newport News, Virginia, but she found that conditions were no better than Glasgow. She tried Philadelphia and then traveled across to Seattle on the other side of the United States. Having left Scotland as a ten-year-old, Williamson went to school in Seattle until he was fifteen and then started an apprenticeship as a pattern-maker in the shipyards. Shipbuilding was thriving during the First World War and 32,000 people worked in Seattle's yards, including a sizable contingent of Scots. They were 100 per cent union-organised, the great majority belonging to the Boilermakers Union.

Two of Williamson's early influences were Scotsmen who worked in the yard. Jim Harris in the pattern shop had been a member of the

John Williamson, National Labor Secretary, Communist Party of the USA was born in Glasgow. He was responsible for the strategy and coordination of the work of Communists in American trade unions. In 1948, along with a number of other Communist Party leaders, he was jailed for five years, fined $10,000 and deported back to Scotland when he finished his sentence. (Courtesy International Publishers, New York).

Socialist Labour Party in Scotland, and told him stories about Red Clydeside and the shop stewards' movement. Bob McCallum, a close friend and next-door neighbour, worked as a rigger and was a militant trade unionist and socialist.

Williamson joined the Socialist Labor Party and then, in 1922, signed up to the fledgling Communist Party, which operated underground at that time. He became active in the youth wing, the Young Workers League, and it was not long before he was made national industrial organiser, based in Chicago. At the start of the CIO recruitment drive he was Communist Party Secretary in Ohio, one of the most industrialized states in the US. In 1946, Williamson became National Labor Secretary, responsible for the strategy and coordination of the work of communists in American trade unions.

Williamson and Charlie Doyle were arrested in 1948, along with two other prominent trade union leaders. Refused bail, they went on hunger strike for six days until pressure built up on the authorities to release them. Four months later Williamson was rearrested after the FBI burst into the Communist Party HQ and led away a number of Party leaders in handcuffs. They were charged with being members of the Communist Party and with conspiracy to organise and advocate the violent overthrow of the United States Government. They were all found guilty and sentenced to five years' imprisonment and fined $10,000. When Williamson finished his sentence in 1955, he was deported back to Scotland, which he had left when he was a boy of ten. Charlie Doyle was deported as an undesirable alien in 1954, along with his American born wife Mikki, whom he married while in prison.

America became consumed with stamping out Communism and sedition in the 1950s. Communists were notching up victories in Eastern Europe and China, and the war in Korea was going badly wrong for America. Senator Joseph McCarthy, the most determined anti-Communist of all the leading politicians, was put in charge of investigating subversion. He shifted the witch-hunt against the left to those Democrats who were associated with the New Deal or who were soft on dealing with Communism. The tidal wave of reaction helped the Republican, Dwight Eisenhower, defeat Harry Truman and win the presidential election in 1952. Philip Murray knew that American trade unionism owed as much to sympathetic governments as to the industrial power of the trade unions. He feared the worst, as Eisenhower owed the trade unions no favours.

Philip Murray (left), with Mayor Lawrence of Pittsburgh (centre), and President Harry Truman at a Democratic Party election rally in 1952. Murray had exhausted himself during the campaign, and four days after the election, he suffered a heart attack and died. (Courtesy Murray papers, box 5, folder 21, Historical Collections and Labor Archives, Special Collections Library, Penn State University)

During the election campaign, Murray had travelled across America by train in support of President Harry Truman. On the morning after Eisenhower's election, a depressed Murray boarded a train at Pittsburgh to travel to San Francisco to preside over the fourteenth convention of the CIO. Four days later, exhausted by the election campaign and another long steel strike, he suffered a heart attack and died at the age of sixty-six.

Tributes flowed in from industry, government and unions. The rival trade union centre, the AFL, sent its condolences at the passing of an outstanding leader. John Lewis eulogised about Murray's contribution to trade unionism. Obituaries in the media recorded the distinguished place Murray held in the economic and public life of the United States. The chairman of US Steel and other steel company leaders expressed their sympathy. A requiem Mass was held in St Paul's Cathedral, Pittsburgh, attended by dignitaries from all walks of American life. As the Mass was starting, whistles blew at steel mills throughout the United States and workers stood for a minute's silence. Company executives and office workers joined in the tribute, while outside the cathedral thousands gathered to pay their respects. The roofs of nearby buildings were crowded as the coffin was taken into the church, and steelworkers lining the streets wept openly at the passing of their leader.

Charlie and Mikki Doyle settled down in London and Charlie became a shop steward at Battersea power station. He was described by the *Daily Mirror* as the most dangerous man in Britain when he led the first national industrial action in the electricity supply industry in 1963. John Williamson was given a rousing welcome when he returned to Scotland. Over 250 communists cheered his entry to a meeting in Glasgow, including the general secretary, the Scottish secretary, and Willie Gallacher, Communist MP for Fife. Williamson went on to work full time for the Communist Party of Great Britain.

Philip Murray's place in US history is assured and he has been given prominence in the Hall of Fame in the Department of Labor in Washington. A bridge in Pennsylvania where the steelworkers rallied in the 1930s was named after him and Lanarkshire Council honoured him by naming a street in Bellshill Philip Murray Road. His last public speech was at a banquet given in his honour at a San Francisco hotel in 1952. He joked with the six hundred steelworkers present that the reason he agreed to attend was his 'graspy Scottish desire to get a free meal'. All who met him testified to his decency and personal warmth. Even those who disagreed with his policies regarded him with affection and reverence.

Chapter 3

Doug Fraser and Detroit's Auto Workers

The wheels were about to come off the American auto industry when Doug Fraser took over as president of the 1.4 million-strong United Auto Workers in 1977. The oil price increases of the 1970s had encouraged the import of fuel-efficient Japanese cars, which gradually captured a greater share of the American market. By the end of the decade car companies started closing plants and laying off workers in record numbers. The weakest of the big producers, the Chrysler Corporation, was on the verge of bankruptcy and hundreds of thousands of jobs were threatened. Fraser's role was crucial for its survival. Using his connections in the Democratic Party, a package was put together to keep the company afloat. Despite opposition from the Republicans and most of the financial press, Congress backed the rescue plan and the company's future was secured.

But the deal meant an enormous sacrifice for the Chrysler workforce. They were being asked to give up their most cherished conditions, some of which they had fought for years to achieve. In exchange for a reduction in pay and benefits, Fraser negotiated agreements on job security. He was deeply hurt at having to concede so much but felt he had little choice. Twice the proposals were rejected by the membership in ballots. Some activists described them as the biggest sell-out in union history. A third and final ballot was held in a last-ditch attempt to persuade the membership. Chrysler executives waited by their phones for the result as Fraser and senior union officials nervously paced the floor of his office. One of his of his colleagues asked, 'Doug, what the hell will we do if they turn it down?' The tension was broken when Fraser shot back, 'I'll jump off that bridge when I come to it.' The laughter continued until they heard that 55 per cent voted to accept the changes.

Fraser was renowned for his quick wit and sense of humour, traits that he says he inherited from his mother, Sarah. Born in Kilmarnock, she was remembered by all who met her as an unconscious comedian: even on her deathbed she had the family in stitches. Fifteen years older than her husband, she never liked to tell anyone her age, and when the priest came to administer the last rites and hear her confession, he asked how old she was. 'I am seventy-five, Father', answered the ninety-two-year-old Mrs

Fraser. When the priest left, the relatives scolded her for not telling the truth. She replied, 'Tell that nosy old bugger nothing about my age. I'd rather do a stretch in purgatory first.'

Born in the Gorbals district of Glasgow in 1916, Doug Fraser lived in a small tenement flat with his parents, his elder sister Sally, and his younger brother Kenneth. He was six years old when his father had to leave Scotland. Sam Fraser was an electrician and worked in the Clydeside shipyards. He had been unemployed for some time and had little prospect of a job during the depression that followed the First World War. His wife reluctantly accepted that there was no future in Scotland, and preparations were made to travel to America. The father went in advance of the family and found a job and lodgings in Paterson, New Jersey. Sarah had always worried about the crime rate in America and her worst fears were confirmed when her husband wrote to tell her that one of the lodgers in his boarding house had been murdered in his room. He admitted afterwards he was so nervous he couldn't sleep at night and put a chair behind the door to jam the handle. Anxious months passed before enough money was saved for the fares and the family could be reunited. Then, in April 1923, the family sailed from the Broomielaw in Glasgow on the steam ship *Caledonia*, bound for New York. Not long after the happy reunion, they moved to Detroit, a city where many other Scots had settled.

They left behind their many friends in the Gorbals, an area that was home to large numbers of immigrants. Sarah's family had been driven there from Ireland by the famines and the Frasers had been forced from the Highlands by the Clearances. They found refuge and work in Glasgow at the heart of Clydeside, the most renowned shipbuilding and heavy engineering centre in the world. But its industry was prone to huge market fluctuations that often resulted in large-scale unemployment. During the First World War the area produced guns, shells, warships and every other form of military hardware. By the time peace was declared in 1918, a vulnerable urban economy had become even more exposed by the temporary boost in wartime demand.

During and shortly after the war, Glasgow and the industrial areas of Scotland had been in ferment. Waves of strike action and political agitation organised by shop stewards challenged the state and paralysed industry. More worrying for the establishment was the political consciousness developing amongst the workers, particularly in light of the revolution in Russia in 1917. John McLean, a schoolteacher and one of Scotland's foremost political intellectuals, founded the Scottish Labour College, which organised Marxist classes for workers. Marxist ideology heavily influenced the leadership of the shop stewards and industrial action for economic goals was combined with rent strikes, anti-war activities and other political initiatives. This high level of left-wing political activity resulted in the area being christened 'Red Clydeside'.

However, Britain's economic collapse after the First World War had a devastating affect on the area, closing shipyards and factories and leaving a quarter of the labour force without work. This time it was no mere fluctuation, but a lengthy crisis that forced 400,000 people to leave Scotland during the 1920s. Most settled in England, but some of the most highly skilled workers were amongst the 60,000 who elected to travel further. These workers took with them not only the skills of their trades, but also a class-consciousness that had been developed through militant trade union struggles and political education.

Detroit in the Roaring Twenties

Like Glasgow in its heyday, Detroit was a thriving industrial city when the Fraser family arrived. It was one of America's fastest-growing cities, increasing from 300,000 at the turn of the century to 1.5 million by 1923. Its auto industry was booming and its workers earned the highest rates of pay in the USA. Car manufacturing, dominated by Ford, General Motors and Chrysler, was centred in Detroit and the southern Michigan towns of Flint and Pontiac, with secondary assembly and parts plants spread through a number of other states. Most of the Scottish immigrants were single men in their twenties when they arrived. They generally stayed in boarding houses run by Scots, or lodged with Scottish families. From here advice was given to new immigrants and information on job vacancies was shared. Scottish neighbourhoods were established and shops sold food imported from home. Even the car companies contributed towards making the Scots feel at home. The Ford Motor Company gave a generous subsidy to the St Andrew's Society, and kitted out a pipe band that they toured around America when showing their latest car models. Much of the social life revolved around Scottish customs and traditions, the Scotia Hall and the St Andrew's Hall being favourite meeting places for the ex-patriot community.

Unlike Glasgow, only a small proportion of the Detroit workers had trade union experience. Only amongst the skilled workforce was there any background of solidarity, class consciousness and collective bargaining.

But mass-production techniques in car manufacturing had reduced the number of skilled workers required to around 10 per cent of the workforce, who mostly worked in the tool rooms. The rest were unskilled and could be taught the main elements of their job in a few days. The bulk of unskilled assembly workers were from agricultural backgrounds in the southern United States or from eastern and southern Europe. Very few of them had any industrial experience, and little or no understanding of trade unions. Working practices were very different from Scotland. Instead of a relaxed one-hour lunch break, with time for a chat or a game of cards, Detroit workers had to wolf down their food in fifteen minutes before going back to work. Some companies were worse than others, and although Ford paid top wages, they dealt harshly with their staff.

Sam Fraser worked at Ford for a short time, but was so appalled at the way the workers were treated, he left as soon as he could. He described how they were herded like cattle and not even allowed to wash above their wrists because they would be wasting company time. He swore he would never drive a Ford car, and years later when his son Kenneth mentioned he was thinking of buying a Ford, he was told never to bring it near the house. The boy bought a Chevrolet instead. Some workers tried to encourage the formation of a union, but with the car companies hostile to any workplace organisation, and most of the unskilled workers apathetic, no meaningful trade union activity took place.

Regardless of his experience at Ford, Sam Fraser liked the American way of life but his wife Sarah was often homesick. Both Sam and Sarah were Catholics and Doug was an altar boy. The children attended Holy Redeemer School, where Doug was teased because he wore short trousers. He refused to go to school until his mother bought him long trousers like the other kids. A popular boy, he easily made new friends and quickly adapted to the American way of life. At home in Scotland his father had taken him to watch Celtic, but he soon forgot about football and became a baseball fanatic. Happy in his new environment, Doug played sports, street games with his friends, and got up to the typical mischievous pranks of lads his age. Indeed, something of the little boy remained in him throughout his life. Even when he was president of the auto-workers, he sometimes ran up the down escalator in hotels for a laugh. Or he would jump up and touch an overhead canopy, or toss a crunched-up piece of paper over his shoulder to try to land it in the waste-paper basket. This impish quality endeared him to his family, friends and staff.

Throughout the Roaring Twenties, skilled Scottish immigrants enjoyed increasing wealth as demand for cars rose and profits soared.

They moved into substantial homes with garages and large gardens in leafy neighbourhoods of low-density housing. The Fraser family lived in a large house in comfortable surroundings where they even rented out a couple of rooms. But this period of affluence came to a sudden halt with the Great Depression, which followed in the wake of the 1929 stock market crash.

The Fraser family and the Great Depression

The auto industry, dependent on consumer buying power, proved highly vulnerable to the Depression and Detroit suffered more than any other major US city. By 1932, 80 per cent of the auto-making capacity lay idle. For those lucky enough to find work, average wages dropped by 37 per cent. Funding for welfare payments dried up, leaving thousands of families in desperate straits. The Depression hit the Fraser family hard and Sam Fraser was unemployed for long periods. They were evicted from their large rented accommodation and moved to a smaller house in a Polish neighbourhood. Before long they were forced to move on once again to a cheaper flat in an Italian area. Their main preoccupation was keeping a roof over their heads and finding enough food to eat and fuel to keep warm.

Around them, other families had their gas and electricity supplies cut off during the freezing winter conditions. Furniture, banister rails, floorboards and porches were broken up for fuel. Many of the recent immigrants, including the Scots, moved back home, some never returning. Tens of thousands of people moved around the country searching for jobs. Those who were evicted from their homes lived in the city's shantytowns made of cardboard and corrugated iron and many were reduced to begging or stealing in order to survive.

Doug Fraser, a tall, dark-haired fourteen-year-old at the start of the Depression, saw how humiliating it was for his proud father to be unable to provide for the family. Doug joined other young men scavenging for anything that could burn, often stealing coal from railway cars. He queued for three-day-old bread, which his mother fried with dripping and onions for the main meal of the day. With no prospect of work, they were about to be evicted once again, and faced the prospect of joining the thousands of homeless. Then they had a stroke of luck. Their former landlord offered them a chance of moving back to the upper floor of their original house. The new tenants had been evicted after they had broken up part of the property for fuel. The Frasers could live there if they looked after his property and if they paid the rent whenever they could manage.

Despite all the suffering, Fraser later explained that he was glad he was brought up during the Depression because it gave him a tremendous education about life and about people. It also helped him to make up his mind to become an active trade unionist. 'I was a teenager during the Depression. I saw misery and despair. I was angry at the injustice of it all and it had an impact on me the rest of my life,' he explained to his daughter Jeanne when she was a teenager. 'The greatest lesson of my life, the most valuable experience, was going through the Depression,' Fraser told a Detroit magazine in 1979. 'The lesson of the Depression is how an economic system can be so cruel that people can be robbed of their rights and their dignity because they have to beg for jobs and grovel for jobs, do favours and bribe for jobs … in our neighbourhood so many people were on welfare. No one had a job. No unemployment compensation. People were in desperate economic straits.'

Initially the rise in unemployment and the spread of poverty did not lead to automatic growth in trade unions or action to defend jobs. With jobs scarce, and an abundance of willing workers, circumstances were not favourable to strike action, and workers felt vulnerable enough without putting their heads above the parapet. The first political responses to the Depression were mainly organised by the Communist Party, and included demonstrations by the unemployed, resistance of evictions and campaigns for increases in welfare assistance involving thousands of people. Billy McKie, one of Detroit's leading Communists, courageously edited and distributed the only union publication in the city, *The Ford Worker*. McKie, who learned his politics in Edinburgh, worked at the massive Ford Rouge Complex just outside the city, on the banks of the River Rouge. The Rouge was the biggest integrated factory complex in the world, employing over 100,000 people in the 1930s. It had a railroad with 100 miles of track and sixteen locomotives, and a hospital. It also had its own police force, a scheduled bus network, and 15 miles of paved road. Henry Ford was well aware that the Rouge could be a key target for union action.

In 1932, with the help of the Communist Party, McKie organised a demonstration of three thousand unemployed workers, who marched on the Rouge Plant to demand jobs. In the highly charged political environment even this simple demand provoked an alarmed reaction from the establishment. At the factory gates, the police, backed by Ford's security services, attempted to break up the gathering. During the ensuing fighting, the police drew guns and opened fire on the demonstrators, killing

Bill McKie, a sheet metal worker, was chairman of the Edinburgh Strike Committee during the 1926 general strike. A founding member of the Communist Party of Great Britain, he edited and distributed the Ford Worker in Detroit. He was sacked for his union activity in 1936, reinstated several years later, and was forced to resign his union positions in 1949 because of his Communist Party membership. (Courtesy International Press, New York)

Seventy thousand people attended a funeral procession following the deaths of four people killed by the police during an unemployment demonstration at Ford Rouge, Detroit, in 1932. (Courtesy W P Reuther Library, Wayne State University)

four and wounding nineteen. Seventy thousand people turned out at the funerals of those who were killed, as outrage at the deaths swept America.

The shock of the Depression gradually awakened a political and trade union consciousness throughout America, especially in industrial cities like Detroit. Doug Fraser's family were surrounded by radical political activity. The Communist Party opened a hall directly behind their home and Fraser joined in some of the Communist youth activities. In common with many of the Scottish community, Fraser's father took him along to union and political meetings, which he saw as an essential part of his education. Many years later, after he became president of the United Auto Workers, Fraser explained that trade unionism had been part of his life from his earliest memories. 'I suppose you could say I belonged to the union before I went to work because we talked about it all the time.' Along with thousands of others, the Frasers attended debates about the political situation sponsored by a range of Socialist and other left-wing organisations. Sam Fraser had been a member of the Labour Party in Glasgow and joined the American Socialist Party soon after arriving in Detroit. In the 1932 presidential election, he campaigned for Norman Thomas, the Socialist Party candidate.

Bill McKie: experienced and fearless leader

However, Roosevelt's victory in the 1932 election gave some hope. The New Deal offered a favourable legal climate for the establishment of unions, and by 1933, after four years of suffering and anger, the auto-workers were ready to fight back. Thousands took part in a series of strikes organised by a short-lived auto-workers union set up by the Communist Party and led by Billy McKie. With thirty years of experience as an active trade unionist in Scotland, McKie was highly respected by his colleagues, and fearless in his advocacy of trade unionism. Born in Carlisle in 1876, he started work when he was twelve as an apprentice sheet-metal worker. His parents were dedicated Salvation Army volunteers, and McKie played tenor horn in the brass band. His life changed when he arrived in Edinburgh aged nineteen and was involved in a strike. He became active in the sheet-metal worker's union and joined Britain's first Marxist party, the Social Democratic Federation. As propaganda secretary of the Edinburgh branch and education organiser of its successor organisation, the British Socialist Party, McKie came into contact with Scotland's leading Marxists. He helped run the Edinburgh section of John McLean's Scottish Labour College, which was responsible for teaching an entire generation of shop stewards. In Edinburgh, 350 students – including dockers, engineers and miners – enrolled for McKie's classes.

He crossed swords with another famous Edinburgh activist, James Connolly, who formed a rival Marxist organisation, the Scottish Socialist Party. Connolly spent seven years in the United States from 1903 until 1910. For a short time he was a full-time organiser for the Industrial Workers of the World (IWW), and founded the IWW Propaganda League. In the year before he left to return to Ireland, he was one of six national organisers of the American Socialist Party and travelled around the US addressing meetings and giving advice to branches. It was in Ireland, of course, that Connolly achieved his illustrious place in history as a political and trade union leader, ending with his role in the Easter Rising in 1916. Venerated as a national martyr after his execution in 1916, Connolly's significance is beyond the scope of this book.

Billy McKie became a well-known figure at national and local level in the British trade union movement. He was a member of the national executive of the Sheet Metal Workers Union and was one of Edinburgh Trades Council's most respected luminaries. During the 1926 general strike he was chairman of the Edinburgh Strike Committee and was a founding member of the Communist Party of Great Britain in 1920. McKie's daughter lived in Detroit and in 1927 he and his wife sailed over on a visit. Perhaps disillusioned by the outcome of the general strike, or perhaps wishing to be close to his daughter, he decided to stay and work in Detroit. He had no difficulty finding a job at Ford and settled in quickly, despite being in his fifties. His age, politics and vast experience set him apart from most of the other union activists in America.

The Communist Party set up a trade union organisation that led a number of auto-workers strikes in 1932 and 1933. They won partial gains, but for the most part were met by strong resistance from the employers who isolated and victimised many of the leaders. Other efforts to form unions in the auto industry met with limited success. Skilled workers set up the Mechanics Education Society of America, a craft union disguised as an educational body. James Murdoch, originally from Paisley, was its president in 1935 and many other Scots were prominent at local level. It served a useful purpose in pulling together 34,000 skilled workers into a coherent unit. Over 14,000 members took part in a series of strikes in Flint and Detroit, closing a hundred tool shops for periods of up to six weeks. Internal arguments over the restrictions of membership to skilled workers dominated much of the policy discussions and led to splits.

Shortly after the strikes, the American Federation of Labor formed the United Auto Workers (UAW) and McKie became president of the local at the Rouge complex. But the Federation appointed all the senior officers, none of whom had any experience in car plants. Their efforts to organise the workforce seemed half-hearted and it was not until the Congress of Industrial Organizations launched the campaign for industrial unionism that a substantial proportion of the workforce began to respond (see Chapter 2, pages 49-50).

A new tactic – the sit-down strike

Despite the New Deal's improved legal environment for trade unions, the American employers mounted ferocious opposition to any attempts to establish them in the workplace. However, in January 1936 a major breakthrough took place in the town of Arcon, Ohio after a sit-down strike by the Firestone tyre workers. British workers had no knowledge of the sit-down strike tactic, but it had been used in other parts of Europe. The Firestone workforce knew that if they went on strike they could be easily replaced from the vast pool of unemployed in the area. Instead of walking out, they decided to stay in the factory, but refused to work. The company feared removing them would cause damage to their expensive equipment and machinery. A month later, another sit-down strike at the neighbouring Goodyear Tyre Plant was described as one of the greatest battles in American labour history. Firestone and Goodyear were eventually forced to negotiate a settlement with the newly formed Rubber Workers Union. These successes were a tremendous morale booster for unions throughout America and the sit down tactic became most famously associated with the United Auto Workers. The UAW's first significant victory using this tactic came in November 1936 at the Midland Steel plant, a supplier of chassis frames to Ford and Chrysler.

The tool-room workers at Midland were well organised and were led by John Anderson, an electrician from Glasgow who had emigrated in the early 1920s. Highly popular with the skilled workers and an outstanding orator, Anderson's speeches were delivered with a rich Scottish accent that had his audiences captivated. It was said he deliberately thickened his brogue for effect. He was also a prominent member of the Communist Party and once stood as its candidate for Governor of Michigan. Midland's 2000-strong workforce was highly disciplined and the company already recognised the union. But Anderson's grand plan was to kick-start a union recognition campaign throughout Detroit and he knew that a strike at Midland would quickly cripple production at the main car plants.

A number of demands were tabled by the union for pay and conditions improvements, and when these were only partially met, Anderson gave the signal to start the strike. The sit-down was well planned and started quietly and smoothly, taking the company and most of the leadership of the UAW by complete surprise. Five days after it began, Chrysler's assembly operations closed down. Management agreed a settlement acceptable to the union and other auto-workers followed the precedent set by the Midland workforce. During the next six months, the auto industry was hit by a wave of sit-down strikes, bringing thousands of workers into action.

At GM's flagship plant in Flint, a company town where 80 per cent of the families depended on General Motors for their livelihood, there were only a small number of union members. The union's national leadership had drawn up plans to strike for recognition, but following the Midland victory, a sit-down happened spontaneously. It closed down the main section of the plant, but the company refused to negotiate. Police used tear gas to try to dislodge the workers, but were met by a hail of rocks, bottles, and car body parts. The police withdrew, but opened fire as they retreated. Fourteen workers were shot and nine police injured by missiles in what was called 'the battle of the running bulls'. After the police launched another abortive attack, the National Guard was called in.

This provoked other GM plants to join the fray and soon over 125,000 workers were involved. At the GM Cadillac plant in Detroit, Dave Miller from Dundee was the leader of the strike. He was an experienced union activist in Scotland and had started work in a Dundee textile mill at the age of twelve. In his teens he laid tramlines in the city and was a member of the Tram and Vehicle Workers Union. A dedicated Socialist, he refused to serve in the armed forces during the First World War and was jailed for three-and-half years. Miller had been Billy McKie's vice-president at Ford Rouge but was sacked in 1936. The workforce at Cadillac and the rest of the GM plants stood firm and it became clear to management they had lost the battle. A recognition agreement with the UAW was signed and pay increases granted. The first of the big three had been won over, and the union turned its attention to the Chrysler Corporation.

Chrysler's massive Dodge Plant in Detroit employed 25,000 workers and was second only to Ford Rouge in size. It was the target for what became America's biggest sit-down strike. A plant of this size

*Demonstration in Cadillac Square, Detroit in support of sit-down strikes at
Chrysler plants in 1937. America's biggest sit-down strike took place at Chrysler's
Dodge Plant where David MacIntyre, a welder from Alexandria, Dunbartonshire
was chairman of the plant committee. (Courtesy W. P. Reuther Library, Wayne State
University)*

United Auto Workers badge

presented a logistical nightmare, as a sit-down strike required much greater organisation and preparation than a traditional walk-out. But the workforce at Dodge were already well organised, with 800 shop stewards led by 180 chief stewards reporting to the plant committee. David MacIntyre, chairman of the plant committee, had been a Clydeside shop steward and organised the car plant using the same structure as the Scottish shipyards. He was a welder from Alexandria, Dunbartonshire and had emigrated when he was twenty-seven. After introducing education classes for stewards, he produced a shop steward's handbook. An Irishman, Pat Quinn, and Bert Manual, an ex-coalminer from Bothwell in Lanarkshire, shared leadership responsibilities with MacIntyre. Known in the plant as 'Mr Union', Manual emigrated in 1923 and had been organising union meetings since 1935.

In March 1937, three weeks after the victory at Flint, a secret signal was given to start the sit-down strike at Dodge. Within half an hour all 25,000 workers had left their machines, bringing production to a standstill, but only two thousand remained in the plant, as that was the maximum that could be fed and organised. Discipline had to be enforced and strict codes of conduct were drawn up. Outside of Dodge, union leaders called sit-down strikes at other Chrysler plants. Sam Fraser was chairman of the shop committee at Chrysler's De Soto plant and was one of the leaders of the sit-down strike. His son Doug, twenty years old at the time, also worked at De Soto, where he had a job as a metal finisher.

After three days, Chrysler stated that it regarded the strike as a revolutionary challenge and sought an injunction against the occupations. It announced that the strikers had terminated their contracts and were no longer employees. On the eighth day of the strike, an injunction was issued and the court ordered the men to leave the plants by the following day. The men at Dodge voted to resist the injunction and each department was assigned responsibility for defending an entrance. Similar preparations were made at the other plants. Barricades were reinforced and the strikers prepared for an onslaught by the National Guard. When the deadline expired the county sheriff found ten thousand pickets outside the gates of Dodge with at least two thousand barricaded inside. The sheriff was powerless to enforce the injunction and the Governor was reluctant to call out the National Guard. A compromise was eventually reached and two weeks later Chrysler agreed to recognise the UAW.

This led other vehicle parts manufacturers to accept the union without a fight. But the last of the big three, the Ford Motor Corporation, was a tougher nut to crack. At the start of the UAW campaign, Henry Ford declared, 'We will never recognise the United Automobile Workers or any other union.' Over four thousand workers suspected of union membership were sacked between 1936 and 1941, including Bill McKie and Dave Miller. In a famous clash between union and management that became known as the 'Battle of the Overpass', national union leaders stood alongside McKie and fifty others to distribute leaflets to the Ford employees at the Rouge plant. Bodyguards employed by Ford, including gangsters, wrestlers, boxers and Ford servicemen attacked the union members, leaving some of them badly beaten. When photographs and reports of the assault appeared in national newspapers, public support for the union increased, and Ford's reputation diminished. But the success with GM and Chrysler could not be matched at Ford, and it was several years before it finally recognised the UAW.

The success of the 'strategy strike'

Nevertheless, UAW membership now stood at 300,000, but a battle to control the union began to develop between competing factions, which at one point threatened the very existence of the organisation. Right- and left-wing caucuses emerged and the two sides literally fought it out in the locals. Meanwhile, membership plummeted and both General Motors and Chrysler used the opportunity to walk away from any further union negotiations. It became critical for the survival of the union to re-establish collective bargaining at both GM and Chrysler, but both managements thought they held all the cards. Their confidence was high because legislation was introduced to outlaw the sit-down strike, and a conventional strike of production workers would take a long time to have an impact in the depressed conditions of the car market. The union came up with an alternative industrial action method. The 'strategy strike' was launched, using only the skilled tool-room workers. They produced the tools and dies for the new car models a year ahead of production.

General Motors was targeted, and the union waited until the tools and dies for GM's 1940 model were needed. The tool-room workers walked out, but production workers assembling the old models were not affected. The production workers could afford to support the smaller number of skilled members on strike for an indefinite period. There was a 100 per cent response from Detroit's tool rooms, and after four weeks the company settled because it would lose ground to its competitors if the following year's model was not ready on time. Bargaining rights were re-established and Chrysler followed suit after a ballot of its employees.

Credit for the 'strategy strike' idea is often given to Walter Reuther, who later became UAW president. But according to Bill Stevenson, who was chairman of the GM bargaining committee, the tactic emerged from discussions amongst the activists at local level and was then put to Reuther. Stevenson, from Glasgow, was instrumental in the conduct of the strike and the negotiations with GM. An American colleague once asked him when he became interested in unions, and he explained that he was born into the movement. His father was a shop steward and the family discussed politics constantly. When he was serving his apprenticeship as a fitter/turner at a Clydeside shipyard during the First World War he attended lunchtime classes on politics and economics delivered by shop stewards. In 1919 he was one of the one of the leaders of an apprentices' strike over pay and training. Post-war unemployment forced Stevenson out of Scotland and he ended up in Detroit. At the time of the strategy strike, he was president of the powerful skilled workers' local on Detroit's west side, which had several thousand members.

A further and final attempt was made to win recognition at Ford in a campaign that started in 1940. Thousands of union members were signed up at the Rouge plant and the union then applied to the National Labor Relations Board for representation elections under new legal provisions. Suddenly management provoked a strike by sacking members of the company grievance committee. The union called an all-out strike and most workers walked out. After ten days a temporary settlement was negotiated and it was agreed to hold a ballot on union recognition. Almost 70,000 workers at the Rouge plant voted and overwhelmingly opted for the UAW. In 1941, much to the astonishment of the press and politicians, Ford offered the most progressive agreement of all the car companies. Not only was the UAW recognised, but a union shop was established, requiring all new employees to join the UWA; all sacked workers, including Billy McKie, were given their jobs back; union subscriptions would be deducted from salaries; and the Ford Services Department, the hated private police force, was disbanded.

Henry McCusker, from Tannochside near Bothwell in Lanarkshire, became president of Ford Rouge, which was now the biggest local in the United States. An ex-coalminer, he was involved in the Lanarkshire miners' strikes of the early 1920s. One of the 50,000 who left the mining industry in Scotland in the decade after the First World War, he emigrated to Pennsylvania in 1923, where he worked in the deep anthracite coalmines. The wages offered in Detroit drew him to the

Local 600 UAW (Ford Rouge) ballot stations. The Rouge was the biggest integrated factory complex in the world, employing over 100,000 people. After a ten day strike in Ford management agreed to hold a ballot on union recognition in 1940. Almost 70,000 workers at the plant voted and overwhelmingly opted for the UAW. (Courtesy W. P. Reuther Library, Wayne State University)

Motor City in 1925, and he bluffed his way into a job as a grinder at the Rouge. Within a few years most of his family and half of Tannochside had landed in Detroit. Joe McCusker, his younger brother, left Scotland after the 1926 general strike and the nine-month long miners' strike. Joe started work at the Rouge in 1928 and entered the Ford Apprentices School to train as a tool and die maker. After Ford recognised the union, he became the tool and die unit secretary and a member of the plant negotiating committee. The vice-president of the Rouge local was George Campbell from Parkhead in Glasgow, who had been a shop steward in the Amalgamated Engineering Union. Born in 1898, he attended Quarrybrae School before serving an apprenticeship as a fitter at the Parkhead Forge and Steel Works. A keen sportsman, he was an amateur boxing champion, a useful skill to have in Detroit trade union circles.

By the time the United States entered the Second World War the overwhelming majority of Detroit's auto-workers were members of the UAW. In almost every local in Detroit and in other car plants across America, Scottish workers held prominent positions. It was said that every tool shop had a shop steward who answered to the name Jock or Scottie. However, the auto industry changed dramatically during the war and no cars were produced for civilian use from 1942 until 1945. Military equipment, including tanks, trucks, bombs, arms and ammunition took the place of cars on the production lines. Nevertheless, by the end of the war UAW membership had swollen to 1.2 million.

During this time the Scots consolidated their positions in the union. George Campbell joined the full-time staff of the union as assistant director of the skilled trades department. John Anderson and Bill Stevenson continued as leaders of Detroit's skilled workers. Anderson was president of Local 155, which organised tool and die shops on the east side of Detroit, and Bill Stevenson was president of Local 157, which took care of the west side. These were the locals that had revived the union with the strategy strikes and whose members were the most political and best organised. Stevenson's closest ally in the west side was John Fairbairn, a Glasgow engineer who was financial secretary of the local. Fairbairn emigrated in 1925, but during the Depression he almost starved to death and had to return to Glasgow until economic circumstances in the US improved. The vice-president of Local 157, George Handyside, also came from Glasgow and, like Fairbairn, struggled through the early 1930s and often considered returning home permanently. Dave Miller, was elected president of the Cadillac local after leading the sit-down strike at the plant. At Ford, Joe McCusker took over from his older brother as president of the giant Rouge local in 1945. Billy McKie was the tool-room organiser at the Rouge and was a senior member of the Ford National Council negotiating body.

In 1942, Bill Stevenson was promoted to regional director of Detroit, with a seat on the international board, the exectutive body of the union. He joined two other Scots on the highest body of the union, Alex McGowan and William McAulay. McGowan was a former shipyard worker from Glasgow. He worked in the GM assembly plant at Tarrytown, New York State where he became president of the UAW local. He moved through the ranks until his appointment as regional director for the north-east states and a member of the executive board. McAulay joined the executive in 1940 and was director for Flint and Pontiac, two motor towns to the north of Detroit. Until he settled in Pontiac, he had a somewhat itinerant life. A former Lanarkshire miner, he transferred to Fife when a new coalfield opened up. He married and had two children before the family emigrated to Springfield, Illinois in 1911. He only stayed there for a year until he was lured to the silver mines in Park City, Utah. Three years later he moved to Roosevelt, Utah when oil was discovered, but was back in Springfield by 1920. He finally moved to Pontiac to work for General Motors as a body-trimmer. His leading role in the recognition battles propelled him on to the executive board.

Walter Reuther causes divisions

After the war, demand for cars went through the roof. With a prosperous industry there was a secure future ahead, but the biggest problems affecting the UAW were internal divisions. This time the issue was not confined to the auto-workers. The international trade union movement was torn apart by the fallout from the Cold War, and nowhere was this more keenly felt than the United States. In 1946 Walter Reuther, director of the General Motors department of the union, made an opportunist bid for power. He had support from the GM locals and launched a campaign against the incumbent president of the union, R. J. Thomas. Colleagues who had previously stood shoulder to shoulder in the recognition disputes were now set against each other as the union split once again into two factions. Reuther's ambitious streak was common knowledge. Even US President Harry Truman told Congress of Industrial Organizations president Phil Murray to watch out. 'Phil, that man is after your job,' said Truman. 'No, Mr President,' Murray replied, 'he is after yours.'

When the UAW was being formed, Reuther had just returned from the Soviet Union where he worked in the Molotov Auto Works in Gorky. A member of the Socialist Party in 1936, he owed his position on the executive board of the union to Communist support, and his relations with the Communist Party until 1938 had been cordial. In 1938 he was named by the DIES Committee, the predecessor to the House Un-American Activities Committee, as a Communist. But by 1938 tensions within the leftist faction began to surface, firstly over Roosevelt's New Deal and then a year later over the non-aggression pact between Germany and the Soviet Union. By 1940 Reuther had left the Socialist Party and openly attacked Communists at the UAW convention. By 1946 his strategy was to attack the left-of-centre leadership of the UAW. Reuther accused it of being pro-Communist and gathered a number of right-wing groups around his push for the leadership.

The Association of Catholic Trade Unionists, in which some of the Scots were active, supported Reuther's anti-Communist position. Henry and Joe McCusker were committed Catholics and supported Reuther. So also was John Fitzpatrick, another Scotsman on the Rouge executive. On the other side of the religious divide, George Campbell, the Glaswegian vice-president of the Rouge, was a leading freemason and also sided with Reuther's anti-Communist agenda. Other anti-Communist groups like the Ku Klux Klan supported Reuther, although he did not openly acknowledge their support.

However, the bulk of the other leading Scots supported the leadership against Reuther's right-wing caucus. These included Doug Fraser, who had quickly risen to the top of his local at De Soto, where he had started as a metal finisher. Much to the dismay of his father, he had dropped out of high school before graduation. After spending several months in hospital with rheumatic fever, he left school in his final year, and later admitted this was one of the most foolish things he had ever done.

Doug was fired from his first two jobs because of union activity. At his first job at Bryant Motors, he became friendly with another boy of the same age. The lad always seemed in agreement with many of Fraser's views, so he decided to ask him to join the union. However, the boy was the owner's nephew, and Fraser was quickly shown the door. He did not last much longer in his next job with Ever-Hot Heaters, where he was suspected of having union sympathies. His toolbox was broken into and some union cards he was planning to distribute were found. At Ever-Hot he experienced one of the many indignities workers regularly faced at that time. 'The toilet was square in the centre of the shop and from the waist up was plain glass, so when you went to the toilet … the bosses could see you at all times,' Fraser recalled. His next job was beside his dad at the De Soto stamping and assembly plant.

Elected president of the local in 1943, Doug Fraser admitted his father's reputation at the plant had helped him win the position at the age of twenty-five. He joined the Michigan Commonwealth Federation, a left-wing Social Democratic party which had some limited union backing in early forties. In 1944 he left to join the army, but returned at the end of the war and went straight back to De Soto. His father had pleaded with him to go to law school and offered to fund him, but Fraser refused. De Soto executives, who had been impressed by his energy and drive when he was president of the local, offered him a position in management, and gave him time to think it over. 'There's no point,' replied Fraser, 'I don't need any time. I've made up my mind what I want to do with my life.' On his return he was re-elected president and thrust into the internal union struggle.

Reuther clears out the left

Reuther won by a whisker and the divisions in the union widened and deepened. Against a background of anti-Communist hysteria that was sweeping the country, he routed the left within a year of his victory. Over a hundred staff were sacked and replaced by Reuther's supporters, although some of his opponents were bought off. Reuther was greatly assisted by the Taft-Hartley Act, which required union officials to sign an affidavit stating they were not members of the Communist Party. This finished off any left-wing opposition that remained.

Amongst the casualties in the cull of the left were many of Detroit's Scottish contingent. Bill McKie, who was on the Ford negotiating committee, refused to sign the affidavit. When the UAW directed its local leaders to comply and the Rouge local agreed with the order, McKie resigned, stating that he intended to remain a member of the Communist Party. Not even John Anderson's prestige amongst the skilled workers could save him from defeat when he was challenged for the presidency of his local in 1949. He was offered a job in the personnel department of Midland Steel and he spent the rest of his working life in a management role. David Miller was called before the House Un-American Activities Committee. Joe McCusker had picked the winning side and was rewarded accordingly, becoming a member of the international board.

George Campbell continued as assistant director of the skilled trades department and remained there until he retired in 1959.

Bill Stevenson lost his seat on the executive board in 1947 and returned to the tools before bouncing back ten years later. In this remarkable comeback, Stevenson was appointed to a full-time position in 1957 in the skilled trades department and then in 1963 took over the job George Campbell had left four years previously. Most of the other Scots survived at least for a few years. Doug Fraser was one of Reuther's opponents who emerged unscathed from the carnage. Despite aligning with the left against Reuther's revolt, he was appointed to a full-time position in the UAW's Chrysler department in 1947. Reuther admired his attitude and forgave him for siding with the opposition, putting it down to youth and inexperience.

With the internal situation stabilised, the UAW was in a powerful bargaining position at a time when profits for car companies were around twice the average level of the rest of American industry. For the next two decades the UAW set the standards in collective bargaining and other unions followed. The union then started looking at pensions as its key objective and concluded deals with Ford and GM before moving on to Chrysler in 1950. Doug Fraser was on the Chrysler negotiating team and both sides reached swift agreement on the amount of pension to be paid. But the company refused to set up a separate pension fund to meet their commitments. It wanted to pay the pension out of its general fund, but given the past uncertainties in the car industry, the UAW wanted the security of a separate, independent fund. With no agreement on this principle, a strike was called. Much to the frustration of the union it dragged on for 104 days, the longest in Chrysler history. It was a completely unnecessary strike according to Fraser, who believed the company were just being pig-headed. Many years later it still angered him to think of the wages auto-workers lost for no reason. In the end an agreement was reached, based on the funded model the union proposed in the first place.

Fraser impressed Reuther during the lengthy negotiations, exhibiting a shrewd bargaining sense and winning crucial concessions from the GM management team. The following year Fraser negotiated a new five-year contract, which guaranteed annual wage increases, a cost of living escalator and a healthy pension. Reuther was now convinced of his potential and offered him a job as his administrative assistant, essentially his right-hand man. The two worked closely for the next eight years and Fraser was involved in all major negotiations and executive board meetings. After the death of Phil Murray in 1952, Reuther became president of the Congress of Industrial Organizations, which gave Fraser an opportunity to view the wider trade union movement from the centre of power. In 1959, with Reuther's encouragement, Fraser stood for election as co-director of Detroit's biggest region. In 1962 he was elected to the executive board and in 1970 he became one of two national vice-presidents.

The 1960s: prosperity, racism and Vietnam

Many landmark agreements in the industry were reached without strike action. Auto workers moved into the middle class, as measured by earnings, home ownership, security of employment, and of course, ownership of cars. Detroit was one of the highest ranked cities in the United States for average family income, and as the prosperity spread, memories of the struggles of the 1930s began to fade. Union tactics changed again and deals typically lasted three years, after which one of 'the Big Three', Ford, Chrysler or General Motors, would be targeted by the union for the next campaign, the choice of company dependent on its relative economic strength. Meanwhile strike funds were amassed to sustain disputes that often lasted several months. But once a deal was struck with one of the Big Three, the others generally followed suit.

The nature of the membership of the UAW was changing rapidly. Between 1962 and 1967, half of the workers in the auto industry left, and by 1970, one third had less than five years' service. Those who were in the plants when the recognition battles had been fought were rapidly passing out of the union. The leaders of the locals were no longer Scots, and only at senior levels were there still familiar faces. This transformation of the union composition coincided with the heightening of tensions caused by other developments in America. Race conflict became the most pressing domestic issue.

Detroit had expanded by a further 230,000 people during the war. Many of the newcomers, 80,000 of whom were black, had come from the southern states. The lack of housing and services gave rise to tensions that were often manifested in racist attacks and rioting. One of the worst incidents occurred in 1943. The mayor of Detroit estimated that 100,000 whites took part in rioting during a two-day period that left twenty-five blacks and nine whites dead. UAW officials tried to keep racial tensions out of the workplace, but unofficial 'hate strikes' often broke out over black men being promoted or given what some saw as 'white men's work'. The Ku Klux Klan actively encouraged many of the strikes and had

Doug Fraser was appointed to a full-time position in the UAW's Chrysler department in 1947. Although he had been against Walter Reuther in the leadership struggle, Reuther admired his attitude and ability. (Courtesy W. P. Reuther Library, Wayne State University)

positions in some locals. The UAW attempted to tackle racism through progressive policies, education programmes and literature, but despite many initiatives, they were unable to contain the problem.

By the late sixties, black workers comprised a quarter of Detroit's auto industry. An alternative black trade union movement developed in Chrysler's Dodge plant. The Dodge Revolutionary Union Movement attacked the auto companies but reserved its sharpest invective for the UAW, which it depicted as racist. Other plants followed the Dodge lead, and although it fizzled out two years later, the movement was a real threat to the UAW. After the assassination of Martin Luther King in 1968, white workers in some plants threatened strikes if company flags were lowered to half-mast. The car plants in the southern states were particularly troublesome for the UAW leadership. They resented attempts by national union officials to make them comply with UAW policy, dismissing them as northern liberals. In Tennessee, a local led by segregationists built a UAW hall with separate facilities for black and white workers.

Doug Fraser volunteered to visit the local to outline the union's policy towards such reactionary practices. When he arrived in Tennessee, he was greeted by an angry mob, resentful at his presence. He addressed the most hostile audience he had ever faced in his life. More worryingly, at the end of the meeting they stayed behind, blocking his exit and refusing to let him leave. Then George Holloway, a black activist, pointed to the car park, which was full of black union members who were ready to come to Fraser's assistance. Holloway told him that if he had the guts to come down and challenge the segregationists then the least the black workers could do was make sure he got home safely.

The other major issue that divided American society during this period was the Vietnam War. The American trade union movement had united into the AFL-CIO, and the right-wing traditionalist George Meany was president. Despite Walter Reuther's anti-Communist past, he found the movement's foreign policy and its old-style leader out of touch with the feelings of union members. Reuther felt that the AFL-CIO had become narrow and negative, and its foreign policies were much further to the right than the American public. Reuther's brother, Victor, exposed a connection between the CIA and the AFL-CIO. The UAW was represented by Victor Reuther at the National Labor Assembly for Peace in 1967, the largest ever gathering of trade union leaders opposed to the Vietnam War. Major UAW locals, like Ford Rouge, issued their own statements against

Doug Fraser (left) and Walter Reuther at press conference during Chrysler pay negotiations, 1964. The two worked closely together and Fraser was involved in all major negotiations. In 1959 Fraser became a director of Detroit's biggest region and in 1962 he was elected to the executive board. (Courtesy W.P. Reuther Library, Wayne State University)

the war, and when Walter Reuther pulled the UAW out of the AFL-CIO over its Vietnam policy, locals applauded the decision.

Walter Reuther died in a plane crash in 1970, not long after Doug Fraser had been elected vice-president. Reuther had been grooming Fraser to take over the presidency when he retired, but his death left the executive board in a dilemma. Another candidate came into contention, an older man called Leonard Woodcock, who had been the other vice-president for a number of years before Fraser. There was an equal split on the board between supporters of each, until the acting chairman cast the deciding vote for Woodcock. With the executive recommending Woodcock, Fraser decided not to contest the position at the following convention, although many thought he would have won. But he did not want to risk splitting the union again.

Disappointed by his loss to Woodcock, Fraser considered throwing his hat in the ring for the Democratic nomination for the Michigan Senate seat. He had been frequently mentioned as a possible candidate, but his liberal views were at odds with the majority of voters. In any case, his heart and soul was in the UAW and he could continue as a major influence in Democratic Party politics as UAW vice-president. When the first black mayor of Detroit was elected in 1973 he had to appoint a chairman of the Detroit Police Commission at a time when police–community relations were extremely challenging. To unite the city he chose Fraser, whose judgement and integrity were universally respected.

Fraser becomes president

When Leonard Woodcock retired, Fraser was the unanimous choice of the executive board, and sole candidate for president at the 1977 UAW convention. His first task was to lead a delegation to press President Jimmy Carter for health security legislation. Next he testified before Congress on health and energy bills. The government appointed him to the Labor-Management Group, a top-level national forum for union and industry leaders, but he resigned a year later. Business leaders had wrecked a proposal for some modest employment legislation reforms and Fraser, frustrated by a new aggressiveness of corporate America, accused them of waging 'a one-sided class war against working people, the unemployed, the poor and minorities, the very young and the very old, and even many in the middle-class of our society.' In response, he warned that 'we in the UAW intend to re-forge the links with those who believe in struggle: the kind of people who sat down in the factories in the 1930s and who marched

Doug Fraser was the unanimous choice of the executive board and sole candidate for president at the 1977 UAW convention. During a difficult period in office American car manufacturing slumped and tens of thousands of auto-workers were made redundant.

in Selma in the 1960s.' After his resignation he called a conference to discuss the establishment of a new left progressive organisation. Over one hundred organisations were represented, including trade unions, environmental groups, women's organisations and consumer groups. The Progressive Alliance was formed, rallying liberals and the left around a programme of full employment, workplace health and safety, alternative energy, women's rights, and consumer protection. Fraser aligned the UAW with international solidarity movements and withdrew UAW funds from banks that dealt with apartheid South Africa, declaring 'We in the UAW don't believe that the hard-earned money of our 1.5 million members should wind up being used to aid a country that practises such racist, repressive and undemocratic policies.'

However, it was Fraser's misfortune that he became president of the UAW in the union's most difficult period since the organising days of the 1930s. The oil-price increases of the 1970s had encouraged the import of more fuel-efficient Japanese cars that gradually captured a greater share of the American market. By the end of the seventies plant closure announcements became commonplace, with tens of thousands of auto-workers made redundant. The Chrysler Corporation was the weakest of the Big Three and in 1979 was about to go to the wall. Republicans and the right-wing press called it a lame duck and argued against any government loans to keep it afloat. But the union organised a grassroots lobbying campaign and, together with Fraser's Democratic Party connections, convinced Congress to provide $1.2 billion in loan guarantees. But the loans came at a price for Chrysler's workers. They were forced to sacrifice many gains they had made over the previous twenty years and they were not easily persuaded. It was estimated that the concessions they were being forced to make were worth $1.7 billion. Twice they threw back the deal in membership ballots and only when modified proposals were put to them in a third ballot did they vote to accept it. Opposition in the union ranks argued it was the biggest sell-out in union history.

Fraser was deeply hurt at having to concede so much and could not sleep at night during the negotiations. Only his immense popularity with the rank and file allowed him to pull off the settlement and survive in office. They respected him because he never forgot where he came from. When visiting a factory he would go to the canteen for a coffee with the workers or talk to men and women on the line, sometimes leaving management waiting. He was comfortable talking to ordinary people and had a close relationship with the up and coming younger leaders in the locals. As part of the Chrysler bail-out deal, Fraser was given a seat on the board of the company, an unprecedented arrangement. Years later he felt that the contributions he made to save Chrysler were the proudest of his career, and never had any regrets about his decisions.

Just keeping the lights on at Chrysler occupied much of Fraser's time. However, car workers in other companies were not ignored. Under incessant pressure to accept pay cuts because of low-wage competition, Fraser said 'Competing on wages with countries that share only minimally the benefits of productivity with their workers can hardly be an appropriate national goal for America. The true spirit of our democracy embraces the fundamental rights of workers to organise and to have safe and secure jobs.' But financial problems at GM and Ford led to changes in contracts requiring concessions by the union. Fraser launched a successful charm offensive to lure Japanese car manufacturers to open plants in the US.

In 1981 Fraser led the UAW back into the AFL-CIO. It happened shortly after the Republican government sacked striking air-traffic-control officers and police marched their leaders into court in handcuffs and leg irons. The re-affiliation allowed UAW members to participate in Solidarity Day, a giant demonstration in Washington against Ronald Reagan's anti-labour policies. The Reagan years were as grim for the US trade union movement as the Thatcher years were for Britain's unions.

Throughout this dismal period, Fraser's sense of humour kept everyone's spirits high. His jokes and witty remarks were legendary and were used to put people in their place as well as to take the sting out of an awkward situation. He had his staff in fits of laughter when an overambitious lay officer from one of the locals phoned to inquire about the death of a full-time official. Fraser confirmed that the man had passed away a few hours ago. Without another word the lay officer asked, 'So can I take his place?' An astonished Fraser retorted, 'Well if it's OK with the undertaker, then it's OK with me.' Fraser's mischievous side was also renowned. On one occasion he was amongst a group of politicians having photographs taken when he noticed a senator beside him standing up on his toes to make him look taller. Fraser, a six-footer and several inches taller than the senator, then rose up on his toes with a wry smile for the camera.

Of course there was much more to Fraser than wit and humour. He was also a very tough negotiator and had an explosive temper. During one round of negotiations he threw a chair against a blackboard and in another he threatened to kick down a locked door in the employer's bargaining room. These angry outbursts found their way into the media and delighted the rank and file of the union. He was totally honest in his dealings with management, and consequently could be brutal when deceived. One car-company vice-president gave him misleading information during negotiations, and Fraser cut him to ribbons before ignoring him for the rest of the meeting. The company was forced to withdraw the errant VP from the rest of the pay talks. He did not hold back when it came to personal insults against employers, calling the president of GM 'a horse's ass', and describing the Chrysler chairman as 'an honest, honourable, incompetent man'. Despite his attacks on the employers, they respected him greatly. Henry Ford II said Fraser would make a good senator, and Chrysler's chief negotiator described Fraser as 'probably one of the most talented, multi-faceted individuals the labor movement has ever produced'.

Fraser's other achievements as president were considerable. He was frequently in front of Congressional committees testifying on behalf of civil rights legislation, strengthening social security, enactment of equal rights and other matters of social concern. He served on a number of Democratic Party commissions and Walter Mondale, Democratic presidential candidate in 1984, had plans for 'high office' for Fraser, had he become US president.

Doug Fraser's retirement

After twenty-nine years Fraser's first marriage ended in divorce and he later married his second wife Winifred, a dean at Wayne State University. She accompanied him on a visit to Scotland after he retired and he took her to see the street where he was born. It was a Sunday afternoon and they decided to go for a quiet drink in a local Gorbals pub, but they were astonished that it was so busy they could not get a seat. It was Fraser's seventh visit home and he never lost his love for Scotland or his interest in the country. The family even had their own crest on a Fraser tartan. When he read that Glasgow was the European City of Culture in 1990, he was so excited he couldn't wait to tell his colleagues. But they had to be shown a copy of the article before they would believe him. Compared to Detroit in the 1990s, Glasgow, in his opinion was a much cleaner, vibrant, modern city. Its new image and self-belief, the designer shops, restaurants and bars impressed him greatly.

By contrast, Detroit's centre in the 1990s was an eerie place dotted with gap sites of land contaminated by previous industrial activity and buildings that had stood empty for years. All the automobile plants had moved to the suburbs, and much of Detroit's population had left as well.

After the racial disturbances, most whites moved to the suburbs. The mass departure was termed 'white flight' and it left the city with an 80 per cent black population. The exodus of jobs and workers trapped Detroit in a downward economic spiral, leaving the city without sufficient funds for its management. Poverty, crime and infant mortality increased as a result. Buildings that were burned down in race riots in the 1960s were never replaced and some were never even demolished. The inadequate public transport system was typical of many American cities, but in Detroit's case was partly caused by the supremacy of the car in the 'Motor City'. The city failed to attract new business and attempts at establishing metropolitan-wide planning also failed, with political decisions breaking down between the white suburbs and black inner city. However, more recently attempts have helped to revive the downtown area and the riverfront has been the focus of much development.

In 1983 Fraser reluctantly retired at the UAW convention. In his final speech as president he said, 'This union has been my school, my college, and my education. This union has opened the door to worlds I never dreamed of. I met with presidents and with prime ministers and other leaders of the world, and engaged in important and stimulating meetings … because you let me be leader of this great institution.'

After his retirement from the UAW Fraser joined the staff of Wayne State University teaching undergraduate and masters-level classes in employment relations. A member of staff at the university said of Fraser, 'Students loved him. Doug had a keen intellect and a wealth of experience in the labour movement and American politics, and the ability to teach from that vast experience. He was a great professor.' His work as a teacher earned him recognition from top universities and various honorary degrees. Long after his retirement he was still in hot demand for media interviews and as a conference speaker. He told a convention in 1991 that, 'In every single democracy in the world you will find a vibrant, vital labour movement. The reason is that in a democratic society, where you have a system of checks and balances, a labour movement is absolutely indispensable … There will always be unions as long as there are bosses.' In a National Public Radio interview in 1997 he said, 'The labour movement, the whole movement, is a constant struggle. It's been a never-ending struggle. And you have to view it that way. And if you rest on your oars, then you're going to witness the demise of the labour movement. Practically, I can't see it happening.'

Doug Fraser died on 23 February 2008. His widow and the UAW HQ received floods of tributes from trade union leaders, politicians and car-company bosses, including Bill Ford, Chairman of Ford Motor Co. UAW President Ron Gettelfinger was the first to make a statement in his honour. 'It was because of his background and ethics that he was able to serve the membership of our union in a manner that was above reproach. Doug never forgot the "sacred trust" that was bestowed on him 'to serve the best interests of our members and their families.' Former Michigan Governor James Blanchard said, 'He was probably the most respected labour leader in America, and had a great political charm, as well as a substantive commitment.'

To honour Doug Fraser's leadership of the UAW, the Douglas A. Fraser Center for Workplace Issues was established in Detroit's Wayne State University. It was opened in 1988 thanks to donations from Ford, GM, Daimler Chrysler, the UAW and other organisations. Its research and teaching are aimed at providing the best workplaces and environments to improve the quality of life of workers. Underlining the huge esteem for Fraser in the automobile industry and the US labour movement, the board of advisers of the Center include the president of the AFL-CIO, president of the UAW and the vice-president of Ford. The Center is a lasting tribute to Doug Fraser and a lifetime of exceptional leadership dedicated to improving the lives of generations of people in the car industry.

Chapter 4

J. B. McLachlan and the Nova Scotia Miners

The 1886 Lanarkshire coalfield strike was one of Scotland's most violent industrial confrontations and proved to be a watershed for Britain's trade unions. The miners had called a strike over cuts in pay, and the Coal Masters Association immediately rushed in scabs who were protected by large numbers of police. Two months into the strike the miners became more desperate and shops were looted to feed their starving families. Mounted police charged into any gathering of more than a few people, including children and the elderly. As attacks on strike-breakers increased, the government grew alarmed and sent in the army to assist the police. Miners' cottages were raided and union activists were arrested. The Lord Provost of Glasgow called for an urgent meeting between miners and mine owners to try to resolve the dispute and the Coal Masters Association reluctantly agreed to speak to the miners' representatives.

Sixteen miners sat opposite the same number of coal owners at the meeting presided over by the Lord Provost. The owners outlined their requirement for a sliding scale of wages, which would regulate pay in harmony with coal prices. This was the accepted principle for determining wages at that time. James McLachlan, the fiery, red-haired miners representative of the middle ward of Lanarkshire, rose to address the meeting. He was only eighteen years old, fairly small, but highly confident. Waiting until the room fell silent, he then launched a tirade against the coal masters and their pay cut. A religious fanatic, he spoke with the same uncompromising certainty he heard from the preachers in the small fundamentalist Presbyterian sect to which he belonged. He rejected the coal masters' arguments and reiterated the miners' original demands that the cuts in pay be withdrawn. The meeting ended in hostility, with the coal owners yielding no ground.

James Bryson McLachlan was born in 1869 in Ecclefechan, Dumfriesshire, 8 miles north of the English border. The village of around eight hundred inhabitants was also the birthplace of the celebrated writer Thomas Carlyle. The son of a stonemason, Carlyle was born in 1795 and educated at the village school before going on to Edinburgh University. His highly influential books and articles inspired social

James Bryson McLachlan was the fifth child of an Irish immigrant weaver (James McLachlan) and his wife Esther Bryson. He was born in Ecclefechan in one of a row of small cottages in Carlyle Place. McLachlan was born in the property (above, on the left) which abutted the left hand gable of the Arched House, two doors away from the birthplace of Thomas Carlyle himself. These cottages were built by James Carlyle (Thomas Carlyle's father) and his three brothers; McLachlan was proud of his association with the family. He often recounted the tale of his birth in later life and frequently carried a copy of Thomas Carlyle's Sartor Resartus.

reformers throughout the Victorian era. McLachlan's father, the son of Irish immigrants, lived in a cottage built by Carlyle's father. He was a cotton weaver, but the depressed conditions in the trade forced him to leave Ecclefechan and move to north Lanarkshire, an area of industrial growth. When he was just ten James McLachlan joined his father down the coal mines, having completed only a few years of schooling.

McLachlan's mother belonged to the small fundamentalist Cameronian sect of the Reformed Presbyterian Church and James was brought up in her faith. Long hours were devoted to Bible study in the strict religious household, and in later years, after he became an atheist, he astonished clergymen with his knowledge of scripture. Many aspects of McLachlan's religious youth shaped his understanding of society. The obstinate religious fanaticism of this period found expression in political forms later in life, and when he believed in a cause, no level of harassment could break him. When he was twenty, influenced by a preacher who roused the crowds at street-corner meetings, he left the Cameronians and joined the Baptist Church. The evangelical preachers taught him the art of public speaking and persuasive argument.

When he was twenty-four he married Kate Greenshields, who was a member of his local church. She was a beautiful, intelligent, black-haired girl who had received a good education and was well versed in poetry and drama. Her father was a stonemason, a trade which at that time was regarded as the aristocracy of labour. Kate's family felt that marrying a miner was beneath her station, but the objections were overcome when it became clear how much in love the two young people were. They remained devoted to each other throughout their lives, despite many periods of suffering and hardship. Their children later spoke of the close bond between them, their daughter explaining, 'I have yet to meet another couple who *loved* and *liked* each other as my father and mother.' McLachlan hated to be parted from her for any length of time. The day before he was released from a six-month prison sentence he wrote a poem that ends with the lines, 'Just twelve more hours and the days are o'er that from Katie I've been riven, / Just twelve more hours then grudging sun, it's Katie, me and heaven.'

McLachlan was such a confident young man that he volunteered to become secretary of his local union when he was only fifteen. However, it was not long before he found himself on the employers' blacklist and, like most miners' leaders, was forced to move around the coalfields to find work. For the first eight years of his marriage the family moved house constantly through Lanarkshire and Ayrshire, ending up in the east end of Glasgow. In 1902 they decided to move to Nova Scotia, Canada.

Located on the eastern coast of Canada near the mouth of the St Lawrence River, Nova Scotia comprises a mainland peninsula and the adjacent Cape Breton Island. Latin for New Scotland, Nova Scotia was named by Sir William Alexander, Earl of Stirling, in the early 1600s, who obtained a charter from King James the Sixth of Scotland for its colonisation. Some Scottish settlers arrived in 1620 but were removed when the area was turned over to the French. The first substantial migration from Scotland occurred when a shipload of Scots sailed from Ullapool on the *Hector* in 1773. The anniversary of the landing is still celebrated in both Nova Scotia and in Ullapool, but for those who survived the crossing and the subsequent battle for survival, it was a harrowing experience. Emigration arising from the Highland clearances and the Irish famines gave the Province its predominantly Celtic character.

Coal deposits were found in various parts of Nova Scotia and small mining operations began at the start of the nineteenth century. The end of the century saw a rapid expansion of coal mining when the Dominion Coal Company took over most of the mines and invested in modern plant and infrastructure. Nearby deposits of limestone and iron ore provided the ingredients of a steel industry and when the first steel mills opened in 1900, families from all over North America and Europe flocked to the province looking for work. Most of the unskilled workers were from farming backgrounds and had little understanding of trade unions. But the Scots arrived with the experience of many labour confrontations behind them, and consequently played a leading part in the organisation of unions.

The McLachlan family settled in Sydney, Cape Breton, whose population had doubled from three to six thousand between 1901 and 1905. A new steel plant had been built, but housing was scarce and facilities in the town had not been developed. It was a primitive frontier settlement with the buildings made of wood and homes lacking light and ventilation. Water and sewage pipes were still to be laid and the dirt roads and footpaths turned to mud after rainfalls. The insanitary conditions led to outbreaks of smallpox, scarlet fever and tuberculosis.

Nova Scotia's first unions

Strikes had taken place in the 1860s and '70s, but no proper union organisation existed until 1881, when Robert Drummond set up the Provincial Workmen's Association (PWA). Born in Greenock, Drummond emigrated to Nova Scotia in 1865 when he was twenty five. He found work as a miner and in 1874 was promoted to supervisor at the Springhill colliery in Cumberland County, where 44 per cent of the miners were Scottish. Several years later the Springhill Mining Company announced reductions in wages two years in a row at a time when coal prices were rising. Drummond was incensed and, despite his management position, joined in secret discussions at the pit about forming a union. He was immediately accepted as the miners' leader and spokesman. A strike was called and a quick victory achieved, boosting the union's reputation throughout the province. Before long every mine in Nova Scotia was organised, and soon workers from other industries were clamouring to join. The union's influence was then extended to cover steelworkers, railwaymen and others.

The son of a middle-class grocer, Drummond had a distinctive Scottish accent and wonderful sense of humour. He exuded confidence as a speaker and eloquence as a writer, becoming full-time secretary of the union and editor of its journal. The union's constitution, which was drafted by Drummond, strongly reflected the ritual and language of freemasonry. Passwords, solemn oaths, titles and regalia revealed the influence of secret societies, which had also been a feature of the some of the earlier Scottish unions. Drummond's guru was Alexander MacDonald, and Drummond ensured that the PWA followed the same philosophy as the Miners National Association in Britain (see Chapter 1, pages 7-8). It acknowledged that there could be times when wage reductions would have to be agreed and promoted arbitration as more sensible and less expensive than strikes for dealing with differences between employers and employed. He was also anxious to ensure that the PWA cultivated habits of thrift, industry, economy and sobriety amongst its members.

However that did not mean that the PWA refrained from supporting strike action. Indeed, during Drummond's period as Grand Secretary, seventy strikes took place, which were normally one-pit disputes. He publicly defended the strikes, even when violence was used against management or strike-breakers. The longest strike at a pit lasted a full year, during which management tried to bring scabs from Scotland, who refused to work after Drummond intervened.

Robert Drummond was born in Greenock and set up the Provincial Workmen's Association of Nova Scotia in 1881. He became full time secretary of the union, which organised the miners and other workers in Nova Scotia. After he joined the Legislative Council in 1891 he turned against the union's more radical policies. (Courtesy Beaton Institute, Cape Breton University, 79-977-3957)

Politically, Drummond was a radical liberal, but after the government sent in troops to break a strike, he concluded that the PWA should stand its own candidates in elections. In the 1890s he was among the most forceful voices raised on behalf of full female enfranchisement. He was an excellent propagandist and used his dazzling rhetoric to bring about recognition of trade unionism as a legitimate force in social and economic life. Collective agreements represented an important new approach to industrial relations in Canada, and through his efforts the country's first compulsory arbitration legislation was introduced. As the chief lobbyist of the union, and later as a senator, Drummond campaigned successfully for mine-safety legislation. After a tragic explosion at Springhill, which claimed the lives of 125 men and boys, the use of gunpowder in mines was abolished. In some Nova Scotia collieries over a quarter of the underground workforce were boys, and legislation was passed raising the minimum age for working underground and stipulating a minimum standard of training and qualifications to become a collier.

Drummond became a pillar of the establishment in the town of Stellarton, Pictou County. He was a leading member of St John's Presbyterian church, a justice of the peace, a town councillor and, later, mayor. However, when he joined the Nova Scotia Legislative Council in 1891, it seemed to distance him from the workers he represented. He became less comfortable in the PWA, and eventually resigned in 1898 after stubbornly refusing to accept his members' views on the truck system (miners hated the arrangement that allowed employers to pay them in scrips, or currency substitutes, to be used only at the company store).

His early radicalism gradually vanished while on the legislative council, and he became a proprietor of his own paper, the *Maritime Mining Record*. He began to write on mining affairs from a business perspective, and his support for the coal companies during later disputes meant he was loathed by the new wave of militants who took over the PWA. He denounced left-wing union leaders and blamed them for damaging the coal industry by their strikes and propaganda. When James McLachlan became one of the union's main figures, Drummond sarcastically commented that 'some wise men from the east, in other words some recently arrived Scotsmen, have taken possession of the PWA lodge at Sydney and are trying to introduce some new old-fangled notions'. He branded the PWA leadership as 'insane radicals whose wage claims threatened to destabilise the entire coal industry'. Even during periods when wages were cut and the miners' families suffered great hardship, he was an apologist for the coal companies, arguing that workers had forgotten the habits of industry, sobriety and thrift. Such comments ruined his reputation amongst trade unionists and made him an object of contempt in the mining community. Nonetheless, his record beforehand made him one of the most significant figures of nineteenth-century Canadian labour history.

John Moffat rebuilds the PWA

In the period leading up to Drummond's resignation, the very existence of the PWA was threatened. Because of Drummond's intransigence, he antagonised the miners to the extent that they deserted in droves to join the Knights of Labor (see Chapter 1, pages 16-17), taking with them property owned by the PWA lodges. In 1898 the PWA had less than one thousand members when another Scotsman, John Moffat, took over from Drummond as Grand Secretary.

Moffat was only sixteen years old when he left Ayrshire to come to Cape Breton in 1882. He had been an activist in the Ayrshire Miners Association when it was formed in 1880. However, the union, which was led by Keir Hardie, was abandoned after an unsuccessful strike and, perhaps because he was victimised, Moffat decided to emigrate. His experience in Ayrshire did not weaken his resolve and he was soon in conflict with his first mine manager over working conditions. He then tried to organise a lodge of the PWA but was sacked and blacklisted from the pits in Cape Breton. He moved to the mainland of Nova Scotia to find work before returning to Cape Breton in 1893. Settling in the town of Dominion, he became a respected member of the community, participating in church and school affairs, and was elected president of his local PWA lodge.

Once he took over from Drummond, he set about stabilising the ailing organisation. He firstly had to wage a lengthy legal battle to get back the PWA property from the Knights of Labor. The next year, he submitted a 10 per cent pay demand, which the coal company conceded without a strike, and the following year claimed a further substantial rise in wages. Members flooded back, and by 1903, Moffat had rebuilt the PWA into a well-organised union with thirty-five lodges. The revitalised union was not restricted to miners. Several thousand workers at the Dominion steel plant joined in the hope that they would win recognition from their employer. Dominion had gradually acquired most of the coal-mining capacity in Nova Scotia as well as steel mills, shipping, and other industries. It recognised the PWA for negotiation in its mines, but it categorically denied trade union rights for its steelworkers.

John Moffat, who was sixteen years old when he left Ayrshire to go to Nova Scotia, took over from Robert Drummond as secretary of the Provincial Workmen's Association. He fought a bruising battle with J B McLachlan for the support of the miners and resisted attempts to merge with UMWA. (Courtesy Beaton Institute, Cape Breton University, 79-975-3955)

Men in the Dominion steel plant worked long hours with little time off. Some worked without a day off throughout the year on alternate eleven- and thirteen-hour shifts, which at changeover meant a twenty-four-hour shift once a fortnight. The PWA called a strike in 1904 after the company reduced pay by a substantial amount. But it ended in disaster and cost most of the steelworkers their jobs. Dominion hired strike-breakers, and requested federal troops to protect them from pickets. The seven-week-long strike left the union bankrupt and incensed that state forces had been used to break their strike.

After this defeat, the PWA decided once again that political representation of workers was essential to ensure protection during disputes. As an experiment it stood an independent Labour candidate at the provincial elections. They had high hopes that their candidate would triumph in a predominantly coal and steel community, especially with the bitter experience of the strike still fresh in everyone's mind. However the candidate lost his deposit and after this rebuke from its own supporters, the mood in the PWA turned against direct involvement in elections. John Moffat's response to the failed steel strike and the subsequent political rejection was to return to Robert Drummond's philosophy of accommodation and conciliation. He concluded agreements with the coal companies that allowed them to adjust miners' wages with variations in the price of coal.

James McLachlan was horrified at Moffat's change of strategy. He was working at the Princess Colliery, the biggest mine in Nova Scotia, where half the workers were under twenty. MacLachlan was an experienced miner in his thirties, which helped him win the confidence of the other miners. He became the union representative for the pit and was viewed as an intellectual for his regular contributions to the Nova Scotia daily newspaper, the *Halifax Herald*. His letters on social, economic and mining issues were sprinkled with references to Thomas Carlyle and Robert Burns. Some of them were highly critical of the leadership of the PWA and called for changes in union policy.

McLachlan leads a contentious split

The price of coal had been falling and with it the wages of the miners. The agreements between the PWA and the coal companies were based on the price of coal and until that rose, the PWA accepted there could be no increase in wages. Miners were becoming impatient with their union and McLachlan concluded that the PWA had had its day.

Although McLachlan was only five years younger than Moffat, he had left home much later and witnessed changes in the philosophy of the union in Scotland. The rise of large integrated coal and steel companies, the rapid growth of the industry, and the flood of new workers all represented a challenge to the established policy of the PWA. The notion of an equal partnership between mine owners and men was difficult to recognise in the new circumstances, and McLachlan had already seen the future with the more advanced development of the industry in Scotland.

He favoured joining the United Mine Workers of America (UMWA), and started corresponding with their headquarters. The UMWA had grown rapidly to over 400,000 members in the USA and Canada and was led by a militant executive, which the Americans called the international board. Unions in the USA had been encouraging Canadian unions to join them and the UMWA had already established District 18 of the union in western Canada. Peter Patterson, a Scotsman who had previously worked in Nova Scotia, represented District 18 on the union's international board, and was sent to Nova Scotia to encourage the PWA to affiliate. Patterson reported that many miners were put off joining the PWA because of John Moffat's restrained approach to pay bargaining, but would join the UMWA in droves if given the chance.

Most of the miners felt that joining the UMWA would give them more strength in negotiations and McLachlan had hoped for an agreed formula for amalgamation. However, in the face of hostility from Moffat, a diplomatic agreement was difficult. The Grand Council of the PWA eventually agreed to hold a referendum to determine whether or not they should amalgamate. A majority of voted in favour of amalgamation, but as less than 50 per cent of the membership participated, the Grand Council ruled that the vote was inconclusive. When they decided not to join the UMWA, McLachlan attempted to mount a legal challenge, but Moffat outmanoeuvred him.

McLachlan bitterly attacked Moffat for not accepting the vote and told PWA members they had been betrayed. He felt it futile to continue to work within the PWA and concluded that a breakaway was the only option. In 1908, McLachlan led thousands of miners out of the PWA and established Nova Scotia as District 26 of the United Mine Workers of America. Amongst those who left and affiliated to the UMWA were the Springhill miners, whose lodge was the birthplace of the PWA. McLachlan was elected secretary/treasurer, a full-time, salaried position, and in his first report to union delegates, he claimed a membership of seven thousand for the new union, organised in ten locals. Two Scotsmen were now leading rival Nova Scotia mineworkers' unions of approximately the same size.

Glace Bay, twelve miles from Sydney, was chosen as the HQ of District 26. The McLachlan family was once more on the move, renting a house from Dan McDougall, the new President of District 26. Known as 'Orange Dan' for his membership of the Orange Order, McDougall was a Scotsman who had been a PWA stalwart before he was persuaded to join the UMWA. He was a well-known and highly respected town councillor and had a distinguished record in PWA activity.

The coal companies were happy to deal with the PWA, but viewed the UMWA with alarm. Not only did they refuse to enter discussions with the UMWA, but sacked all known members. In total a thousand miners were fired, and despite several attempts at reconciliation, the coal companies, dominated by Dominion Coal, refused to reconsider. Even the international president of the UMWA was ignored when he came to Nova Scotia to reassure the coal companies about the union's intentions. While he was there, he attempted to persuade John Moffat to reconsider his views on a merger, but had no success.

The Dominion Coal strike

A strike was inevitable. A demand for a substantial increase to halt falling living standards was tabled, but the main issue for the union was recognition and reinstatement of the sacked miners. It was decided to target the Dominion Coal Corporation, limiting strike action to the seven Dominion lodges. The Corporation was prepared for the strike. One of the 625 special constables sworn in by the county council was John Moffat. His PWA members were instructed to work normally during the strike. Strike-breakers were recruited and coal companies in Britain promised to supplement these if needed. Barracks were constructed for the strike-breakers inside the perimeter fence of the mining complexes. Five hundred soldiers were prepared for action and a train loaded with machine guns, light artillery, rifles and ammunition was despatched to Cape Breton. When the mayor of Glace Bay protested at the arrival of troops to the federal authorities, John Moffat and thirteen PWA lodge secretaries wrote to the government requesting that the troops remain.

Soldiers escorted the PWA men and the strike-breakers from their homes to the pit in large groups and back again after their shift. Such class collaboration by Moffat provoked a fierce attack from McLachlan, who

Dan McDougall was the first president of District 26 of the UMWA (Nova Scotia). McDougall was arrested during a strike and taken to Montréal, and although he was eventually acquitted, he never recovered from the beatings he received in jail. Blacklisted from the mining industry, he became postmaster for Glace Bay (Courtesy, Sheddon Studios, Beaton Institute, Cape Breton University, 80-712-4892)

denounced him in his inimitable way. 'By birth a Scotsman; by adoption a Canadian; by nature a traitor; by profession a scab organiser; and by long and continued habit, the arch lickspittle of the Dominion Coal Company.' The coal companies tried to recruit miners from Europe and the USA, but the UMWA countered by placing adverts in newspapers urging men not to accept the jobs.

The strike was one of the longest and most bitter in Canadian history and resulted in defeat for the UMWA. The troops evicted strikers from their homes, helped break up demonstrations, and had orders to shoot to kill if anyone defied their instructions. Dan McDougall, president of District 26, was woken at 5 a.m. by police and whisked off in leg irons to Montreal, where he was jailed. His 'crime' was a statement that the housing conditions in the strike-breakers' barracks were sub-standard. This was considered a criminal libel against Dominion Coal and the legal authorities agreed. Although McDougall was eventually acquitted, he never recovered from the beatings he received in jail.

McLachlan tried every conceivable tactic during the strike, and at one stage managed to turn the tables on Dominion. Showing an exceptional knowledge of legal matters, he laid a series of charges against the coal company and its executives. Claiming that they were involved in price-fixing and limiting production from 1900 to 1909, McLachlan forced the court to order the impounding of the company records for the nine years in question. Warrants were served on the president and chief executive of Dominion and although the company was eventually cleared, the directors, exhausted by the whole episode, announced their retirement. Hopes were raised when a new syndicate bought Dominion, but were dashed when they announced they were not prepared to recognise the UMWA.

The strike ended after ten months, with the UMWA having contributed approximately $1.5 million in strike relief. For a period District 26 continued to function, but by 1913 the total paid-up membership stood at only 176. The UMWA, which had also paid out a large sum to support a strike on Vancouver Island, decided to close down its Canadian districts.

McLachlan after the strike

Dan McDougall found a job in the post office and rose to become postmaster for Glace Bay until his death in 1924, but McLachlan, no longer paid by the union, had limited employment opportunities. In addition to the four children who had emigrated with him from Scotland, five more were born in Canada. To make a living he bought a 6-acre dairy farm. The family grew a few crops, and with fourteen cows and some chickens, they were able to start a business selling milk and eggs. The farm did not produce enough income to sustain the family, but his three eldest daughters had other jobs and their contribution was enough to maintain the family unit. On the positive side, McLachlan was left with enough spare time to teach his children and to study history, mathematics and economics. Despite the difficult financial situation, McLachlan, who was a voracious reader, built a sizeable library. It included a large collection of Scottish and Socialist publications, including the novels of Walter Scott, Robert Louis Stevenson, and the main works of Marx and Engels.

Although his life was devoted to improving working-class living standards, McLachlan was modest in his own tastes and was highly generous with the little money he had. If his children asked for something, he gave them every cent he had. The same applied to anyone he met. Even complete strangers were beneficiaries of his kindness, for example, a man he had never met before was loaned his horse and cart. Sometimes he came home having emptied his pockets for a penniless soul and on one occasion came back without shoes because someone he met needed them more. This characteristic made him totally incorruptible. Very often coal-company agents would try to bribe union officials, but they realised very soon that they were wasting their time trying to buy off McLachlan. A poem written by a Cape Breton miner alludes to his honesty with the lines: 'They knew they could not buy you Jim, / With money, stolen votes or booze.'

One of the many visitors to the McLachlan home was his old friend Keir Hardie, who had come to North America in 1908, campaigning for the Socialist candidate in the American presidential election. The Canadian Trades and Labour Congress was meeting in Halifax that year, and Hardie took the opportunity of addressing the convention. Along with his wife and daughter, he then travelled on to Cape Breton to stay with McLachlan. Their discussions carried on into the wee small hours, talking about Scotland, trade unions and politics. McLachlan was a member of the Socialist Party of Canada, and later became president of the Independent Labour Party when it was formed in Cape Breton in 1917.

Despite the legacy of the 1909 defeat, McLachlan remained positive that the economic and political pendulum would swing in the left's direction. His optimism strengthened with the changing economic conditions created by the First World War. Industry was booming, but inflation left wages far behind price increases. Throughout the country, workers were pressing for pay rises to catch up. However, in Nova Scotia, John Moffat had negotiated a two-year deal with Dominion Coal, which left no scope for a wage increase. Moffat, faced with angry members demanding action, insisted that wage increases would have to wait for a rise in coal prices.

McLachlan started secretly organising another union, the United Mine Workers of Nova Scotia, and waited patiently for the right moment to attack. He had gained support from his old comrades and some of the younger miners. During the summer and autumn of 1916 the new union launched a recruitment drive, with a demand for a 25 per cent across-the-board increase. By the end of the year, half of Nova Scotia's coalminers had joined his union. Concerned about this development, Dominion offered the PWA a 10 per cent rise. But even the PWA knew that this was not enough to stem the tide of unrest, and in a desperate attempt at survival demanded 30 per cent. Faced with pay claims from both the PWA and the new union, Dominion Coal once again geared up for a lengthy dispute. But the government was concerned at the implications for wartime coal production and looked for a way to avoid a strike.

A Federal Fuel Board had been created at the start of the war and one of its members was James Watters, president of the Canadian Trades and Labour Congress (see Chapter 5, pages 139-140). Watters, a Scotsman and a close political colleague of McLachlan, persuaded the government to set up a royal commission to look at problems in the mining industry, including the difficulties caused by having two unions in Nova Scotia. The commission met and recommended a large pay rise for the miners. It also concluded that an amalgamation of the two unions was in the best interests of the miners and the industry. This time the now-discredited PWA agreed, and a new trade union was formed, representing all the miners in Nova Scotia. In his final remarks as Grand Secretary of the PWA, Moffat stated that the miners should 'close up our ranks and join forces with the brothers for the common good of all'. The evening after the merger, Moffat announced he would not be contesting any position in the new union. He retired from trade union activity, and later became the Nova Scotia correspondent of the *Labour Gazette*.

The merged union became the transitional organisation for affiliation to the UMWA, and in 1919, District 26 of the UMWA re-emerged. This time the miners were united, with the backing of the government, and Dominion Coal had little choice but to recognise it. McLachlan was the sole nomination for secretary/treasurer and Robert Baxter, his

James B McLachlan, one of Canada's most illustrious labour leaders, was born in Ecclefechan, Dumfriesshire. He was president the Nova Scotia district of the United Mine Workers of America, but was expelled from the union by John L Lewis. He was a leading spokesman for the Communist Party of Canada but resigned in 1937 over policy differences. (Courtesy Prof David Frank)

closest lieutenant, was elected president. Baxter came from Lanarkshire and emigrated to Canada at the turn of the century when he was twenty-two. He had supported McLachlan's leadership since he first challenged Moffat and had led one of the locals during the 1909 strike. However, it was not long before the two comrades came to blows.

Baxter and McLachlan: from comrades to bitter enemies

After the First World War, economic conditions began to deteriorate, leading to wage cuts, falling coal prices and unemployment. Baxter and McLachlan clashed over the 1922 pay settlement, which entailed a pay cut. Baxter felt a strike was not appropriate during these general economic conditions and was reluctantly in favour of doing a deal with the company. The majority of the District 26 board supported Baxter, but McLachlan defied them and launched a vigorous campaign against the offer. Once again he was prepared for a yet another bitter struggle against a fellow Scotsman.

But McLachlan had read the mood of the miners correctly. Regardless of the economic situation, they voted overwhelmingly to reject the company offer. But since conditions did not favour a prolonged strike, McLachlan proposed a go-slow. Scottish miners had adopted this tactic – which was in effect a restriction in output – during the nineteenth century. The Nova Scotia trade unions had never used this method before and although it required a high level of discipline, it proved an extremely effective device. After a few weeks the confidence of the miners grew and the mood began to harden. A conference was convened and calls were made for an all-out strike. It was traditional to allow maintenance work to be carried out during strike action to avoid damage to the mines, but on this occasion the delegates went over the heads of their leaders and decided to stop all work. This meant that within a few weeks some mines would be destroyed. The mine owners, fearing the loss of their investment, panicked and agreed a settlement acceptable to the miners.

After celebrating their victory, the miners then directed their attention towards Baxter and his supporters on the board. A vote of no confidence in the leadership was carried and fresh elections were held. McLachlan and his allies won a resounding victory, with McLachlan re-elected and Baxter heavily defeated by 'Red' Dan Livingstone for the presidency.

A district committee of like-minded socialists now surrounded McLachlan. In 1923 McLachlan, Livingstone and most of the District 26 board joined the Communist Party. They also affiliated District 26 with the Red International of Trade Unions, an organisation set up by the Communist International. However, the president of the UMWA, the fiercely anti-Communist John L. Lewis, was carefully monitoring events in Nova Scotia. McLachlan and District 26 were beginning to create other problems for the UMWA board by threatening to repudiate a pay agreement. In the summer of 1923, Lewis was in crucial talks with the anthracite coal operators in the US for recognition of the union. He was at pains to point out that the UMWA could be trusted to uphold any agreement it reached on behalf of the 158,000 anthracite miners. The coal operators were citing the problems in District 26 and the issue was threatening to become an embarrassing obstacle to an agreement. Lewis was determined to prevent strike action in Nova Scotia and show his ruthlessness with any district of the UMWA that broke ranks. However, when a strike took place, it was not over pay, but was in support of the steelworkers.

Cape Breton steelworkers, almost 60 per cent of whom were in a union, had been fighting for union recognition but with no success. In 1923 a strike was called over a 20 per cent pay reduction. Armed company police clashed with steelworkers, but the brutality of the provincial police caused uproar. Eyewitnesses described them indiscriminately attacking anyone in their way, including women, children and the elderly. Reports of their vicious behaviour spread throughout the Cape Breton community. In the coalfields, miners met to discuss the events and urged their officials to call a sympathy strike.

In response, a telegram signed by Livingstone and McLachlan was sent to all locals in District 26. It condemned the police brutality, criticised the Nova Scotia Premier, and called every miner out on strike. But the Premier responded by ordering the arrest of Livingstone and McLachlan for publication of false information. In the middle of the night, police raided their homes. The pair were arrested, shackled in handcuffs and leg-irons, and rushed out of Cape Breton to a jail in Halifax, where they were held incommunicado for several days.

Robert Baxter, still smarting from his election defeat, urged Lewis to take action against McLachlan and force District 26 to toe the line. While the two leaders were behind bars, Lewis ordered the District 26 committee to end the strike. When they refused, he expelled McLachlan and Livingstone from the union and revoked the District 26 charter, which in effect stripped the district of its powers. The other leaders were removed from office and Baxter was put back in office. Assisted by the courts, he ended the strike in a few weeks.

However, within a year, District 26's independence was restored. Threatened by desertion of the Nova Scotia miners to Bob Russell's 'One Big Union' (see Chapter 5, pages 147-148), Lewis agreed to hold elections for the Board. McLachlan was ineligible to stand, as he had been expelled, but his supporters won all the positions contested. Robert Baxter was again heavily defeated in the election for president. After a further unsuccessful attempt for office a couple of years later, he retired from union activity.

McLachlan turns to journalism

McLachlan was eventually charged and convicted of publishing a seditious document. However, he was acquitted on appeal, having spent almost six months behind bars. Thousands gathered to greet him on his release, and he stopped in several towns in Nova Scotia to address huge public meetings. He then went home to a hero's welcome in Cape Breton, where he was feted by the miners and the steelworkers. Forman Waye, the steelworkers' leader, described him as 'the greatest exponent of the cause of labour in the Maritime Provinces ... whose word was his bond ... who was utterly fearless in fighting the tyrants who exploited the poor; and who possessed a brilliant and analytical brain that was tireless in labour's cause'.

Expelled from the union, he was offered the job of editor of the *Maritime Labour Herald*, which gave him an excellent platform to air his views. He conducted colourful attacks on the coal companies and on John Lewis. Other right-wing union leaders were not spared his legendary sarcasm. A brief notice written by McLachlan appeared in the paper announcing the death of Samuel Gompers, the founder of the American Federation of Labor and arch enemy of the left. 'Sam Gompers, after serving the master class faithfully for forty years, is dead. We shall be unable to attend his funeral, but heartily approve of the event.' His ferocious attacks on business interests and right-wing trade union leaders made him many enemies, and on four occasions the offices of the *Herald* were attacked by arsonists.

During this period, police agents reported that although McLachlan was no longer a union official, he was as active and radical as ever, and was now even more influential in the mining community. Interest in McLachlan began to spread throughout North America, and a journalist from one of Canada's most popular publications, *Maclean's* magazine, came to Cape Breton to interview him towards the end of 1924. He described McLachlan as 'a short bow-legged little man with a face lined and pitted with years of struggle, keen eyes beneath a shaggy red moustache, a soiled collar much too large for him and a wrinkled suit rather the worse for wear'. Impressed by his sincerity and intelligence, the journalist thanked McLachlan for his time. As he was leaving McLachlan made a prediction: 'The company's goin' for tae try another wage cut in the spring, but mark ye, bye, the miners of Cape Breton'll be flat on their backs afore they'll tak'it! Mind that!' He was referring to the British Empire Steel Company, which had taken over the assets of the Dominion Coal Company. During its eight-year history it was in constant financial crisis due to the inordinate amount of debt it had taken on to finance mergers. Huge profits were required to meet these financial commitments forcing management to seek impossible levels of productivity from its workforce.

His prediction proved accurate. Miners were working reduced hours and conditions in the Cape Breton coalfields were so atrocious that they were debated in the Federal parliament. When further pay cuts were announced, the union called for a royal commission to examine conditions in the mining communities. Alarming descriptions of the suffering were reported by neutral sources. The Baptist minister of Glace Bay wrote that some children wore clothes made from flour bags, and that families were surviving on black tea, molasses and soup bones. Then, at the beginning of March 1925, the coal company announced a suspension of credit at the company stores. The move shocked even the Nova Scotia Premier, who stated that the whole purpose of credit at the stores was to help people through difficult times. With many families already dependent on relief, the union felt there was nothing to lose by calling a strike.

The bitterest strike of all

The British Empire Steel Company immediately took their horses and equipment from the mines and prepared for a long strike. As the strike dragged on, the company's attitude became more bullish and its vice president was quite blunt about the situation. He stated in a newspaper interview that the longer the strike went on, the stronger the company's position became. He added a further comment – 'They can't stand the gaff!' – a colloquialism meaning that the miners' resolve would eventually be broken by starvation and privation. The quote became notorious in the labour movement, but its effect was to gain widespread sympathy for the strikers. Appeals were made for assistance to prevent starvation, and an outraged public responded. The company's callous and confrontational attitude prompted newspapers to organise collections that raised thousands of dollars. Support came from churches, including the Catholic Church, whose parish priests throughout Nova Scotia were instructed to raise money for the strikers. The Salvation Army and the Red Cross gave assistance, as did hundreds of voluntary organisations and trade unions. Miners from all over the world sent donations, including $5000 from the miners of the USSR. Even some corporate organisations joined in, with the Quaker Oats Company sending several railway cars full of oats and flour. The UMWA eventually agreed to send $10,000 per week after John Lewis was satisfied that maintenance of the mines was still being covered.

But it was not easy to 'stand the gaff'. Over 30,000 people were dependent on relief and by the third month of the strike supplies had reduced substantially. Starvation was beginning to have an effect on morale. An offer by the union to accept arbitration was rejected. Drastic action was needed to prevent total defeat. The strike had been relatively peaceful and the union had allowed maintenance work to proceed without interference. This had helped maintain public sympathy and the support of the UMWA international board. But as they faced humiliation, the miners upped the ante and withdrew all co-operation. Once again the mines faced total destruction.

A power plant supplying electricity to the pumps at the collieries had been allowed to operate during the strike. On 11 June 1925, the union men walked off the job and company police were despatched to the plant. In the defining moment of the strike, thousands of miners, joined by their wives and children, converged on the power station. Faced with a hostile demonstration marching towards them, the police panicked and opened fire. The effect of this seemed to embolden the crowd. Undaunted, they charged towards the power station, overwhelmed the company police and chased them in every direction. The power-station pumps and boilers were then closed down. But the miners suffered numerous casualties, including a father of nine, William Davis, who was shot dead. Later that night, the coalfields were engulfed by rioting as word of the death spread. Company stores were looted and then burned to the ground. Coal-company buildings were set alight as crowds of people rampaged through the streets. One Cape Breton newspaper described the unrest as the 'result of five months of government inaction, corporation obstinacy, and the accumulated desperation of hungry men'.

A few weeks later there was an election in Nova Scotia and the Conservative opposition promised to settle the strike. They won by a landslide and set up a royal commission, exactly the proposal suggested by the union before the dispute began. Despite bitter opposition, the commission forced the company to negotiate with the UMWA. The union came out of the episode with dignity, but the 1925 strike is still remembered as the saddest, most difficult struggle in the history of Cape Breton unions. However, the strike proved to be a watershed in industrial relations in Canada. Both the Liberal and the Conservative parties accepted the need for legislation to give rights and protection for trade unions and their members. Every year on 11 June, Cape Bretons mark the events of 1925 with a public holiday, named Davis Day in honour of the dead man. The hated company stores, burned down in the riot, never reopened.

Despite the unity created during the 1925 strike, internal conflict within District 26 was a continuing theme. There was a constant battle between the left and right and often those who were elected on a left-wing ticket later moved to the right. The combination of internal issues and the ongoing problems in the relationship with the international board led to a further split and the creation of yet another union. James McLachlan had played no direct role in the strike and for most of the period he was confined to bed with pleurisy. The *Maritime Labour Herald's* offices had been set on fire during the strike and never opened again.

The Depression and anti-Communism

The UMWA membership had begun to drop alarmingly, and there was widespread disquiet about its leadership and its policies under John Lewis (see Chapter 1, page 38). In 1932, miners in Nova Scotia opted to leave the UMWA and form their own Nova Scotia union. The split had the backing of McLachlan, but he took no role within the new organisation. Instead, he toured the country speaking on behalf of the Communist Party. During this period, McLachlan was the Communist Party's best-known working-class leader. He was installed as president of the Workers Unity League, which was set up by the Communist Party in 1929 as a revolutionary trade union centre in an attempt to rival the existing Trades and Labour Congress (see Chapter 5, pages 141, 151-156). He led a protest to Ottawa to outline the poverty-stricken conditions of the miners. The Tory Prime Minister, R. B. Bennett, agreed to meet a deputation and opened the proceedings by explaining at length how the coal companies were not making any profits and kept the mines open just to provide the miners with work. McLachlan listened patiently until the PM had finished his defence of the coal owners and then quietly observed 'Ah yes, Mr Bennett, you know all about profits, you are sure an authority on profits – but you don't know anything about digging coal.'

One of the most captivating orators in Canada, McLachlan was seen as a dangerous revolutionary by the state. He was described in his police file as 'a great reader, a fluent speaker and a mob leader. [He is] witty, sarcastic and yells with a Lowland Scots burr that is worth hearing.' The Canadian authorities devoted large resources to prevent the growth of the Communist Party, deporting or jailing leading members. They were particularly anxious about their Russian, Ukrainian and Finnish immigrants, whom they suspected of Bolshevik sympathies. Police agents attended every Communist public meeting. To enable them to follow proceedings and report on speakers, meetings were banned in languages other than English. At a mass meeting in Toronto, attended by a large proportion of Scots, McLachlan decided to have a bit of fun. He deliberately thickened his accent so that the police agents could not understand a word. As they cast anxious looks at each other, wondering if they should close the meeting down, hundreds of Scots roared with laughter as McLachlan ridiculed the authorities and poked fun at the law. However, the anti-Communist operation was not a joke. In 1931 eight Communist leaders were arrested and jailed for five years (see Chapter 5, page 152). But the police missed James McLachlan, as he was in the Soviet Union at the time. Attempts were made to detain him on his return, but he managed to evade the police.

The period was one of significant growth for the Communist Party of Canada. Like its sister parties throughout the world, it was increasing in size and influence and its members were confident that the world was on the verge of Socialism. The Workers Unity League had organised a number of strikes in 1934 and was gaining members during the Great Depression. But in the autumn of 1935 the strategy of the Canadian Communist Party, like those throughout the world, was turned on its head by a decision of the seventh congress of the Communist International. The expected world revolution had not materialised and Fascism was now the main threat to the working class and to the Soviet Union. Anti-Fascist alliances were sought with Liberals and Social Democrats. Communists now required to work within existing union structures. The Workers Unity League was wound up, and the Nova Scotia miners were urged to rejoin the UMWA. John Lewis was now seen as an ally.

Banner of UMWA New Victoria local, Nova Scotia (Courtesy David Frank)

McLachlan endorsed the idea of the united front, but was disturbed that the Nova Scotia miners were being encouraged to merge with the UMWA on John Lewis's terms. It was personally galling for McLachlan that the Communist Party had embraced his nemesis, and McLachlan refused to accept the Canadian Communist Party's interpretation of the Communist International's policy. He began to drift from the Communist Party, accusing it of moving to the right and betraying its principles. He felt he had no choice but to resign.

Later that year, British Communist MP Willie Gallacher, who was on a speaking tour of North America, came to Nova Scotia. One of the Red Clydeside leaders during the First World War, Gallacher was MP for the mining constituency of West Fife. A year earlier, Gallacher's visit would have been the cause of great jubilation for McLachlan. Gallacher addressed a public meeting, and the audience asked him about McLachlan's resignation. He answered that all Communists, regardless of any disagreements they had with party decisions, must loyally carry them out if the majority votes for them. McLachlan, who was in the audience, rose to say that he loved the Canadian Communist Party, but would not accept orders contrary to his beliefs. He could not support John Lewis, and left the party so that he could have freedom to express himself.

McLachlan's legacy

McLachlan died in 1937 at the age of sixty-eight. His funeral was one of the largest witnessed in Cape Breton, with over three thousand mourners present. Although no Communist Party officials attended, the party's newspaper, *The Worker*, was full of praise for McLachlan's contribution to the fight for Socialism. Eulogies were written about his life in national newspapers and trade union journals. True to Celtic tradition, two songs were written about him, 'The Jim McLachlan Song' and 'The Ballad of J. B. McLachlan'. A monument in his memory was erected in Glace Bay showing McLachlan with a child. Beside his biographical details is one of his quotations which states: 'I believe in education for action. I believe in telling children the truth about the history of the world. That it does not consist of kings, or lords, or cabinets. It consists of the history of the mass of the workers. A thing that is not taught in the schools. I believe in telling children how to measure value. A thing that is not taught in school.' Cape Breton University holds an annual J.B. McLachlan memorial lecture and awards a J.B. McLachlan scholarship in his honour.

J B McLachlan Monument, Glace Bay. The monument shows McLachlan with his grandson. Beside his biographical details is one of his quotations about education. (Courtesy Paul Prendergast, Beaton Institute, Cape Breton University, 92-427-23602)

More than anyone else in Cape Breton, McLachlan was responsible for its reputation as a stronghold of radical politics and militant trade unionism. After the reconciliation with the UMWA, McLachlan's sons, Tom and James, became active in the union. Tom was elected president of District 26 from 1954 to 1958, and was also president of the Nova Scotia Federation of Labour for ten years. He joined the Co-operative Commonwealth Federation, a left-wing Social Democratic party (see Chapter 6, page 180) and became its Nova Scotia president as well as serving several terms as a councillor for Glace Bay.

Chapter 5

R B Russell and the Canadian Trade Union Centres

Many of today's pupils at the R. B. Russell Vocational High School in Winnipeg, Manitoba will be unaware that their school was named after a Scotsman who was once seen as the most dangerous man in Canada. Bob Russell was jailed for two years after leading the Winnipeg General Strike in 1919, when the establishment thought that the country was on the verge of a Bolshevik-style revolution. Russell was also the figurehead of a trade union centre that at one point threatened to become the predominant force in Canadian trade unionism. Called simply One Big Union, it was established as a revolutionary industrial union, aimed at organising both skilled and unskilled workers. One Big Union was only one of a number of trade union centres created to organise Canadian workers, with Scots prominent in the leadership of them all.

Robert Boyd Russell was born in 1888 in the Springburn district of Glasgow, the hub of the British railway manufacturing industry. Massive factories, each employing several thousand, together with scores of smaller workshops, made Springburn the biggest centre of railway manufacturing in the world. Thirty thousand people lived in the area's high-density tenement accommodation, and most were dependent for their living on the production, repair and maintenance of trains. Russell served his engineering apprenticeship at a time when Springburn built a quarter of the world's locomotives and rolling stock, and exported them to every corner of the globe. The factories were well organised by trade unions and Russell was a member of the powerful Amalgamated Society of Engineers. In 1911, at the age of twenty-three, Russell emigrated to Winnipeg, and found a job with the Canadian Pacific Railway at the Weston railway workshops. Once settled, he arranged for his childhood sweetheart, Margaret Hampton, to join him. They were married in Winnipeg and later had two children, a boy and a girl.

Although it was built in the middle of the prairie, Winnipeg was the third largest city in Canada, with a population of 175,000 and growing fast. The Canadian Pacific Railway dominated the city, and provided many of the jobs. It owned railway yards, a foundry, locomotive and rolling-stock workshops. Other industries followed, including the Ogilvie

The Winnipeg council named the R B Russell Vocational High School after one of the city's most celebrated labour leaders. Three years after Bob Russell's death, construction of the school started, and the opening ceremony was attended by his wife and children. (Courtesy Christian Cassidy, Winnipeg)

flour mills, Vulcan iron works, sawmills, farm-machinery factories and machine shops. Almost all industry was located at the northern end of the town and, with the railroad dividing the city, a distinct class division developed between its north and south sides. Immigrants usually settled in the north end, where living conditions were appalling, the density of housing was high and pollution was a problem. Drains and sewers were inadequate, rubbish was seldom collected and there were few parks or open spaces for children to play. Predictably, discontent erupted sporadically, and by the time Russell arrived, Winnipeg had a reputation as the most militant city in Canada. Employers had been to the courts so often for injunctions forbidding strikes or picket lines that Winnipeg became known as 'Injunction City'.

Canadian Trades and Labour Congress

Russell had been highly influenced by his Socialist father, and was a member of the Independent Labour Party in Scotland. He joined the Socialist Party of Canada when he arrived, but there was no established union in the railway workshops. Craft unions in Canada had developed during the nineteenth century, but their existence was mainly local and very often short-lived. The British Amalgamated Society of Engineers had established several branches in Ontario and Quebec but, gradually, Canadian workers looked towards the unions in the United States for organisational support. The craft union movement in the United States had been extremely successful in negotiating industry-wide agreements and had created a national assembly of trade unions, the American Federation of Labor (AFL). The AFL co-ordinated activities among member unions, sorted out disputes between them, and represented the union's political interests at government level.

Canadian workers were impressed by the AFL's track record and the large funding reserves available to support strike action. Since many skilled workers travelled back and forth across the border searching for work, the idea of a union that covered Canadian and US workers made sense. Canadian membership of what became known as international unions gradually began to rise. The Canadian Trades and Labour Congress (TLC), which had been established in 1883, began to model itself on the AFL. However, the American domination of the internationals, and the imposition of their policies on the Canadians, was a perennial problem.

The International Association of Machinists (IAM) was a well-organised craft union similar to the Amalgamated Society of Engineers in Britain. Russell contacted their HQ and they helped him set up the Winnipeg local, Lodge 122. He took on the role of secretary and soon he became well known in Winnipeg labour circles. In 1918 a vacancy arose for secretary/treasurer of the Canadian district of the IAM, and he was the overwhelming choice of the membership for the position. This thrust him into the limelight at the Trades and Labour Congress, where his eloquent speeches captured the attention of the delegates.

James Watters was the president of the Trades and Labour Congress and had held the position since the year Bob Russell arrived in the country. Born in Edinburgh in 1869, Watters worked as a miner and left Scotland to go to the West Virginian coalfields. In 1893 he moved to Vancouver Island, which was the scene of many epic battles between coal owners and miners. The British Columbia labour movement had a radical history and some early successes. At the turn of the century, workers had achieved an eight-hour day, regulation in the coal industry and other labour legislation far in advance of other parts of Canada. Several Socialist organisations thrived, and Watters joined the Socialist Party of Canada, standing unsuccessfully as a candidate in the 1903 election. He became secretary of the Victoria Trades and Labour Council and when British Columbia became the first province in the country to establish a Federation of Labour, Watters was chosen to lead it.

Respect for his leadership qualities spread throughout the Canadian trade union movement. In 1911, the Trades and Labour Congress, despite its conservative reputation, elected the left-wing Watters as its president. His leadership was unchallenged, especially when the onset of the First World War brought about full employment. With the trade unions in a strong bargaining position, militancy increased and membership of the TLC shot up from 160,000 to over 400,000. However, in common with other countries, as the war continued, a split developed over the issue of conscription. Watters led the anti-conscription coalition and as a result lost the support of many conservative trade unions. There was also a distinct division between trade unionists in the western and eastern provinces, with those in the west much further to the left. Other disagreements arose, particularly between the supporters of exclusive craft unions, and those who advocated organising all workers in an industry, regardless of their skill. Watters had been treading a careful line between the conservative majority and his Socialist colleagues in the west. But Bob Russell and the radicals accused him of selling out, and denounced his attempts at conciliation. At the 1918 convention, the conservatives stood a candidate against Watters and he lost the presidency. Bob Russell stood for secretary/treasurer, but was heavily defeated.

One Big Union and the Winnipeg general strike

The divergent views expressed at the 1918 annual meeting of the TLC made a split in the movement almost inevitable. The traditionalists were in control of the TLC, but some on the left felt they should continue their attempts to transform it. Watters challenged for the presidency the following year but was again defeated. Other radicals, especially those from the western provinces, decided the time had come for a breakaway. They agreed to convene a special conference in Calgary in 1919 to draw up plans to reorganise the labour movement into industrial rather than craft unions, and to form a radical alternative to the TLC. They called the new organisation One Big Union (OBU) and declared it a revolutionary industrial union with the general strike its principal weapon. Among the list of immediate objectives were a six-hour day and a five-day week. Bob Russell left his full time job with the IAM to become general secretary of the new organisation.

Previous attempts had been made to organise industrial unions, but had petered out. The Knights of Labor spread from the United States to Canada in the 1860s but declined by the 1880s. The Industrial Workers of the World (IWW), also known as the Wobblies, was set up by a group of American Socialists to organise all workers in a single union. Many Canadian workers joined, but in the depression before the First World War it lost most of its members. Russell supported the ideals of the Wobblies, but hoped to learn from its mistakes.

The main intellectual driving force for OBU was an Aberdonian, William Cooper. Born in 1860, Cooper was the chief theoretician of the movement, and his extensive writing for OBU created much of its distinctive philosophy. A cabinet-maker by trade, he had helped found the Aberdeen branch of the Social Democratic Federation. He was elected to Aberdeen City Council and served for eleven years before emigrating to Canada in 1907. Cooper established the Worker's University in Winnipeg, where he taught classes in economics, history and politics.

A few weeks after OBU's inaugural convention, events in Winnipeg took on their own dynamic. Winnipeg had been a hotbed of militancy and radical politics throughout 1918, with strikes involving firemen, water workers, telephone operators, and electricians. In December 1918, a mass meeting had been called to protest against the policies of the

Robert B Russell was born in the Springburn district of Glasgow and became secretary/treasurer of the Canadian district of the International Association of Machinists. He left this full time position to become general secretary of 'One Big Union' when it was formed in 1919. (Courtesy Prof Ken Osborne, Winnipeg)

federal government, during which speakers called for an end to the capitalist system and expressed support for the Bolshevik Revolution in Russia. British Secret Service reports warned of Russian plans to promote revolution in Canada, prompting the Canadian authorities to ban publications in Russian, Ukrainian and Finnish. Secret police investigated trade union activists and Socialists.

Against this background, the Winnipeg general strike began. Although many of the strike leaders were prominent members of OBU, it did not organise the strike. A simple labour dispute about a pay claim between metalworkers and their employers started the ball rolling. Negotiations broke down, and as a show of solidarity with the metalworkers, the Winnipeg Trades and Labour Council called sympathy strikes. On 15 May 1919, thirty thousand workers walked out, closing the city's factories, crippling its retail trade, and stopping most of its transport. Public-sector workers joined in, with policeman, firemen, telephone operators, employees of waterworks and other utilities voting to join the strike. A central strike committee took over the running of the city. They gave authority for the movement of food and provision of essential services, and persuaded the police and indispensable public servants to go back to work. In a letter to the OBU leader in Vancouver, Russell described some of the events:

We pulled a strike on Thursday morning, which tied up the entire City – everything has come to a complete standstill. From reports we had received, we knew they intended declaring martial law, and for that reason we left the policemen on the job. We also decided to leave in enough men on the water works to keep the pressure on the mains at 30 pounds, enough to give a domestic supply to working-men's homes. ... we decided to allow the music halls and picture shows to remain open, providing they displayed a card, stating that they were open with permission of the Strike Committee ... after having tied up the City completely, we realized the necessity of opening up some restaurants, providing also that they displayed a card, stating that they were open with the authority of the Strike Committee. The same prevails with the supply of gasoline necessary to carry on those industries we had exempted – everything that is running is advertising the fact that it is by authority of the strikers.

Business leaders were convinced the strike was a Communist plot. They formed a committee of bankers, manufacturers and politicians, and with the assistance of the local newspapers, organised opposition. The federal government, worried that the strike would spread to other parts of Canada, decided to intervene. Government ministers met with the

Mural in the Exchange District of Winnipeg depicting some of the major events of the 1919 general strike, as well as the images and names of the imprisoned strike leaders.

Winnipeg general strike leaders at Stony Mountain prison after their arrest (Russell is fourth from left of back row). Eight strike leaders were arrested and most were sentenced to a year's imprisonment for conspiracy. Bob Russell was given two years as he was seen as the ringleader. (Courtesy Provincial Archives of Manitoba)

business leaders, but refused to speak to the strike committee. The local police force were fired for refusing to sign a no-strike pledge, and 1,800 special constables were recruited to work alongside the mounted police. On 17 June at 2 a.m., armed police raided the homes of eight strike leaders, charged them with conspiracy to overthrow the government, and took them to Stony Mountain penitentiary.

The arrests only served to heighten the tension in the city. During a demonstration on 21 June, on what became known as Bloody Saturday, tempers flared when a non-union driver tried to force a tramcar through a crowd that had gathered on the main street. Demonstrators smashed its windows and set it on fire. Mounted police were called in and made three charges into the crowd. Initially, they used clubs, but the crowd counterattacked with rocks and stones. When two of the police officers were pulled from their horses, the police opened fire, killing two people and wounding thirty.

As the shooting began, the crowd panicked and began to run away from the main street, only to be met by hundreds of special constables pouring out of the police station nearby. In the hand-to-hand fighting that followed, hundreds were injured and eighty people were arrested. The response from the federal government was immediate. They despatched troops to the city, and for the next few days the centre of Winnipeg was placed under military control. Armoured cars with machine guns in position patrolled the streets, and armed soldiers took up positions along the pavements. On 26 June, after six weeks, the strike was called off.

The strike leaders faced trial and were accused of planning to 'introduce to Canada by other than lawful means, the Soviet form of government similar to that now in force in portions of Russia'. The Prime Minister, Sir Robert Borden, was convinced, 'that the strike was a definite attempt to overthrow the organisation of government and to supersede it by crude, fantastic methods founded upon the absurd conception of what had been accomplished in Russia'. Although the police commanding officer at the time stated that the strike was nothing more than an ordinary labour dispute, the National Director of Public Safety, C. H. Cahan, thought otherwise. He stated that, 'the Bolsheviks were firmly behind the labour disputes in the West'. The trial ended with several leaders being found guilty and given prison sentences ranging up to a year. Bob Russell was thought to be the ringleader and most dangerous. He was tried separately and sentenced to two years' imprisonment.

Russell and the other Scots involved in the Winnipeg strike would have been aware of remarkably similar events that had taken place at

The general strike leaders encouraged Winnipeg's citizens to enjoy walks in the parks during the strike where they were entertained by orators like R E Bray. (Courtesy Provincial Archives of Manitoba)

The 1919 general strike leaders avoided organising pickets or demonstrations for fear of provoking clashes with the mounted police. But on Bloody Saturday mounted police made three charges into a crowd. When two of their officers were pulled from their horses, the police opened fire, killing two people and wounding thirty.

home a few months before. With Scottish unemployment rising after the First World War, a campaign was launched for a forty-hour week to help share the available work. Led by the shop stewards' organisation, the Clyde Workers Committee, and supported by the Glasgow Trades Council, a general strike was called to begin on 27 January 1919. All the main factories in Glasgow closed down as over seventy thousand walked out. Other cities in Scotland and Northern Ireland joined in. On Friday 31 January a mass demonstration was organised in Glasgow's George Square. Thousands of police lined up to control the estimated ninety thousand demonstrators filling the square and surrounding streets. Strike leaders addressed the crowd and then formed a deputation to meet the Lord Provost. Suddenly, police launched a ferocious baton charge into the crowd. Some eyewitnesses believed that the attack was unprovoked; others said that it was in response to attempts to stop tramcars being driven by strike-breakers in the streets near George Square.

Police and demonstrators fought pitched battles. The Sheriff attempted to read the riot act, but had torn it out of his hand. Strike leaders were in the thick of the fighting, and one of them, Willie Gallacher, landed a punch on the Chief Constable as a police baton felled one of the other leaders, Davie Kirkwood. The crowd drove the police back and started marching out of the square towards Glasgow Green. At the front of the march ex-servicemen continued to fight with police, and for the rest of the day and into the night, clashes took place throughout the city. The Secretary of State for Scotland described the event as a Bolshevik uprising, and asked the government to send troops to restore order. The nearest Scottish regiment, the Highland Light Infantry, were based at Maryhill, a short distance from the city centre. But when it became known that they had expressed support for the strike, orders were given to lock them up in their barracks. The next day, armed soldiers from English regiments arrived, along with tanks and artillery, which were stationed at strategic points in the city.

The strike leaders were arrested and sentenced to several months' imprisonment. Later Willie Gallacher talked of the atmosphere at the time of the strike and what was called the Battle of George Square. 'We had forgotten we were revolutionary leaders of the working class. Revolt was seething everywhere, especially in the army. We had within our hands the possibility of giving actual expression and leadership to it, but it never entered our heads to do so. We were carrying on a strike when we ought to have been making a revolution.'

Like the Battle of George Square, the events in Winnipeg went down in labour folklore. They also gave an impetus to recruitment for One Big Union, with over seventy thousand joining in the first year of its existence. There was immediate success across western Canada and northern Ontario, where loggers, miners, construction workers, longshoremen, metalworkers and many others joined up. Craft workers left their international unions to join OBU and, for a time, the supremacy of the Canadian Trades and Labour Congress was threatened.

After a year in prison, Bob Russell was released on parole and returned to building One Big Union. One of his first assignments was to address a meeting of railroad workers in the town of Dauphin in Manitoba. As part of his parole conditions, Russell was required to inform the Winnipeg police of his movements. Arriving in Dauphin at 2 a.m., with the temperature at minus 20 degrees, he was met by a constable, who ordered him to accompany him to the police station. He tried to explain that he had fulfilled the conditions, but the policeman took no notice. Russell later recalled the incident. 'I'm protesting like hell ... I was refusing to accept this damn stuff. I was demanding my rights, and he didn't worry – just kept marching me up the damned street, and we landed in his office. Then he takes off his coat and he gets out a bottle of whisky and gives me a shot.' He had been a police officer in Winnipeg and had been fired for refusing to sign a no-strike pledge. In the warmth of the police station they talked politics for the rest of the night and finished off the bottle.

From 1921 until 1925 Russell travelled around the country mobilising support for the new union. Often the meetings were emotionally charged affairs with heated arguments about which direction the trade union movement should take. Russell described one gathering in Nova Scotia where the auditorium was packed to the rafters and the platform was a ring in the centre. The speaker before Russell had said something derogatory about another trade unionist whose colleague took offence at the remarks. 'He was a boxer ... the middleweight champion of Nova Scotia. He hooked him one and he landed down in the audience in the lap of a woman ... a riot started ... I threw off my jacket, I rolled up my sleeves and I tried to get quiet and order in there ... I said, "Now look, if it's a fight you want it's a fight you'll get. But we in the west fight a different way ... we fight with our tongues and our heads."

But OBU was unable to capitalise on its moment of opportunity. The threat to the established unions provoked a very effective counter-offensive by the TLC to win back its craft members. Employers refused to negotiate with any OBU affiliate and often there was collusion between the employers and the international unions to undermine it. Many of Russell's closest lieutenants began to have second thoughts about the OBU. Some of them had joined the newly formed Communist Party of Canada, which condemned breakaway organisations. It called on radicals to remain in existing unions and to concentrate on changing their policies. This line cost the Communist Party the support of Russell, who fitted the profile of a Communist in every other respect. He had been a member of the Socialist Party until it folded, and then joined the Independent Labour Party. In 1927 he stood in the Manitoba Provincial election and came close to winning a seat.

OBU had begun to decline, and by the end of the 1920s it only existed in a few workplaces in Winnipeg. From time to time it made a breakthrough and even opened a few locals in the textile industry in the USA. Sometimes when an international union refused to support a strike, OBU recruited disillusioned members. During 1926 Russell had high hopes of recruiting the Nova Scotia miners en masse when they clashed with John Lewis, but a resolution to the dispute meant further disappointment for Russell. Although OBU fizzled out, its existence pointed to the inadequacy of the TLC structure to meet the needs of the growing numbers of unskilled and semi-skilled workers in the mass-production industries.

Tom McEwan and the Workers Unity League

The opportunity to engage hundreds of thousands of disenfranchised workers was seized by the Communist Party, which had changed its industrial strategy at the end of the 1920s. The policy of radicalising established unions from within had met with some success, and in a number of unions Communists won key positions. But in 1929 the Communist International (Comintern) decided that revolutionary trade union movements, under Communist leadership, should be established in the advanced capitalist countries. However, there was no reconciliation with Bob Russell and the OBU. A new Canadian trade union centre, the Workers Unity League (WUL), was formed and Tom McEwen was chosen to lead it. McEwen had been a Communist Party organiser in Winnipeg for just a couple of years before he was summoned to Toronto to become general secretary of the new union. His only trade union experience before this was as a member of the Winnipeg Trades and Labour Council.

Tom McEwen, general secretary of the Communist trade union centre, the Workers Unity League, was born in Stonehaven. He was arrested in 1931 along with seven other leading Communists, found guilty of belonging to an illegal organisation, and jailed for five years. In 1950 he moved to Vancouver where he edited the Pacific Tribune, a labour–movement newspaper. He died in 1988, at the age of ninety-seven.

McEwen was born in the Stonehaven poorhouse in 1891, the illegitimate son of an itinerant farm labourer and an impoverished young mother. His mother died of TB when he was five and he hardly knew his father, who was killed in the Boer War. Brought up by caring foster parents for several years, he was taught the poetry of Robert Burns and the history of Scotland. Later, he moved in with his aunt and uncle, but no matter how much they tried to make him feel at home, McEwen could not settle. He left home at an early age and by his own endeavours started an apprenticeship under a master craftsman who was one of the best blacksmiths in Scotland. Testament to his teaching was the first prize McEwen won in a horseshoeing competition years later in Canada.

Although he was an accomplished blacksmith, work in the north-east of Scotland was scarce and wages poor. As a teenager McEwen married a local girl, Isabel, who worked in a textile mill. When a daughter was born, McEwen decided it was time to move on. There were adverts in newspapers about emigration to Australia and South Africa, but there was no way the couple could afford the cost of the passage. However, agents distributed leaflets detailing the great opportunities in Canada that were available to anyone prepared to work on a farm. And the passage was free provided the emigrant worked for the farmer for a year. McEwen set out for Canada alone and his family joined him once he had prepared a home for them. He later recalled his feelings as he left Scotland: 'I sailed from Glasgow in 1912. I had just turned twenty, a young man with a trade, bound for a new country, with something less than five dollars in my pocket, and the certainty of a great future in a great land.'

The ship embarked at the port of Quebec City after a gruelling ten-day voyage. McEwen and the other immigrants were then unceremoniously herded onto a train to take them west. After a further four days' journey, in suffocating heat during the day and freezing cold at night, the train reached Winnipeg. The ordeal did not end until McEwen's destination near Morden, where he had arranged a job on a farm. Morden, cultural capital of Canada in 2008, was then a beautiful town in the Pembina Valley, one of the oldest and most prosperous settlements in southern Manitoba. In the surrounding area, a variety of unorthodox immigrant groupings had settled, including Mennonites, Hutterites and Doukhobors.

After an unhappy term on the farm, McEwen sent for his family, but moved around various jobs. He started his own blacksmith's business twice, only to go bankrupt on both occasions. The second time was in 1920, which was also the year his wife died in the Spanish flu pandemic.

It was estimated that a third of the world's population were infected by Spanish flu and as many as fifty million people may have died. The death of his wife was a devastating blow to McEwen, who by then had two sons and two daughters. Despite offers from neighbours and friends to take care of the children, McEwen was determined that the family unit would stay together. Under no circumstances was he prepared to condemn his motherless children to the same fate he had experienced as a child. McEwen credits the love, dedication and courage of his six-year-old daughter, Isabel, in helping him hold the family together. 'This wee lass of six years, endowed even then with great human qualities, took upon her own small shoulders the role of "Mother" to all of us – a role she carried with deep and steadfast devotion all the years of her short life.'

The proud family remained close throughout their lives and all followed their father's footsteps into the Communist Party. His two sons fought in the Spanish Civil War with the Canadian section of the International Brigade, and his older daughter Jean, a nurse, went to China to attend the soldiers of Mao Zedong's revolutionary army. Isabel died in Toronto when she was only thirty-six, well known for her work in the Canadian trade unions and with the unemployed. The loss of the daughter they worshipped was another crushing blow to the family. For McEwen her death was unbearable. 'It was she who taught me many of the simple characteristics of a good Communist by her great-hearted devotion, loyalty and love, not only to her own family, but to all humanity, neighbour and stranger alike. This staunch rebel woman, from her earliest childhood days down to the last hours of her life ... loved all humanity. When people suffered, Isobel suffered; and with each victory her joy and happiness were as infectious and real as the fragrance of a heather-clad mountainside.'

McEwen had joined the Communist Party in Saskatoon, where he moved after the death of his wife. In 1927 he was made a full-time Communist Party organiser for Manitoba and Saskatchewan, based in Winnipeg. He was closely associated with the developing party line and intimately connected with Tim Buck, the man who was about to become the new party leader. After only two years as a party organiser, McEwen was given the job of industrial director, with the task of organising and leading the Workers Unity League.

During the ten years of the Great Depression, Canada was one of the worst-affected countries in the world. At one time 28 per cent of the working population was unemployed and in industrial centres like

Winnipeg, it was estimated that half of the families in the city relied on welfare at some stage. For those lucky enough to find work, wages were low and only a small number were in unions. The inability of the mainstream trade unions to mount an effective challenge left an organisational and political vacuum, which was partially filled by the WUL.

At the inaugural conference in 1930, McEwen was elected general secretary. James McLachlan, the Scottish miners' leader from Nova Scotia (see Chapter 4, pages 130-131), became president and served in that position throughout the life of the WUL. The first national convention was held in Ottawa a year later, with delegates from factories, mines, lumber camps and also from unemployed workers' organisations. McEwen travelled across Canada addressing meetings and recruiting members. Throughout its existence, the WUL faced heavy resistance from employers and repression from the state, reaching levels never seen before or since. It was subjected to frequent police raids on its national and local offices, attacks on strikers and imprisonment of activists. Many immigrants were deported, including Scottish WUL activists Alan Campbell, David Chalmers and James Huston. In the summer of 1931, the national offices of the Communist Party and the WUL were raided and all documents seized. Eight leading Communists, including McEwen, were arrested and found guilty of belonging to an illegal organisation. They each were jailed for five years and sent to Kingston penitentiary to serve their sentences.

Although nominally general secretary while in prison, McEwen relied on key organisers to co-ordinate the strategy and day-to-day tactics of the WUL. His chief lieutenant was Fred Collins, a Glaswegian, who was based in Ontario. Collins was often harassed by the police, but led scores of strikes, including the famous Stratford strike in 1933, which received national publicity when troops were rushed to the small town. It started when workers in seven small furniture factories joined the WUL. They went on strike for higher pay in a dispute that lasted two months. At a nearby chicken factory, some of the lowest-paid workers in Canada were encouraged by the action of the furniture workers and also joined the WUL.

Trouble started when pickets attempted to stop management removing partly finished goods from the furniture factories. The workers at the chicken factory then decided to walk out for their own pay claim. They surrounded the chicken factory, adding to the congestion and confusion in the town centre. A battle between police and pickets erupted that lasted the whole day, causing the city authorities to panic and call for army support. The next day two companies of the Royal Canadian Regiment arrived with machine-gun carriers. Canadians were appalled when they saw pictures of the troops in what appeared to be tanks, for use against unarmed workers fighting for a living wage. The outcry was so vociferous that the troops were never used, and indeed this was the last time troops were ever involved in a labour dispute in Canada.

The event was a propaganda victory for the WUL and for the strike leader, Fred Collins. Collins had been a tram driver in Glasgow before the First World War and after his demobilisation from the British forces he emigrated to Canada, settling in Toronto. He became involved in the trade union movement, joined the Communist Party, and was appointed Ontario organiser of the WUL when it was formed. Collins also organised the Ontario contingent of the Canadian section of the International Brigade, which fought in the Spanish Civil War. He was a prominent figure in the unemployed workers movement, and was the main organiser of the 'On To Ottawa Trek' in 1935, one of the most celebrated demonstrations of the unemployed during the Depression. Collins served several terms as president of the Toronto Trades and Labour Council, and was on the executive of the Ontario Federation of Labour.

The inimitable Sam Scarlett

The WUL organiser in the Prairie Provinces was one of the most fascinating and colourful labour activists in Canada. Sam Scarlett was a well-known veteran of many epic trade union struggles in North America. Born in Kilmarnock, he served an apprenticeship in engineering and left Scotland at the turn of the century to settle in Galt, Ontario. He was also a highly skilful footballer and played semi-professionally for the town's championship-winning team while working in a local engineering factory. However, politics and trade unionism were his main interests and he became an active member of the International Association of Machinists in Canada. When he moved to Chicago in 1908, he met some of the leading members of the Industrial Workers of the World. A trusted friend of IWW leaders Joe Hill and Bill Hayward, he became a full-time organiser and was soon the target of the police. Sent to organise the iron miners in Minnesota, he led them in a series of major strikes, which earned him his first arrest. Police harassment was a problem he faced throughout his life. The authorities hounded him so often that he lost count of the number of times he was arrested and imprisoned, but some put the figure at over ninety.

In 1917 Scarlett was arrested by Chicago police in a round up of IWW members and charged with conspiracy. Over one hundred Wobblies were found guilty and sentenced to between five and twenty years imprisonment. Scarlett, deemed to be one of the most dangerous, was framed on a murder charge and sentenced to thirty years. However, after the intervention of a senator, whose daughter had been wooed by Scarlett's charm, he was released from prison and deported back to Scotland after serving three years. But he had been away from the old country for too long and all his connections were now across the Atlantic. He returned to Canada in 1920, worked as a harvest hand and became an organiser of the agricultural workers section of the IWW. Around this time he joined the Communist Party.

Scarlett was one of the best platform speakers of his day, and had audiences riveted at street corners and in meeting halls. Jack Scott, a fellow Communist from Ireland, recalled an occasion when Scarlett addressed a couple of meetings in Toronto. A Sunday afternoon meeting which began at one o'clock finished at five with Scarlett speaking non-stop. After something to eat, the next meeting started at seven o'clock, and he talked until ten. The two then adjourned to the home of a young Scottish carpenter and over a couple of bottles of whisky Scarlett entertained them until dawn with his tales and finished off proclaiming 'One of the wonders of the Soviet Union is that for one dollar you can buy enough whisky to get the whole of Scotland drunk.'

When the WUL was formed, Scarlett was happy to throw his energy into organising the Prairie Provinces. He had some early successes, including an agreement with coal operators in Alberta. Then in 1931 miners in the Souris coalfield of south-eastern Saskatchewan contacted the WUL, desperate to join a union. Conditions in the coalfield were appalling and the mine company was notorious for not replacing damaged or rotten timber supports, which often caused roof cave-ins. Miners worked in two feet of water in some mines, and in others there was inadequate ventilation. Smoke from blasting hung in the air, and carbon dioxide gas caused frequent illness. Living conditions were just as bad. The company houses were timber shacks with flimsy roofs and no insulation or running water. The dwellings were infested with lice, bed bugs and cockroaches. Despite the fact that the miners were paid less than other western miners, the owners announced wage cuts.

When the miners contacted Scarlett, he immediately left for the Souris coalfield. Once everyone was signed up to the union, a strike was called. To publicise the desperate plight of the miners a motorcade was organised through the coalfield villages. But the local mayor banned the demonstration and called in the Royal Canadian Mounted Police to back up the local police force. Scarlett ignored the mayor and went ahead with the protest.

There was a carnival atmosphere as miners and their families packed into old cars and trucks with little thought of the banning order. The motorcade passed through towns and villages gathering support for their cause in a peaceful protest until they reached the town of Estevan, where the demonstration was due to end. A contingent of forty-five heavily armed mounted police officers blocked the road into the town. Skirmishes broke out and the police started making arrests. After stones were thrown at the Mounties, they attacked the protesters mercilessly. They then opened fire, killing three unarmed miners and injuring twelve more. The following morning the homes of strike leaders were raided and thirteen men were arrested. Sam Scarlett was among those detained, and was later jailed for twelve months for causing a riot. However, the miners continued their fight, and eventually a royal commission awarded them a pay increase and a reduction in hours. No action was taken against the Royal Canadian Mounted Police.

In 1935, the Communist Party decided to disband the WUL. The Comintern, alarmed by the spread of Fascism, called on all Communist parties to build popular fronts with anti-Fascist organisation and to unite with established unions. Tom McEwen, who had been released on parole in 1934, took responsibility for winding up the WUL. He negotiated mergers between the WUL affiliates and their equivalents in the Trades and Labour Congress. McEwen claimed that WUL members consented with the dissolution and that mutual agreements were reached about sharing leadership positions in the merged unions. But some WUL activists dispute this. Jack Scott maintained the members were not consulted about the organisation's liquidation and claimed that TLC affiliates simply took over the WUL unions without any leadership deals being struck.

Although it was in existence for only five years, the WUL fulfilled an important role during a difficult period for trade unionism. Its membership never exceeded forty thousand, but the WUL took on battles and campaigns that none of the established trade unions would have attempted. It provided a national focus for the unemployed, organising them behind petitions, demonstrations and protests for welfare relief and unemployment benefit. Some groups of workers were involved in unions for the first time, including many immigrant communities. Most of the eighty-five strikes officially recorded in 1931 were led by WUL. By 1934, there were 189 disputes, of which 109 were led by the WUL. Many of its officials became seasoned organisers and were soon to play a key role in a new-style trade union movement which was about to exert its influence across Canada.

CIO unions form the Canadian Congress of Labour

The new organisation spread from the United States and was formed from some AFL unions who believed in industrial unionism. This time the foundations of the new movement were well-established unions, particularly the United Mine Workers of America, which had sufficient resources to ensure its success. Seven AFL unions established the Congress of Industrial Organizations and brought the philosophy of industrial unionism to a receptive and enthusiastic audience of men and women amid the Depression (see Chapter 2, page 50). The traditional craft unions opposed the spread of this organisation and expelled the seven unions from the AFL. A reluctant Canadian Trades and Labour Congress was forced to do likewise, but the expulsions only served to galvanise the recruitment crusade of the CIO unions.

Thousands of workers in the mass-production industries of rubber, auto, steel, clothing, meatpacking, logging and electrical goods responded to the union recruitment drive. Many of the organisers were former WUL officials. Their leadership skills were put to the test in some of the conflicts they faced in the early years of the CIO, as employers refused to recognise the new unions. Communists held many of the leading positions, but encountered further state oppression.

Just after the start of the Second World War the Canadian government again outlawed the Communist Party, this time because of its anti-war position. Internment camps were set up across the country, and in 1941, ninety-eight active Communists were interned. The list included the presidents of the Seamen's Union and the United Electrical Workers, who were both involved in crucial pay negotiations at the time of their arrests. Tom McEwen and Fred Collins were among those interned. But Sam Scarlett decided he was too old and too ill to face another period of incarceration, and fled to the USA to avoid the round-up. By September 1942, after the USSR joined the Allies, all Communists had been released, but shortly before this, Scarlett died in Detroit.

The banished CIO unions in Canada joined forces with some independent unions to form another Canadian trade union centre. The Canadian Congress of Labour (CCL) was formed in 1940 and elected Miners' Union leader Pat Conroy as secretary/treasurer. Born in 1900 in Baillieston, Glasgow, Conroy worked as a miner from the age of thirteen. His father died when Conroy was only eight, leaving a wife and seven children. Although he had won a scholarship to high school, his mother was dependent on her son's earnings and he was forced to go down the pit. His two elder brothers had emigrated to Drumheller, Alberta before the First World War, and in 1919 Conroy joined them. Soon after arriving, he left to travel around the USA for two years, drifting from job to job. He worked as a lumberjack along the west coast and as a labourer in construction gangs in the Midwest. In Kentucky and Colorado he was a coalminer, before coming back to Alberta in 1922. When he returned he became active in the miners' union and rose from secretary of his local to vice-president of the western Canadian district of the United Mine Workers of America.

Conroy became the undisputed authority in the Canadian Congress of Labour during a period when membership increased from 78,000 to over 300,000 in less than a decade. The Second World War signalled the end of the Great Depression and brought full employment to most of Canada. Many enlisted in the armed forces, while women and farm workers found jobs in the munitions factories in the cities. Union membership expanded rapidly, but unlike the British and American governments, the Canadian government did not invite the unions to join coalition decision-making. Therefore there was no obligation to offer no-strike pledges during the war, and a number of major disputes took place. A series of strikes in the 1940s followed, with highly advantageous reforms of industrial relations legislation. Workers won the right to belong to a union and employers were compelled to establish collective bargaining and grievance procedures. In addition, an arbitration ruling to settle a strike in the auto industry had major implications for the Canadian trade union movement.

The United Auto Workers called a strike of its ten thousand members at the Ford plant at Windsor, Ontario in 1945. Among the union's list of demands were a closed shop and automatic check-off of union dues. After two months, another eight thousand workers from nearby Ford plants walked out in sympathy. The strike lasted ninety-nine days, after which both sides accepted arbitration. Mr Justice Ivan Rand of Ontario's supreme court was appointed to arbitrate. In a momentous ruling, Justice

Rand granted the union the automatic check-off of union dues. He also ruled that, since all workers benefited from union-negotiated contracts, they must pay union dues, even if they decided not to join the union. His ruling became known as the Rand Formula, and from then on, every union in Canada sought its application in their negotiations.

The extra finances gained by the unions allowed them to hire more staff and develop greater expertise in negotiations. However, there were problems below the surface. The Cold War created hostility towards the Communist Party, and after the CIO expelled several Communist-led unions, the Canadian Congress of Labour followed suit in 1949. This gave the green light for raiding by other unions, causing ferocious and often violent confrontations. Conroy decided he had had enough of the infighting and resigned abruptly and unexpectedly in 1951. In a final speech, he lambasted union leaders for the divisions they had caused. He had been the main influence and driving force for over a decade, and although he was urged by all sides to reconsider, he refused to withdraw his resignation. He was appointed Labour councillor to the Canadian Embassy in Washington, a post he held until his retirement in 1972.

Fred Collins suffered more than most as a result of the expulsions. After his release from internment, he was appointed a full-time official of the Fur and Leather Workers. When it was kicked out of the CCL in 1950, he lost his job and moved to Vancouver, where he started work as a welder in a shipyard. However the fumes from his welding equipment exacerbated a heart condition and caused his death soon after he started. Tom McEwen spent the next twenty-five years of his life as editor of the *Pacific Tribune*, a labour-movement newspaper based in Vancouver. He died in 1988, at the age of ninety-seven.

A new harmony: the Canadian Labour Congress

Gradually, the divisions that had split the labour movement began to recede. Joint activity brought the leaders closer, and the Trades and Labour Congress softened its position regarding industrial unionism. Its membership had risen to 350,000, almost the same number as the CCL, and the two organisations recognised that the constant raiding of each other's members was divisive and costly. By 1956 an agreement was reached on a merger, by which time combined membership exceeded one million. The inaugural convention of the new organisation, the Canadian Labour Congress (CLC), met in Toronto. Bob Russell was invited to attend the convention as a mark of respect for many years of dedication to the labour

Pat Conroy from Baillieston, Glasgow, was a leader of the Canadian miners before becoming secretary/treasurer of the Canadian Congress of Labour when it was formed in 1940. He was the undisputed authority in the organisation during a period when membership increased from 78,000 to over 300,000. (Courtesy Canadian Labour Congress)

R B Russell, circa 1960. When 'One Big Union' merged with the Canadian Labour Congress in 1956, it allowed Russell to spend the rest of his life as secretary of the Winnipeg Trades and Labour Council. (Courtesy Canadian Labour Congress)

George Schollie, from Glasgow, was secretary of the Canadian District of the International Association of Machinists and also vice-president of the Canadian Labour Congress. (Courtesy Canadian Labour Congress)

movement. Shortly afterwards, One Big Union, still in existence with a few hundred members, affiliated with the new trade union centre.

Not all of the major issues were solved by the creation of the CLC. Political activity, which historically had caused much conflict between Canadian unions, was still a problem. Some believed that the reform of labour law was best achieved through support for a political party, and the Canadian Congress of Labour had actively supported the Co-operative Commonwealth Federation, a Social Democratic party (see Chapter 6, page 180). The Trades and Labour Congress, following the more conservative philosophies of the American-dominated international craft unions, believed in remaining politically neutral. A compromise was adopted between the two factions, allowing autonomy in political activity at provincial and local level, but no endorsement or affiliation nationally. But significantly, the inaugural convention asked the political education committee to initiate discussions with the Co-operative Commonwealth Federation (CCF) about the possibility of forming a new political party.

George Schollie, a vice-president of the new Canadian Labour Congress, was a key member of the political education committee. Born in Glasgow in 1900, Schollie served his apprenticeship at the Queens Park locomotive works and studied history and economics at the Scottish Labour College. He was a member of the Amalgamated Society of Engineers and joined the Independent Labour Party when he was a teenager. His brother bought a farm near Yorktown, Saskatchewan and invited him to come to Canada. After a year working on the farm, he found a job with the Canadian Pacific Railway in its Weston workshops in Winnipeg, the same shop Bob Russell had worked in ten years before.

Schollie was probably involved with One Big Union when he first arrived, but in 1927 he joined Lodge 122 of the International Association of Machinists (IAM), the local that had been established by Russell. He became lodge president and during the 1930s he was secretary of the Winnipeg Trades and Labour Council. Again following in Russell's footsteps, Schollie was appointed secretary of the Canadian District of the IAM in 1943. In 1949 he was elected international vice-president of the IAM, a position he held until his retirement in 1961. He also served as a vice-president of the Canadian Trades and Labour Congress, and his seniority and background assisted in winning over the craft unions to participate in the creation of a new party.

At a key point in the talks, a new director of political education, George Home, was appointed. Home had been secretary of the British Columbia

George Home was appointed director of political education for the Canadian Labour Congress in 1960. Home delivered milk in Glasgow when he was a kid and participated in his first strike when he was ten. (Courtesy Canadian Labour Congress)

Federation of Labour for ten years, and was a Co-operative Commonwealth Federation activist. Born in Glasgow in 1911, he emigrated to Vancouver with his parents in 1926. He once told an interviewer, 'As a kid, when I was delivering milk in Glasgow, we formed a union, and I participated in my first strike when I was about ten years of age. Anyone coming from Glasgow has his roots in trade unions.' He worked as a meat-cutter, and then in a gold mine, but was sacked for trying to organise a union. During the Second World War, he was one of the leaders of a huge local of the Boilermakers Union, which organised the Vancouver shipyards. However, shipbuilding contracted steeply after the war and he was laid off. He found a job in the packing-house industry and before long was president of the local. He had been active in the CCF throughout his time in Vancouver and was highly regarded within the party.

In 1948 he became president of the Vancouver Trades and Labour Council after a long-running battle between the CCF and the Communist Party. Later that year he was elected secretary of the British Columbia Federation of Labour, a full-time position. He was totally committed to trade union involvement in the political process and strongly supported the British Labour Party model. With ten years experience of co-operation between the CCF and the trade union movement in British Columbia, his appointment as director of political education was of key importance. It took place just as plans were being discussed about the formation of a new party.

In 1961 agreement was reached between the CCF and the CLC to found the New Democratic Party (see Chapter 6, page 195). It represented a triumph of the British tradition of support for a political party by the trade union movement. Scottish immigrants played a decisive role in its establishment and it is one of the distinguishing features between the Canadian labour movement and that of the United States. Working alongside Home on the staff at the CLC headquarters was a fellow Scot, Joseph McKenzie, the director of organisation and another great believer in the political involvement of the trade union movement. Born in Glasgow in 1910, McKenzie arrived in Canada with his parents as a young boy and served an apprenticeship as a compositor in Toronto. He was made redundant during the first years of the Depression and then found a job in a rubber factory, where he tried to organise the plant. Although he was fired for his efforts, he eventually rose to become the Canadian director of the United Rubber Workers and president of the Ontario Federation of Labour. 'Joe Rubber', as he became known,

Joseph McKenzie, from Glasgow, was Canadian director of the United Rubber Workers and president of the Ontario Federation of Labour before his appointment as director of organisation for the Canadian Labour Congress. (Courtesy Canadian Labour Congress)

was dismissed after he lost a power struggle within the union, but was appointed to the staff of the Canadian Congress of Labour. Following the merger, McKenzie's job was to ensure the effective integration of the two organisations and smooth over any obstacles. He was also highly successful in spearheading efforts to recruit members in new sections, particularly among white-collar workers. McKenzie continued as director of organisation for twenty years until his retirement in 1975, which was a period of constant growth for Canadian trade unions.

The structure of the Canadian trade union movement remained much the same after 1956. For Bob Russell, the decision to wind-up One Big Union after thirty-seven years was heartbreaking. It was never the success he and others had hoped, but he lived to see the achievement of many of its objectives. When it merged with the CLC, it allowed Russell to spend the rest of his life as secretary of the Winnipeg Trades and Labour Council. He was appointed to the Manitoba Labour Relations Board, the Fair Wage Board, and was invited to serve on the boards of community groups and charities. Before he died in 1964, the Manitoba government honoured him for his services to Labour and in 1967 the cornerstone of the R. B. Russell High School was laid. His wife Margaret, and his two children, David and Margaret, attended the school's official opening.

Plaque inside the R B Russell Vocational High School, which was unveiled by the Winnipeg and District Labour Council, recognising Russell's work as a labour leader and activist for vocational education. (Courtesy Christian Cassidy, Winnipeg)

Chapter 6

Tommy Douglas and the Canadian politicians

In 2004 the Canadian Broadcasting Corporation asked its viewers and listeners to vote for the person they considered to be the greatest Canadian of all time. For several weeks before the ballot advocates made their case on radio and TV for various outstanding people. When the votes were counted there were three Scots in the top ten. The inventor of the telephone, Alexander Graham Bell from Edinburgh, took ninth place. Canada's first prime minister, Sir John A. Macdonald from Glasgow, was eighth. But first place went to Falkirk-born Tommy Douglas, former premier of the province of Saskatchewan, who instigated the Canadian healthcare system. Douglas never became Canadian prime minister, but for ten years he was leader of the New Democratic Party.

The son of an iron-moulder, Douglas was born in 1904. His father followed several generations of the family who were employed at the world famous Carron Iron Works in Falkirk, which was opened in 1759, and was once the largest smelting works in Europe. James Watt's first steam engine was made at Carron, and the Adam brothers designed fireplaces and domestic appliances for the company. However, the foundry concentrated mainly on munitions. Henry Shrapnel developed his explosive shell in Falkirk, and Alfred Nobel ordered many of his materials from the foundry. The famous small naval cannon, called the carronade, was developed and produced by the company. The success of the Carron foundry drew others to the area, and by the middle of the nineteenth century dozens of ironworks had sprung up around Falkirk, attracting thousands of workers. By the end of the nineteenth century, Scotland produced almost half of Britain's steel and a quarter of its coal.

However, by the start of the twentieth century, the Scottish economy was beginning a long-term downward slide, and foundry workers were the first to feel the pinch. Douglas's father decided to look around for other opportunities, and Canada seemed to promise a brighter future for iron-moulders. In 1910 the family moved to Winnipeg, Manitoba, but they did not stay long. When the First World War broke out, Douglas's father, who was an army reservist, was called up, and the family moved back to Scotland. With his father in France, Douglas and his mother stayed with

Tommy Douglas, born in Falkirk and the son of an iron-moulder, was voted the greatest Canadian of all time in 2004. He was formally premier of Saskatchewan and leader of the New Democratic Party. (Courtesy of the Douglas-Coldwell Foundation)

her parents in Glasgow. During the First World War Clydeside was a cauldron of political activity, with protest marches, rent strikes and shop stewards' militancy. Douglas spent four formative years of his youth in this highly charged atmosphere, listening to radical Socialists like Jimmy Maxton, Willie Gallacher and John McLean, who were frequent speakers on street corners and in meeting halls in Glasgow.

Douglas's mother was from Highland stock and had previously worked in a Paisley cotton mill. Both her parents were deeply religious, her father a member of the Plymouth Brethren and her mother a strict Presbyterian. The grandparents encouraged Douglas to attend church regularly and he noted the affinity between the minister's sermons and some of the speeches by Socialist politicians. This combination of religious and political understanding was the foundation of his political philosophy.

Douglas was a small, sickly child, suffering bouts of illness, which frequently confined him to bed for lengthy periods. Injuries sometimes failed to heal properly, and one of these, a small cut on his knee, almost led to the amputation of his leg. He spent years on crutches until an eminent orthopaedic surgeon in Winnipeg took an interest in his case and agreed to treat him for free. The leg was saved and the experience convinced him that healthcare should be provided free of charge to all. Years later he explained, 'I felt no boy should have to depend either for his leg or his life upon the ability of his parents to raise enough money to bring a first-class surgeon to his bedside.' Despite his problems, he remained cheerful and optimistic, determined to overcome any handicaps, a characteristic he displayed throughout his life. Most sports were out of the question for him then, but he instead developed an interest in amateur dramatics, an activity that flourished in working class areas in Scotland. He even started elocution lessons to assist his delivery, and continued them when he returned to Canada.

During his school holidays in Glasgow, Douglas found a job as a labourer in a cork factory. The owner was so impressed by his enthusiasm and friendly manner that he gave him an office job and offered to train him for management. Douglas enjoyed the work and the wages, which were higher than his father had ever earned as an iron moulder. Against the wishes of his parents, he dropped out of school, but he never trained for management. When his father returned at the end of the war, the family decided to move back to Canada. Nevertheless, the old country's influence on Douglas was deep and lasting. He was absorbed by Scottish history and his boyhood hero was Robert the Bruce. Not surprisingly, his favourite poet was Robert Burns, who had an immense effect on him, and throughout his life he was a devotee of Scotland's bard.

The Douglas family arrived back in Canada in time to observe the 1919 Winnipeg general strike. Indeed, towards the climax of the strike, fourteen-year-old Douglas was an eyewitness to Bloody Saturday, when two people were shot dead by police and many others were injured (see Chapter 5, page 144). Douglas had been walking through the middle of Winnipeg when a riot broke out. Along with a friend, he found a vantage point on a rooftop from which he had a clear view of the scene. He recalled later: 'We saw the mounted police … riding the strikers down and breaking up their parade. There had been a good deal of shooting. Most of the mounted police were shooting into the air, but some of them shot into the crowd.'

Many of the strike leaders were Scottish, and the speeches had a familiar ring. Douglas attended some of the outdoor meetings and by the time he started an apprenticeship as a printer at Richardson Press, he was already well versed in political and trade union matters. He worked on a voluntary basis for labour politicians and joined the Typographical Workers Union. Away from work and politics, he enjoyed a range of sport and leisure activities that would have been unthinkable before the skill of the surgeon saved his leg. He played football, was a keen cyclist, and went camping at weekends with the Scouts. He joined a Winnipeg boxing club run by the Trades and Labour Council. At five feet six inches tall, and weighing in at nine stones eight pounds, he won the 1922 Manitoba amateur lightweight boxing championship. Despite a broken nose, the loss of several teeth and damage to his hand, he continued in the ring and held the title the following year. But the sports activity did not interfere with his love of the stage, and he found time to join an Amateur Dramatic Society in Winnipeg.

William Irvine unites farmers and industrial workers

During his teens, Douglas's thoughts began to dwell on religious matters, with long and intense discussions with friends about the concept of the social gospel. This was an attempt to apply Christian principles to the social problems caused by industrialisation, and was a major force in North American religious circles during that period. He began to seriously consider dedicating himself to the church and sought advice on becoming a minister. He was an avid reader, and one of the books that influenced him most was *The Farmers in Politics*, written by a Scottish clergyman,

William Irvine. Irvine was one of the key intellectual forces within the left in Canada for nearly fifty years, and his role in the Canadian labour movement cannot be overstated. His book contained an analysis of social Christianity, the main topic of discussion among the young theologians, and his political activity amongst farmers and industrial workers laid the groundwork for the birth of a Socialist party.

Born in the village of Gletness in Shetland in 1885, Irvine was the son of a fisherman who had a small croft. He left school at fourteen and served an apprenticeship as a carpenter in a boatyard. He shared the Shetlanders' love of music, and was an accomplished singer and fiddle player. His interest in the Church came mainly from his grandfather, a Congregational minister, who coached him in the art of preaching. He grew up in a political family; his father was a Socialist, and his three cousins, who were compositors at the *Shetland Times* in Lerwick, were leading members of the Marxist Social Democratic Federation. They were active in their trade union and formed the Lerwick Workingmen's Association, which campaigned for better housing conditions, helped form trade union branches, and ran candidates in the town-council elections.

Typically of many young Shetlanders, Irvine had an urge to seek wider opportunities than existed at home. When he was only sixteen, a chance arose to work in St Louis, Missouri, which was hosting a trade fair. Along with two other young men from Gletness, he travelled to the USA and spent a year and a half working on construction sites. However, on his return to Shetland, he decided to devote his time and energy to the Church. He had begun preaching in his local church from the age of fourteen, and was already an able speaker. He now ventured further afield to other parts of Shetland as a lay preacher, developing an eloquent public speaking style and gaining an understanding of the life and problems faced by farmers, fishing communities, artisans and industrial workers. This experience was put to good use in his political work in Canada, when he became the driving force in building a political alliance between farmers and industrial workers.

In 1907, Irvine met the father of James S. Woodsworth, a well-known Canadian clergyman and left-wing activist, who later became leader of the main Socialist organisation. He was in Britain recruiting young men for the Methodist ministry in Canada and was suitably impressed by Irvine to offer him a place at a Methodist college in Winnipeg. Irvine jumped at the chance to take another trip across the Atlantic to study his favourite subject. By the time he left for Canada, Irvine's Socialist

William Irvine, from Shetland, was one of the key figures within the left in Canada for nearly fifty years. Initially a clergyman, he later left his ministry for full time political activity. He was an MP, edited a newspaper, and wrote a number of books and pamphlets. (Courtesy Glenbow Archives, na-5123-1)

convictions were already well established. On his arrival in Winnipeg, he was introduced to Woodsworth and, with so many things in common, they immediately struck up a close relationship, which lasted throughout their lives. Although Woodsworth was a practising minister, he had stopped believing in much of the Christian creed. Similarly, Irvine was often in conflict with conventional Church thinking, and rejected traditional Christian dogma.

Irvine's theology course was not confined to the cosy cloisters of the college in Winnipeg. Practical experience was part of the course, and his first winter in Canada was spent as a preacher in a lumber camp, where temperatures of minus 30 degrees were normal. Very few students wanted to go to the camps to rough it with the hard-drinking lumberjacks, who often mocked the preachers and just about tolerated their presence. But Irvine volunteered and made an immediate impression. After a couple of months in the camp, he got the chance of a free train trip to Winnipeg. Although he had little money, he looked forward to the break.

The train, full of lumberjacks heading for a few days' holiday, stopped at the town of Dauphin, halfway to Winnipeg, where travellers could buy lunch. Irvine ordered his, but found he was a nickel short when he was handed the bill. Embarrassed by his predicament, he asked the man next to him if he could borrow a nickel and pay him back when they got to Winnipeg. 'A nickel?' replied the lumberjack, a little surprised. He then turned round and shouted at the rest of his colleagues in the canteen, 'Brothers, here is our sky pilot. He wants a nickel. Can we spare it?' He took off his hat and passed it round and came over to Irvine with the collection, which amounted to over $100. It was the most money he'd ever had in his life. Back on the train, Irvine brought out his fiddle and played for them all the way to Winnipeg.

After his ordination he was given a temporary assignment in a church serving a farming community in south-western Ontario, where he witnessed the poverty and suffering of the small farmers. Most were heavily in debt to the banks for machinery, land and livestock. Interest rates were high and credit was hard to come by. Railroad companies charged exorbitant rates for transporting produce, and the grain exchange was dominated by five companies, which manipulated the market to the disadvantage of the farmers. Irvine organised a farmer's co-operative, which provoked a fierce encounter with the merchants of the town. When his position came to an end, his departure was greeted with mixed emotions in the community. His next posting was in Calgary,

Alberta, where there was an established Labour Party. After joining the party, he set up a debating forum, which attracted leaders of the Calgary trade unions. He then produced and edited a newspaper, the *Nutcracker*, with the objective of developing an understanding between farmers and industrial workers, which in Canada was crucial for any party on the left.

The farmers were well organised, with eleven thousand members enrolled in the United Farmers of Alberta (UFA). Also, the Calgary Trades and Labour Council was highly active politically, and its chairman, Alec Ross, a Labour Party activist, was eager to support any joint initiative with the farmers. Ross, a thirty-six-year-old bricklayer, came to Canada from Scotland in 1906, a year before Irvine. A joint farmer-labour ticket was agreed for the 1917 election to the Alberta parliament, with Ross and Irvine standing for Calgary seats. The joint ticket was successful in four constituencies, with Ross winning in Calgary Central, but Irvine lost in Calgary South.

By the time of the 1919 Winnipeg general strike, Irvine had resigned from his ministry. He now devoted his attention to political action and journalism, with spells in between when he returned to his trade as a carpenter. He wrote his first book, *The Farmers in Politics*, which had such an influence on Tommy Douglas. The book's main purpose was to assist the farmers' movement, but it also enabled Irvine to outline his own social philosophy. After the First World War, the plight of the farmers was as bad as that of the industrial workers. Drought, depression and the collapse of agricultural prices made the Alberta farmers fiercely hostile to the establishment. They despised the wealthy elite who manipulated the two main Canadian parties. Irvine urged them to organise as a class to fight exploitation by business and financial interests. He encouraged them to look towards a government that would root out abuse, improve public education and health, and secure control of Alberta's natural resources. Co-operation, not competition, was the message he preached to a largely receptive audience.

In 1921 a federal by-election was called in the Medicine Hat constituency of Alberta. Irvine and Ross quickly brought together farmers, farm labourers and industrial workers and formed a progressive alliance to contest the election. Robert Gardiner, a farmer from Aberdeenshire, was chosen as the candidate, and he went on to win a resounding victory. He continued to serve for over fourteen years in the federal parliament and became a founder member of the 'Ginger Group' of Socialist MPs. Membership of the UFA leapt to 33,000 as a result. UFA and labour branches mobilised for the provincial elections in 1921, and to the astonishment of most Canadians, the joint ticket won a majority of seats and formed a government. Alec Ross became minister of public works and Alfred Speakman, a Dundonian, was also elected. He was highly instrumental in the unity movement of farmers and urban workers and served four terms in the Alberta legislature.

Shaken by the results in Alberta, the federal government called a general election. This time the farmers produced another famous election result. Sixty-five farmers were returned from different provinces in Canada, marking a decisive moment in breaking the two-party system at national level. Donald Kennedy, from Perthshire, was one of the winning UFA candidates, and joined the Ginger Group. However, only two Labour Party candidates were successful. William Irvine won in Calgary East, and in Winnipeg, his close friend James Woodsworth triumphed.

Irvine was quickly noticed as one of the finest orators in the House. In the first of many eloquent speeches he defended the miners in Nova Scotia, who were on strike over pay cuts. After only a year in Parliament, he proposed a private members' bill for the abolition of the death penalty. His speech introducing the bill lasted almost two hours and was one of the most memorable of his career. He argued, 'It is degrading and demoralising to humanity; it is an outrage upon the finest sensibilities; and in addition it fails to deter people from the commission of any crimes … I think it is due to Canada as well as to this Parliament, that if the nation is going to continue to occupy the position of the avenger of blood with regard to criminals, there ought to be no doubt whatsoever about the efficacy of the system in securing the civilised end for which we retain it … I want the minister of justice to bring proof – if he opposes me – that capital punishment has hindered one single criminal from committing a crime … nothing short of absolute proof can be accepted as an excuse for Canada retaining the death penalty and placing our nation in the position of an executioner.'

Irvine made an unforgettable impact on the House of Commons, his talents winning him the admiration of his colleagues and the respect of his enemies, including the prime minister. However, he and Woodsworth had a limited amount of influence in the House, and the lack of Labour Party representation was the main weakness when challenging the government. In addition, some of the farmers' MPs began to stray from their original objectives.

The Canadian Labour Party had been founded in 1917, on the initiative of the Trades and Labour Congress. It was modelled on the

British Labour Party, but it soon ran into problems when some of the union leaders, under pressure from the American AFL, withdrew support. Although it achieved a degree of success in some provinces, it never became a coherent national organisation. At local level, it was composed of trade unions, labour councils, co-operative societies, and a number of independent political organisations. These included Socialist societies and the Communist Party.

The birth of the Communist Party

After the Bolshevik revolution the Canadian government declared Communist organisations illegal, forcing activists underground. In 1921 delegates from different parts of Canada met in secret at a farm near Guelph in Ontario to found the Communist Party of Canada. A year after it was established, the party was formally launched at a convention in Toronto. To allow it to function openly, it went under the name of the Workers Party of Canada. The convention elected John MacDonald as general secretary and also voted to affiliate to the Canadian Labour Party.

Born in Falkirk, the same town as Tommy Douglas, MacDonald excelled at school, and his teachers pleaded with his parents to send him to university. However, economic conditions prevented the luxury of higher education, and instead, MacDonald served an apprenticeship as a patternmaker. As a teenager he became involved in the Socialist Party, and later the Social Democratic Federation. He was a member of the Patternmakers Association, and was elected President of the Falkirk Workers Federation. Arriving in Toronto in 1912, aged twenty-four, MacDonald continued his political and trade union activities. He soon became the leading voice of the Patternmakers Union local and by 1919 he was vice-president of the Metal Trades Council. At its formation in 1917, he joined the Canadian Labour Party, and became Ontario vice-president. By the time he joined the Communist Party in 1921, he was one of the best known figures in the Ontario labour and trade union movement. Many of his trade union colleagues followed him into the Communist Party, and with his background, trade union experience and personal prestige, he was elected general secretary.

The main character in the days leading up to the formation of the Communist Party was another Scotsman, Tom Bell. Not much is known about Bell's early life in Scotland or where exactly he was born, although the year of his birth is known to be 1895. He was a printer by trade and was the prime mover in bringing about the unification of several Socialist organisations to form the Communist Party. He was arrested in Alberta in 1918 for involvement in Communist activity and given a suspended sentence. A year later he was arrested again in Toronto when a Communist meeting was raided, and this time was given a two-year sentence. Released after seven months, he attended meetings of the Communist Party of the USA, which had been driven underground. Learning from his US comrades, and with the experience of his arrests, Bell developed a passion for clandestine activity and covert action, which was essential in the initial stages of the Communist Party. He helped form the Plebs League, which organised lectures and discussions on Marxism, the first phase of a cautious, and legal, approach to the formation of the Communist Party. After its formation Bell became organiser of the party's Manitoba district until 1923, when he was transferred to Nova Scotia. There he worked closely with James McLachlan and became business manager of the *Maritime Labour Herald*. Both Bell and John MacDonald, who came to Nova Scotia on a speaking tour, were arrested during the bitter miners' strike in 1923, and were charged with conspiracy (See Chapter 4, page 126)

Bell was an intellectual who could speak seven languages, but was often at odds with the other five members of the Communist Party's central committee. He began to feel isolated and in 1925 he resigned his position before moving to the United States, where he became active in the US Communist Party. There, he wrote an influential booklet, *The Movement for World Trade Union Unity*. He was given a place at the Lenin Academy and moved to Moscow, where he wrote a commentary on the sixth congress of Comintern, which was published in 1928. Despite his undoubted ability and commitment, he lost the confidence of his comrades because he was seen as a factionalist who was constantly involved in internal party intrigue. However, he is remembered for his efforts in bringing about the formation of the Communist Party of Canada.

During the mid-1920s Communists were allowed to have membership of the Labour Party and in Ontario they dominated it. John MacDonald was elected chairman of the Canadian Labour Party in 1924 and in that capacity attended the British Commonwealth Labour Conference in London in 1925. However, opposition to the Communists began to grow and in Quebec a resolution from the railway workers union calling for the Communists' expulsion was carried. Similar motions to expel Communists at the Ontario and other provincial conferences were put forward but defeated after heated debate. Ultimately, however, the policy of Communists working inside and alongside social democratic and socialist organisations was ended by a decision of the Comintern.

In 1928, the sixth Comintern Congress concluded that capitalist stability was coming to an end, and that the actions of Social Democratic parties would help maintain the capitalist system. It was the duty of Communists to unmask the role the Social Democrats played in the labour movement. 'Class against class' was the new slogan for the struggle throughout the world. Derogatory terms were used to describe members of Socialist and Social Democratic parties such as social Fascists, labour fakirs, and class traitors.

John MacDonald was more interested in labour organisation and had no pretensions as a theoretician. He attended the Comintern Congress in Moscow in 1922, but he paid little attention to their publications or Marxist literature. He had doubts about the 'class versus class' tactic and was accused of not carrying out the decisions of the Comintern with the degree of enthusiasm expected of a general secretary.

He was attacked by some senior party figures who had the support of the young Communists. Many of them were eager to adopt new and more radical policies for promoting the Communist cause. They felt that fresh faces were needed, and that the leadership were incapable of shedding their Social Democratic background. The majority of members and delegates to the party congress still supported MacDonald, but against him were the Comintern, the Young Communists International and the United States Communist Party. MacDonald was removed from his post and was eventually expelled in 1930, along with several other party leaders. He later joined forces with Maurice Spector, a former chairman of the party, who founded the Canadian Trotskyist Movement. The new Communist line urged party members to be continually focused on the menace of social reformers. They described James Woodsworth as the most dangerous enemy of the working class, and Winnipeg was seen as the centre of parliamentary reformism.

William Irvine did not escape attacks from the Communist Party either, regardless of the far-left picture painted of him by the media. Although he was was an outstanding parliamentary performer, he lost in the 1925 general election as a Labour candidate. He took a job as organiser of the United Farmers of Alberta and when another federal election was called a year later, he stood as a UFA candidate. He won his seat and remained in parliament for the next nine years. In 1929, he published his second book, entitled *Co-operative Government*.

The Co-operative Commonwealth Federation, a new socialist party

The United Farmers of Alberta won the provincial elections in 1926 and 1930. The Prairie Provinces had the best wheat-growing land in the world, but at the onset of the Great Depression the farmers' conditions became unbearable. The price of wheat fell from $1.60 a bushel to 40 cents. Farmers were transporting wheat and livestock to markets across the country, only to find the haulage costs were greater than the value of their products. Conditions became worse when they were hit by a prolonged drought and insect infestation that devastated the land. Fertile land was turned to dust that blackened the sky when there was a storm. With no water they couldn't even raise chickens or grow enough vegetables to feed themselves, let alone pay off their debt. Farmers and farm hands were evicted and machinery repossessed. Destitute farmers and the industrial unemployed marched together, sometimes in defiance of legal bans on protests.

When Richard G. Reid became premier of Alberta in 1934, the United Farmers' government was in decline. Reid was born in Glasgow in 1879 and educated at Hutchesons' Grammar School before emigrating in 1903. Elected to the Alberta Parliament in 1921, he served as a cabinet minister for fourteen years, including a decade as finance minister. But the Depression had made him more conservative and, when he took over as premier, he was at odds with the radical members of the UFA, and in particular the Aberdonian MP Robert Gardiner.

Gardiner took over as president of the United Farmers of Alberta in time to play a crucial role in the launch of a new left party. Leading activists felt that the time was right for the creation of a national party uniting the farmers with the industrial workers. Gardiner invited representatives of farmers and trade unions from Saskatchewan, British Columbia and Manitoba to the convention of the United Farmers of Alberta in 1932. An agreement was reached to form a new party, which was named the Co-operative Commonwealth Federation (CCF). James Wordsworth became chairman, and Angus MacInnis, a Scotsman and delegate from British Columbia, was elected vice-chairman. There were two more Scots out of the five members of the national council, John Queen of Manitoba and William Irvine.

Angus MacInnis initially emigrated from Scotland to Prince Edward Island, before moving to Vancouver. He was a member of the Independent Labour Party and worked as a tram driver before becoming a full-time union official. When the Labour Party was formed he became the British

Columbia secretary and won the Vancouver South seat for Labour in the federal parliament election in 1930. He was one of the most passionate and forceful speakers in the House of Commons and was described by journalists as a Marxist revolutionary. He was a dour and serious man, not noted for frivolous behaviour, and completely dedicated to Socialism. Tommy Douglas was once asked where MacInnis was born, to which he replied, 'He was not born, he was quarried!'

John Queen, the other Scot on the National Council of the CCF, was the first Socialist mayor of Winnipeg. Born in Lanarkshire in 1882, his Plymouth Brethren family moved to Dunfermline, where he went to school. He was a cooper by trade and emigrated to Canada in 1906, where he found a job at the Prairie City Oil Company. Two years later he married Katherine Ross, who had emigrated from Scotland the year after him. An active trade unionist before he left home, he joined the Social Democratic Party, helped found the Winnipeg Socialist Sunday School, and was business agent for the *Western Labor News*. Elected to the Winnipeg City Council in 1916, Queen was leader of the Manitoba Independent Labour Party. He came to national prominence when he was arrested as one of the leaders of the 1919 Winnipeg general strike, along with Bob Russell (see Chapter 5, page 144). Sentenced to a year's detention for sedition, he was elected to the Manitoba Parliament while in prison. He was described as a man with a magnetic personality, whose rich Scottish voice could charm the birds off the trees. He was particularly remembered for the housing reforms he introduced, which were recommended as a model for the rest of the nation. He held office until 1942, when he was unexpectedly defeated due to a split vote on the left, caused by the Communist Party fielding a candidate. He spent the remainder of his working life as a trade union official, and his daughter Gloria became a prominent feminist. Queen Street in Winnipeg is named after him.

William Irvine was the intellectual driving force behind much of the activity of the Co-operative Commonwealth Federation, producing two pamphlets outlining the distinctly Socialist programme of the party. But the results of the 1935 federal election, the first after the launch of the CCF, were disappointing, with only seven successful candidates. Robert Gardiner and William Irvine both lost narrowly. But thirty-year-old Tommy Douglas, the CCF candidate for Weyburn in Saskatchewan, won the seat by the narrow margin of 301 votes.

Douglas had completed his apprenticeship as a printer in 1924 (see page 124 above). However, he had made up his mind to become a church

John Queen, from Lanarkshire, came to national prominence when he was arrested as one of the leaders of the 1919 Winnipeg general strike and was sentenced to a year's detention. While in prison he was elected to the Manitoba Parliament, and later became the first socialist mayor of Winnipeg. (Courtesy Provincial Archives of Manitoba)

minister and started an arts degree at Brandon College, a Baptist university. He immersed himself in college sport and politics, making a name for himself as a superb debater. On completion of his degree he was ordained and given a parish in the prosperous town of Weyburn, which had a population of five thousand. Shortly after graduation, he married Irma Dempsey, a petite, brown-haired woman with sparkling eyes. But during the Depression, he had become more involved in campaigning against poverty than saving souls. He spent the summer of 1931 in Chicago, where he was deeply disturbed by the destitution he witnessed. While in the USA, he met Norman Thomas, leader of the American Socialist Party, and established a friendship that lasted throughout their lives. Douglas attended Socialist Party meetings and assisted in some organising, and when he returned to Weyburn, he was determined to devote more of his time to political campaigning. He formed the Weyburn Labour Party in 1931 and helped set up the local Unemployed Workers Association. During a miners' strike near Estevan he helped organise food parcels and financial support. For these efforts the media branded him a Communist, a charge he faced throughout his political career.

After the formation of the CCF, Douglas stood in the elections for the Saskatchewan Parliament in 1934, but was defeated. Disheartened by his showing, he resolved to quit politics and move to Milwaukee, where he was offered the ministry in a large Baptist church. However, when a federal election was called in 1935, the CCF leadership urged him to stand. Just then he received a visit from a superintendent of the Baptist Church, who was clearly opposed to the CCF. He told Douglas in no uncertain terms that if he stood for the CCF in another election he would not be accepted for a Baptist ministry anywhere. The defiant response from Douglas was, 'You have just got the CCF a candidate.'

A few months before the election in 1935, the Communist Party made overtures to the CCF about joint activity, but was rebuffed by the CCF leadership. After years of attacks, the CCF had a policy of non-co-operation with Communists. However, at grassroots level, members ignored the policy and worked alongside Communists in campaigns against Fascism and support for the Republicans in the Spanish Civil War. Tommy Douglas never nursed a grudge and felt it was more important to stop Fascism than argue over past differences. Along with members of the Young Communist League, he attended the Geneva World Youth Congress, where he heard Spanish delegates speak about the threat to democracy from Franco and the Fascists. After the Geneva congress he accompanied the Spaniards to the British Labour Party Conference in Edinburgh, and helped facilitate meetings where they spoke to delegates about the impending civil war. Douglas was also vice-president of the Communist-led Canadian League Against War and Fascism. These activities were later highlighted by opponents desperate to label him a Communist sympathiser. Douglas dismissed the taunts, stating, 'I have never abandoned a cause because Communists were involved.'

Membership of the Communist Party increased as a result of its activity with mass organisations during the 1930s, particularly the campaigns against unemployment, although its electoral successes were limited. James Litterick, however, secretary of the party in Manitoba, had the distinction of being the first openly declared Communist to win an election at state or federal level in North America. Litterick was born in Glasgow in 1901 and followed his father's footsteps into the British Socialist Party when he was only sixteen. In 1920 he was arrested during a demonstration against rent rises in Clydebank. That same year he became a founder member of the Communist Party of Great Britain. Emigrating to Canada in 1925, he worked as a miner in Alberta and British Columbia, and became secretary of the Communist Party in British Columbia in 1926. When the general secretary was arrested in 1931, Litterick moved to Toronto and took over some of his duties and in 1934 became secretary of the Manitoba Communist Party. At the height of Communist popularity in 1936, he was elected to the Manitoba Parliament. As well as winning much of the working-class vote, he won considerable support from the Jewish community in the city. His spell in parliament was curtailed, however, when the Communist Party was again declared illegal in 1940. Litterick was expelled from the legislature and was the subject of a police man-hunt after he escaped arrest and went into hiding. Nothing is known of him from then on, but rumours persisted that he was murdered by the police.

Douglas: Master of the political stage

As one of the few CCF members of parliament, Tommy Douglas quickly gained a national profile. He became a popular character in parliament and was in great demand throughout Canada as a public speaker. Cheerful, energetic and full of wisecracks, he used his experience in amateur dramatics to turn political meetings into enjoyable and, at times, hilarious events. He began telling jokes to liven up his audience, in the belief that when they were laughing, they were listening. He could

James Litterick was the first person to win a parliamentary election in North America on an openly Communist ticket when he was elected to the Manitoba legislature in 1936. He was born in Glasgow and was a founder member of the Communist Party of Great Britain. (Courtesy Provincial Archives of Manitoba)

put down a heckler or take the heat out of any awkward situation with a witty one-liner. It was an ability he retained throughout his life, as his relatives found out when they visited him in hospital after he was struck by a bus. It was not long after his eightieth birthday, and as he lay there, bandaged from head to foot, with multiple injuries, he looked at his visitors and said to them 'If you think I'm in bad shape, you should see the state of the bus.'

People came from miles around to hear his performances. He was in his element when handling hecklers or drunks, and his anecdotes were hilarious. Opposition politicians found to their cost that it was dangerous to tangle with him in parliamentary debates. Deriding Douglas's efforts on behalf of farmers, the agriculture minister pointed out that Douglas was no farmer and suggested he knew nothing about farming. Douglas shot back, 'No and I never laid an egg either, but I know more about omelettes than most hens.'

One of Douglas's most famous yarns was the Mouseland story. 'Every four years in a democratic country, the mice held an election and would elect one group of cats or another. The cats were smart and they passed good laws – for the cats. One year, they would elect the black cats, and oh, the conditions for the mice were terrible! So four years later, the mice would rise in protest, throw out the black cats and elect the whites. But the white cats were even hungrier and crueller, so in the next election they gave the black cats another chance. And so it went on until one day a small mouse had a bright idea. 'Say, why don't we elect mice?' The cats, and even some mice, called him a radical, a Commie, but the idea spread, until one day — and Douglas would finish the story with a wink — 'My friends, look out for the little fellow with the big idea.'

Douglas was in constant demand as a speaker at Burns Night socials and St Andrew's Day banquets. He travelled the length and breadth of Canada, meeting his compatriots and toasting the immortal memory of Burns. The life and writings of Burns had a powerful influence on him and his favourite poem, 'A Man's a Man For A' That', to him encapsulated the spirit of Scottish democratic ethics. But like any politician in high demand, Douglas frequently ran the risk of pushing himself too hard. All the travelling and his conscientious constituency work took its toll on his health. He developed a duodenal ulcer in his first term in parliament, a problem that troubled him throughout his career. But as he had shown before, he had extraordinary stamina and resilience in coping with physical setbacks and health problems.

The CCF's support in the early days of the Second World War increased rapidly. In Saskatchewan, the party had been the official opposition for three years, and looked close to a breakthrough in the province. However, the party leader in the province lacked charisma, and many members felt that Tommy Douglas could do much better. Despite his great popularity, Douglas was extremely modest. It took a great deal of persuasion to convince him to take over, and reluctantly he accepted the challenge in the interests of the party. When he became the Saskatchewan CCF leader in 1942, he was obliged to resign his seat in the federal parliament and the next two years were spent preparing his party for the 1944 provincial election.

The CCF was predicted to do well, but when the results were announced a gasp of astonishment could be heard throughout Canada. The Co-operative Commonwealth Federation, fighting on an overtly left-wing manifesto, won over 50 per cent of the vote. They captured a staggering forty-seven seats out of fifty-two in the legislative assembly in a result that was beyond their wildest dreams. All eyes then turned on the forty-year-old Tommy Douglas as he took over as premier, with sceptics predicting a one-term wonder. His enemies were to be disappointed, because he remained at the helm in Saskatchewan for the next seventeen years and presided over one of the most creative and innovative provincial governments Canada had ever witnessed.

The CCF's Saskatchewan reforms

The government's first priority was reform of the healthcare system. Douglas had witnessed many people in Canada become bankrupt or lose their homes to pay hospital bills. He was determined to introduce a compulsory hospital insurance system that did not depend on ability to pay, and added the office of minister of health to his role as premier. The Saskatchewan healthcare plan was put into operation at the beginning of 1947, and it proved so popular that ten years later the federal government took steps to apply it nationwide.

Education was another major CCF policy and Douglas chose a young schoolteacher to lead the department. Teachers' salaries were increased and students were provided with free textbooks. The education system was reorganised, and the cost was more evenly spread between the wealthy and poorer districts. Rural children began to receive the same educational opportunities as their city cousins, a move that delighted the farmers. Loans were granted to young people enrolling in university or

Headline of the Saskatchewan Commonwealth, 1944, which understates the CCF victory by one seat. The Co-operative Commonwealth Federation, fighting on a left-wing manifesto, won over 50 per cent of the vote for the Saskatchewan legislative assembly and captured forty-seven seats out of fifty-two.

CCF — Co-operative Commonwealth Federation logo

Pat Conroy, secretary/treasurer of the Canadian Congress of Labour addresses the CCF conference in 1945. (Courtesy Canadian Labour Congress)

technical school, and Saskatchewan's education system became one of the best in the country by the end of the 1950s.

Three new ministries were created: labour, social welfare, and co-operatives. The department of social welfare brought about many reforms in child welfare, assistance for the aged, housing and the prison system. Farmers were protected from eviction for unpaid debts. Rural electrification and road-building programmes were undertaken, and water and sewerage facilities were extended to farm homes. Crop insurance made life much more secure for the Saskatchewan farmer and the Trade Union Act gave Saskatchewan the most advanced labour code in North America. It guaranteed the right of collective bargaining, and outlawed some anti-union practices. An employee could not be fired for union activity and Saskatchewan became the first province to ensure workers were given a minimum of two weeks' paid holiday per year.

Talented civil servants and economists from other parts of Canada, the United States and Britain flocked to Saskatchewan to become involved with this great innovative government. The economic developments programme included the creation of publicly owned utilities like Saskatchewan Telephones and the Saskatchewan Power Corporation. However, private, public and co-operative ownership all had important roles to play in the province's economy.

Not all the decisions of the government were popular, but Douglas was fearless of opposition if he believed a policy was right for the whole community. Not long into its first term of office, the government raised the road tax for heavy goods vehicles by a substantial amount. Within a few days furious truckers organised a protest rally against the decision and an angry crowd of demonstrators converged on the government buildings in Regina. His predecessors would normally have ignored any protests, but Douglas decided to go out and confront the truckers face to face.

As soon as he appeared at the door of the buildings, the enraged mob booed and hurled abuse. Douglas stood silently until the noise died down, and when a sudden hush fell over the gathering, he spoke to them quietly. He told them how much he sympathised with them about the state of the roads in Saskatchewan. He explained how he was going to introduce cheap vehicle insurance, which would benefit them and business in general. They fell about laughing at some of his funny stories, and he soon had them eating out of the palm of his hand. By the time he had finished, they had forgotten the purpose of their protest.

Throughout the years of reform, the CCF faced a constant battle against big business, which did everything possible to sabotage their programme. Douglas responded mockingly, 'Nothing can be quite so resentful as a man who has ridden on your back for fifty years and then you make him get off and walk.' At times Douglas was taken aback at the depths his enemies sank in attacking the government. 'I never thought politics could be so dirty,' he later wrote. 'They threw everything they had into it ... we were Communists, we were atheists, we were anti-religion; this was the beginning of the Soviet Union being set up in Canada.' But Douglas fought back with some scathing comments. 'There's no lie too preposterous for them to spread, and no tactic too despicable for them to adopt. Don't let them deceive you again. If they fool you once, shame on them. If they fool you twice, shame on you.'

The federal election in 1945 offered the tantalising prospect of further success for the CCF at national level. An opinion poll showed the party ahead of both the Liberals and the Conservatives and it was expected to win between seventy and a hundred seats. This would not have been overoptimistic if compared with the UK election result the same year, which the Labour Party won by a landslide. However, the CCF came in a poor third, with just over 15 per cent of the vote, and with only twenty-eight MPs.

Alistair Stewart from Buckhaven in Fife won the Winnipeg North seat for the CCF, maintaining the city's radical traditions. He joined another Manitoba victor, William 'Scottie' Bryce, who was elected for the Selkirk constituency, fifteen miles north of Winnipeg. Bryce was born in Lanark and raised in Glasgow. Unemployment forced him to leave Scotland just after completing an engineering apprenticeship in 1919, but he left his trade to become a farmer. The political education he received on Clydeside was put to good use in organising the farmers, and he became president of the Manitoba Farmers Association in 1941. For a brief period in the early 1950s he was leader of the Manitoba CCF and served several terms in the federal parliament until 1958.

Irvine's return to parliament

William Irvine was another of the successful candidates, and at the age of sixty re-entered the House of Commons.   From the time of his electoral defeat in 1935 to his re-election in 1945, Irvine had produced a constant output of political articles for the *People's Weekly*, the newspaper of the Alberta CCF, where he was associate editor. In addition, his writing found a new outlet – the theatre. He wrote a play about contemporary Canadian politics, the subject – of course – being the class struggle.

In Brains We Trust was performed to some acclaim in Toronto and Edmonton, encouraging Irvine to write another. *You Can't Do That* was a political comedy performed in Edmonton and other parts of Alberta. It received good reviews, with general agreement that it was clever, witty and entertaining. Although he was a warm and charming person, Irvine's forceful and lively writing provoked debate and controversy, which he seemed to relish. He did not mind if he was in conflict with conventional opinion and was frequently labelled a Red or accused of being un-Canadian. In any case, he was indifferent to personal ambition and was happy to work in the shadow of others. But for a time during the late 1930s, Irvine was in a precarious financial position. Against his principles, and simply to feed his family, he took a job as an advertising executive, using his writing skills to entice customers to buy products. The salary was more than he had ever earned before, but once his debts had been paid, he went back to being an organiser for the CCF.

During the Second World War his thirty-year-old son, Harry, was killed in action. A CCF candidate for a constituency in Alberta, Harry enlisted in the Royal Canadian Air Force at the start of the war. In 1944 he was piloting a plane over enemy territory and was shot down. Although his body was never recovered, he was presumed dead, leaving a wife and two children. Harry was very close to his father and the loss was a bitter blow to Irvine and his wife, neither of whom was able to come to terms with the tragedy.

Irvine's third stint in parliament only lasted one term. At the next federal election in 1949 the CCF vote dropped by 2 per cent, but the impact on the number of MPs was more pronounced. They only won thirteen seats, and fifteen CCF MPs were defeated. Irvine returned to journalism, but he remained president of the Alberta CCF. He became increasingly concerned about the shift in the CCF's international policies, as they gradually became identical to those of the Liberal government. In essence, both backed the United States in all the important issues. Irvine supported the concept of peaceful co-existence with the Soviet Union and wrote a pamphlet on international co-operation. The CCF leadership never published the radical document, which was a critique of capitalism's warmongering.

In the frenzied atmosphere of the Cold War, the leadership of the CCF banned members from involvement in any organisation that could be seen as a Communist front. The media and opposition politicians condemned Irvine for his support for the World Peace Congress, which was viewed as pro-Soviet. Courageously, he proposed a CCF delegation to the Soviet Union in 1954. The leadership ignored the proposal, but Irvine proceeded to organise a six-member delegation from the Alberta CCF. They met with top Soviet officials, including Premier Nikita Khrushchev, but were faced with a barrage of criticism when they returned. Irvine responded with another book, entitled *Live or Die with Russia*.

Other CCF policies were watered down though the 1950s, especially in relation to public ownership. Emphasis was on the useful place for private enterprise in a mixed economy, rather than nationalisation. Nevertheless, none of the policy changes brought about any improvement in the party's electoral standing, which had dropped to less than 10 per cent. Only eight MPs represented the CCF in the House of Commons and membership was falling. Outside Saskatchewan and British Columbia, the party had only pockets of support.

In British Columbia, where the CCF consistently won more than a third of the vote, it was led by Robert Strachan. Born in Glasgow in 1914, Strachan emigrated to Nova Scotia on a farm labour scheme, and from there he moved west to British Columbia. Working as a carpenter, he was active in his union local and was later elected leader of the Brotherhood of Joiners and Carpenters for the province. In 1952 he was a successful CCF candidate for the Legislature, and became leader of the British Columbia CCF in 1956.

In Ontario, Canada's most populous state, with the largest concentration of industry, the CCF was polling less than 20 per cent. In other provinces the vote was down to single figures. National party leaders concluded that the base of the party organisation had to shift more towards organised labour. In most of the advanced capitalist countries, Social Democratic parties were established on a trade union foundation. The exception, of course, was the USA, where the trade union movement rejected affiliation to any party. Many of Canada's unions were created as districts of US-dominated international unions and this had hindered attempts to win trade union affiliation in the past. However, a new trade union centre, the Canadian Labour Congress, had just been created and this was seen as an historic opportunity to ally with the CCF. This time, organisers were confident there were sufficient unions on board to make a success of a Social Democratic party. A national committee was formed to create a new party, with equal representation from the CCF and the Canadian Labour Congress.

Two thousand delegates attended the founding convention in Ottawa of the New Democratic Party in 1961 where Tommy Douglas was elected leader. (Courtesy Canadian Labour Congress)

The New Democratic Party

In August 1961, two thousand delegates attended the founding convention of the New Democratic Party (NDP) in Ottawa and Tommy Douglas, the party's most charismatic figure, was elected to lead it. But he was deeply concerned at the decline of the left-of-centre parties throughout North America, and sensed that the mood in the country did not favour the NDP. However, the new structure provided a decent opportunity to challenge the two main parties, and he felt duty-bound to accept the challenge. After five successive election victories, Douglas left his home in Saskatchewan where he enjoyed a status other politicians could only dream of. But he was content that he had put in place legislation that secured his last major and most significant initiative. His hospital insurance scheme had been well received when it was set up at the start of his first term. But the establishment of Medicare, a comprehensive health insurance service, was the greatest achievement of his career. However, it was also the cause of his worst political nightmare.

When Medicare was about to be introduced the following year, Saskatchewan was hit by a strike, not by trade unionists, but from the medical establishment. Doctors were opposed to a compulsory, government-controlled scheme and made it clear that they would refuse to work if it was introduced. Their main claim was that Medicare would interfere with doctor–patient relationships, but the real reason was the effect it would have on their wallets.

The British Labour government had faced the same reactionary opposition when it introduced the National Health Service in 1948. Doctors were worried that their private patients would start using the NHS. Outraged at the prospect of doctors becoming state employees, the British Medical Association mounted vitriolic opposition. In a ballot held just a few months prior to its introduction, GPs and hospital doctors opposed the NHS by a huge margin, with forty thousand votes against and only five thousand in favour. Nye Bevan, architect of the British NHS, was determined that no sectional interest would derail the reforms. He described the BMA as 'a small body of politically poisoned people'. But it was only after he agreed to allow consultants to work in the NHS and at the same time treat their lucrative private patients that opposition dwindled. In Bevan's own words, he bought them off 'by stuffing their mouths with gold'.

In Saskatchewan, the doctors were encouraged to hold out by private medical-insurance companies based in the United States. The doctors'

Tommy Douglas addresses an NDP Convention in the mid-1960s. When he retired he was presented with many honours, including a silver tray from the Socialist International, which only Keir Hardie had received before. (Courtesy Douglas-Coldwell Foundation).

campaign won support from the opposition parties, and protest groups were formed throughout the province. Rallies, petitions and advertisements raised the temperature of the debate, which divided communities and, sometimes, families. Doctors attempted to frighten people on welfare, telling them that they would be unable to treat them again. The New Democratic Party, which had not yet faced its first election, experienced the hostility of people who believed their healthcare was about to end. New Democratic Party members, including Tommy Douglas himself, received threatening phonecalls and hate mail. There was almost a sense of civil war in the province as the well-oiled right-wing machine poured out smears and downright lies.

When the act came into force, most doctors closed their surgeries, forcing the Saskatchewan government to bring in doctors from Britain, the US and other parts of Canada. After twenty-three days, the strike ended after more money was offered. Some doctors left Saskatchewan for the USA, but by 1965 most doctors accepted the scheme and it eventually became the model for the rest of Canada. Nevertheless, a great deal of political damage was done to the New Democratic Party and to Tommy Douglas. During the doctors' strike a federal election was called. It was the worst possible time for the NDP to attempt its first general election. The party won nineteen seats with 13 per cent of the vote. However, it failed to win a single seat in its Saskatchewan heartland and Tommy Douglas was humiliated in Regina, losing by ten thousand votes.

After this crushing blow to his reputation, Douglas offered his resignation as party leader. This was immediately rejected by the party's MPs and one of them resigned his seat to enable Douglas to enter parliament at a by-election held a few months later. During the 1960s, four general elections were held, placing an enormous strain on the NDP's finances and organisation. The best result produced no more than twenty-five MPs, with less than 20 per cent of the popular vote. The new phenomenon of TV domination of elections was not advantageous to Douglas. The confidence that Douglas exhibited when faced with a live audience was absent on television. Master of the political stage, Douglas was not telegenic and appeared ill at ease in front of the cameras. However, in face-to-face debates, he was more like his old self and in one the televised debate during the 1968 election, he came out best against the Conservative Party leader, and the charismatic new leader of the Liberal Party, Pierre Trudeau. However, in 1971, with NDP support stagnating at around 15 per cent of the popular vote, Douglas decided to give up the leadership.

After Douglas left a few other Scots represented the NDP at federal level, the most prominent amongst them being Ian Waddle and Ian Deans. Waddle was born in Glasgow and came to Canada as a child. He won the Vancouver Kingsway constituency in 1979 and in 1989 challenged unsuccessfully for the NDP leadership. After losing his seat in 1993, he moved into provincial politics, becoming a BC government minister and writing a political thriller, *A Thirst To Die For*, which was published in 2002. Ian Deans was a firefighter from Kilmarnock who stood for the leadership of the Ontario NDP in 1979. Narrowly defeated, he then turned his attention to federal politics and won the Hamilton Mountain seat in 1980. He became House Leader of the NDP, which meant dealing with day to day parliamentary business on behalf of the party. However, he surprisingly left parliament in 1986 when he was offered the chairmanship of the Public Services Relations Board.

Although the NDP never broke through as a national force, peaking at just over 20 per cent in 1988, their vote in the provincial elections, although inconsistent, was much healthier. In British Columbia, the NDP won the election in 1972. Robert Strachan had given up the leadership three years before, but was appointed minister of transport and communications. In Saskatchewan, the NDP re-established themselves as the natural party of government. In Alberta, the NDP formed a government in 1986. The biggest prize of all, Ontario, was won in 1990, but the NDP government only lasted one term. In Nova Scotia they came close to winning with a vote of around 35 per cent.

Analysing the failure to emulate the European Social Democratic parties at federal level, Douglas concluded it was impossible to achieve a united movement of industrial workers in Canada. He was dubious about the class-consciousness of North American industrial workers and solidarity among the working class. He said, 'If anyone is class conscious, it is the big middle class with which people in many occupations identify, and which is hinged with disdain for greasy plumbers and mere manual workers. But those blue-collar workers are not proud of their class and loyal to it; they are, individually, either anxious to get out of it, or at pains to deny any distinction between their occupation, and any other. They are part of the upwardly mobile syndrome of North America.'

William Irvine, who was such an inspiration to the young Tommy Douglas, devoted the rest of his years to campaigning for world peace. He was still politically active in his seventies, continued to write lengthy pamphlets, and in defiance of conventional opinion, organised a delegation to China in 1960. He never forgot his roots and on three occasions he returned to Shetland. The Woodsworth–Irvine Socialist Fellowship, an affiliated body of the NDP, was established to spread Socialist education and study in Canada, and was named in honour of the two guiding figures of Canadian Socialism. On the eve of the Cuban missile crisis in 1962, Irvine died in his sleep, working on another publication on peaceful coexistence. In total he wrote twenty-two books and pamphlets, as well as two plays.

When Douglas bowed out as NDP leader, he was overwhelmed with mailbags full of good wishes from members of the public. Other party leaders spoke highly of his integrity and his ability as a parliamentarian. He received a plethora of awards, including honorary degrees from various universities and the Companion of Order of Canada. Perhaps his most treasured accolade was from the Socialist International, which presented him with a silver tray, honouring his service on the executive council. The tray was a very special tribute, which only one person, Keir Hardie, had received before. Handing over the award, the secretary of the Socialist International said to Douglas 'Please accept the thanks of the Socialist International for having made the sun of Socialism rise in North America.'

Douglas returned to Scotland as often as he could, visiting his relatives in Falkirk on several occasions. He carried on in the House of Commons until 1979, the same year he led a delegation to China. Two years later, aged seventy-six, he discovered he had cancer. However, he continued to campaign on behalf of the NDP and in his final speech to the 1983 convention he received thunderous applause from several thousand delegates when he finished by telling them 'We are seeking to get people who are willing to dedicate their lives to building a different kind of society ... a society founded on the principles of concern for human well-being and human welfare.' When he died in 1986, the response to his death clearly showed that he was one of Canada's most loved politicians. His status as the greatest Canadian of all time is testimony to the contribution he made and the esteem with which he is now held in Canada.

Harry Hynd of the United Steelworkers speaks to NDP supporters during an election campaign in Ontario, a province that the NDP won in 1990.

Chapter 7

Joe Davidson, Harry Hynd and the post-war Ontario immigrants

One of the greatest ever waves of emigration from Britain took place between the end of the Second World War and the early 1980s. A widespread decline in heavy engineering affected Scotland, the North-East of England and Wales, and many workers were forced to move home. A large proportion settled in the Midlands and the South of England, where jobs were plentiful, and others moved farther afield. Future prospects, adventure and the promise of a better lifestyle all played a part in attracting the Scots to Canada. Ontario was one of the most popular destinations in Canada, where more than two million people claim Scottish descent. The 'Golden Horseshoe', a band of land curving around Lake Ontario's western shore and on to the US border, was the base for over 50 per cent of Canada's manufacturing industry. An abundance of natural resources and good transportation links to the American heartland made manufacturing the principal industry, with electrical goods, iron and steel, paper, chemicals and cars the main products of the area. Indeed, Ontario surpassed Michigan in car production in 2004, although the industry has subsequently been hit by massive closures.

Although Ontario was a magnet for Scottish industrial workers, Canada's public services were also expanding rapidly and many Scots joined the increasing numbers who were employed in that sector. True to form, they made their presence felt in the public sector trade unions but, as in every country, they became easy targets when they led strike action. In the 1970s, the post office workers seemed to symbolise everything the public disliked about trade unions. And the Canadian press painted a picture of their union president as a man mired in the class struggle of a bygone age and ill equipped for modern, sophisticated labour relations. Joe Davidson, from Shotts in Lanarkshire, led two national postal strikes and numerous local skirmishes. He was accused of irresponsible radicalism and was designated by the media as the most hated man in Canada, although more discerning members of the public pointed to incompetent management and inadequate funding in the service. But, irrespective of the way others viewed him, the members of the postal workers union saw

Davidson as a fierce advocate of their cause, and although he made some major mistakes in handling the media, they loved him for the way he fought on their behalf.

Davidson leaves Scotland

Joe Davidson came to Canada to start a new life at the age of forty-two, not long after his wife died. He was born in 1915 and lived in Shotts, Lanarkshire, a coal and steel town midway between Glasgow and Edinburgh. The first ironworks opened in 1802, and by the beginning of the twentieth century there were over twenty coalmines. The population of the town grew to fifteen thousand, a large proportion of them from Ireland. Some of Scotland's greatest working-class leaders were born there, including the miners' leader Mick McGahey. Joe Davidson's father was a miner but died while he was still at school. His mother was adamant that he would not follow his father down the pit and, with the assistance of her brother, found him a job as an apprentice moulder at the Shotts Iron and Coal Company. His uncle worked at the same foundry and was a staunch Labour Party member and trade unionist. He was an important influence on Davidson and encouraged him to read Socialist literature, starting with *The Ragged Trousered Philanthropists* by Robert Tressell.

Like many young men, Davidson dreamed of earning a living as a professional footballer. He played at junior level alongside miners like Jock Stein and Willie Waddell and although scouts from senior professional sides often watched him, no offer ever came. In 1936, after he had finished his apprenticeship, he married Elizabeth Brown, whom he had been courting from the age of fifteen. The Brown family were highly political and Elizabeth's mother added a number of left-wing books to Davidson's collection. His work experience and instinct forged a general set of Socialist beliefs without any intellectual understanding of economics or Marxism. He described himself later in life as an evolutionary Socialist, with the proviso that evolution needed a shove at every opportunity.

For the next twenty years Davidson, a member of the Amalgamated Union of Engineering Workers, moved around different foundries but took no active role in union affairs other than attend branch meetings. He was content with life and had never considered leaving Scotland or, indeed, leaving Shotts. Everything changed in 1956 when Elizabeth died of cancer. The loss of his lifelong sweetheart left him depressed and his only child, Catriona, had just been married. He could not bear to stay in Shotts as it stirred up too many memories, and decided make a clean break by moving to Canada. Sailing from Liverpool in 1957, he made his way to Toronto, where he had arranged to stay with a young Shotts couple who had emigrated several years before. Contrary to expectations, it was not easy to find employment and Davidson was rejected for a number of jobs. Eventually he found work at the Canada Iron Foundries in the steel town of Hamilton, south of Toronto.

Harry Hynd: the making of a future leader

Another recent Scottish émigré ended up in Hamilton after experiencing the same problem finding work. Before he left Methil in Fife, Harry Hynd had arranged a job with Westinghouse, a large electrical goods manufacturer in Ontario. However, he reported for work only to discover that the company had just laid off 1,200 staff and there was no job for him. Unemployed for months and with no dole money, he was forced to rely on close friends to help him through. He applied unsuccessfully to several other firms, and was about to give up and go back home when he heard that the Steel Company of Canada was hiring workers. To Hynd's relief he was chosen from a long line of unemployed workers and given a start at the company's Hamilton plant. Known by its acronym STELCO, it was the biggest steel company in Canada.

One of five children, Hynd was brought up in a room-and-kitchen in the Methilbrae district of Methil. When he was eleven the family moved to one of the newly built houses a mile away in Kirklandwalk, which seemed to be the height of decadence, with inside toilets. He had a room to himself. His father was a coalminer and secretary of the local branch of the National Union of Mineworkers. His mother was well known in the tight-knit mining community, active in the women's guild, the co-operative and the Labour Party. Both parents had enormous influence on Harry as he grew up, although they were unable to persuade him to stay on at school beyond fifteen years of age. After leaving Aberhill School, he started an engineering apprenticeship with Balfour's of Leven. An active and outgoing teenager, he was a member of the local athletic club, a keen gymnast and amateur boxer. At eighteen he moved to the mining industry, where he completed his apprenticeship as a mechanic. Young workers in the mining industry were encouraged to become actively involved in the union and anyone showing an interest was allocated a mentor who taught them the basics of trade union representation. There were no courses, seminars or workshops; they learned everything by experience, under the guiding influence of a knowledgeable trade union official. Hynd grasped the opportunity and remains grateful to his mentor, who was a skilful negotiator and an excellent teacher.

At the time, national service was compulsory, but men working underground in the mines were exempt. Hynd had been employed in the engineering shop on the surface but volunteered to work underground rather than join the forces. However, he was uncomfortable working in conditions that he regarded as dangerous and unhealthy. But if he left he was liable to be called up and his only alternative was to leave the country. With the encouragement of friends who had emigrated to Canada, he left Scotland in 1957, when he was twenty-four. Sailing from Greenock on an old American troopship called the *Fairsea*, he arrived in Halifax, Nova Scotia, before completing his journey to Hamilton by train.

The town of Hamilton was named after George Hamilton, the son of a wealthy Scottish businessman and politician, who owned the land on which it was built. Near the town there were abundant supplies of iron ore and limestone, and coal could be cheaply imported from the Appalachians. These ingredients gave rise to Hamilton's steel industry and its population expanded from fifty thousand at the start of the twentieth century to over 500,000 today. Although the city became synonymous with steel, it was also a major producer of textiles, electrical goods and shoes. However, it was severely affected by the Great Depression in the 1930s, and thousands of workers lost their jobs as steel-making capacity was slashed. The formation of the United Steelworkers of America (USWA) gave renewed hope to the community when it started to organise in Canada. Its Canadian HQ was set up in Hamilton, but after the failure of several strikes to gain negotiating rights, a breakthrough was made when John Mitchell was appointed its Ontario director in 1942.

Mitchell was born in the mining village of Auchenheath, in Lanarkshire. He started working down the mine at the age of twelve and became a member of the Lanarkshire Mineworkers Union. While still a teenager, he was elected president of the district organisation of the union, which encompassed several pits in the area. Extremely popular in the community, he was also active in the co-operative movement and became director of the local co-op society. His powerful oratory and platform presence made him one of Lanarkshire's best-known and most articulate advocates of Socialism. He was a member of the Independent Labour Party and stood as a candidate in parliamentary elections.

In 1908 he left Scotland to work in the Illinois coalfields but then

John Mitchell, Canadian director of the United Steelworkers of America in the 1940s, was born in Auchenheath, Lanarkshire. He was a founding member of the Co-operative Commonwealth Federation and was its Ontario president for eight years.

moved to Cape Breton, Nova Scotia, where he was active in the United Mine Workers of America. But he missed home and in 1912 returned to Scotland. However, by the end of the 1920s he decided to give North America another try and settled in Hamilton in 1929, just as the Great Depression struck. When he found himself out of work, he became involved in the unemployed workers' movement and threw himself into political action. He joined the Co-operative Commonwealth Federation (CCF) when it was established in 1932, and his experience proved invaluable to the newly formed party. He was elected president of the Ontario CCF, and held the position for eight years. He stood for election to the Hamilton City Council, and served three terms. Before he was asked to become Ontario director of the United Steelworkers, he was working for the Boot and Shoe Workers Union, which was affiliated to the Congress of Industrial Organisations (CIO). But the CIO felt that winning recognition in the steel industry was a more pressing task and they needed an experienced head to steer the campaign in Ontario.

STELCO dominated the industry and was one of the most fiercely anti-union companies in Canada. After an unsuccessful strike in 1943, the USWA prepared plans for a national strike in 1946, which proved to be the breakthrough the union desperately craved. Two of the steel companies closed their plants during the strike, but the STELCO management insisted on continuing production. But they could not get enough strike-breakers through the picket lines to produce the steel to fulfil their contracts. After ten weeks, supplies of steel to the construction and manufacturing industries began to run out. The federal government was forced to intervene, and demanded that the steel companies negotiate with the USWA. The steelworkers won almost all their demands including the recognition of their union. The 1946 strike firmly established the United Steelworkers of America in Canada.

Davidson's career change

By the time Joe Davidson and Harry Hynd arrived in 1957, trade unionism was firmly established. Wages were much higher in Canada than in Scotland, but Davidson found it difficult to accept the customs and procedures, and thought of going back home. However, he dreamed of an office job, with a salary and a secure pension and, more in hope than expectation, he applied to the civil service for a job as a clerk. He was astonished when they replied, offering him a position as a postal clerk in Toronto. But it was not the cushy nine-to-five job he had dreamed of. He was based in the sorting office of the main post office in Toronto. Along with dozens of others, he worked eight-hour shifts, separating letters into various sizes and stacking them into machines. Management refused to allow them to sit, so the clerks perfected a stork imitation, standing on one foot at a time, with a knee on a case for balance. But the job paid much the same as he had earned working in a foundry, and he was happy with his new career. In 1960 he married Ellen McLachlan, a Glasgow woman, who coincidentally had sailed to Canada on the same ship as him.

In 1959, Davidson accepted a position as a staff representative in the Canadian Postal Employees Association, because no one else wanted it. This was the first time he held office of any sort in a union. The staff association was one of three organisations in the post office, and the Toronto branch was the biggest in Canada. The branch committee spent as much time discussing fundraising and social activities as they did on terms and conditions of service. The biggest issue they dealt with was the air-conditioning in the sorting office. At national level, there was no collective bargaining and the civil service pay commission merely recommended annual increases.

Throughout the rapidly expanding public sector the situation was the same. Most of the workforce belonged to staff associations, but they had no provisions for collective bargaining and no legal right to strike. Gradually, wages began to lag behind the private sector. In addition, the introduction of private management practices to improve efficiency, coupled with imposed technological changes, caused a build-up of resentment. Frustration began to boil over and, by 1965, the postal workers had had enough. Despite threats from their employer, and in defiance of the law, they took strike action. It was the first of eighteen major disputes in the post office over the next twenty years.

At the beginning of the 1950s, postal workers were paid on the same grades as the police and the fire service. But as the public sector grew in size and complexity, the simple method of across the board pay increases attracted more and more criticism. As the government tried to grapple with a better way of determining pay, they postponed and then cancelled pay increases that were due to civil servants in the late 1950s. Although angry noises were made, the staff associations took no action. They lobbied the government to allow collective bargaining, but were ignored. The 1960s saw pay differentials between postal workers and their former comparators widening with every annual award. Then in 1965 a pay offer, which was well below expectations, sparked a rank-and-file rebellion. It changed the face of employment relations in the post office and stunned the government every bit as much as it surprised the leaders of the staff associations.

It started with a walkout in Montreal. The leaders of the staff association refused to endorse the strike and told everyone to remain at work. However, workers in Vancouver and Hamilton ignored the instruction and joined their Montreal colleagues. In Toronto the branch leadership were divided and confused, but the members ignored them anyway and walked off the job. Within a few days half the postal workers in Canada were on unofficial strike, forcing the government to offer more money to settle the dispute. Legislation was later introduced to allow collective bargaining, but the circumstances in which strike action could be used was limited.

The leaders underestimated the militancy of the members. They felt caught between a government that would not listen and a membership whose patience was exhausted. At an historic union convention following the strike, significant changes were made to the organisation. Most of the leadership were defeated in the executive elections and replaced by those who had led the militant action. The name of the organisation was changed to the Canadian Union of Postal Workers, to reflect the change from a staff association to a proper trade union, and the rules were changed to give greater powers to the membership. Membership subscriptions were increased and more full-time officers were appointed. Public sympathy had been with the postal workers during the strike and at last they felt respected for their work and proud of their new trade union.

The Toronto leadership had dithered during the strike and were under attack in the local branch elections. Joe Davidson, who had become treasurer of the Toronto branch in 1962, had been torn between loyalty to the national leadership and the militancy of his Toronto members. He had been confused at different times during the dispute, and his inexperience as a trade union officer was apparent. Nevertheless, he was unchallenged for his relatively minor position and was respected for his honesty. But two years later, his Toronto colleagues regarded Joe Davidson as the best candidate for the branch presidency. At the age of fifty-two he accepted his first full-time position in a union.

Montreal postal workers meet during 1965 strike. The 1965 unofficial strike was the first of eighteen major disputes in the post office over the next 20 years. The strike also paved the way for collective bargaining in the Canadian public services. (Courtesy Peter Whittaker, CUPW)

Steel strikes of the sixties

Meanwhile, Harry Hynd settled quickly once he started work at STELCO. Through his friends in Hamilton, he was introduced to his future wife Margaret, who had emigrated from Scotland along with her parents when she was twenty-one. Within a year, Harry and Margaret were married and soon saved enough money for a deposit to buy a house. But he had a grievance with the local STELCO management, which he asked his union representative to resolve. The local official, who was well meaning but highly emotional and totally inexperienced, made a hash of dealing with his case. When Hynd explained how it should have been handled, the official suggested he should take over the role. Hynd then found himself handling grievances on behalf of several hundred steelworkers. Two years later, he became the chairman of the grievance committee and member of the executive of the twelve-thousand-strong local.

There was a considerable Scottish presence in the steel plant and a high proportion were involved in the union. The secretary of the grievance committee, Harry Greenwood from Ayrshire, eventually became secretary of the local. Others on the grievance committee were Bill English from Fife and Bob Reilly from Glasgow. John Lennie had a full-time union position responsible for health and safety, and his brother Jim was on the job evaluation committee. A number of other Scots were on the executive committee.

STELCO continued to be the pacesetter for the steel industry in Canada, and the ruthlessness of their management had not changed. A year after Hynd started, he was called out on a strike that lasted eighty-six days. He learned that strikes of this length were commonplace in the steel industry in Canada, and it was to be the first of many that affected the main plant in Hamilton. In the 1960s, the number of strikes in all industries increased. Some were unofficial and usually took the form of immediate walkouts. In 1966, one in three disputes in Canada fell into this category and did not receive union authorisation. That year an unofficial strike at the STELCO plant broke out and shop stewards ignored instructions from their union to go back to work. Pickets blocked the entrances to the plant and the dispute turned violent. Although negotiations resulted in an increase in pay, thirty-five employees were fired for incidents on the picket lines.

Another landmark strike at the Hamilton plant in 1969 lasted eighty-five days and resulted in huge pay rises and increases in benefits. Other steel companies followed suit, putting Canadian steelworkers, for the first time, on higher rates than their United States counterparts. Larry Sefton, who had replaced John Mitchell when he retired, was impressed with Hynd during the strike and offered him a full-time union position. Sefton had played a leading role in the STELCO recognition strike in 1946, and was looked upon as a hero by the steelworkers. Without hesitation, Hynd accepted the job, delighted to work alongside someone he admired so much.

In contrast to Harry Hynd's lengthy trade union apprenticeship and subsequent support, Joe Davidson was learning the ropes as he went along. With few to guide and advise him, he made a series of mistakes. Not long after he became president of the three-thousand-strong Toronto local, he was faced with a problem about how best to deal with casual workers, most of whom were women. Many casuals had crossed picket lines during the 1965 strike, and were expelled en masse from the union. Davidson's attitude was anything but enlightened. He felt that postal work was 'men's work', and he intended to keep it that way. He foolishly told the casuals in Toronto that the union did not want part-time workers, and if there were layoffs, it should be the part-timers who went first. These statements came back to haunt him when another union started recruiting the women. A quick change of policy and approach from Davidson just managed to prevent causing a long-term recognition problem. Years later the Canadian Union of Postal Workers became a great champion of women's rights, completely transforming its attitude to women. In particular, it fought for maternity leave and after a forty-two-day strike, it became the first union in Canada to win maternity pay for its workers.

The turmoil in the union continued for several years, with changes of leadership and shifts in alliances. No tangible progress had been made since the 1965 strike, and questions were being asked about the competence of some of the leaders. The Toronto branch was the largest in the country and was in a position to influence policy and leadership positions. When a vacancy occurred for national vice-president, Davidson was lobbied to stand. After less than a year as Toronto branch president, he won the election and moved from Toronto to the union's headquarters in Ottawa. Although he recognised his own lack of experience as a negotiator, Davidson was staggered to find out that he was not the only one. None of the new leadership had much knowledge of pay systems, job values and the politics of negotiations at national level. Indeed, the union employed someone from outside the post office to conduct their pay talks.

Harry Hynd was born in Methil, Fife and worked as a mining mechanic. He found a job at the huge STELCO steel mill in Hamilton and later became a United Steelworkers of America full-time official.

Times of crisis for postal workers

Inflation had eaten into postal workers' salaries, and once again resentment had built up. By 1970 the postal workers, like the rest of the public sector, found themselves caught up in national pay restrictions. Governments throughout the world were imposing similar policies as a way of controlling inflation. But, generally, the pay guidelines for the public-service workers were enforced, while the private sector found ways round them. The Canadian government introduced a 6 per cent wage guideline, well below inflation and the demands of the postal workers. The mood was militant, and a dispute was inevitable.

This time the union used rotating strikes, playing cat and mouse with the post office, calling out one local after another on twenty-four-hour walkouts. This cost the members less financially, and kept the pressure on the government for a longer period. Most locals were on strike for between six and eight days in a dispute that dragged on from May until September. Finally, an acceptable package was agreed, giving postal workers a 10 per cent increase and a range of fringe benefits.

The union leadership had every reason to feel smug, but were not allowed to for long. By the next national convention in 1971, the major issue now facing the members was automation, and the leadership was condemned for taking its eye off the ball. The discontent at the convention resulted in some casualties on the national executive, including the president. Joe Davidson survived unscathed, but he was unsure how long he would last as vice-president. The Montreal local were particularly vocal at the convention. They had been conducting an aggressive campaign against casual employment and new technology, and urged others to do likewise. However, soon after the convention, their campaign escalated into a strike when local management suspended a number of activists. The local then occupied the main post office, and demanded the suspensions be rescinded.

The new national president attempted to negotiate a way out of the crisis with government officials. But the embattled Montreal group did not trust him and refused to allow him to speak on their behalf. The exasperated president felt his position untenable at this challenge to his authority, and resigned. Vice-president Joe Davidson was now propelled into the most important position in the union. It was a job he did not seek, and one he knew he was not qualified to do. Until that moment, Davidson had been seen as honest Joe, one of a nine-member board, and not a particularly influential voice at that. Now he was on his way to becoming 'that Scottish bastard', the media's favourite hate figure.

In 1974 Joe Davidson from Shotts, Lanarkshire was elected to his first full time union position at fifty-two years of age. After the sudden and unexpected resignation of the president of the Canadian Union of Postal Workers, Davidson took his place. As the number of strikes in the post office increased, he became the media's favourite hate figure. (Courtesy Peter Whitaker, CUPW)

Despite the animosity he felt towards the Montreal branch, and the temptation to let them stew in their own juice, Davidson knew that this was the biggest crisis in the union's history. An illegal strike was taking place in the second biggest branch of the union, and post office premises were being occupied. There was the threat that every union official in Montreal would face dismissal and prosecution, and with the second biggest branch in the country disbanded, the entire union would have suffered in its wake. But the Montreal management were refusing to negotiate, so there was little option but to escalate the dispute. Fully aware that further illegal strike action could make the situation worse, Davidson telephoned Toronto president Lou Murphy the following morning. He explained 'Our backs are to the wall. If they beat us in Montreal, they beat the whole union and we just can't let them hang. I want Toronto out right away.' Without hesitation Murphy responded 'OK, Joe, we'll be out by noon.' Murphy was a good as his word and once he was sure the Toronto members had walked out, Davidson then issued a general strike call to all branches. Before long the national post office system had ground to a halt.

The next few days were the most nerve-racking of Davidson's life. Applications for injunctions against the union amounting to hundreds of thousands of dollars of compensation had been tabled. If the action failed, the union was finished and the leadership were likely to be imprisoned for calling an illegal strike. The executive board were tense and pessimistic about the outcome. It was time for a cool head, courage and determination, and Davidson rose to the occasion. He boosted confidence when others had doubts and convinced the executive that the fight could be won. After five days, a breakthrough came. Government representatives offered a settlement, which included the lifting of all suspensions, and also agreed to discuss methods of dealing with new technology and automation. The sigh of relief could be heard across Canada.

The next union convention took place two months later in Quebec City. It was an opportunity to celebrate the united action that won such a famous victory. Normally in such circumstances, the Montreal workers would have thanked the rest of the organisation for responding to their call for help, and in turn the delegates would have congratulated Montreal for the militant stand. But there was no celebration of unity and success. Instead, Davidson spent five exhausting days in the chair, presiding over procedural battles between the union's two main centres of power, Montreal and Toronto. French-speaking Quebec was at war with the English-speaking provinces. Davidson was about to offer his resignation by the end of the gruelling convention as floor fights took place over every conceivable issue. However, the convention ended with Davidson being declared president for the next three years and a French-Canadian elected as vice-president.

Davidson had little experience as a public speaker and no understanding of dealing with the media. The public relations of the union had been abysmal, and it was relatively easy for post office officials to blame the union for any impasse in negotiations. The importance of the post office to the public, and the impact of industrial action, resulted in intense media attention on the union. With another strike looming in 1975, Davidson was in demand for radio and television interviews and what little public sympathy was left for the postal workers soon evaporated. He struggled in front of the cameras, finding it difficult to stay calm and sound confident. With his gruff manner and a difficulty explaining complex issues to a wider public audience, it was easy to cast Davidson as the villain of the piece.

As the union edged towards a strike, public interest in the negotiations intensified, and Davidson was pursued for quotes by a hungry media. Dozens of journalists, TV crews, and radio interviewers appeared for press conferences during the negotiations. At one of these frenzied events Davidson wrote his own epitaph, and helped label himself as the most hated man in Canada. A journalist began questioning him about public inconvenience as a result of the strike. Davidson replied 'If the public were fully informed, it would support us.' The journalist persisted 'What if they were fully informed and still wouldn't support you?' An exasperated Davidson responded 'I am convinced the public would see the justice of our cause.' With Davidson biting at the bait, the experienced journalist went on 'And if they still didn't?' Davidson lost his cool and blurted out, 'Then to hell with the public!' The room suddenly emptied as journalists rushed to the telephones with their headline and main story. And that was before the strike even began! The dispute lasted forty-two days and received solid backing from the post office members. There was a compromise settlement in the end, but Davidson never recovered.

Discontent continued over the next two years, with sporadic strike action becoming commonplace and constant threats of injunctions against the union. By the triennial convention of the union in 1977, Davidson had had enough. He had suffered a major coronary and for several months during his presidency was laid low with exhaustion. With

Joe Davidson (front left) on a picket line in Vancouver during the 1975 strike. Davidson was pursued for quotes by the media throughout the 42-day dispute and received solid backing from the post office members. Peter Whitaker (front right), whose mother was from Dundee, became national director for western Canada. (Courtesy, Peter Whitaker, CUPW)

another round of negotiations and strikes over the unresolved issue of automation, it was time for someone else to take the helm. No one doubted Davidson's courage or commitment and his members forgave his foibles in the knowledge that he was dealing with challenging circumstances and obstinate management. It is doubtful if anyone could have done any better than Davidson during those grim years for postal workers.

The fight against job losses

In contrast to Joe Davidson, Harry Hynd spent the next ten years working in different parts of Canada, gradually taking on more responsibility. In the longest strike in STELCO's history, the company closed its Canadian operations for 125 days in 1981, with Hynd in charge of some of the smaller plants in Ontario. He was being spoken of as a future leader until his fortunes changed when he backed the losing candidate for director. Dave Patterson was the leader of the Sudbury miners, who had been involved in a nine-month strike against the International Nickel Company. The strike had cost the union much of its reserves, and had bankrupted many of the miners involved. Hynd was involved in winding up the dispute and did not rate Patterson very highly. When elections for director were held, Patterson won, but Hynd had supported his rival. The victor banished Hynd to the union equivalent of Siberia. However, Patterson was defeated in the next election, and in 1988 Hynd was brought back from the wilderness and appointed deputy director. Three years later he won the election for director, representing ninety thousand members in three hundred locals across Ontario and the Atlantic provinces.

His biggest problem was the continuing loss of manufacturing jobs. The North American Free Trade Agreement weakened union bargaining power. It enabled employers to force unions into accepting reductions in pay and conditions. The concessions did not prevent the closure of hundreds of manufacturing plants and the loss of thousands of jobs as employers moved production to the southern states of the USA and Mexico, where labour was cheaper and environmental regulations were minimal.

Later, manufacturing jobs were lost to Asian countries, while foreign companies took over Canadian steel plants and other manufacturing establishments. Some of these companies had different views of collective bargaining, and refused to recognise unions. Jobs in manufacturing were reduced further with the introduction of new processes and technology. Numbers at STELCO's Hamilton plant dropped to two thousand, but

Harry Hynd was elected leader of 90,000 Canadian steelworkers in 1991.
Top: Hynd addressing the USWA Conference, Ottawa in 1996. (Courtesy Murray Mosher, Photo Features Ltd, Ottawa)
Bottom: Hynd addressing trade unionists at Toronto City Hall 1996 (Courtesy David Hartman, Silverlight, Hamilton)

it produced more steel than it did with twelve thousand workers. The United Steelworkers campaigned along with the Canadian Labour Congress against these policies throughout the 1990s, but despite their efforts, jobs in manufacturing became scarcer.

The adventures of John Donaldson

However, the construction industry remained fairly buoyant and trade union membership among skilled workers was still at high levels. In most construction sites in Toronto and other cities it was impossible to get a job without a union card. For over a decade, until he retired in 1990, John Donaldson from Glasgow was one of the key union leaders in construction. He had worked as a steel erector in major sites such as the CN Tower before he became president of the Ontario district of the Ironworkers Union. He was also elected vice-president of the Building Workers Federation, which pulled together over 100,000 construction workers.

Donaldson was born in the Possilpark district of Glasgow in 1936, an area that was a hive of left-wing political activity, especially at weekends. At every corner of Saracen Cross speakers on soapboxes enlightened and entertained the locals. Donaldson enjoyed the speeches and often discussed them with his grandparents, who heavily influenced his thinking. His grandfather was a shop steward at a nearby ironworks, and his grandmother had been a suffragette and a member of the Independent Labour Party. An industrious boy, he delivered milk in the mornings before he went to school and groceries in the evening. After school he served four years of an apprenticeship as a joiner. But he was bored with his work and his surroundings, and longed for adventure. His quest took him a bit further than he had intended: answering an advert for a window-fixer in Toronto, he sailed from Greenock on the *Hibernia* in 1955. A few months in Toronto only whetted his appetite for more travel, so he began moving across Canada, picking up any work he could find. Eventually, he stopped when he reached the beautiful city of Vancouver.

However, with the country going through a recession, there was little work in Vancouver, and Donaldson was forced to live in Salvation Army accommodation. He looked everywhere for a job until he found an unlikely position as an able seaman on a Danish merchant ship. The only ship he had ever been on before was the *Hibernia* but he managed to bluff his way into the job. The vessel was sailing to South Africa, and Donaldson spent the next year as a seaman, working on different ships sailing along the African coast. Then came a highly eventful return to Scotland.

In the port of Dhaka in Nigeria he encountered a thirsty group of Scotsmen who were sailing to the UK the next day. They had a good drink together, sang a few songs and Donaldson recited some Burns poems. When the bar closed he was invited to join them for a nightcap on their ship. Encouraged by his newfound pals, and fuelled with alcohol-induced homesickness, Donaldson decided to stow away. Before he had a chance to sober up, the ship was at sea. Without a passport or other means of identification and with only the clothes he was standing in, he presented himself to the captain. His erstwhile pals swore on their children's lives they had never seen him before. The ship was too far from port to turn back and the enraged captain told him in no uncertain terms that he was in deep trouble when they arrived in the UK. He gave him the worst jobs on board during the ship's voyage. When she docked at Middlesborough, Donaldson braced himself for the worst. The captain escorted him off the ship and took him to the immigration office where he explained the situation to a grim faced official. The captain was told that the immigration service would hold Donaldson in detention and deal with him sternly. As soon as the captain left, the immigration officer burst out laughing. As luck would have it, he came from Glasgow and knew Donaldson's grandfather. He not only let him off, but gave him the train fare to get back home. When he returned to Canada a decade later, Donaldson was just as gallus, but a wee bit more responsible.

This time he had a wife and four children, and the Canadian government paid for their plane fares. The family settled in Toronto, where Donaldson met up with some old friends who arranged a job for him as a steel erector. The construction sites in Toronto were well organised by the unions and Donaldson was usually elected shop steward wherever he worked. He brought plenty of union experience from Scotland, where he had organised a non-union factory in Glasgow and signed up the 350 workers. The company's first reaction was to dismiss him, but when the workforce threatened to walk out, a recognition agreement was reached.

His union work on Toronto's construction sites won him a scholarship to the Labour College in Montreal in 1976. After completing an eight-week course in trade union studies, he was appointed a full-time official of the Ironworkers Union. Highly respected by his fellow ironworkers, he was then elected president of the three-thousand-strong Toronto local and for eight years was vice-president of the Ontario Federation of Labour. As in most countries, construction had the worst accident record of all occupations, and Donaldson's efforts to build a safer workplace

John Donaldson, from Possilpark, Glasgow, at top of the CN Tower in Toronto. Donaldson, a steel erector, was union convener for one and a half thousand workers during the construction of the 1,815 ft tower, which was the tallest building in the world when it was completed in 1976.

environment brought him recognition and respect throughout Canada. His heart always remained in Scotland and he frequently visited his sisters in Irvine, Ayrshire. A great Robert Burns enthusiast, he was a much sought-after speaker for Burns suppers.

The growing strength of public sector unions

The construction industry continued to expand but the changes in the composition of the labour force in Canada were reflected in the growing importance of the service industries and the public sector. Some of the new industries in the service area were smaller, anti-union, and difficult to organise. However, the public sector provided a rich source of membership for trade unions, especially after the postal workers' strike in 1965.

The aftermath of that strike brought major changes in the way the federal and provincial governments dealt with their employees. An Act of Parliament in 1966 extended collective bargaining to all public sector workers, and permitted the use of the strike weapon under specific circumstances. With these new constitutional rights, public sector workers joined unions in their thousands. Federal employees joined the Public Service Alliance of Canada, whose membership rose to 180,000 by the 1980s. As provincial governments allowed their workers the same rights, the National Union of Provincial Government Employees expanded to 300,000. The Canadian Union of Public Employees, which recruited at municipal level and in hospitals, became the biggest union in Canada, with 460,000 members. Many of the new members were professionals, such as teachers, social workers and nurses. Over 50 per cent of them were women and this resulted in many of the public-service unions becoming ardent campaigners for women's rights.

At the 2006 Convention of the Public Service Alliance of Canada, a Scotsman with a softly spoken but distinct Dundee accent was elected president. John Gordon was born in the Hawkhill district of Dundee before moving to a new house in the Fintry area of the city in 1952. His father, Jackie Gordon, was a full-time official with the Transport and General Workers Union and was chairman of the Dundee Trades Council for many years. During this period, Dundee was seen as a model of left-progressive trade union thinking and action.

Gordon was one of eight children and attended Creigie primary and Linlathen secondary school. He then completed a pre-apprenticeship course in building at Kingsway Technical College and chose plumbing as a trade. After serving an apprenticeship with Galloway's, a local plumbing

John Donaldson was one of the key union leaders in construction. He was president of the Toronto local of the Ironworkers Union and vice-president of the Ontario Federation of Labour. He was also a sought after speaker for Burns Suppers.

firm, he decided to emigrate. Many of his friends were desperate for a change from the usual haunts in Dundee. There was plenty of work in the town at the time, but they wanted a bit of adventure and most went to London. Gordon was twenty-one, and married with a young son. He had relations in Canada who spoke highly of the country and he made up his mind to give it a try. Travelling ahead of his wife and child, he flew to Toronto, where he lived with an aunt and uncle. He was not allowed to work as a plumber until he completed a course on the Canadian plumbing code, but as soon as he was given his plumber's licence he started at his trade. In 1976 he applied for a job with the federal government.

Working alongside other tradesmen in the public works department, he soon became involved in the Public Service Alliance of Canada. The Alliance was formed from sixteen staff associations in 1966 when collective bargaining was introduced for the public sector. The issue that most concerned his colleagues when he started was premium payments for overtime, which were accepted practice in the private sector, but denied to public sector workers. A strike was called that ended in victory for the union. Gordon had been appointed the strike organiser for his unit at the beginning of the dispute, and after the success of the strike he gradually took on more responsible positions in the union. In 1982 he was elected president of the nine-thousand-strong public works section, a full-time position based in Ottawa.

The Canadian government was monitoring the privatisation policies of Thatcher and Reagan in the 1980s and began introducing similar initiatives in Canada. The public works section was badly affected by the privatisation programme and membership gradually diminished until it was merged with another component of the union. In the year 2000, after leading the section for eighteen years, Gordon decided it was the right time to leave. However, he was a popular figure in the union and was persuaded to stand for national vice-president. With some reluctance he agreed to let his nomination go forward at the union's national convention and, much to his surprise, was elected. It was a strange turnaround. Two months after deciding to give up active trade union work, Gordon found himself in the union's second top job. Many of his professional and highly qualified members took some convincing that a plumber should hold such a senior position. However, he won round his doubters and, after six years as vice-president, received strong support for a bid for president in 2006. Four other candidates were in the frame, but Gordon won on the third ballot to lead one of the biggest unions in Canada. He also joined the executive of the Canadian Labour Congress (CLC).

John Gordon, a plumber from Dundee, fought off four other candidates to become president of the Public Service Alliance of Canada in 2006. His father, Jackie Gordon, was a full time official with the Transport and General Workers Union and chairman of the Dundee Trades Council.

Canadianisation of the labour movement

The influx of public sector workers into the labour movement changed the nature of the CLC. For the first time in history, Canadian unions surpassed the membership of the US-based international unions. They began to develop their own identity, independently of the internationals, in a process that was named the 'Canadianisation' of the trade union movement. The weakening of unions in the United States during the 1980s accelerated the process. There were tensions along the way, with some international unions resentful at the policies and organisational issues. The construction trades unions, all of which were international unions, withdrew from the CLC. But they rejoined several years later, with John Donaldson leading the fight to establish a distinctive Canadian character and a greater degree of autonomy. He felt that this was particularly important in relation to the political identity of the unions. He explained 'Most of the US-based unions were right-wing compared to those in the UK and Europe, especially in relation to international issues. For example, the American unions supported the Vietnam War and this policy was forced on the CLC even though most Canadian unions opposed it. American unions gave their usual automatic backing for US policy in Nicaragua, and supported the Contras. But the CLC sent planeloads of materials to assist the Sandinistas.' Donaldson's efforts helped establish a structure for Canadian policy-making within the Ironworkers Union and prevented a split.

Some unions, however, decided to break away completely from their colleagues in the United States, including the Canadian auto-workers. In an acrimonious divorce, they left the United Auto Workers in 1985, condemning the American leadership for concessions they made in pay negotiations. Others broke away from their US-based unions on amicable terms. Three unions in the communications, energy and paper industries left their internationals in the 1980s. With a combined membership of 154,000, they then merged in 1992 to become the Communications, Energy and Paper Union. It was the eighth largest union in Canada, and soon after the merger Eddie Nelson was elected secretary/treasurer.

Nelson was born in 1935 in the village of Moffat in Dumfriesshire. His father was the village gravedigger, and the family lived in a cottage attached to the cemetery. His father was a huge influence, and was badly missed by Nelson when he was conscripted in 1939. The family did not see him again until he was discharged in 1945. He had been an accomplished athlete in the army and a heavyweight boxing champion. Tempting offers of jobs in England were considered, but his mother refused to move from Moffat. His father remained a gravedigger and stayed in the same cottage for the rest of his working life. After leaving Moffat Academy, Nelson's first job was cleaning trains in Beattock. When he transferred to Maryhill in Glasgow, he began to understand how trade unions operated. He admired the vigilant shop stewards and the way they defended and supported their members. Later he reminisced about his time in Maryhill. 'I was impressed by the confident manner in which shop stewards imposed themselves on the bosses. They ensured that there were no violations of our agreements, and no one was picked on. There was a great sense of solidarity in the Maryhill depot. As I was fairly rebellious myself, and did not accept authority lightly, I looked upon the shop stewards with great admiration, and became determined to adopt their attitude. What I learned in Maryhill inspired me for the rest of my life.'

Restless and longing for travel and adventure, Nelson answered an advert for a job in Rhodesia, now Zimbabwe. He then moved around southern Africa, New Zealand, Australia and Papua New Guinea, before finally settling in Canada in 1969. Not long after he started work with the International Nickel Company in Ontario, he was so disgusted by the way its workers were treated that he nearly left Canada. Nelson recalled the incident years later. 'One of the guys who was on probation was sacked for reading a newspaper in the change room of the mine – before his shift started! I was told there was nothing the union could do, as he was on probation. If that had happened in Scotland, there would have been a riot. I was so annoyed that I nearly left Canada, feeling that if they could treat people like this, then I wanted out. I vowed that nickel mine was the last I would ever work in.'

Nelson moved around jobs, becoming active in the trade unions wherever he went. When the Communications, Energy and Paper Union was formed in 1992, he was appointed Ontario organiser, his first full-time union position. Two years later he became Ontario vice-president. Then in 1997, he was elected secretary/treasurer, one of the key positions in the union. During his period in office, major disputes took place against the closure of paper mills, which had a damaging effect on rural areas. Other high-profile strikes included a three month stoppage at Manitoba Telephones. He was responsible for distributing more than $100m in strike pay. A member of the New Democratic Party, Nelson

Ed Nelson, from Moffat, Dumfriesshire, was secretary/treasurer of the Communications, Energy and Paper Union. He was chosen from the Canadian Labour Congress to act as a UN observer when the first South African elections were held in the post-apartheid era.

never lost his interest in Africa, and kept a close watch on developments in South Africa. When the first elections were held in the post-apartheid era, the UN sought representatives from the Canadian Labour Congress to act as observers, and Nelson was the first to be chosen. In the run-up to the election the ANC headquarters were bombed and the day before he arrived in Johannesburg, a bomb had exploded at the airport. Undaunted, he carried out his task, which was to enforce the rules of the election. On several occasions he had to exercise his authority over white reactionaries, including police and army officers.

Nelson felt that the establishment of separate Canadian unions was a positive development, arguing 'The formation of the Communication, Paper and Energy Union gave us a stronger political voice, and the ability to play a greater role in shaping Canadian society.' Harry Hynd, on the other hand, was totally opposed to any split from the United Steelworkers of America. He never experienced interference in Canadian affairs from the US headquarters of the union. 'Never once were we ordered to end a strike, and we could adopt our own policy on issues such as Vietnam. The Canadian section of the union has always been very strong and recently, two Canadians have become presidents of the international union. The USWA was born during the Great Depression, and many people sacrificed their lives for the union, on both sides of the border. There has always been a great bond and immense feeling of unity between steelworkers, regardless of their nationality.'

Hynd also believes that it makes more sense to be part of an international today than ever before. He reasons, 'If companies are organised as giant international corporations, then so should unions. International unions should mean just that, capable of organising out-with their own country and merging or forming bonds with unions in other countries'. He thinks that the work the USWA are doing in organising workers in Mexico gives Mexican steelworkers the benefit of vast experience.

As the Canadian workforce changed, trade unions had to find ways of expanding into other areas to survive. The USWA sought mergers with other unions, and started recruiting in areas outwith its traditional base. They merged with unions in the furniture industry, electronics, chemicals, plastics and auto parts. Later they moved into organising white-collar workers in banks, restaurants, hotels, universities, airports and many other industries. Other unions did likewise and Scottish emigrants continue to play a prominent role maintaining the tradition set by some of Canada's foremost union activists.

John Gordon and union colleagues at a demonstration against unemployment and privatisation. The protest took place in Toronto in 2010 when the G8 and G20 summits were held in Canada.

Chapter 8

William G. Spence and the Australian Workers Union

Many Australians believe that their country's democracy has its roots in an armed uprising that took place in Victoria in 1854. The Eureka Rebellion is seen as a key event in the development of an Australian national identity. It was caused by the dictatorial attitude of a government that seemed oblivious to the injustices suffered by gold miners. Despite numerous attempts to negotiate with the Victoria government, the miners, known as 'diggers', failed to resolve any of their grievances. Exasperated and infuriated, they decided that armed rebellion was their only option. However, the uprising ended with a military attack on five hundred diggers who had barricaded themselves into a small area of the Ballarat goldfield. An eight-year-old Scottish boy watched the events unfold. He listened to the fiery orators addressing thousands of angry diggers. He watched while they built a wooden fortification and swore an oath to a flag he was told was the 'Southern Cross'. A few days later the assault on the stockade began. The battle was over in twenty minutes, leaving twenty-two diggers and five soldiers dead.

William Guthrie Spence was born in 1846 on the island of Eday in the Orkneys. Only 8 miles long by 3 miles wide, Eday had around two hundred inhabitants. During the nineteenth century, the Orkneys, like the rest of the Scottish Highlands and Islands, experienced high levels of emigration. The Highland clearances had forced thousands off their land and when the potato blight hit the area in 1846, the crofting communities were highly vulnerable. From 1846 to 1855, thousands of families were threatened with malnutrition. The potato blight did not cause nearly as many deaths as it did in Ireland, but it resulted in a huge exodus from the stricken areas.

Around a third of the Highland population left their homes, and many found their way to the mining, engineering and shipbuilding industries of the Clyde. But by 1851, the sixth year of potato crop failure, the British government began to encourage large-scale emigration. North America was the preferred choice of the majority, and very few were interested in the expensive and lengthy journey to Australia. However, a government promotion with heavily subsidised fares made the long voyage more attractive. The new enticements coincided with the news that gold had been discovered in Victoria and New South Wales. The press carried exaggerated accounts of easy fortunes being made, and the chance of instant riches was enough to lure people from every walk of life. Crofters left their land and tradesmen, teachers, bank clerks and labourers quit their jobs to try their luck at the 'diggings'. During the 1850s, it was estimated that over 90,000 Scots departed for Australia.

William Spence was six years old when his father decided to join the exodus, and in 1852 the family left the Orkney Isles on a sailing ship bound for Victoria. Travelling steerage, the Spences were allocated a small partitioned area of 6 feet by 3 feet for their sleeping quarters. There was a toilet for women and girls, but men and boys had to go up top and use the lee side of the ship. In bad weather, the hatches were closed, portholes shut, and passengers were confined to their quarters, sometimes for days at a time. After a harrowing four-month voyage, the family disembarked at Port Philip, near Melbourne.

They arrived to find Melbourne almost deserted, with most of its population having departed to the goldfields. Coal miners, butchers, bakers, farm labourers and bank clerks were among the first to go. The government struggled to cope, as most of its employees had left their posts, including nearly all its teachers and 80 per cent of the police force. Ships lay deserted in the harbours of Sydney and Port Philip as the crews joined the passengers and headed inland towards the diggings. Buildings in the process of construction were abandoned and flocks of sheep were left unattended. The scarcity of labour caused wages to rise dramatically and some skilled workers made a quicker fortune than the diggers themselves. Spence's father was a stonemason and worked at his trade for a year before moving on to the diggings.

The nearest goldfield was 75 miles from Melbourne across sparsely populated territory. Those who could afford it hired horses and carts to transport themselves and their possessions. Those with little money walked all the way, sometimes pushing a wheelbarrow loaded with the bare necessities for gold digging: a tent, a pick and shovel, and a prospecting pan. Along the journey, bushwhackers lay in wait for opportunities to steal anything of value.

The Spence family moved to Creswick, a settlement of several thousand prospectors living in tents, huts and makeshift accommodation. The whole area was perforated with ditches where men had been digging. The creeks were muddied and there was no clean water available or sanitary methods of sewage disposal. Diseases, particularly typhoid and dysentery, were rife and there were few doctors to treat those infected. Irritating insects like mosquitoes, March flies (clegs) and flying ants often made life unbearable.

During the gold rush years of the 1850s, the colony of Victoria (the Australian states were six separate colonies before 1900) grew from 76,000 to 540,000. Few had experience of any form of mining. Initially, the gold was extracted from shallow alluvial deposits on or near the surface. These offered the most accessible and easily extracted gold, but they were soon worked out. A few lucky diggers made fortunes, some made a decent living, but others suffered abject poverty. Some became bitter about the misleading information they were given, abandoning the quest for gold to go back home.

As the gold became more difficult to extract and the goldfields became more crowded, discontent began to build. Miners had to buy a licence for 30 shillings, which entitled the holder to work a single 12-foot-square claim. But most of the miners did not dig enough gold to cover the cost. The police used the enforcement of the licence as an excuse for harassment and extortion. Bribes and favouritism settled many disputes over claims and a general atmosphere of privilege, patronage and corruption permeated the goldfields. Unlicensed miners who were caught in police raids were fined £5 for a first offence and repeat offenders were sentenced to hard labour.

The Eureka Rebellion

The diggers had no political rights and they were unable to buy land, so they decided to organise. Tom Kennedy, a Scotsman who had been a prominent Chartist at home, led the Creswick miners. A few miles away in the larger town of Ballarat, an Irishman, Peter Lalor, and Duncan Gillies from Glasgow helped set up an organisation whose demands included the right to vote, the reform of property laws, and the abolition of the licence. Kennedy was part of a three-man deputation sent by the Ballarat Reform League to Melbourne to meet the governor of Victoria to put forward the proposals. But the governor sent them back empty-handed.

A crowd of ten thousand gathered in Ballarat to hear the deputation's report. The Southern Cross, a flag designed by the diggers as a symbol of rebellion, flew defiantly behind the speakers and the militant speeches matched the belligerent mood of the mass meeting. They voted to burn

Gold miners on alluvial workings. Initially gold was extracted from shallow alluvial deposits on or near the surface, but these were soon worked out. As the gold became more difficult to extract and the goldfields became more crowded, discontent began to build. (Courtesy State Library of Victoria)

Image of the Eureka Stockade, an armed uprising that took place in Victoria in 1854. The rebellion ended with a military attack on five hundred diggers who had barricaded themselves into a small area of the Ballarat goldfield. Twenty two diggers and five soldiers were killed. (Courtesy State Library of Victoria)

their licences and to resist any arrests. Peter Lalor led them in taking an oath: 'We swear by the Southern Cross to stand truly by each other and fight to defend our rights and liberties.' They were ready to take on the army and the police. Tom Kennedy rode to Creswick and rounded up three hundred men. Onlookers cheered as he led them into Ballarat the following day, riding a white horse and brandishing a sword. The armed men marched behind him singing the Marseillaise and chanting Chartist slogans.

Construction of a defensive stockade started in the predominantly Irish quarter of Eureka. Guns and horses were requisitioned and military drills commenced. However, despite the emotion and enthusiasm, there was a lack of discipline and strategy. During the daytime there were around fifteen hundred in the stockade, but at night most of the rebel army went back to their tents and huts. Only a few hundred remained behind the barricades when the authorities made their move. At dawn, three days after the start of the rebellion, a party of 276 police and military personnel left a government camp and approached the stockade. The subsequent battle was short and one-sided. Taken by surprise and outgunned, the miners were quickly routed. Twenty-two of them were killed and twelve wounded. Most of those killed were Irish; John Robertson was the sole Scotsman. On the government side, five were killed and twelve wounded. The surviving rebels were taken prisoner, martial law was declared, and soon all armed resistance crumpled.

However, what appeared to be a decisive victory for the government proved to be a temporary success. As word spread of the events at Eureka, there was a groundswell of public indignation at what was seen as the brutal overreaction of the troops and police. A few months later the government put thirteen of the imprisoned rebels on trial for treason, amid great controversy throughout the colony. Their defence lawyer, James Grant, was born in Alvie, Invernesshire in 1822, and emigrated with his parents to New South Wales when he was fourteen. At the time of the Eureka rebellion he was practising as a solicitor in Melbourne. He supported the diggers and organised a demonstration that drew a crowd of five thousand. At the trial he defended the diggers without taking a fee and became a national hero when the men were acquitted.

After the trial, a commission of enquiry into the administration of the goldfields was set up and most of the diggers' demands were met. The licence was abolished and replaced with a Miner's Right, which cost a small annual fee. Grant's reward was a seat in the Victoria legislature in 1855 and a position in the government led by the Liberal Premier of Victoria, James McCullough. Born in Glasgow in 1819, McCullough only had a primary-school education, but worked his way up to become a junior partner in a merchant's firm in Dennistoun in the east end of Glasgow. Before he left for Australia in 1853, he had been Collector — the second most senior official — for the Glasgow Trades House, an influential institution that incorporated the main trades and crafts of the period. He was Premier of Victoria for four terms, from 1864 until he retired in 1878, and he encouraged James Grant to pursue land reform favourable to the diggers and other immigrants. The subsequent Land Act gave miners the right to 20 acres at an annual rental of 2 shillings per acre. Grant earned great popularity throughout Victoria for the proposals and served in various administrations.

The Irishman Peter Lalor was also elected to represent Ballarat and later became Speaker of the Legislative Assembly. His friend and business partner, Duncan Gillies, joined him some years later. Gillies was born in 1834 at Overnewton on the west side of Glasgow. He attended secondary school until he was fourteen and started work as a clerk in the city centre. Bored with office routine, his spirits rose when news of the gold discovery reached Scotland, and he joined thousands of other young, single men who sought to get rich quick. After landing at Port Philip in 1852, he set off for the diggings at Ballarat. One of the youngest leaders of the diggers, he was elected to the Ballarat Miners Board when it was set up in 1858. Three years later he was elected to represent Ballarat West in the Legislative Assembly. It was not long before he was given ministerial responsibilities, and his portfolios included railways, land and agriculture. In 1886 he became Premier of Victoria and, interestingly, refused to accept the customary knighthood offered to premiers. However, his government was blamed for the depression that started in 1890 and he lost office the following year.

William Spence followed the political developments in Victoria with great interest. The Eureka rebellion had left a vivid impression on him that lasted throughout his life. He was a bright, cheerful boy, who worked as a shepherd and later as a butcher's assistant. When he was fourteen, he began working as a miner in lead mines which were several hundred feet deep. With no formal education available in the tented goldfield communities, Spence was virtually self-taught. However, he became an avid reader, and devoured the works of the most radical writers of the period, such as Bellamy, Ruskin, Blatchford and Morris. He not only

William G Spence, born on the island of Eday in the Orkneys, became known as the 'father of the Australian trade union movement'. He was the driving force in the building of unions for miners and for sheep shearers. The latter became the core of the Australian Workers Union in 1894, which was unrivalled in size and influence until the Second World War. (Courtesy National Library of Australia)

grasped advanced social and economic theories, such as Darwinism and Socialism, but had a great ability to explain them to his fellow workers. Later, he became an author himself, writing a total of seventeen books and pamphlets. His intellectual capacity and determination to succeed, together with a passionate belief in justice for the working class, made him a natural trade union leader.

By the age of twenty-eight, Spence was one of the most prominent of the union activists in Victoria. Local unions had already been formed in gold, lead, silver and coal mining, and attempts were being made to establish a mining organisation for the whole of Victoria. A typical local union existed in Clunes, the town where gold was first discovered in Victoria. The surface deposits had been exhausted after a few years' digging by prospectors and further extraction was only possible by large mining companies using advanced equipment. The main company employed several hundred miners and in 1873 attempted to introduce Saturday afternoon and Sunday shifts. But the miners refused to accept the new conditions, formed the Clunes Miners Association, and went on strike. The company brought in Chinese strike-breakers, but when they arrived under police protection, rioting broke out and the dispute was soon settled. Spence had advised the Clunes miners during the strike, and afterwards affiliated them with the newly formed Amalgamated Miners Association of Victoria.

He later moved back to his base in Creswick, where he became secretary of the Creswick Miners' Union, and also took them into the the new Victoria union. Several strikes followed and in 1882 Creswick miners won an eight-hour day and a union closed shop. However, Spence, who had married in 1871, had begun to suffer from silicosis, a lung disease caused by the inhalation of dust containing silica. Further underground work was a risk to his life and he knew his mining days were numbered. But his success in building the Amalgamated Miners Association meant that the union could now employ a full-time secretary and there was never any doubt that Spence would be the miners' choice. During the next twenty years he rose to become the pre-eminent figure in Australian trade unionism.

A monument to commemorate the Eight-Hours Movement stands in the Carlton district of Melbourne. In 1856 stonemasons in the city established the principle of eight hours work, eight hours recreation and eight hours rest, symbolised in the three 8's at the top of the monument. (Courtesy Roisin Kelly)

Eight-hour day procession, Melbourne 1914. Unions began celebrating their eight-hour day victory with demonstrations on April 21, the anniversary of the breakthrough. In 1879 the Victoria government declared the day a public holiday. (State Library of Victoria)

Eight-hour day victory

Other Australian unions had been established earlier and had won some of the best conditions for the working class in the world. Skilled workers were in high demand for the building boom that followed the gold rush. Taking advantage of these circumstances, stonemasons in Melbourne called for the introduction of an eight-hour day, at a time when a sixty-hour week was standard in Britain. The principle of eight hours work, eight hours recreation and eight hours rest was a claim put forward by radicals in Britain and other European countries, but was seen by many as a utopian dream. However, in 1856 the Melbourne stonemasons made it a reality.

They were led by James Galloway, a Scotsman, and James Stevens from Wales. Galloway was born in Springfield, Fife in 1828 and moved to Glasgow where he joined the Chartist movement. He emigrated to Melbourne in 1854 and two years later became secretary of the Stonemasons Union whose main aim was the introduction of an eight hour working day. In 1856 the stonemasons decided to restrict working hours to eight hours a day, six days a week. Galloway, who was secretary of the union, also informed employers that they would strike if there was any reduction in their pay. As a show of strength, the stonemasons working on the construction of Melbourne University staged a well organised and well executed protest. They stopped work and proceeded to march to Parliament House carrying banners with three figure 8's depicting 8 hours each for work, recreation and rest. As they passed building sites along the way, other construction workers downed tools and joined them in a growing procession towards parliament. Galloway and Stevens started negotiations in earnest with the city's construction companies and within a few weeks every building contractor had conceded the stonemason's claim. Soon carpenters, bricklayers, plasterers and other building trades in Melbourne were working an eight-hour day. Unions began celebrating their victory with demonstrations on the anniversary of the breakthrough and in 1879 the Victoria government declared the day a public holiday.

Sadly, Galloway did not live long enough to enjoy the benefits of his achievement. Five years after his success in leading the eight-hour day breakthrough, he died from pneumonia at the age of thirty-three. He was survived by a wife and two daughters, his only son having died three years earlier, aged twelve months. In 1880 a monument was erected in his honour by the working men of Ballarat. In Melbourne's Carlton district, near to the Trades Hall, a memorial monument to the eight hour day movement was erected in 1903. On top of its pedestal and granite column are three figure 8's, and a sphere representing the earth inscribed with the words 'Rest, Labour, and Recreation'. More recently, unions raised funds to restore the graves of some of those who led the historic victory, and an impressive memorial monument was built at Melbourne general cemetery in Galloway's honour. It was unveiled in 1992 by Gough Whitlam, former Prime Minister of Australia. Another monument to the eight-hour pioneers stands outside the HQ of the Construction, Forestry, Mining and Energy Union in Melbourne.

Another Scottish leader of the Stonemasons Union became the first trade union representative in any legislature in the British Empire. Charles Don, who was one of Melbourne's best-known figures, came from Coupar Angus. He left school at the age of twelve and began work as a handloom weaver, but later started an apprenticeship as a stonemason. Encouraged by his father to read widely, he studied the works of radicals like Tom Paine, John Cartwright, and William Cobbett. In 1842 he joined the Chartist movement, and spoke regularly at the Market Cross in Edinburgh. In 1847 he moved to Glasgow, where he was prominent in radical debating societies. Lured to Australia by the discovery of gold, he emigrated with his wife and daughter in 1853.

Leaving his family behind in Melbourne, Don travelled to Ballarat in a fruitless attempt at the diggings. His gloomy departure from the goldfields turned to tragedy when he arrived back in Melbourne to discover that his wife had died when he was away. He returned to his trade as a stonemason and once again became active in the trade union movement. After remarrying in 1855, he took over James Stevens' position as president of the Melbourne stonemasons in 1858. He became the leading advocate of the working class in Melbourne, speaking at street meetings about their conditions and campaigning on land and fiscal policy. When Melbourne trade unions decided to field a candidate for the Victoria Parliament, Don was the popular choice. Elected to represent the Collingwood constituency of Melbourne in 1859, he used his position to support the inclusion of eight-hour-day clauses in all government contracts and advocated many other progressive proposals.

The Victoria building workers helped spread the eight-hour day to other parts of Australia. They succeeded in New South Wales and this prompted the engineers to launch a campaign in their own industry. In Sydney, engineers made some ground in reducing the working week, but were unable to sustain the position. Then William Miller, a patternmaker

Group of miners, circa 1880s. William Spence took over as full-time secretary of the Amalgamated Miners Association and it soon became the largest union in Victoria. From his Victoria base he launched the Amalgamated Miners of Australasia in 1884. (State Library of Victoria)

from Glasgow, took over as leader of the Sydney engineers. However, he felt that conditions were not favourable for an offensive on the eight-hour day, and decided to bide his time. In 1873, during a boom in the industry, he made his move, catching the employers by surprise. He tabled a demand for an eight-hour day and a 15 per cent increase in wages, and gave them a deadline of three weeks to introduce it. The employers initially thought the union was bluffing, but when Miller's members in the Sydney dockyard walked out, the employers realised they were in for a fight. The dockyard quickly settled, and soon the rest of the Sydney employers fell into line. Although the employers fought back the following year, the eight-hour day became established in the engineering shops and spread to other parts of Australia.

The victory raised Miller's status and propelled him to president of the New South Wales Trades and Labor Council, where the secretary was also a Scot. Angus Cameron, a carpenter, came from Edinburgh and emigrated with his parents in 1854. He became the first trade union representative on the New South Wales legislature not long after Miller's promotion. Cameron won the seat of Sydney West and used the position on the legislative assembly to support legislation for the eight-hour day and other labour issues.

Mining unions had also negotiated an eight-hour day and, after William Spence took over as full-time secretary of the Amalgamated Miners Association, more local unions began to affiliate. It soon became the largest union in Victoria with a membership of eight thousand. Spence liked to describe the union as moderate, but during the ten years he was in charge he sanctioned twenty-nine strikes, some of which lasted over two months. Compulsory levies for strike pay were introduced and the union won some major gains, including the formation of a union–employer joint conciliation board.

Spence spreads the word

But Spence's vision did not stop at uniting the Victoria gold miners. Described by some contemporaries as 'a man of genius in his organising and negotiating skills', his aim was to build a union throughout the colonies of Australia and New Zealand embracing all types of mining: coal, gold, copper, silver, etc. From his Victoria base he launched the Amalgamated Miners of Australasia — the term used to cover the colonies in Australia and New Zealand — in 1884. An intercolonial council was set up to deal with major issues and arrange financial support for strike action.

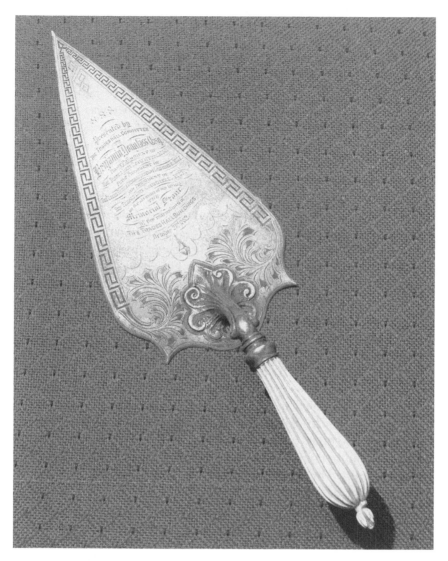

A silver trowel commemorating the laying of the foundation stone of an extension to the Melbourne Trades Hall in 1882. Trade unions were proud of one of the most impressive buildings in Melbourne which was the head quarters of the unions in Victoria. It was dubbed 'the Temple of Labour' and 'the Workingman's Parliament'. (Courtesy CFMEU)

The New South Wales coalminers enthusiastically embraced the idea. They had established a union in 1860 and were involved in the colony's first major strike a year later. Several local unions had been active in collieries along the Hunter River Valley, near Newcastle. They merged to form the Hunter River Miners' Association, and elected James Fletcher as president. Born in Dalkeith, Midlothian, Fletcher was the first of many Scottish leaders of the New South Wales coalminers. He started work down the Lothian mines when he was a young boy, and left for the gold diggings in 1851, when he was only seventeen. He then moved to the more familiar surroundings of the Newcastle coalfield.

His leadership skills and negotiating ability were shown when he organised a strike after coal owners announced a wage cut of 20 per cent. Fletcher managed to divide the coal owners and pulled off an unlikely victory for the union. The union then attempted to set up a co-operative coal company, with Fletcher as chairman and manager. The venture failed, but Fletcher went on to become manager and part-owner of another mine. In the 1870s he was elected mayor of Wallsend and Plattsburg, two mining villages outside Newcastle. He then turned his attention to newspapers and became proprietor of the *Newcastle Morning Herald and Miners Advocate*. He represented Newcastle in the New South Wales legislature in the 1880s, and was appointed minister for mines and public works. However, his whole life seemed plagued by financial worries. When he died in 1891, an editorial in the New South Wales newspaper, the *Daily Telegraph* stated 'He has advanced the prosperity of Newcastle as no other man has done. He has improved the condition of the miners and in doing all this he has impoverished himself.' In 1897 a statue was erected by public subscription in Newcastle 'to commemorate James Fletcher, a friend of the miners'.

After the New South Wales miners joined Spence's all-Australia union, the copper miners of South Australia also affiliated, boosting its membership to thirty thousand – a giant organisation for the era. Overcoming the problems created by different occupational traditions was a remarkable organisational achievement. It was even more extraordinary because of the distance and political boundaries between the colonies at a time when the nation of Australia had yet to be created. The union was loosely based and allowed autonomy within its sections, but during a major coal strike in New South Wales in 1888, the Victoria metal miners levied their members a shilling a week to support their colleagues.

Having achieved a measure of success with the miners at intercolonial level, Spence was keen to promote his vision of closer unity between all trade unions throughout Australia. He proposed an Intercolonial Council of Trades Unions and convinced the Melbourne Trades Hall Council to back the idea. He also argued for direct labour political representation and suggested parliamentary committees be established for each colony.

By his early forties, Spence had become Australia's best-known trade union leader. He commanded the respect of the employers for his ability as a shrewd negotiator and as a statesman. Despite embracing the political and social concepts of some of the most radical thinkers of his day, he remained a deeply religious man and was a pillar of the community in Creswick. A lay preacher and secretary of the Presbyterian Church, he was also leader of the temperance movement, a borough councillor and a justice of the peace. Noted for his warmth and unflappable temperament, Spence enjoyed a status that few others in Australia could match.

In 1886 a young sheep shearer approached him for advice about forming a union. David Temple outlined the problems faced by workers in the industry. Vast numbers of men worked in the Australian shearing sheds, travelling extensively between the sheep stations during the shearing season. Most had other jobs as farm labourers or miners and some were members of unions in these industries. A number of attempts had been made to unionise the shearers, but the itinerant workforce from different backgrounds made it difficult to organise. However, after listening to Temple, Spence agreed to lend his support to building a shearers' union.

His first act was a letter to the *Ballarat Courier* announcing the intention to set up a union for shearers and inviting anyone interested to attend. Only thirty men turned up and, of those, thirteen joined. At a second meeting, a constitution was agreed and the Amalgamated Shearers' Union (ASU) was established, with David Temple as secretary and Spence as president. A few stalwarts travelled throughout Victoria and New South Wales, gradually signing up members. Meanwhile, Spence made the case to the wider public at a series of meetings, which were given detailed coverage by local newspapers. Acknowledged for his talent to present a reasoned and persuasive argument, he reinforced the favourable impression he had created as the leader of the miners. His association with the new union ensured that it would be taken seriously by both employers and workers.

Once a core of shearers had been recruited, a set of rules were drawn up specifying the terms and conditions under which shearers could be employed. This included a maximum working week of forty-eight hours

Group of shearers at work circa 1890. Sheep shearing employed vast numbers of itinerant workers who were difficult to organise. But William Spence and David Temple formed the Amalgamated Shearers Union in 1886 and within a few years it had 20,000 members. (State Library of Victoria)

and a defined level of skill for shearing. Just before the start of the shearing season, this was put to the landowners (known as pastoralists), who were also informed that they had to obtain their shearers through the ASU. Taken by surprise, the pastoralists signed agreements accepting the union's terms. Shearers began to join the union in their thousands. As part of the agreement, a union representative was elected at each sheep station (ranch), to deal with grievances. In cases where pastoralists refused to recognise the ASU, a strike was called and organisers were sent to the recalcitrant station. A strike camp was set up just outside the station boundary, and pickets positioned. If non-union shearers worked at the station, they were invited to join the ASU. Many of them had no understanding of what a union was, and usually joined when they were given an explanation. The owners had no choice but to pay the minimum rate or else their sheep would not be sheared.

Some pastoralists used repressive colonial laws to have strike leaders arrested, but the vast majority went along with the union rate. Even those who employed non-union labour found they were left with an inferior job that ended up costing them more. By the fourth conference of the union in 1890, it reported a membership of twenty thousand across Victoria, New South Wales and South Australia. In Queensland, the shearers formed their own union, which had several thousand members. Shearers ceased to be a nomadic pack of poorly paid casual workers and became part of an organised and influential body with pride in their skill and their trade union. They gave hope to similar groups of outback workers, known as bushmen. In his book *Australia's Awakening* Spence wrote 'unionism came to the Australian bushmen ... bringing salvation after many years of tyranny'.

Employers organise against the unions

The birth of the ASU had come at a favourable time. Throughout the prosperous years of the 1880s most unions made progress. The ASU and the Amalgamated Miners Association, the two giant unions so heavily influenced by Spence, advocated solidarity across union and colonial boundaries. They also helped to transform trade unionism in the cities by giving unskilled workers an example to follow. But Spence and the more astute union leaders knew that many of the advances could be reversed during adverse economic conditions. By the end of the 1880s the long period of economic boom that had started with the gold rushes in the 1850s began to burst. The landowners established a powerful Pastoralists'

Union, and were determined to break the power of the ASU. They announced they would no longer co-operate with the ASU and would employ only non-union labour.

Other employers began to develop their own well-financed associations. National federations linking employers' organisations were formed, mirroring those of the trade unions. Both sides prepared themselves for the inevitable battles as pay rates were cut and workers were laid off. Employers were determined to withstand attempts by unions to negotiate pay and conditions and began to issue ultimatums to their workers. Major grievances affected every industry and the scene was set for a bitter confrontation. The chairman of the Steamship Owners Association summed up the situation from the employers, stating: 'All owners throughout Australia have signed a bond to stand by one another ... never before has such an opportunity to test the relative strength of labour and capital arisen.' The great maritime strike of 1890, the biggest confrontation between unions and employers in nineteenth-century Australia, was about to begin. On the fifteenth of August 1890, the Marine Officers' Union affiliated to the Melbourne Trades Hall Council. This was seen as a provocative act by the ship owners, as it took place in the middle of pay negotiations. With the implied threat of solidarity action by other workers, the employers terminated negotiations. Immediately, marine officers walked off their ships in Sydney, Melbourne and Adelaide. The employers fought back and recruited non-union labour.

Meanwhile, with unemployment rising, the pastoralists were successful in attracting sufficient shearers willing to work on the landowners' terms. The ASU called for a boycott of any wool produced by non-union workers and the trade union federations responded to the appeal. Inevitably, the two disputes converged. Dockers joined the strike in sympathy with both the marine officers and the shearers. Coalminers joined in, refusing to supply coal for non-union ships. Spence called out the militant New South Wales shearers and later wrote 'to the astonishment of the public, 16,500 men stopped work at once without a question as to the why and wherefore except that it was necessary in the interests of unionism. It was one of the finest examples of loyalty the world has ever seen'. Seamen, gas workers and others walked out and within a short time over fifty thousand were directly involved, either in sympathy with the marine officers or against the loading of non-union wool. A Labour Defence Committee was set up, led by William Spence.

Newspapers carried alarmist reports raising the fear of revolution. Military units were called in for the first time in a labour dispute. The sense of panic was epitomised by the response of the Victoria government to the call for a demonstration in Melbourne in support of the strike. Machine-gun nests were set up on the parliament buildings and a thousand military personnel were deployed. The night before the demonstration Colonel Tom Price told his men 'You will each be supplied with forty rounds of ammunition and leaden bullets and if the order is given to fire, don't let me see one rifle pointed up in the air. Fire low and lay them out.' Despite the intimidation, sixty thousand protesters defiantly marched through Melbourne in support of the strike. In another show of strength, a demonstration in Sydney stretched for 1½ miles.

The colonial governments used the full force of the state to assist the employers and landowners. They did not hesitate to use the courts, the police and the military against the strikers. The shearers took the worst punishment. Using the Masters and Servants Act, a draconian piece of convict-era legislation, employers dragged striking shearers before the courts. The clauses 'neglect of duty' and 'breach of contract' carried sentences of up to three months in jail and heavy fines. In one county, sixty men were fined £10 (more than two weeks' wages) and forfeited wages for work done before the strike. Altogether 1,377 shearers were dealt with under the Act, but special treatment was reserved for union organisers, who were given fines they could not possibly pay. In one case, Arthur Rae, a future general secretary, was fined £320, and sentenced to two-and-a-half years' imprisonment for failure to pay. He was released a month later after a public outcry.

The economic conditions were against the strikers and employers found a ready supply of labour from the growing ranks of unemployed casual labour. The strike ended after four months when the merchant naval officers returned to work on employers' terms in November 1890. Other unions followed suit, although some coalminers stayed out for another two months. Spence and the other leaders had seriously overestimated the strength of the trade union movement. They also misjudged the power of a united employers' front, backed up by the forces of the state. Unions were seriously weakened and took a long time to recover their pre-strike membership. Wage cuts of up to 30 per cent followed, the worst being in the maritime industry.

Despite the setbacks, Spence remained optimistic that history was on the side of the trade union movement. In 1892 he delivered a lecture entitled *The Ethics of New Unionism*, which was later published to widespread acclaim. He continued to look for areas of expansion and targeted the unskilled shed hands, who worked alongside the shearers in the woolsheds. They were not unionised but, rather than recruit them directly into the ASU, it was decided to assist them to form their own union, and amalgamate some time later. This proposal was later extended to include all farm labourers, and in 1891 the General Labourers Union was formed. ASU organisers enrolled over five thousand members into the new organisation before its inaugural conference. There were many more farm hands than shearers and it was clear that the new union had the potential to dwarf the ASU. William Spence was chosen as general secretary and he set an ambitious target of sixty thousand members in three years. Spence was now the leading figure in three unions: the ASU, the Amalgamated Miners Association, and the General Labourers Union.

The officials of the General Labourers Union came mainly from the ASU, but other organisers were employed from the labourers' ranks. One of the fresh intake was a fascinating character who had participated in the formation of a number of political organisations, including the Melbourne Anarchist Club and the Social Democratic League. Larry Petrie, a notorious trade union and political activist, was born in Scotland in 1859 and was a close friend of William Spence. He was well educated but when he arrived in Australia he took a job as a labourer. On the Melbourne docks, he set up a union branch and led an unsuccessful attempt to launch a six-hour-day campaign. Sacked by his employers after the failure, he found a job in a quarry but had to quit when his arm was badly injured in a workplace accident. The arm was amputated a few years later after it was broken in a fight with a non-unionist.

Described as a wild rebel and a mad revolutionary, Petrie was nevertheless appointed secretary of the General Labourers Union in Sydney. His devotion to the cause of the working class and commitment to the union were indisputable. Covering a large area of New South Wales, he worked tirelessly for his members, but his fanatical exploits caused panic in the union hierarchy. In 1892 he planted a bomb at Circular Quay in Sydney during a dispute. When Spence heard about the plot he was incensed and immediately arranged for two of his lieutenants to locate and defuse the device. The following year Petrie was charged with attempted murder and causing an explosion on a non-union ship during a seamen's strike, but was acquitted through lack of evidence. After his release he decided to join a utopian Socialist settlement that had been founded in Paraguay. He was a warm-hearted, lovable rogue, who despite his ultra-leftist tendencies retained the affections of William Spence and other mainstream trade union leaders. He died in Paraguay in 1901 when he jumped onto a railway line to save a child from an oncoming train. The child was unharmed, but the rescue cost him his life.

Financial crisis, more strikes and Waltzing Matilda

The financial crisis that started in 1890 deepened. Property values collapsed and overseas investment dried up. Prices for wool and wheat fell dramatically and unemployment soared. Banks folded, government tax revenues collapsed, and public works programmes were abandoned. To make matters worse, a long drought began, heaping further damage on an economy that was still predominantly dependent on agricultural exports. Unemployed shearers and other workers were forced to tramp across Australia looking for work and thousands of men arrived at shearing sheds only to be turned away. Their numbers were swelled by impoverished industrial workers from Sydney and Melbourne searching for any kind of employment. For some the fight for survival was too much, with reports of men found dead from exhaustion after months of wandering through the bush looking for work. In such circumstances, there was little prospect of any union advances.

Nevertheless, Spence pushed ahead with his organisational goal of uniting the bush workers into one union. But organising the general labourers and merging with the shearers proved to be more complex than Spence had envisaged. Many shearers were fearful of diluting the union's strength by accepting unskilled workers into its ranks. But Spence was adamant that unity of all workers in the same industry was the only way to defeat the employers, and pushed ahead with the proposals. However, David Temple disagreed and resigned before the vote on amalgamation was taken. When the new organisation was established in 1894, Spence took over as general secretary. Named the Australian Workers Union, it went on to become the predominant union in the country. Up until the Second World War no other union could rival its size and breadth of coverage.

Soon after its formation Spence led the new union into a debilitating dispute after pastoralists proposed a further reduction in pay. Against his better judgment, Spence was resigned to taking a stance after failing to reach a compromise. 'You can only make capitalism think or look at you at all by hitting it in the pocket,' he maintained. In a speech to launch the strike he told his members 'It is time to give capitalism a lick in the lug.' The 1894 strike was one of Australia's most violent industrial conflicts, particularly in Queensland. Spence wrote in the union journal, the *Australian Worker*, that members had to prepare for the struggle by 'playing cunning till we get out in the wind and dodging the enemy till we see a certainty of wiping him out altogether'. During the strike woolsheds were burned to the ground, riverboats transporting scab labour were attacked, and some scabs were tarred and feathered. Gun battles between the military and strikers were frequent, and in every town fighting and brawling broke out between union and non-union men. As the strike dragged on, the police and government troops became more involved. Trade unionists were given harsh sentences for riot, damaging property and unlawful assembly. Sometimes they were simply detained without trial for thirty days, even if no offence was committed. One man convicted of setting fire to a riverboat was jailed for seven years. The number of unemployed men who were willing to work at any price made it a difficult strike to win and it fizzled out towards the end of the shearing season.

The 1894 strike has a lasting legacy in the famous Australian folk song, 'Waltzing Matilda', which was written by the poet Andrew 'Banjo' Paterson. Shortly after the strike Paterson visited the Dagworth station which was owned by the McPherson family. In the surrounding area eight shearing sheds had been burned down, including the woolshed at Dagworth. The chief suspect was Samuel Hoffmeister, one of the strike leaders. Bob McPherson and three police troopers left Dagworth to track him down, but when they found him beside a billabong he was dead. It is alleged that he shot himself rather than face capture and certain hanging. Banjo Paterson was facinated by the story and wrote a poem about the incident. Bob McPherson's sister, Christina, had been playing a tune on the harp called 'Thou Bonnie Wood of Craigielea', a Scots song written by Robert Tannahill in 1805 and set to music in 1818 by James Barr. Paterson put the words to the tune and it became one of the world's favourite songs, although not many know its origin.

Spence described the years from 1895–98 as the union's dark days. Membership almost halved, forcing the closure of district offices and reducing the general secretary's status to unpaid honorary officer. The blatant use of the state apparatus to defeat the strikes in the 1890s led politically conscious workers to conclude that trade unions alone could not defend their interests. In the Trades and Labor Councils there was a growing tide of opinion in favour of forming a political party to represent the interests of the working class. From the late 1880s Spence had advocated the formation of an Australian Labor Party 'to root out the class representatives from the colonial parliaments'. He had no difficulty convincing the Australian Workers Union to support him, but was less successful with the miners. His Victoria base of the Amalgamated Miners Association rejected his pleas to launch a new party and he was forced to resign as its general secretary in 1892.

W G Spence MP

The Trades and Labour Councils committed trade union funds to form Labor Electoral Leagues, the forerunner of the Australian Labor Party. Spence was one of the early successful candidates and entered the New South Wales Parliament in 1898. On taking up his seat, he resigned as general secretary of the Australian Workers Union, but was appointed president of the union, a position he held until 1917. When the six colonies federated to form Australia in 1900, Spence was elected to the first parliament. He started writing a number of books and pamphlets. Two of his books, *Australia's Awakening* and *The History of the AWU*, were personal accounts of the early days of the Amalgamated Miners Association and Australian Workers Union. He produced pamphlets on private enterprise, Socialism and child welfare. In 1907 he stood for the leadership of the Labor Party, but was defeated by fellow Scot Andrew Fisher. His political achievements were not on a par with his record in the trade union movement but he attained cabinet rank in 1914–15 as Postmaster General and was vice-president of the Executive Council in 1916 (See Chapter 9, page 279).

The election of a Labor government transformed the fortunes of trade unions, especially after the introduction of the arbitration system. Although a supporter of arbitration, Spence believed that union leaders ran the risk of taking their eyes off the ball by relying too heavily on its application. Addressing the Workers Educational Association in 1915, he talked of the changed nature of the trade union movement. 'Today it is recognised as an institution in the community and even considered respectable. It no longer calls for the self-sacrifice and suffering which was the lot of its active members in the past; but its work is still unaccomplished, and its mission in our social economy is not yet fulfilled.' Unions had become too conservative, according to Spence, and had fallen into the bad habits of the old days when the craft unions dominated. Criticising the unions for their sole emphasis on wages and hours, Spence reminded them of 'the real work which lies before the workers ... the overthrow of the capitalist system'.

Within a year of this speech, the Labor Party was in turmoil over its response to the First World War and Spence had done a complete U-turn. After a split over military conscription, the Prime Minister, William Hughes, was expelled from the party. Twenty other members of the Parliamentary Labor Party who supported him suffered the same fate, Spence included. This rump then formed the National Party and Spence continued in parliament until 1919. In his last speech to parliament in 1919 at the age of seventy-three, Spence had changed his mind about capitalism. He declared that its overthrow was no longer necessary, as the workers now had the arbitration system, giving them an equal say with the employers. He died in 1926, aged eighty, and was survived by his wife, four daughters and three of his five sons.

The Australian Workers Union survived the critical struggles of the 1890s and began to grow again. It merged with other unions in the pastoral, mining and timber industries, which were the key business sectors in Australia at that time. With over 100,000 members it was the biggest union in Australia and the most powerful Labor Party affiliate. It was strongly opposed to military conscription during the First World War and the leadership were deeply disturbed that William Spence took a different view. The union was instrumental in expelling the rebels who campaigned against Labor Party policy and it was with a heavy heart that they asked Spence to resign as president. Despite his ignominious exit from the union and the Labor Party, Spence was regarded as one of the country's most inspirational figures and fully deserved his moniker 'Father of the Australian trade union movement'.

The Australian government acknowledged his unique contribution to the nation by naming a district of Canberra 'Spence' in his honour. But he had a long wait for the trade union movement to recognise his achievements properly. After lying in an unmarked grave for seventy-four years, the unions gave him the burial he deserved. In 2001 a monument to him was unveiled in the Melbourne cemetery where he was buried. Two years later the new Victoria Headquarters of the Australian Workers Union was named after him.

Chapter 9

Andrew Fisher and the Australian politicians

There was a sharp intake of breath throughout Australia when the results of the 1910 general election were announced. For the first time in political history a party with an avowedly Socialist manifesto had won an outright majority in a national parliament. Throughout the world, Socialists rejoiced as the scale of the Australian Labor Party's victory became known. With 50 per cent of the vote, Labor had won forty-two out of seventy-five seats in the House of Representatives and all of the Senate seats contested. The eyes of the world were fixed on the new Prime Minister, Andrew Fisher, and his epoch-making government.

Born in the Ayrshire mining village of Crosshouse in 1862, Fisher was brought up with his seven siblings in a one-bedroomed house in a typical miners' row. Toilets and washhouses were shared with other families and water was collected in buckets from a communal tap at the end of the street. School ended for Fisher at ten years of age when his father developed pneumoconiosis, or 'black lung', a debilitating disease caused by breathing in coal dust. Along with his elder brother, Fisher started down the mines and was soon working a twelve-hour day from Monday to Saturday. His father, who had been a union activist, was also a founding member of the Crosshouse Co-operative Society. The co-operative played an integral part in the Crosshouse community, especially when it opened a shop with a reading room and library. Andrew Fisher was a prodigious reader and made good use of these facilities to enhance his education. The reading room also provided the opportunity for people of the village to debate the affairs of the world, and Fisher revelled in the discussions.

His father was a deeply religious man and taught his children the values of honesty, trust and class solidarity. Attempting to gain advantage at the expense of others was seen as an act of betrayal. Personal ambition had to be directed for the benefit of the community. Alcohol was the scourge of the working class and gambling was its twin evil. These strict Puritan teachings of his father and the church elders helped form Fisher's character, but he was urged to think for himself. He read the works of radical authors like Thomas Carlyle and Ralph Emerson and as a young man was confident in his set of beliefs, harbouring no doubts about right and wrong. At seventeen he was appointed Crosshouse branch secretary of the Ayrshire Miners Union. Tall and good-looking, with deep-set eyes and sandy hair, Fisher was a warm and friendly young man who was highly respected in the community. Despite his youth, he already had seven years' experience of underground work and was trusted to lead the miners from the twelve pits in the village. He knew the consequences of sticking his head above the parapet, but never let the threat of victimisation deter him from taking a leading role. Two years later he lost his job after a ten-week strike led by Keir Hardie, the Ayrshire Miners' Union Secretary, ended in defeat. It was the first of several occasions when Fisher was sacked for his trade union activity.

Although he managed to find work after the 1881 strike, Fisher was sacked for a second time in early 1885 and put on the employers' blacklist. There now seemed little prospect of another job in Ayrshire. Around the same time Thomas McIllwraith, Premier of Queensland, addressed a public meeting in Kilmarnock and extolled the great opportunities in the colony. McIllwraith came from Ayrshire and was keen on others joining the community of Scottish miners that had been established in Queensland's Burrum coalfield. After family discussions, Fisher and his younger brother James decided to emigrate, and later that year they sailed to Brisbane.

Within two months of his arrival in Burrum, Andrew Fisher was promoted to mine supervisor, and looked forward to a career in mine management. However, after he was denied a further promotion three years later, he decided to move 80 miles south to the town of Gympie, where he found work in a goldmine. He settled down in Gympie and became involved in the co-operative society, the local defence force, the church and its Sunday school. He also took over as president of the local branch of the Amalgamated Miners Association, but in 1890 he was sacked once again for leading a strike. During the period of enforced unemployment that followed he turned his attention to the exciting political developments that were taking place.

The founding of the Labor Party

The Australian Labor Party is often described as the infant child of the maritime strike of 1890 (see Chapter 8, page 256-257). The colonial governments (Australia was, at the time, made up of six separate colonies) openly supported the employers during the dispute, and the state apparatus was used to ensure the defeat of the unions. The trade

William Kidston, an iron moulder from Falkirk, became premier of Queensland in 1906 when the Labor Party formed a government. But Kidston later split with his Labor colleagues, founded a new party, and continued as premier until 1911. (Courtesy State Library of Queensland)

union movement was taught a lesson in class politics and became convinced of the need for parliamentary representation. Shortly after the strike, key trade union leaders met with representatives of some of the Socialist organisations to prepare the ground for candidates in the 1891 election. They formed Labor electoral leagues, ten years before Labour representation committees were set up in Britain.

Over the following years Labor parties emerged in the colonies. They soon captured the imagination of the Australian working class, and within a very short period had transformed the political landscape. The results of the first colonial elections after the maritime strike astounded the Labor candidates and their opponents alike, and marked a watershed in Australian political history. In Queensland, Labor won sixteen seats, making it the second largest party. Labor candidates won fifteen seats out of forty-two in New South Wales. In Melbourne, ten seats were won in the Victoria Assembly and notable successes were scored in South Australia, Tasmania and Western Australia.

By the end of the decade, Queensland boasted the first ever Labor Party to hold office anywhere in the world, albeit very briefly. Andrew Fisher was appointed secretary for railways and public works in a minority Labor government, but the administration only lasted a week before the opposition parties joined forces to remove it. But it sent the signal throughout Australia that Labor's time was approaching. Another Scotsman, William Kidston, held office in the transient government. Kidston, from Falkirk, was treasurer and postmaster general. Born in 1849, he served an apprenticeship as moulder in a local ironworks. Exhausted by the long hours and heavy labour, he emigrated to Queensland when he was thirty-three, and left his trade to open up a bookshop. He set up the Workers Political Association and helped found the Labor Party in Rockhampton. In 1906 he became premier when the Labor Party once again formed a government in Queensland. But he later split with his Labor Party colleagues, founded a new party, and continued as premier until 1911.

Arguably the most influential figure in Queensland Labor politics during this period was another Scotsman, Matthew Reid. Reid was a carpenter and joined the Social Democratic Federation when he worked in Glasgow. His political experience was invaluable to the Queensland Labor Party. Soon after arriving in Brisbane in 1887 he was elected to represent the carpenters on the Brisbane Trades and Labor Council. After being sacked for his union activity, he was appointed to a full-time union position with the Australian Labor Federation and during the 1890s steered the Queensland Labor Party through its formative years. He won a seat in the legislative assembly in 1893 and campaigned on behalf of the unemployed, in support of land reform and for educational opportunities for the working class. During the 1894 shearers' strike he was denounced as a dangerous revolutionary for vociferously defending the union's tactics. During a debate about the strike in the Queensland legislature, he was ordered out of the House and suspended for a period for unparliamentary behaviour.

In New South Wales, George Black was one of the successful Labor Party candidates at the 1891 election, winning in West Sydney. Born in Edinburgh in 1854, Black had a middle-class upbringing and attended Edinburgh University. However, he failed to graduate, and emigrated to Australia. He tried various occupations and locations before settling down to work as a journalist in Sydney with the *Bulletin*. An excellent public speaker and a member of the Socialist and Republican Leagues, he was well known in Labor circles in Sydney. After his election in 1891, he set his sights on becoming party leader, but was thwarted mainly because of problems in his private relationships. He left his wife, with whom he had the first five of his twelve children, and set up home with a married woman. However, his talents were greatly admired and he remained one of the most influential figures in the fledgling New South Wales Labor Party. He edited two newspapers, and amongst his many publications were books on Robert Burns and a *History of the Australian Labor Party*.

In South Australia, a breakthrough was made in a by-election in 1892 when John McPherson became the first Labor member of the Assembly. Born in Aberdeen in 1860, he attended St Paul's secondary school and the Mechanics Institute before being apprenticed with the Free Press Printing and Publishing Company. In 1882 he and his wife emigrated to South Australia and settled in Adelaide, where he started work with the *South Australian Register*. In Aberdeen he had been an active member of the Scottish Typographical Association and continued his trade union involvement in Adelaide. He was sacked during a dispute at the paper, but continued to have a high profile with the South Australian Typographical Society. McPherson held his East Adelaide seat at the 1893 general election, and became chair of the Labor Group on the Legislative Assembly, where he was renowned for his tact and astute political skills. Sadly, he was diagnosed with cancer aged thirty-seven, and decided to resign at the next election. His closest friend and compatriot,

James Hutcheson, who had worked beside him in Aberdeen, replaced him as the member for East Adelaide. Hutcheson had followed him to Australia in 1884 and was also fired during the strike at the *Register*.

A new century and a new nation

The Labor Party's emergence had occurred when the momentum for the creation of a federated nation of the six Australian colonies was at its peak. The labour movement was enthusiastic about the founding of the new country and when the nation of Australia was born on the first day of the twentieth century, the Labor Party was well placed to challenge the established parties. In the first all-Australia election it won fourteen of the seventy-five seats it contested in the House of Representatives, and eight seats in the Senate. A number of Scots were successful in that historic election, and went on to play prominent roles in government during the first stages of the new nation's history. Andrew Fisher was one of the successful candidates, winning Queensland's Wilde Bay constituency with 55 per cent of the vote.

Since his arrival in Queensland, Fisher remained in touch with all his family. Three years after he left home, his father died and Fisher sent his mother as much money as he could afford. But this was only the first of a number of bereavements the family had to endure. His brother James left the Burrum coalfield in 1892 to work in India, but was killed in a mining accident a year later. Another family heartbreak followed in 1895 when his youngest brother, Robert, a mining engineer, was killed in an accident in Canada. Fisher had paid for Robert's studies in colliery management, and his death was extremely hard to bear. Then, shortly after his general election triumph, he received further tragic news of the death of another brother, John, who was chief constable in Grimsby, Lincolnshire. On a happier note, at the end of 1901 he married twenty-seven-year-old Margaret Irvine, the daughter of his landlady. He had evaded personal relationships until almost forty, but became a devoted husband and a loving father of five sons and a daughter.

The Labor Party mounted an effective opposition during its first period in parliament. At the next election in 1903 it increased its representation to twenty-three seats in the lower house and won ten Senate seats. For a few months in 1904 the Labor Party even formed a minority Government with Chris Watson, a former activist in the Australian Workers Union, becoming prime minister. During the five-month period the Labor Party was in government, Andrew Fisher held office as minister of trade and customs, ranked fifth in the cabinet hierarchy. Although highly regarded for his ability, he was not noted for his eloquence as a public speaker. His harsh voice and pronounced Ayrshire accent made him difficult to follow, and he often spoke too fast when he was nervous. His speeches in parliament lacked humour and were described as a mixture of Presbyterian righteousness and trade union demagogy. However, he was capable of scoring telling points in a debate, and his attacks on his opponents could be ruthless. His main strengths were his sincerity, modesty, and tenacity. When party discipline became strained by some of the difficult decisions that had to be taken during its period in office, Fisher demonstrated his skills as a politician, showing a talent for conciliation and knowing when to compromise. This was recognised in 1905 when he was elected deputy leader of the party with specific responsibility for party unity.

Scots were also prominent in the Senate. Gregor MacGregor, a native of the village of Kilmun in Argyllshire, led the Labor group in the Upper House. Born in 1848, MacGregor worked as a labourer in the Clydeside shipyards and took part in a successful union campaign for a shorter working week. In 1877, he emigrated to South Australia, where he worked in the building trade. He was elected secretary of the Building Workers Union, and also president of the South Australia Trades and Labor Council. Shortly after his arrival in Australia, McGregor was in an accident at work that left him almost blind. But the disability forced him to develop a prodigious memory for facts and figures, which he put to good use throughout his political career. In 1894 he was elected to the South Australia Legislative Council before moving to the Senate of the Federal Parliament in 1901. He was appointed leader of the Labor Group in the Senate and deputy chairman of the Parliamentary Labor Party. Admired for his tactical shrewdness, he became vice-president of the executive council, until failing health forced him to give up his position in 1914.

Labor's chief whip in the Senate was a Scottish miner, Hugh de Large, who came from Airdrie. After losing both parents when he was very young, de Large left St Margaret's primary school at ten to work in the Lanarkshire mines. As a youth he developed a keen interest in politics and became active in the local miners' union. When he was twenty-eight he emigrated with his wife and family, firstly to Queensland in 1887, and then to Newcastle in New South Wales. Blacklisted for his trade union activity, he moved to Western Australia where he worked in the goldfields. Described as a composed but humourless man who spoke

Group photograph of the federal Australian Labor Party MPs elected to the House of Representatives and Senate at the first election in 1901.

Andrew Fisher is sixth from the left in the middle row, with Hugh de Large beside him in seventh place. William Spence is first from the left in the front row and Gregor McGregor is third in same row.

with a pronounced Scottish accent, de Large served as Labor chief whip in the Senate for seven years.

One of the highest-ranking trade union officials in Australia was elected to the Senate in 1903. Bob Guthrie, former president of the Seamen's Union and secretary/treasurer of the Federated Council of Australian Unions, was born in Partick, Glasgow in 1857. With the probable assistance of a bursary, he was educated at Allan Glen's School in the city's Townhead district. He left school at fifteen to become a ship's apprentice and spent many years at sea before settling in Adelaide. In 1888 he became full-time secretary of the South Australian branch of the Seamen's Union and had a high profile during the maritime strike in 1890. He was one of the most influential advocates of working-class representation in parliament and was a member of the South Australian legislature before winning election to the Senate. A fine public speaker with a strong Scottish accent, he pursued legislation around maritime and trade union issues. Later referred to as the 'Australian Plimsoll', he served on a royal commission on maritime safety, and the resulting act of parliament became known as 'the Guthrie Act'.

In 1907, after the resignation of Chris Wallace, parliamentary Labor Party leader, three candidates emerged to succeed him: Billy Hughes, president of the Waterside Workers Federation, William Spence, president of the Australian Workers Union, and Andrew Fisher, deputy leader. Although he lacked the charisma of the other challengers, Fisher was the most engaging of the candidates, pleasant to his colleagues and easy to get on with. His qualities of good judgment and personal integrity appealed to Labor parliamentarians and the party's rank and file alike. He was modest enough to admit his failings and did not hesitate to seek advice from others. But when it came to supporting basic labour principles, his resolution was unbreakable and his victory in the leadership election was a triumph of his character and integrity.

Fisher: from coalminer to prime minister

Labor was the largest party in parliament, but had been sustaining a Liberal government since 1906. After two years it withdrew support, and the Liberal prime minister was forced to resign. Fisher was then asked to form a government, and in November 1908 the former coalminer from Crosshouse took over as Prime Minister of Australia.

At the age of forty-six his hair was going grey, but his handsome features made him look young for his age. He was tall, broad shouldered

Andrew Fisher became prime minister in 1908 and led the Labor Party to an outstanding general election result in 1910. But he was not comfortable as leader during the First World War and resigned as Prime Minister in 1915 to become the Australian High Commissioner in London. (Courtesy Talma Studios, (PAC-10003578), State Library of Victoria)

and muscular, giving him a commanding presence in the House. There were limited opportunities for radical reform in the minority government, but Fisher's initial goal was to make Labor acceptable to the Australian electorate as a party of government. He pursued a number of popular issues for which he could get majority support and gradually gave the public confidence in Labor's ability to govern. The maturity and astuteness of the Labor government began to be recognised by those who had doubted its ability to rule. Labor looked forward with confidence to the 1910 election, but when the results were announced, they exceeded all expectations. Labor romped home with forty-two seats in the House of Representatives, a majority of eleven. In the Senate it won all the seats up for election, giving it twenty-three out of thirty-six constituencies. Fisher was the first Australian prime minister with majorities in both Houses, giving him total control of the legislative programme. He doubled up as minister of finance and a detailed programme of social and economic measures followed, shaping Australia's political and fiscal policy for many years to come. During the next three years 113 acts of parliament were passed, achieving many of the party's basic objectives.

The creation of a nationalised bank was one of Labor's major goals, and in the first session of the new parliament the Commonwealth Savings Bank was formed. In Fisher's words it was 'a bank directly belonging to the people and directly managed by the people's own agents'. There was furious opposition from the private banks, especially when the Commonwealth Savings Bank was given sole responsibility for the issue of banknotes. Fisher came in for heavy personal criticism from opponents who dubbed the banknotes 'Fisher's Flimsies', wrongly predicting they would end up worthless. The following year, the government focused on employment law, strengthening conciliation and arbitration. It introduced tax reforms, industrial relations legislation, a workers' compensation act and also reformed the voting system. Old age pensions were increased and extended, maternity benefits were introduced, and medical support to the poor provided. Some of these reforms were not available in Britain until after the Second World War.

The 1910–13 Labor government captured the imagination of the Australian people and marked its graduation from a party of protest to a party of government. As well as trade unionists and their families, the Labor Party attracted the support of middle-class reformers who had discarded the Liberal Party. It became a broad coalition, appealing to radical nationalists, intellectuals and campaigners of social causes. Many of the poorer rural workers and small farmers also identified with its aims. Its success at federal level was matched by victories in the state legislatures, where Labor controlled most of the governments. In Andrew Fisher, the Labor Party had a leader of distinction, unchallenged within the party, and whose status and reputation was recognised throughout the country. His judgment was proved sound on key issues, conveying an image of trust, competence and stability. He was acclaimed by fellow Labour leaders throughout the world, and was showered with praise and congratulations by his Australian Labor Party members.

At the height of his powers, Fisher came to Britain to represent Australia at the coronation of King George in 1911 and to attend an imperial conference. Although there was concern amongst the establishment about his Socialist credentials, he was given the red-carpet treatment in when he arrived in London. Afterwards he travelled to Scotland by train, where he received a more wholehearted reception from his ain folk. Arriving at Kilmarnock station accompanied by Keir Hardie, he was welcomed by the Lord Provost and miners' union officials. A tour of Ayrshire's Burns country followed before his motorcade entered his home village of Crosshouse. Thousands lined the streets to greet him, many of them old friends and former workmates. Keir Hardie encapsulated the spirit of the homecoming declaring, 'Crosshouse has turned out en masse to welcome Andrew Fisher, whom it had known as a barefoot boy. He has returned with the respect and confidence of five million Australians.' At Crosshouse primary school the children, led by his old schoolmaster, sang 'A Man's a Man for 'A That', Fisher's favourite song. An emotional Fisher responded, 'Whether a man is a lord or a scavenger, test him on his merits and actions and, if these things ring true, then *"let sense and worth o'er a' the earth bear the gree and a' that"*. The great aim of parliament and nations of all kinds has been summed up by Burns. This is all we are trying to do. If there is suffering which can be moved without deterioration to the race, it is the duty of a free country and a free parliament to remove that disability, to give every man his place, not according to his money or position into which he may have been born.'

At a banquet in Kilmarnock, tributes were paid to the former miner who rose to challenge and defeat the establishment. The Lord Provost, Matthew Smith, declared with pride 'Mr Fisher's rise to the position of honour which he has attained marks an epoch in the history of miners as a class.' At a public meeting organised by the Ayrshire miners, Tom

A. FISHER, M.P. (Australia)   J. KEIR HARDIE, M.P. (Britain)

Fraternal greetings from the workers in the Old Home Land to their Comrades in the new. The aim of our world wide movement is the same — the Economic Emancipation of earths toiling millions.

Signed, J. Keir Hardie

14.12.'07

Andrew Fisher and Keir Hardie, 1907. Fisher was born in Crosshouse, Ayrshire. At seventeen years of age he became the local branch secretary of the Ayrshire Miners' Union, which was led by Keir Hardie. When Fisher returned to Scotland in 1911 as Australian prime minister, he was accompanied by Hardie on a tour. (Courtesy State Library of Queensland)

McKerrell, the Ayrshire miners' union official spoke of Fisher's class loyalty. 'It is comparatively easy for an able man to rise to a cabinet position by leaving his own class and joining another ... Andrew Fisher's triumph has been greater. He has remained loyal in his own class ... Some men have risen from the working classes, Andrew Fisher has not. He belongs to them. He is one of them and remains among them.'

First World War conscription

But despite the popularity of the government during most of this period, the Labor Party lost its majority in the House of Representatives in the 1913 election by one seat. Fisher fought off a challenge to his leadership from Billy Hughes, but the minority Conservative government that took office did not last long and was defeated on a vote of confidence. Labor won the following year's election with a clear majority and Fisher became prime minister for the third time on the eve of the First World War. With Australian troops preparing to join the British war effort, anxiety grew within the Labor Party regarding Australian involvement. And as Australian casualties began to mount, the numbers opposing the war increased. Fisher was responsible for sending the first Australian troops into battle, but was uneasy about the war and was opposed to military conscription. However, the Labor Party was dangerously split on the issue and faced its gravest crisis since its foundation.

In Britain the left was also sharply divided, but unlike Australia, the Labour Party was not in power. It opposed the war, with Keir Hardie and Ramsay MacDonald leading peace marches against the conflict. However, once war was declared, the majority of British Labour MPs felt obliged to fall in behind the government and support the troops. This caused a major split, and Ramsay MacDonald resigned as leader. He was replaced by a Glaswegian, Arthur Henderson, who had been a full-time official of the Foundry Workers Union. Labour was invited to join the War Cabinet, and Henderson became the Labour Party's first government minister. But conscription was strongly opposed by most sections of the labour movement, with strike action breaking out on Clydeside when it was introduced.

The Australian unions were equally emphatic in their opposition to conscription, and stepped up their anti-war campaigning. The jailing of some union activists for distributing anti-war leaflets caused uproar on the left of the party. Twelve trade union opponents of the war were arrested and charged with treason, later reduced to sedition, and sentenced to fifteen years' imprisonment. Their most senior figure was Donald Grant from Inverness, who arrived in Sydney in 1910, aged twenty-two. He was a prominent opponent of the war and regularly spoke at public meetings. Described as a fiery mob orator with a thick Scots burr, he drew record crowds to his meetings in Sydney and Melbourne. He was released from prison in 1920, after serving five years of his sentence. Grant went on to become a Labor Party senator in 1943 and advisor to the minister for external affairs. In 1946 he returned to Inverness, where the town council gave him a civic welcome.

Economic problems mounted as the war continued and the government introduced a freeze on wages. But it could not prevent runaway inflation as shortages of basic goods drove up prices. It was not just the left that campaigned against the war: the moderate Australian Workers Union, which could normally be relied on to back the leadership, also opposed Australian involvement and was vehemently against conscription. Divisions opened up in the party at all levels, and at the top there were frequent clashes between Fisher and his deputy leader, Billy Hughes. The strain of leading the party for eight years and the task of leading the country in wartime was taking its toll on Fisher's health. He became morose and withdrawn and the constant stress was affecting his health. He was not comfortable as a war leader and knew that his heart was not in the forthcoming battle over conscription.

This period of soul-searching coincided with a vacancy for a new Australian High Commissioner in London, and the position was his for the asking. Some of his close friends were deeply concerned about his health and encouraged him to apply. The lucrative salary and relatively stress-free position proved attractive to Fisher and his family. And so, under no internal or external pressure to go, he bowed out as prime minister in 1915, just as the Labor Party was about to tear itself apart.

Billy Hughes, who was born and educated in London, became prime minister. He was a more enthusiastic militarist than Fisher and was keen to address the problem of a shortfall in army recruitment. Invited to London for talks on developments in the war, he came back determined to introduce conscription. However, he knew he would lose a vote in parliament, and instead called a referendum in an attempt to gain a mandate. An internal Labor Party agreement was reached, allowing party members to campaign on either side of the issue. The referendum, held in December 1916, produced one of the most acrimonious clashes in Australian political history, with anti-conscription activists subjected to constant police harassment. The Melbourne Trades Hall was raided by military police looking for anti-war leaflets, and the forced entry into a major trade union office by police acting under a Labor government aroused widespread bitterness. When ballot papers were counted, Australians voted against conscription by a narrow margin.

This led to a vote of no confidence in Hughes, forcing his resignation as leader of the Labor Party. Against Hughes were two thirds of the parliamentary party, every state Labor Party, and every trade union. However, half the government ministers and several state Premiers had supported him. When Hughes formed a coalition government with the support of the opposition, twenty-three out of sixty-five Labor MPs in the House of Representatives joined him. Along with other leading party members, they left and formed the National Labor Party, which eventually merged with the Liberals and was renamed the National Party. Hughes continued as prime minister until 1923, and the National Party stayed in power until 1929.

A number of the Scottish parliamentary contingent joined Hughes' National Labor Party. William Spence hesitated before he declared his support for Hughes and was given a cabinet position for the first time. He became Postmaster General and later vice-president of the executive council, but was asked to resign as president of the Australian Workers Union. Hugh de Large, Labor's chief whip in the Senate, continued the same role for the National Labor Party. Bob Guthrie, the Seamen's leader, was re-elected on a National Party ticket in 1917, and was expelled from the Seamen's Union. George Black, who once had pretensions to becoming party leader, became a cabinet member in 1915, when he was appointed colonial secretary and minister for public health. John Newland, a railwayman from Nairn, Morayshire, was elected to the Senate in 1913 and was appointed to the executive of the parliamentary Labor Party. He followed Hughes into the National Labor Party and became president of the Senate.

Labor's losses, Communist gains

The destructive split in the Labor Party resulted in a loss of political power for the next fifteen years. Its monopoly of leadership of the trade union movement had also been challenged by more radical Socialist organisations, which had led a series of strikes before and during the war. After the dust had settled at the end of the war, many on the left took inspiration from the Bolshevik Revolution. In 1920 the Communist

Jock Garden was born in Lossiemouth, Morayshire and was a lay preacher in the evangelical Church of Christ. In 1916 he became secretary of the New South Wales Trades and Labor Council and was the main driving force for the establishment of the Australian Council of Trade Unions in 1927. He was the first chairman of the Communist Party of Australia, but left in 1926 and joined the Labor Party. (Courtesy Search Foundation, Australia)

Party of Australia was formed, and became a rival to the Labor Party within the trade union movement. It would be difficult to envisage the Communist Party of Australia without the Scots who played such a major role in its foundation and development. Indeed, the joke in labour circles was that Australian Communism was a Caledonian conspiracy. Its key founding members were Scots and all the general secretaries from its creation in 1920 until after the Second World War were born in Scotland. Many of its most prominent industrial leaders and its rank and file cadre force emigrated from Scotland. Bill Earsman from Edinburgh was the driving force behind its early development and became its first secretary. He teamed up with Lossiemouth-born Jock Garden, who was appointed party chairman.

Earsman was a top-class tradesman with a certificate in mechanical engineering from Heriot-Watt College. He emigrated to New Zealand in 1908 and moved to Melbourne two years later. He was already a committed Socialist when he left Edinburgh and was an experienced union official. In 1915 he was elected secretary of the Melbourne district of the Amalgamated Society of Engineers, and held various positions in the Victoria Socialist Party. Passionate about working-class political education, he set up Labor Colleges in Victoria and New South Wales. He also wrote a pamphlet, *The Proletariat and Education,* which was published in 1920. During the war he played a conspicuous role in the anti-conscription referendum campaign in Victoria and many contemporaries saw him as the single most important influence in the formation of the Australian Communist Party.

Jock Garden, the Communist Party chairman, was the son of a fisherman from Lossiemouth on the Moray Firth coast, the same birthplace as Ramsay MacDonald. He served an apprenticeship as a sailmaker before emigrating with his family to Sydney in 1904. A preacher in the Church of Christ, he was more interested in evangelical philosophy than Socialism. When he wasn't preaching, he worked at his trade and attended occasional trade union meetings. However, he volunteered to become the Sailmakers' Union delegate to the New South Wales Trades and Labor Council, and his interest in politics developed from there. His natural enthusiasm and highly effective pulpit-style oratory soon attracted attention. In the ferment that followed the referendum on conscription, Garden's newfound passion for radical Socialism propelled him successfully challenge for secretary of the New South Wales Trades and Labor Council, which was the most powerful trade union organisation in Australia at that time.

The Communist Party had an immediate appeal to trade union activists, with most of the executive committee of the Trades and Labour Council following Jock Garden into the new party. The secretaries of the Newcastle and Brisbane Labor Councils also joined, as did key members of the South Australia and Victoria Trades Hall Council. When the all-Australian Trades Union Congress was held in 1921, around 15 per cent of delegates were members of the Communist Party. The same year, Earsman attended the third congress of the Communist International (Comintern) in Moscow and won recognition for his party over a rival Marxist organisation.

Along with Garden, he returned to Moscow the following year to represent the Australian Communist Party at the fourth congress of the Comintern. However, his status in the international Communist movement was eclipsed by that of Garden, who was regarded as the more important working-class leader. To rapturous applause from delegates, Garden boasted that his one thousand Communist Party members influenced 400,000 Australian trade unionists, and could even shape Labor Party policy. As a result, he and not Earsman, was elected to the Comintern executive. His claim was a complete exaggeration and he admitted later that he just gave the audience what they wanted to hear.

The delegates may have had second thoughts if they had known that Garden continued his attachment to evangelical Christianity and was still a deacon in the Church of Christ. Indeed, on his way back from Moscow, he stopped off in Scotland, where he addressed a mass Christian revivalist meeting in the north east, apparently making hundreds of converts for his church. Earsman, who was in Scotland at the same time, read reports in one of the national newspapers about 'the remarkable revivalist scenes at Lossiemouth' and lost no time in reporting the event to Comintern officials. When they questioned Garden, he spun a fanciful story, claiming he was being followed by police and disguised himself as a preacher to shake them off his trail. It is unlikely they fell for the explanation, but no action was taken against him.

Garden made his way back to Australia with advice from Lenin, given during a private audience, that his Communist Party members should work more closely with the Australian Labor Party. He recommended that the Communist Party should apply for membership as an affiliated body, or if that was not accepted, to seek joint membership of both parties. This advice was given to others including the Communist Party of Great Britain. The Australian Labor Party rejected affiliation but approved joint membership of individual communists. Garden was elected to the executive of the New South Wales Labor Party, and other communists won leading positions. But two years later the Labor Party changed their position and in 1924 all communists were expelled. The expulsions had a catastrophic effect and soon the Communist Party began to disintegrate.

The aftermath of the fourth Comintern Congress carried further misfortune for Earsman. Australian security services had categorised him as a dangerous revolutionary and had been tracking him for some time. On his way back, he was stopped in London and told he was barred from re-entering Australia. He then returned to Moscow for a year, where he taught English at the military academy and was made an honorary member of the Red Army. However, when he came back to Britain in 1927, he left the Communist Party and sought re-entry to Australia. Despite the support of some eminent people, he was refused twice. Resigned to remaining in Britain, he found a job in Edinburgh, became active in the engineering union, and joined the Labour Party. In 1937 he was appointed secretary of the Edinburgh Trades Council, a position he held for the next twelve years. Apart from his trade union input, he was a strong supporter of Edinburgh becoming a centre for the arts and culture, and helped found the Edinburgh Festival Society. In 1950, his efforts were recognised when he was awarded an OBE.

Earsman's job as party secretary was given to another Scotsman, Tom Wright, who came to Australia with his parents in 1913 when he was eleven. After finishing his schooling in Sydney, he served an apprenticeship as a sheet metal worker. With just one year's membership of the Communist Party behind him, he found himself elevated to the secretary's position under the guidance of Garden at only twenty-two years of age. It was Wright's misfortune that he took on the role at a time when the Communist Party was in disarray, although the slump in membership was halted and the Party began to grow during the 1920s. But a major change in the Comintern policy led to a split in the Australian Party, with Wright finding himself on the losing side.

Jock Garden stood as a Communist Party candidate at the 1925 election, and received a humiliating vote. He decided he had enough and the following year he left and joined the Labor Party, becoming chief lieutenant of J.T. Lang, the newly elected Labor Premier of New South Wales. He continued to lead the New South Wales Trades and Labor Council, remaining its secretary until 1934. He put his energy into the establishment of an all-Australian trade union centre and, more than anyone else, he was responsible for the foundation of the Australian

Council of Trade Unions in 1927. In 1934 he relinquished his union position when he was elected MP for the constituency of Cook in the federal parliament election. Although he was an effective parliamentarian, his political career only lasted one term. After internal struggles over the control of party radio and newspapers, he was expelled from the Labor Party and lost his seat in the next election.

Throughout his life, Garden had lived on the edge of legality, from time to time facing criminal charges. He had been arrested for incitement to murder for a speech he made during a strike in 1928, but later the charges were dropped. In 1948 he was found guilty, then later acquitted of corrupt business dealings involving large sums of money. His last brush with the law was in 1957, when he and his son were charged with fraud. As joint owners of an astrology journal, they allegedly failed to deliver horoscopes to customers who had already paid for them. Garden was also a racehorse owner and a publisher, and continued to attract controversy until his death in 1968.

The Great Depression

In 1928, Soviet Communist Party leader Joseph Stalin predicted that capitalism was about to face a major economic crisis that would result in Social Democrats supporting cuts in workers' living standards. To distance Communists from their former allies, relationships with the Social Democratic parties were set to change. Instead of co-operating with Social Democrats, Communists would now expose them as enemies of the working class and nothing less than social Fascists. Tom Wright opposed the new policy, and at the 1929 congress he was removed from his position as general secretary. Some time later, when he was given the opportunity to exercise self-criticism, he repented and became a loyal party member thereafter. Still only twenty-seven, Wright's career was just beginning. He became national president of the Sheet Metal Workers Union in 1940 and led it for over thirty years. A campaigner for Aboriginal rights, he wrote a pamphlet in 1939, *New Deal for Aborigines,* arguing that the labour movement needed to recognise and address the government's neglect of aboriginal Australians. Wright served on the executive of the Australian Council of Trade Unions for many years and contributed to the formation of the Amalgamated Metal Workers Union in 1972, ending his career as its national vice-president.

Like Communist parties around the world, the Australian Party began to organise along democratic centralist lines. This meant a much tighter and more disciplined administration, requiring higher levels of obedience and vigilance. The new structures and new policies required new leaders, and from a group of committed working-class socialists, John B. (Jack) Miles was selected to lead the new-style Communist Party. Over forty when he took up the position, he was older than most of the party activists, and was affectionately known as 'The Old Man'. Miles was born in Hawick in the Scottish Borders, and was educated in Edinburgh before serving his time as a stonemason. After marrying, he and his wife Elizabeth emigrated to Queensland in 1913, where Miles joined the stonemasons' union and represented them on the Brisbane Trades and Labor Council. As soon as he arrived he became active in the Socialist League, and then joined the Brisbane branch of the Communist Party when it was formed in 1920. He impressed Comintern officials with his leadership qualities, and in 1931 he moved to Sydney as party secretary.

A demanding leader and a workaholic, Miles's stern demeanour was often a handicap to winning allies and forming relationships with his colleagues. But his caution, prudence and attention to detail helped shape the party into a resolute and robust revolutionary organisation. He restructured it from bottom to top, creating factory branches and concentrating on its industrial working-class base. Although his character was largely shaped by his strict Presbyterian upbringing, he had a long running extra-marital affair with Jean Devanny, a well-known Australian novelist. She was attracted by his powerful intellect and analytical mind, attributes which were about to be put to the test as Stalin's prediction of economic chaos proved correct.

A Labor Party landslide victory at the 1929 election soon began to look like a poisoned chalice, as the economy of the country collapsed amidst the chaos of the Great Depression. The impact on Australian society was devastating, as unemployment rose to 30 per cent in 1932. Men left their wives and children to search the country for work, often fighting with others over a poorly paid job. Families lost their homes and built shacks on the edges of towns, while churches and charities set up soup kitchens to feed the hungry and the destitute. The Labor government, as predicted, did indeed preside over cuts in living standards when faced with demands by the bankers. Splits over economic policy led to a humiliating defeat in the 1931 general election. A similar story unfolded in Britain as the minority Labour government, elected in 1929 and led by Ramsay MacDonald, struggled to cope. They faced the same problems and the same pressures from the bankers. MacDonald tried to

J. B.(Jack) Miles, a stonemason from Hawick, was general secretary of the Communist Party of Australia from 1931–48. Under his leadership the Communist Party built mass popular organisations and expanded its influence. (Courtesy Search Foundation, Australia)

concoct a deal with the Trades Union Congress to cut wages and benefits. When it was turned down, he caved in to the bankers and, like Hughes in Australia before him, left the Labour Party and formed a government with Liberals and Conservatives. In his early days MacDonald was an outspoken opponent of the First World War and an inspiration to the labour movement. For almost ten years he had dominated the Labour Party, but his reputation suffered tragically with his decision to turn his back on the party he helped build.

The Australian Labor Party was trounced in the 1931 federal election, which was followed by defeats in state elections the following year. The only exception was Queensland, which had a habit of bucking the national trend. There, Bill Smith was Labor Party leader, continuing a remarkable Scottish pedigree in the state's politics. Before him, Matthew Reid, Andrew Fisher, William Spence, William Kidston and a number of other Scots had played leading roles in the Queensland Labor Party.

Smith was born in 1887 in Invergowrie, Perthshire and was a painter and decorator by trade. He moved to Glasgow and joined a Socialist discussion group that had been formed in the shipyard where he worked. He suffered from a bronchial condition that caused him severe discomfort, and doctors advised him to move to a warmer climate. When Andrew Fisher toured Scotland in 1911, Smith attended one of his meetings and was so impressed he made up his mind to emigrate to Australia. Six months later he arrived in Queensland and found a job at his trade in Mackay. He joined the Australian Workers Union and was elected president of the local branch in 1913. Two years later he won the Mackay seat for Labor, becoming a member of the Queensland parliament at the age of twenty-seven.

Unlike most other state Labor parties, Queensland was united against First World War conscription and did not suffer the same splits as elsewhere. During the conscription referendum Smith gained a reputation as an outstanding orator and was in hot demand throughout Australia. His anti-war speeches infuriated Prime Minister Billy Hughes, who inaccurately described him as 'an Irishman from Glasgow down here talking Gaelic treason'. Much to Hughes' disgust, Smith became a minister in the Queensland government as Labor started a reign of fourteen years of power in the state. He was a skilful parliamentarian who took over the Labor leadership prior to the 1932 Queensland election. He won against the national swing, the first of four consecutive election victories during the Depression.

William (Bill) Smith – from Invergowrie, Perthshire – was premier of Queensland from 1932–44. Smith was one of a long list of Scots who were prominent in the Queensland Labor Party. (Courtesy State Library of Queensland)

Communist support grows

The Communist Party started to gain more support, especially among trade union activists, as the Depression continued. In 1936 Jack Miles organised a national tour that took him around the Australian mining towns, where he received enthusiastic receptions. Even the Caledonian Societies warmly welcomed him wherever he went. The party began to re-establish itself in industry and started building mass popular organisations through which it expanded its influence and membership. The most important of these were the Militant Minority Movement, the Unemployed Workers Movement, and the Movement Against War and Fascism.

The Militant Minority Movement was designed to appeal to shop stewards and active trade unionists who rejected the compromises of right-wing Social Democratic union leaders. It had notable success in key industries and helped Communists win support in union elections. In 1935 Communists held 375 trade union positions across Australia, mostly at shop-steward level. By 1937 this had risen to a thousand positions, some of which were on the executive bodies of major unions and professional associations, such as those for teachers and actors. The Militant Minority Movement was particularly successful in the mining industry, where the Miners Federation president, Charles Nelson, and the Secretary, Bill Orr, were both Communists.

Nelson was born at Broxburn, West Lothian. Orphaned at the age of two, he was brought up by highly political grandparents. He left school at thirteen to work in the shale mines and three years later he joined the Independent Labour Party. When he was twenty he emigrated to New South Wales, where he worked as a miner near Lithgow. During the 1916 anti-conscription campaign he was one of the most vocal mining-union activists. He also ran Marxist education classes throughout the war and was a founding member of the Australian Communist Party. Many of the students from his Marxist classes followed him, including Scotsmen Jock Jamieson and Jock Lundip, who were both active in the miners' union. Nelson was one of the most vociferous leaders of the Militant Minority Movement, which gradually began to dominate the Miners Federation. In 1934 Nelson won a resounding victory in the election for president.

The Miners Federation secretary Bill Orr was from Bellshill and came to Australia after serving in the British armed forces during the First World War. Born in 1900, Orr left school at the age of nine to work in the Lanarkshire coalmines. He emigrated to New South Wales and settled in Lithgow, where he attended Nelson's Marxist classes. Like Jock Garden, he had been a preacher in a Nonconformist sect, and his stirring oratory assisted his rise to prominence. Orr had never held any position in the Miners Federation, but after he joined the Communist Party, the Militant Minority supported him for general secretary.

The two Scottish friends and Communists worked well together, leading negotiations on pay and conditions, and jointly writing a number of pamphlets on the mining industry. Pay settlements were generally reached through arbitration, but in 1938 the Miners Federation called the first national coal strike since 1916. Substantial concessions were won, particularly on health and safety. The dual Scottish leadership lasted until 1940, when Orr resigned as secretary due to ill health, although he continued to work on behalf of the miners as a member of the Commonwealth Coal Board. Nelson continued as president and was the figurehead in a battle between the right and left of the labour movement for the control of its newspaper. He became managing director of the *Labor Daily*, and continued in the same role with its successor newspaper, the *Daily News*. But he was prone to overwork and on several occasions suffered physical breakdowns.

The Communist International had realised that attacks on Labor Party members and Social Democratic union officials were alienating some of the very people they were trying to convince. The rise of Fascism in Europe made unity imperative, and therefore the line on Social Democrats changed in 1935. The image of party leaders also changed. Jack Miles was given a makeover in an attempt to transform him into an inspiring working-class leader. Jean Devanny, who had once described Miles as tense, volatile and cutting, now spoke of him as a political genius with a deep tenderness underlying his hard exterior.

The advance of the Communist Party during the 1930s was brought to a temporary halt in 1940 when it was banned for its anti-war policy. The party opposed the war when the Soviet Union entered a non–aggression pact with Germany in 1939. The war was condemned as imperialist and some trade union support was lost. Police raided the homes of known party members, publications were removed and all party assets confiscated. The party went underground and Jack Miles wrote articles and pamphlets under the pseudonym of A. Mason. There were also bitter divisions within the party, and when Charles Nelson refused to accept the line, he lost Communist support in the union and was defeated by a loyal party member in an election for union president in 1941. Although the Communist Party reversed its policy when Germany invaded the Soviet Union in 1941, the ban was not lifted until 1942.

Labor returned to government in 1941, with John Curtin as prime minister. There were two Scots with senior ministerial responsibilities. John Dedman from Kirkcudbrightshire was a member of the War Cabinet and had the unenviable task of reorganising wartime production. He had only become a member of parliament in 1940, but his ability was immediately recognised by John Curtin. His role was to ensure resources were diverted to military and essential needs, resulting in unpopular, and sometimes petty, impositions of controls. Dubbed the minister for 'austerity', one of his department's orders was that tails be docked from men's shirts as an unnecessary luxury. 'Lumbago Jack', as Dedman was then called, also won many admirers for his achievements, even among those who criticised his style. After the war he held two of the most important portfolios in the government. As the minister responsible for post-war reconstruction, his department was charged with implementing the government's full employment programme. In 1946 he was made minister of defence, a position he held until he left parliament in 1949.

The only other Scot in government was James Fraser from Forres, Morayshire. A driver with the Western Australian Tramways, Fraser was an official of the Tramways Employees' Union before winning a Senate seat in 1937. Minister for external territories for the first two years of the Labor government, he was given the health and social security portfolio in 1943. He was credited as the architect of Labor's social security reform programme, and later became minister for the army in 1945 and minister for trade and customs from 1946.

Communist influence grew during the rest of the war and by 1944 the membership stood at a record 23,000. The Communist Party won a seat in the Queensland parliament and control of a county in New South Wales. Its support in the trade union movement remained very strong and it was estimated that 40 per cent of unions were influenced by the Communist Party. However, between 1945 and 1950 the Cold War transformed the Soviet Union from great ally to major threat and gravely thwarted Communist parties throughout the world. The time had come for a new party leader, and Miles was replaced as general secretary in 1948. The Australian security service still kept him under surveillance, but in 1953 one of their agents reported 'the grand old man of Australian Communism had developed into a kindly little man, ageing and whimsical'.

The Andrew Fisher Bust in Ballarat Botanical Gardens. Until Bob Hawke took over in 1983, Fisher was the longest serving Australian Labor Prime Minister, winning three elections.

Andrew Fisher's legacy

Andrew Fisher was the longest serving Labor prime minister before Bob Hawke took over in 1983. His three election victories changed for ever the way Australians thought about social aspirations. The fact that a man from a humble mining background was voted into national office and trusted to lead Australia gave them a lasting pride in their country. Fisher disparaged honours and decorations, turning down a knighthood and the French government's Légion d'Honneur. He also refused to allow discussion on the subject of having Australia's capital city named after him. But one honour he did accept was the Freedom of the Burgh of Kilmarnock in 1911.

Fisher's appointment as Australian High Commissioner to Britain ended in 1921 and, torn between Australia and Britain, he chose to remain in London. He sought the nomination for prospective parliamentary Labour Party candidate for Kilmarnock, but failed to win local party support. Disenchanted at the outcome, he returned to Australia and tried to win support for a Sydney seat, but suffered a similar disappointment. The early onset of Alzheimer's disease had a debilitating effect, and by the time of his death in 1930, aged sixty-six, he was unable to write his own name. In 1930 British Prime Minister Ramsay MacDonald unveiled a memorial over Fisher's grave in Hampstead Cemetery in London, and in 1978 a memorial garden was opened by the Australian High Commissioner on the banks of Carmel Water in Crosshouse. It features a cairn bearing four plaques, which together make up a picture of Fisher's life.

Chapter 10

Doug Cameron and the Australian engineers

After the Second World War the Australian government started an extensive immigration scheme that was designed to boost its small population. Australians had felt vulnerable during the war and were concerned that they were unable to defend their vast land mass against military attack. This gave rise to the slogan 'populate or perish' and set the scene for an ambitious programme that included assisted passages for those wishing to make their home in Australia. When it was announced that immigrants could travel for only £10, there was a euphoric response. Hundreds of thousands of Britons registered with the scheme. They sought to escape the harsh post-war economic environment, which was contrasted with tantalising promises of sunshine, opportunity and a new way of life. In the quarter-century following the war 1.5 million people left Britain for Australia.

Initially, old troopships were used to transport the migrants, and conditions on board were spartan, but by the late 1950s the liners were more like floating hotels, with swimming pools, cinemas, dance halls and organised entertainment. Many remember the sea journey to Australia as the holiday of a lifetime. The 12,000-mile voyage took three to four weeks by way of the Mediterranean, passing through the Suez Canal and onwards across the Indian Ocean to the main Australian cities of Perth, Melbourne and Sydney. On the way, the ship docked at exotic places such as Gibraltar, Naples, Port Said, Aden and Bombay. The immigrants felt like wealthy tourists, a great change from the conditions endured by their predecessors the century before.

By the 1970s immigrants began arriving by plane, the route of choice for Doug and Elaine Cameron, who had decided to make a new life for themselves and their thirteen-month-old daughter, Lynne. After he was made redundant by one engineering company, and forced to work nightshifts in another, Cameron had decided that prospects in Scotland were bleak. Born in Bellshill, Lanarkshire in 1951, he attended Bellshill Academy, and by his own admission he underachieved. Desperate to leave school, and with his teachers encouraging him out of the gate, he started an apprenticeship as a fitter at Clyde Crane in Mossend. Two years later he moved to Wie Way Watson in Bellshill, where he finished his time. Watson was a chain-manufacturing company based in England and had come to Scotland on a decentralisation grant. But when the grant ran out, the company packed up their equipment and returned to England, leaving Cameron out of work. Although he had no difficulty finding another job at Stewart and Lloyds' Mossend steelworks, the newly married couple loathed the compulsory night-shift work. With the recently elected Conservative government prepared to allow much of Scottish manufacturing industry to collapse, the lure of Australia became stronger.

After Labour's shock defeat in the 1970 general election, trade unions braced themselves for a period of conflict. The new Tory Prime Minister, Ted Heath, vowed there would be no support for what he described as 'lame duck industries'. Scotland had its fair share of those that fitted Heath's classification, with shipbuilding the obvious example. British yards, which had built half of world shipping in the 1950s, were now responsible for only 6 per cent. Clydeside, which had once been the world's leading shipbuilding centre, was reduced to just seven yards. In 1967 a consortium of shipbuilders came together, with Labour government support, under the title of Upper Clyde Shipbuilders (UCS). However, the new Conservative government decided to allow the yards to go bankrupt, and in so doing, provoked one of the most extraordinary union campaigns of the century.

Refusing to accept redundancy, the workers occupied the yards. They continued to work on the existing order books under the control and management of the shop stewards. The UCS 'work-in' and the 'right to work' campaign that followed captured the imagination and sympathy of the public at home and abroad. Demonstrations of over 100,000 took place in Glasgow, and police chiefs warned the government they would not be able to maintain law and order if the yards closed. The prime minister capitulated and changed the government's industrial and economic policy. Before the government could recover from this humiliation, the miners inflicted even more damage by winning national strikes in 1972 and 1974. The latter ended the Tories' short period in office and heralded the return of a Labour government. The British trade union movement was seen as a formidable force in the country, and reached its peak during this period with a Trade Union Congress membership of over thirteen million.

Doug Cameron was a product of this background and unions were an integral part of his culture. A member of the Amalgamated Engineering

Union, he was a regular attendee at branch meetings and represented the apprentices. Ambitious, self-reliant and energetic, Cameron in many senses displayed the authentic spirit of Australia's working-class immigrants. At twenty-two, he was of medium height and build, and his serious countenance revealed a tough, determined, no-nonsense attitude, characteristics that he put to good use throughout a career which took him to the top position in his union. When he entered the Senate in his fifties he had hardly put on an ounce in weight, but his features reflected a colourful and challenging life. His assured manner and pleasant smile put colleagues at ease, but his eyes carried a warning that he did not suffer fools gladly, and enemies even less.

One of Australia's political bloggers wrote about his presence in the Senate: 'Doug Cameron is a Scottish-born, hard-headed, hard-wired trade unionist ... For my money I don't think there is another parliamentarian who could handle themselves in a brawl quite like Cameron could. Today's Senate committee was classic Cameron. The Adversary was out in full force and effect. Cameron stamped on Professor Sinclair Davidson. It got very ugly in a couple of places. Let me say this for Senator Cameron. He will not back down. Ever. Doug Cameron is the sort of mad Scot you would love to have by your side during hairy adventures. And the sort of guy you'd shit your pants if you were facing him.'

Shortly after arriving in Sydney in 1973, Cameron found a job at the city's Garden Island dockyard, Australia's equivalent of Rosyth. The yard was full of Scottish workers and Doug Rowland, one of the engineering shop stewards, came from Gallowhill in Paisley. He had served his apprenticeship as a fitter/turner at A.W. Smith & Co. in Tradeston, Glasgow and after a spell in the Merchant Navy, he emigrated to Australia in 1971. Soon after starting work at the Sydney dockyard, he became a shop steward, following the footsteps of hundreds of other Scottish engineers. Scots had a proud history in the engineering union, with a number of outstanding figures playing a major part in its formation and its progress. Unknown to Doug Cameron at the time, he was about to add another important chapter to its development.

The growth of the Amalgamated Society of Engineers

The union was established in 1852 as the Australian branch of the Amalgamated Society of Engineers (ASE) by twenty-six engineers who had been blacklisted in Britain after a national strike. The branch was formed at sea, and one of the committee members elected was Daniel

Dalgleish, a native of Alloa, who played a significant role in the growth of the union. He became one of the few working-class representatives in any parliament in the world when he won a seat on the New South Wales legislative council in 1860. Since parliamentary representatives received no payment at that time, a collection was taken by fellow trade unionists. He was presented with 165 sovereigns, accompanied by a testimonial, which stated 'Called as you were from the ranks of labour to represent your own class … we have felt it our bounden duty to assist you to our utmost to carry out this experiment to a successful issue.'

After Dalgleish's election to parliament, other Scottish leaders of the union emerged as it increased in size and divided into various branches. David Bennet from Dundee arrived in Melbourne in 1856 and worked at the Langlands foundry. He became secretary of the Melbourne branch in 1865 and was also president and secretary of the Melbourne Trades Hall Council at different stages of his career. William Miller, a pattern-maker from Glasgow, led the Sydney branch and was a foundation member of the New South Wales Trades and Labor Council in 1871 (see Chapter 8, pages 247 and 250). His most celebrated success was achieving the eight-hour day for Sydney engineers. When a second branch was formed in Melbourne, William Campbell, who had served his apprenticeship at John Maughan and Co. in Glasgow, was appointed secretary. With the growth of the number of branches in the colonies (including New Zealand), the Australasian Council was set up in 1888 to cover most of the functions of the ASE executive council in London. William Campbell became its first chairman, while continuing as Melbourne district secretary.

The employers viewed Campbell as a formidable, militant advocate, and he often only had to threaten strike action to achieve his ends. A tough and highly experienced negotiator, he waited until the engineering shops had full order books before he took on the employers. In 1889 he submitted a list of demands. In addition to a substantial wage increase, he included apprenticeship training and a closed shop covering the whole of Melbourne. He gave the employers a month to respond, catching them off guard. Just before the deadline expired, the Employers Association conceded all union demands. The grateful Melbourne engineers decided to increase their union subscriptions to make his position full time, and Campbell became the first paid official of the ASE in Australia.

The victory in Melbourne served as a tremendous stimulus to other areas as the union became more confident of its strength and more militant in carrying out its objectives. In Sydney, engineers refused to work with non-members and in Adelaide, disputes were won regarding overtime and shift payments. By now Campbell was one of the best-known union leaders in Australia and he began to link political and trade union issues. In 1890 he addressed a rally of fifty thousand people during the maritime strike. Melbourne newspaper the *Argus* carried a report of his speech calling for nationalisation of key industries: 'People possess the railways, and why should the people not also possess the gasworks, and the shipping, and break up those huge monopolies?'

Campbell held every senior position in his union as well as being president and secretary of the Iron Trades Council, trustee of the Melbourne Trades Hall Council and president of the eight-hour day committee. Even the employers accepted him as an ardent fighter for Australian manufacturing and were grateful for Campbell's support on the issue of protectionism. His evidence to the royal commission on customs and excise tariffs helped sway the commission to impose import duties of 25 per cent. Failing health ended his engineering union work and in 1908 he lost his sight. A huge collection was raised for him throughout the trade union movement in Australia. True to form, he then became president of the Association for the Blind, and continued in that role until he died in 1913.

Campbell's engineering union positions were filled by John Smith, an Edinburgh-born blacksmith. An exceptionally talented and highly creative union official, Smith played a central role in the history of the ASE. To encourage open debate on a wide range of topics, he set up the Melbourne Sociological Club, where union members could discuss political, social and economic issues. One of the hot topics was the issue of political affiliation, but the engineers resisted joining the Labor Party until later. The club attracted many younger members, including Edinburgh-born William Earsman, who later became one of the founders of the Australian Communist Party (see Chapter 9, pages 281-283). After suffering the loss of a son in 1911, Smith resigned as secretary of the Australasian Council, but was back within a couple of years as chairman, and was still acknowledged as the pre-eminent figure in the union.

In the ten years he led the engineers, Smith introduced major changes to the structure of the union. During the First World War, thousands of Australian engineers had gone to work in Britain, and those who were based in Scotland had encountered the shop-steward system. The returning workers liked the idea of electing union representatives at their place of work and giving them power to bargain on their behalf.

They demanded the same rights in Australia, and Smith ensured the union constitution was changed to reflect the new role of shop stewards. Some of his ideas were ahead of their time and it was decades before they were implemented. He advocated a union for all metalworkers, embracing engineers, boilermakers, moulders and other associated trades. He went further and suggested widening the union franchise beyond skilled tradesmen to accept semi-skilled workers and labourers into membership. He presided over his last major conference in 1922 and retired as chairman a year later, when the ASE affiliated to the Australian Labor Party.

Affiliation to the Labor Party saw the engineers playing a more important political role, but divisions over policy often caused factional splits. Before, during and after the Second World War the union was a battleground in the power struggle between left-and right-wing ideology. By 1945, the Communist Party and their left-wing allies were in control. A few years later the Groupers, a right-wing organisation founded by the Labor Party, had retaken the union. By the mid-1960s the left had re-established itself, and has had the ascendancy ever since.

In 1968 the Australian engineers gained full autonomy from their British parent organisation, and the opportunity was taken to shape a modern constitution for the union. Five years later, a merger with the boilermakers and sheet-metal workers took place, and the new union of 160,000 members was named the Amalgamated Metal Workers Union (AMWU). This event coincided with the election in 1973 of the first Labor Government in Canberra for twenty-three years.

Housing problems, Cameron roused

It also coincided with Doug Cameron's arrival in Australia. Although jobs were plentiful, his most immediate concern was finding a place to stay. It was ironic that the most common reason emigrants gave for leaving Britain after the war was the shortage of housing when, unbeknown to them, the situation in Australia was far worse. Most new arrivals were forced to live in migrant hostel accommodation, the standard of which was significantly lower than that of housing at home. The Australian authorities seemed to have assumed that British working-class families all lived in urban slums or in rural poverty, and thought the immigrants would be grateful for any accommodation provided. The migrant hostels provided minimum comfort and were often hastily constructed corrugated-iron Nissan huts, refurbished former army barracks, or old wool sheds.

They were cold during the winter and insufferably hot in the summer. Men and women were separated into single-sex barracks, bathrooms were shared, and communal dining rooms served food that was often unpalatable. The intention was that migrants stayed only a few weeks, but some lodged for months, or even years. At times the hostels became cauldrons of seething discontent. For many who had left Britain with high expectations, the appalling conditions in the hostels shattered their illusions of Australia. With their confidence crushed and future plans undermined, a quarter of the migrants returned home, with hostel conditions cited as the main reason.

Most migrants only came with enough money to last a couple of months, so saving a deposit to buy a house was out of the question. There was a two-year waiting list for council housing in the cities and private renting was expensive. Even rent for the hostels amounted to half of a skilled worker's salary. In 1967 they were hiked by fifteen percent, provoking sporadic rent strikes. Carl Kirkwood, a Scottish immigrant, led a rent strike at the Preston Hostel in Melbourne. Despite threats of eviction and deportation, the protest met with partial success and received support from trade unions. However, most Australians thought the British were ungrateful for their provisions and dubbed them 'the whingeing Poms'. But Australia's reputation was tarnished by the controversy over conditions in the hostels and British enthusiasm for emigration waned as a result.

The Endeavour migrant hostel in a suburb of Sydney was the place that Elaine and Doug Cameron called home when they arrived in 1973. By then the situation in the hostels had improved, with advice and support readily available to immigrants. They socialised with other Scots, who helped them fit in to their new environment. They wanted a place of their own as soon as possible, but had to stay in the hostel for a year before they had enough money to move on. However, work was plentiful, and after nine months in Australia, Cameron left the Sydney dockyard, where he'd started his first job, to join General Motors at its Pagewood plant. Within a year, he was on the move again to National Springs in Alexandria. The pay was much better than anything he had earned in Scotland but the cost of accommodation swallowed up the difference in wages. Sydney was particularly costly and to have any prospect of decent housing, Cameron knew he had to find work outside Australia's biggest metropolis. In 1975 he answered an Electricity Commission advertisement for a maintenance fitter near Muswellbrook in the Hunter Valley, New South Wales. The

Doug Cameron, from Bellshill, Lanarkshire was elected AMWU organiser for the Hunter Valley in 1982, his first full-time union position. In 1986 he became Assistant State Secretary and Assistant National Secretary a few years later. He led negotiations with the Australian Metal Trades Federation. (Courtesy AMWU)

job was at the massive Liddell coal-fired power station, which was fed from sixteen coalmines by overland conveyors. The main attraction for the Camerons was the cottage that came with the job.

But when they arrived in freezing winter conditions, they found that the house had been vandalised and was unfit for human habitation. A second daughter, Fiona, had been born the month before they arrived, and Cameron was incensed that no one had checked the property. Management seemed unconcerned that a three-year-old toddler and a month-old baby were forced to live in squalor. The only help came from the local trade union official, who demanded action from the employer. Cameron also observed that housing in Muswellbrook was based on a system of industrial apartheid: the blue-collar workers' houses were built around the sewage works, while the managers lived on the hill overlooking the golf course. Furious about the housing situation, Cameron vowed to become more actively involved in the union, and was elected shop steward for the 160 fitters who worked at the power station.

An authoritarian management style led to a poisonous industrial relations atmosphere. In response, the workforce became more militant and determined, and there was no one more resolute than Cameron. Normally quiet and restrained, the pugnacious side of his character prevailed when provoked by ruthless management decisions. A number of lengthy strikes broke out over allowances, housing and safety issues. Some lasted up to six weeks, placing enormous pressure on family finances and a strain on personal relationships. But at the same time, the power station was an excellent grounding for shop stewards, and a number of them later became full-time officials. Cameron's leadership skills were recognised outside his group of engineers, and when elections for chairman of the combined shop stewards' committee were held, he was the sole nominee.

After seven years in the power station, Cameron was elected AMWU organiser for the Hunter Valley, a new full-time position created to deal with the expanding numbers coming into the area. The next four years were spent travelling extensively throughout rural New South Wales, opening his eyes to the struggle of people trying to survive the extremes of life in the bush. His responsibilities were the negotiation of pay and local agreements in mining, general engineering and construction. With 2,500 highly demanding members to serve, the job required a resilient and dedicated full-time official. Disputes broke out frequently, but the most difficult problems were the pay relativities between groups of workers, which often caused internal union friction. Cameron began to earn the admiration of the workforce and the grudging respect of the employers.

During this period Cameron's mentor was Bob Adamson, a boilermakers' shop steward from Ireland, who was a member of the Australian Communist Party. He saw Adamson as a role model, admiring his integrity, commitment and tireless effort on behalf of his members. In the Hunter Valley there was no meaningful Communist Party presence so Cameron joined the Labor Party and remained a member throughout his career. Adamson made a huge impression and his advice, inspiration and political analysis was gratefully received, particularly in relation to international issues

Australian unions: international and race issues

Australian trade unions have a proud history of supporting international solidarity campaigns. The late 1960s saw the start of mass movements against South African apartheid and the Vietnam War, which stimulated thousands of young Australians into political action. Many of Australia's trade unionists joined in the protests, including John Scott, South Australia secretary of the AMWU.

Scott was from Hamilton in Lanarkshire and had his first run-in with an employer while he was still at St John's Grammar School in the town. He had a milk run in the mornings before school and, after being offered a smaller pay rise than expected, led the rest of the delivery boys out on strike. When he left school he trained as a motor mechanic and won the West of Scotland Apprentice of the Year award in 1954. He completed his national service when he was twenty-four and shortly afterwards settled in Adelaide, South Australia. Not long after he started work at the General Motors plant in the city, a colleague was killed in a workplace accident. Management's disregard for safety sparked Scott's involvement in the union and he became a shop steward shortly afterwards. He came to national prominence in 1963 as one of the left-wing leaders of a successful three-week strike, and was elected to the union's top post in South Australia in 1969.

During a demonstration against the Springboks rugby tour in 1971 Scott was arrested and beaten up by police. Also active in the anti-Vietnam War campaign, he met a delegation from North Vietnam that visited Australia. The Australian trade unions campaigned jointly with the Labor Party for the withdrawal of Australian troops, a policy that was delivered by the Labor government in 1973.

Scott recognised that he did not make the best of his opportunities at school, and became passionate about working-class education. Through a voluntary levy of members, he established union education classes. He was the most prominent member of the executive of the Workers Educational Association and was highly influential on the Adelaide University board of adult education. Throughout this period, he held senior positions in the Labor Party, and in 1980 was selected as the candidate for Hindmarsh in the federal elections. He resigned his union position when he won the contest and joined the House of Representatives, holding the seat until he retired in 1993.

Alongside the support for solidarity movements was an awakening consciousness about racism in Australia. Union policies came under intense scrutiny and the attitudes of their members were examined. Australian unions had a chequered history in relation to non-white immigrants and to the indigenous Australian population. The emerging unions in the 1850s had expressed hostility towards the forty thousand Chinese who worked in the goldfields. Workers from the Pacific Islands, brought in as cheap labour on the sugar plantations in Queensland, were subjected to the same treatment. Unions had advocated a 'white Australia' policy to curb non-white immigration, which found fertile ground with successive governments, including Labor administrations. Alongside the general treatment of the Aboriginal population, this was an embarrassing chapter in Australian trade union history. However, the trade union movement has long since recognised the errors of the past and was in the forefront of the campaigns to change racist attitudes and policies. Many unions now have officers responsible for the indigenous people and committees of indigenous activists. The fact that Australia is now striving to be a multicultural country is in no small part due to the efforts and perseverance of the trade union movement.

Cameron's rise to the top

The Labor Government that had welcomed Doug Cameron to Australia did not last for very long. Under the leadership of Gough Whitlam, it carried out a number of radical changes, including the introduction of universal health insurance, and social reform of policies such as divorce and family law. But its economic policies were challenged by business sections of Australian society. The Senate had a Conservative majority and in 1975 blocked the government's budget. But the government refused to back down and the stalemate prompted the intervention of Sir John

Kerr, the Governor General of Australia, who was a British government appointee. A constitutional crisis erupted when Kerr dismissed Whitlam and ordered a general election. Despite doubts over the legality of the Governor General's actions and the condemnation of large sections of the Australian public, Labor lost the subsequent election. The Liberal victors held power until 1983, when Bob Hawke, former president of the Australian Council of Trade Unions, became Prime Minister.

Doug Cameron was enjoying his job in rural New South Wales and was seen as one of the most reliable and competent full-time officials in the AMWU. When a vacancy arose in 1986 for a more senior position, he stood as the left candidate and had no difficulty in overcoming his right-wing opponent in the election. Cameron now had responsibility for the Metal Trades Federation of Unions and led pay negotiations with the manufacturing employers in New South Wales. One of his first tasks was to break a Government-imposed wage freeze. Success in this was followed by an equally fruitful campaign for compulsory superannuation. His outstanding leadership qualities led to a further promotion to the national office where he now led negotiations with the Metal Trades Federation for the whole of Australia. His key tactical weapon was 'pattern bargaining', a practice in negotiations where a settlement with one employer becomes the precedent for the industry. The first step in the process is to identify an employer with a full order book and high profits. Once a favourable settlement is reached and a contract agreed, the union then declares this to be the 'pattern' for the industry. It then demands the same settlement from other employers. Although tough and unbending in negotiations, Cameron could still take a conciliatory approach and was prepared to compromise when it suited.

Prime Minister Hawke inherited major economic problems from the Liberals. Budget deficits and high unemployment rates initially led to clashes with the unions. But the unions compromised and accepted an incomes policy and more flexible working arrangements. Hawke became the longest-serving and most electorally successful Labor prime minister, winning four consecutive federal elections until the Liberals defeated him in 1996. That year, Doug Cameron became national secretary of the AMWU at forty-six years of age. There was a broad consensus amongst the main groups of activists in the union that Cameron was the natural successor for the leading position. He was the sole nominee for the top position, which was an unusual situation for the AMWU, but this was an indication of Cameron's ability as well as confirmation of the stability of the union.

Initially, the biggest problems he faced as national secretary were internal issues associated with recent amalgamations. The union kept the same acronym, but its name changed to the Australian Manufacturing Workers Union. Draughtsmen and technical employees, printers, vehicle builders and food-packaging workers were all absorbed to make the AMWU the biggest union in Australia. Cameron spent a great deal of time trying to build a cohesive and durable union, but the multiple mergers provoked personality clashes and cultural divisions. This was not surprising, as the component organisations had long and proud histories and traditions. The amalgamations of the vehicle builders' and printing unions were particularly tough.

Prominent Scots in the AMWU

Scottish accents were heard in most parts of the union. At the Garden Island naval dockyard, Doug Rowland, who was a shop steward when Cameron worked there, was elected convener, and then appointed a full-time organiser in 1983. He was later promoted to senior resource officer, co-ordinating health and safety and industrial research. Ian Fraser, a welder from Motherwell, filled Rowland's convener's role at the yard. A member of the Boilermakers Union in Scotland, he became a shop steward soon after he started in the dockyard in 1982 and rose to become secretary of the joint shop stewards' committee. He later became a full-time official for the Newcastle district of the union.

Danny Sibbald from Renfrew arrived in Adelaide in 1973 when John Scott was leading the union in South Australia. He had been a member of the Boilermakers Union and a shop steward on the Clyde, and his experience proved invaluable in South Australia. After a number of years as a steward he was given a full-time appointment as a state organiser. Another Scotsman in the South Australia office was the union advocate David Gray, who had come to Australia with his parents when he was a young boy. Born in Rutherglen, near Glasgow, Gray specialised in compensation legislation and other legal services for the AMWU.

In Queensland the state organiser was George Wilson, who had served his apprenticeship as a compositor at Gilmore and Lawrence in Glasgow. A member of the Scottish Typographical Association, he initially emigrated to Wellington, New Zealand in 1958, where he lived for ten years before moving to Sydney. He was father of the chapel in the *Sun* newspaper group and was branch president of the Printing and Kindred Industries Union. After the merger, he became an assistant

Doug Rowland from Gallowhill in Paisley was a convener of shop stewards at Sydney's Garden Island dockyard, which employed a large number of Scottish workers. He was later appointed a full-time organiser in 1983 and became the AMWU's senior resource officer.

secretary in the printing division as well as state organiser in the Brisbane office of the union.

In addition to Doug Rowland and Ian Fraser from the Garden Island dockyard, John Parkin was another Scotsman in New South Wales to be made a full-time official. Born in Rothesay on the Isle of Bute, he served his time as a fitter and was a member of the Amalgamated Engineering Union. In 1980 he emigrated to Sydney, where he worked at Weir Engineering and then at Avon Products. A shop steward for the maintenance fitters in both companies, he was an AMWU delegate to the Sydney Trades and Labor Council. Appointed the union's health and safety officer, he later specialised in training and education.

In Western Australia a number of Scots were prominent. Jim Davidson from Gartcosh, Lanarkshire served his apprenticeship as a fitter, working on agricultural machinery and heavy goods vehicles. His last job before he left for Australia in 1981 was with Brechin Transport in Glasgow, where he was an active member of the Transport and General Workers Union. Within four years of his arrival in Perth, he was elected convener of the construction site where he worked and then became a full-time organiser, covering a region the size of Scotland. The industries he dealt with included coalmining, the aluminium industry, general engineering, construction, abattoirs, food and the chemical industry.

Jock Ferguson: a labour lion

The leading AMWU figure in Western Australia, and one of Doug Cameron's closest allies, was from Glasgow. Jock Ferguson was a colourful character and a skilful negotiator. He and Cameron enjoyed nothing better than a bit of banter about Celtic and Rangers. Born in the Possilpark area of the city, Ferguson attended St Agnes's primary school and St Augustine's secondary in Milton. His grandfather was a convenor of the Boilermakers Union and a member of the Communist Party. After school he served an apprenticeship as a fitter in a shipyard, joined the Amalgamated Engineering Union, and immediately volunteered to represent his fellow apprentices as shop steward. Later he told the story of his first attempt to lead a strike.

'Keen to get a share of a new pay deal and full of youthful exuberance, the Boilermakers apprentices' steward and I called a strike, with the intention of staying out until the apprentices got their share. It lasted only long enough for us to be summoned to the yard manager's office and informed that, as apprentices, our indentures did not allow us to

George Wilson, who was a compositor in Glasgow, became Father of the Chapel in the Sun newspaper group in Australia. After the merger with the Printing and Kindred Industries Union he became Assistant Secretary of the AMWU printing division.

take strike action, and that all the two hundred apprentices would be sacked. Although shocked, I took the news decidedly better than the boilermaker's steward, who burst into tears, saying, "Ma mammy's gonnae kill me!" Crestfallen, we bumped into my grandfather when leaving the office and told him the story. He then had a brief chat with the yard manager and the threat was not carried out. Needless to say the episode taught me a lot about strategy and negotiations. My grandfather's words still ring in my ears: "Never, ever do that again!" I never have but to this day I don't know if I was set up by my grandfather and the manager.'

Married when he was twenty-one, Ferguson joined the Merchant Navy after he and his wife separated five years later. When his ship docked in New Zealand he liked the look of the country and decided to stay. After a few years, he moved on again before settling down in Carnarvon, Western Australia, where he lived for ten years. Working mainly on construction sites, Ferguson was usually elected shop steward. In the early 1990s he was appointed full-time AMWU organiser on a huge construction site at the Burrup peninsula, where there were several thousand AMWU members. It was the base for offshore gas drilling operations and the largest resource project ever undertaken in Australia.

Although wages were high, the conditions in the isolated outpost were among the harshest on the planet. There were major health and safety problems for the multicultural workforce, and Ferguson had only been in the job for a day when there was a strike over asbestos handling. Three thousand angry workers demanded action from their union official and he admitted later to feeling scared stiff when he faced them on that first occasion. Many of the issues could not be resolved on site and Ferguson flew frequently to the industrial relations commission in Perth to settle outstanding problems. Given the size and strategic importance of the project, disputes were often reported on national TV news. After one encounter, Ferguson's strong Glasgow accent became a source of amusement for his Australian colleagues. Interviewed by a news reporter during a major strike, he adjourned to a pub with the shop stewards to watch the programme – only to find that the broadcasters had given his comments subtitles. Afterwards he wrote, tongue in cheek, to the TV company thanking them for their foresight in supplying the subtitles for those of his members who suffered from industrial deafness.

Western Australia was often used to test anti-union laws before they were implemented nationally. Its legislation forbade more than five people to assemble without permission, a law designed to limit the effectiveness

Jock Ferguson was born in Possilpark, Glasgow and worked as a fitter in a Clydeside shipyard. He was appointed full-time AMWU organiser on a huge construction site and went on to become the union's leader in Western Australia. In 2009, he won a seat on the Legislative Council but died just eight months later. (Courtesy AMWU)

of picketing. Like many trade union leaders, Ferguson fell foul of this law on occasion, and was no stranger to the courts after arrests on picket lines. In 1999 he led a group of fifty trade unionists who occupied the state legislature in protest against the anti-union laws. Government business stopped while the group took over the building for two days and nights. Riot police surrounded the parliament and the incident provoked huge national publicity.

Ferguson was famous for his use of wit and humour to settle disputes, a strength acknowledged by workers and employers alike. He was a popular choice when he was elected secretary of the union's Western Australia branch, a position that also carried enormous influence within the Labor Party. When he took over, the AMWU sponsored only one member of the state legislature, but by 2005 there were ten. Four of them became government ministers, and all were union members who had served as shop stewards or full-time officials.

In 2009 Ferguson left his union position when he won a seat on the legislative council. In his maiden speech he told a captivated House a heartbreaking family story. His mother was an unwed Catholic woman, and such was the stigma attached to illegitimate children then that she was sent to a convent to have him. Ferguson was raised by his grandparents, but for years they let him believe they were his parents. His mother lived with them, but he thought she was his sister. Two years after he was born, she had another child, a girl, who was adopted outside the family and whose existence was never mentioned. She grew up with her adopted parents without being told about her birth family. As a teenager she found out by chance that she was adopted, but no one was prepared to discuss the issue. However, following the death of her adopted mother, she began the search for her birth parents. Despite years of fruitless investigations, she did not give up and kept asking questions, writing letters, and knocking on doors. Eventually she found a link that led to her mother, who unfortunately had died some years before. But it came as a shock to discover that she had a brother. It was an even bigger shock for Jock Ferguson when she phoned him from her Greenock home in 2001 to tell him she was his sister.

The real tragedy of the story was that Ferguson and his sister Monica were believed to have been full blood siblings who had been divided for most of their lives by religious bigotry. Their mother was a Catholic and their father a Protestant, and the two had been forbidden to marry. Ferguson explained to the engrossed members of the Legislative Council that 'the discovery of my sister and parentage has highlighted the truly cataclysmic effect that ignorance and discrimination can have on the everyday lives and experiences of families and individuals. My sister was robbed of ever meeting her mother and we were separated from each other for over fifty years. I intend to work hard in this place to build positive changes out of this personal experience, to ensure that as law makers we are always working to break down some of the barriers and prejudices that exclude people and their families from fully participating in our society and achieving personal fulfilment.'

Sadly, Ferguson did not live long enough to contribute to the changes he was so keen to make. In February 2010, just eight months after making his inaugural speech, he died of a heart attack, aged sixty-four. Thousands of mourners attended his funeral, with Doug Cameron leading the eulogies. He was referred to as a 'labour lion' and a legendary figure in the Western Australian trade union movement. Industry chiefs and MPs from across the political spectrum came to pay their respects to one of the most entertaining and well-liked characters in politics. His eight children were present at the funeral and paid moving tributes to their late father. His sister Monica, who travelled from Greenock for the funeral, told the mourners 'Thank God we were eventually re-united ... and took back some of those years that were stolen from us. We enjoyed more quality time than many brothers and sisters do in an entire lifetime. He returned my love a hundredfold.' A bagpiper played 'Flower of Scotland' before the ceremony and 'Scotland the Brave' at the end.

Leftists challenge Cameron

The Scots in full-time positions were reinforced by many more who were convenors, shop stewards and branch officials. This made Doug Cameron feel a bit more secure as national secretary in the face of internal dissent within the AMWU. He belonged to the National Left group of the union, which had been the dominant political block for some time. But he faced a major problem after a militant group known as Workers First came to prominence in Victoria. The group emerged in 1997 in response to a series of bitter and protracted disputes in Melbourne that resulted in permanent workers being replaced with casual labour. Workers First was led by Craig Johnston, who had been a full-time union organiser since 1990. It did not have any specific ideological views, but was critical of Cameron and the National Left group for not taking more direct action against employers.

In the elections for the Victoria executive in the year 2000, Workers First candidates defeated the incumbent leadership who were National Left supporters. Craig Johnston became secretary of the Victoria branch and the scene was set for a confrontation between the two groups. Cameron indicated that he would try to work with the new Victoria leadership, but warned that the tactics of Workers First played straight into the hands of the enemies of the trade union movement. A year later, his predictions seemed to have been proven. In a protest against the loss of twenty-nine jobs, Johnston and his colleagues occupied a Melbourne engineering workshop, but in the process caused damage worth thousands of dollars. They were charged with riot, criminal damage and aggravated burglary. The press had a field day and launched scathing attacks on the AMWU. Cameron was forced to act quickly and decisively. He immediately condemned the action and suspended Johnston from his position. He later expelled him after he was convicted of the charges. Others in Workers First received the same treatment. The Australian Socialist Party, a Trotskyite organisation sympathetic to Workers First, described Cameron's actions as wily and ruthless. They credited him for his patience in waiting until the right moment to pounce and then systematically isolate and destroy Workers First.

Not all the Scots in the union were on Cameron's side. Jim Reid, secretary of the Victoria printing division, opposed the expulsion of Johnston. Reid, from Glasgow, was a former member of the West of Scotland branch of the print union, SOGAT. Although he was not a member of Workers First, he felt the decisions taken by the national leadership were inappropriate and was incensed a few months later when Cameron sacked the national industrial organiser of the printing division. Reid continued in his position, but was regarded with some suspicion by the majority National Left grouping.

This period was a test of Cameron's courage and resolve. Twice in the space of two years he was physically attacked at his home. On the first occasion, unknown assailants wearing balaclavas threatened to kill him. They tried unsuccessfully to open the doors of his car as he pulled into his driveway, and then hurled a brick through the back window. The second assault occurred as he returned home from a local shop with his wife. The attack left him with a broken nose. Police never caught those responsible, but believed they were motivated by internal union disputes. The attacks on Cameron strengthened his position in the AMWU, adding a personal, moral dimension to the political supremacy of his National Left group.

In 1996 Doug Cameron became national secretary of the AMWU and two years later was appointed vice-president of the Australian Council of Trade Unions. He led high profile disputes and was constantly in demand for media interviews. Top: Cameron addressing AMWU Rally in 1998; bottom: Cameron speaking to press during negotiations with Quantas in 2006 (Courtesy AMWU)

Since no perpetrators had been found, all his opponents remained suspect. The police warned him that if a further attack took place, his life could be in danger. He was advised to change his address and with the assistance of the union he moved to a more secure residence outside Sydney. But his main concern was the effect the publicity surrounding the incidents had on the reputation of the union.

In 1998 Cameron had become vice-president of the Australian Council of Trade Unions (ACTU). That year the ACTU was drawn into a bitter dispute between the Maritime Union of Australia and the Patrick Corporation, a large stevedoring company. The Liberal government had introduced anti-union legislation a year before, and the company used it to its advantage. New employment contracts, known as Australian Workplace Agreements, were introduced to counteract the collective bargaining provisions that were enshrined in previous industrial relations law. The Patrick Corporation, in collaboration with the government, dismissed its entire stevedoring workforce and sent balaclava-wearing security staff with guard dogs to evict the dockers after their last shift. The 1,400 men were replaced with casual non-union labour. As leader of the left on the ACTU executive, Cameron urged full support for the dockers from the whole trade union movement. With public opinion on their side, the Maritime Union of Australia blockaded the wharves owned by the company, gradually causing a pile-up of $500m worth of goods. Several months into the dispute, the federal court intervened and ruled in favour of the union. It also found there was an arguable case that the company and the government had participated in a conspiracy. The company was forced to pay out $7.5m to small businesses affected by the dispute.

Bill Oliver and the fight against anti-union legislation

The 1998 Maritime Union dispute was a major test of trade union resolve and discipline. But the legislation that allowed the company to operate in such an aggressive manner was the forerunner of even more draconian anti-union laws. A Conservative coalition government was elected in 2005 with a clear majority in both houses. The first laws it introduced dealt with the building and construction industry, where accepted forms of industrial action were outlawed. New rules were introduced, which carried heavy fines and imprisonment for any breaches. All unions in the construction industry were affected, in particular the Construction, Forestry, Mining and Energy Union (CFMEU).

Bill Oliver (front right) from Kinning Park in Glasgow, at the head of his union contingent on a May Day demonstration in Melbourne, 2002. Oliver became assistant secretary of the Construction, Forestry, Mining, and Energy Union in Victoria and found that much of his time was taken up fighting anti-union legislation.

Bill Oliver, the Victoria secretary of CFMEU, was born in Kinning Park, Glasgow before moving to Drumchapel. After he finished his apprenticeship as a carpenter at Connell's shipyard in Scotstoun in 1971, he emigrated to Melbourne. Working in the construction industry, he became a shop steward and a convener, before being appointed as a field officer and then assistant secretary of the CFMEU. The union has a rich history, with component groups dating back to the 1850s. One of them, the Melbourne stonemasons, spearheaded the eight-hour day movement. Oliver helped to organise a monument in their honour, which stands outside the union's HQ.

To implement the new laws relating to the construction industry, the coalition government set up the Australian Building and Construction Commission. It spent most of its time handing out penalties against the construction unions for engaging in legitimate trade union activities, as defined by the International Labour Organisation. Oliver found himself summoned on many occasions by the Commission to defend his union's actions.

In 2004, he had a frightening experience when arsonists firebombed his house while his twenty-year-old daughter slept upstairs. Oliver and his wife were not present at the time, but neighbours raised the alarm and his daughter escaped unharmed. The homes of two of his union's shop stewards had been torched the week before, but the police were unable to trace the perpetrators. Shrugging aside threats and intimidation, Oliver was elected Victoria secretary of the CFMEU in 2008, the union's top position in the state.

A number of further amendments, given the title Work Choices, were made to Australian labour law in 2005, amounting to the most comprehensive changes to industrial relations in Australia for almost a century. Employer groups supported the new laws but they were bitterly opposed by the trade union movement and by the Labor Party. The ACTU launched a massive campaign entitled Your Rights at Work, investing over $30m aimed at overturning the legislation. It was the biggest union campaign ever launched in Australia, combining workplace organisation with TV advertising and community campaigning. It also targeted vulnerable parliamentary seats held by supporters of the government. Demonstrations against Work Choices attracted over 300,000 at the beginning of 2005, and more than half a million took to the streets in June 2006. The Workers First faction put aside differences with the National Left group as they faced up to the new challenges from the government.

*Bill Oliver addresses a mass meeting of CFMEU members in the Melbourne
Festival Hall in 2011. In 2008 Oliver was the overwhelming choice of his members
for State Secretary, the most senior position of his union in Victoria.*

The outcome of the 2007 general election was a clear majority for the Labor Party and many argued that the union campaign had a significant impact on the result.

During this period, Doug Cameron became one of the best-known figures on Australian TV. As vice-president of the ACTU he was one of the key figures during the campaign and he also led high-profile industrial disputes by the AMWU. Much of the press coverage was hostile and focused on Cameron's politics rather than the issues. In a dispute with a components company, which threatened production in the whole Australian car industry, the press accused him of endangering the Australian economy, and alleged that he deliberately started the strike for political reasons. A number of strikes at Qantas, the airline, made news headlines and put him in the spotlight to explain union action to an angry public. Like many national union leaders, Cameron was demonised by the press and needed substantial reserves of strength and courage as well as support from his colleagues. He showed his mettle on these occasions, his steely resolve matched by his skill at media handling. His clarification of the reasons for the action won a great deal of public sympathy, and he turned much of the public anger towards management. In a dispute with Qantas over a decision to transfer maintenance work on its aircraft from Australia to China, Cameron warned the airline that it would face the fight of its life if it proceeded. He led the campaign to keep the jobs in Australia, winning widespread public support and forcing the airline to review its decision.

Cameron elected to the Senate

In 2007, after over a decade as leader of the AMWU, Cameron announced his intention to stand for the Senate. Selected as the Labor candidate for a seat in New South Wales, he won the election and joined the Senate in 2008. In his maiden speech, he paid his respect to the Ngunnawal people, the indigenous Australians who inhabited the Canberra area. As someone who failed to fulfil his own potential at school, he pleaded for a national programme to modernise the Australian school system. Climate change and the need for environmental sustainability was another of the issues highlighted in the speech. But much of it concentrated on the importance to democracy of employment laws that are seen to be just and even-handed. In particular, he attacked the hated legislation governing the building industry for its anti-democratic powers and breaches of International Labour Organisation conventions. In 2010 Cameron became convener of the national left of the Labor Party.

Senator Doug Cameron, 2009. After leading the AMWU for over a decade, Cameron won a Senate seat in New South Wales in 2008.

A contest for Cameron's successor as national secretary of the AMWU took place. The Workers First faction continued to support the National Left leadership, but a challenge came from Glasgow-born Jim Reid, secretary of the printing division. Supported by the vehicle division, Reid mounted an effective campaign against National Left candidate Dave Oliver, and mustered 40 per cent of the vote. Reid was required to relinquish his position as secretary of the printing division to stand, and had to go back to the tools after his defeat.

The AMWU has changed from the craft based engineering union set up by Daniel Dalgleish and the pioneers who landed in Australia in 1852. It was always one of the most important industrial and political unions in the country and has adapted to the changing industrial climate by merging with others to remain Australia's key union in manufacturing. Doug Cameron was one of a line of Scots who rose to the leadership of the union, but he may not be the last as Australia remains a highly popular destination for young Scots to live and work. Many will take on trade union responsibilities and some will play prominent roles, continuing the notable contribution Scots have made to the Australian trade union and labour movement.

Chapter 11

Peter Fraser and the New Zealand politicians

The small Ross-shire village of Fearn was all set for the visit of its most distinguished son. The warmest of Highland welcomes awaited the international statesman, with a guard of honour and over a thousand friends and well-wishers assembled in the school playground. It was 4 August 1941 and the Right Honourable Peter Fraser, Prime Minister of New Zealand, was coming home. The ceremony continued with a procession to the kirk, where a special service was held. He was then taken to his former workplace in Tain. Revered throughout the Highlands, he received the Freedom of Tain, Inverness and Dingwall, along with many other awards and tributes.

Fraser was the son of a shoemaker whose family had lived in Fearn for generations. The village had around 160 residents when he was born in 1884. Most people lived in stone cottages with thatched roofs, there was a communal well, a post office, a store, a community hall and a primary school. The Free Church of Scotland had a kirk that stood in the bleak countryside to the south of the village, and there was a railway station nearby. Fraser's father was the leading Liberal Party activist in the area, and was well known throughout the parish. His cobbler's shop was a magnet for those in the village interested in political discussion and was christened 'the House of Commons' by the locals. Fraser's mother was a well-read and refined woman who belonged to a family of McLeods who originally came from Assynt in Sutherland. It was an area that had experienced appalling suffering during the Highland Clearances, with thousands of crofters driven off their land to make way for sheep. The McLeod home was burned down and the family wandered the Highlands in search of food and shelter. His mother's stories about the crimes of the absentee Highland landlords had a profound effect on Fraser and his siblings. He often referred to the crofters as 'a dispossessed people', forced from their land by treacherous and greedy landowners.

Scotland introduced free primary-school education in 1889, the year Fraser turned five. Although he was an outstanding pupil, there was no prospect of him continuing to secondary level. His father's income barely managed to feed his four brothers and two sisters, let alone pay secondary-school fees. Instead, Fraser started work as a post office delivery boy before being apprenticed to a carpenter in the village. After a year he transferred to a builder in the nearby town of Tain. He made up for his curtailed education by attending evening classes, studying maths, history and English literature.

At an early age Fraser joined the discussions in the 'House of Commons', enthusiastically advocating the same radical Liberal views as his father. By the age of sixteen he was tall and slim, with blue-grey eyes, a long face and a prominent nose. Although he was an avid reader, his eyesight was poor, a problem that troubled him throughout his life. He had become secretary of the local Liberal Association and was seen as a courteous, kind-hearted boy who would share his last penny. Despite being a committed Liberal, he subscribed to the Socialist weekly newspaper, the *Clarion,* and read books by Keir Hardie, John Burns, Robert Blatchford and other Socialist authors. When Keir Hardie addressed a meeting in Tain, he was so impressed by questions from Fraser that he took him aside afterwards for a private chat. But politics were not Fraser's sole interest, and most nights were occupied with a variety of pursuits: the temperance movement, farm workers' campaigns, the local football team and the village debating society. But his most enjoyable evenings were spent at the literary society, where he developed a love of Robert Burns that lasted throughout his life. Later in New Zealand, he gave lectures on Burns and was highly sought-after as a Burns Supper speaker.

It was no great surprise, however, when he decided to leave Fearn at the age of twenty-three. There were few opportunities in the Highlands and a high proportion of the young men and women left home and headed south to the Lowlands, to England, or abroad. Fraser's parents had lived in Canada for several years before returning to Fearn, and seven of his eight siblings had departed by their mid-twenties. Fraser initially moved to Edinburgh and then Glasgow, before joining his brother William in London.

Through his connection with the MP for Ross-shire, Fraser found work as a carpenter in the Houses of Parliament buildings, where repair work was being carried out. This gave him ready access to the debates in the House of Commons, where he could listen to the speeches of some of the great politicians of the time. His mother was a resolute advocate of women's rights, and Fraser was proud to write home telling her that he had met Emmeline Pankhurst and other well-known suffragettes. He was heavily influenced by his mother's views on the subject, and throughout his life his commitment to women's rights never wavered. But like many radical liberals, Fraser had been moving gradually to the left, and the intellectual discussions among the London Socialist set persuaded him to join the Independent Labour Party in 1908.

With his carpenter's job in Parliament coming to an end, Fraser began to think of his next move. New Zealand had a reputation for progressive policies and many Socialists had visited the country. Sidney and Beatrice Webb, Tom Mann, Ben Tillett and Keir Hardie had all come back from New Zealand impressed by its enlightened values. Women had been given the vote in 1893, and workers were protected by some of the most progressive labour laws in the world. Much of the labour legislation was introduced in the aftermath of a bitter four-month strike in 1890. The maritime strike affected Australia and New Zealand, and although it ended in defeat for the unions, it changed the face of labour relations for the next twenty years (see Chapter 9, pages 256-257 and 12, pages 354-355).

Strike defeat: Labour Group formed

The collapse of the strike persuaded trade union leaders in New Zealand to focus more on political action. Most of the mainstream trade union leadership backed the Liberal Party and lobbied for the selection of trade union parliamentary candidates. At the general election in 1890 a number of working-class candidates, selected by the trades and labour councils, ran on Liberal tickets. Five of them were successful, and formed a Labour Group in parliament, to be joined by others after subsequent elections. One of the group, T. L. Buick, recorded that almost all the Labour Group members were Scottish or of Scottish descent.

David Pinkerton was typical of the Scots in the group. Born in Kirknewton, West Lothian, in 1836, he served his apprenticeship as a shoemaker in Edinburgh. Lured to New Zealand by the Otago gold rush, he arrived with his wife in 1861. Like most gold diggers he had no luck and settled in Dunedin, where he practised his trade. Factory production of boots and shoes had begun to undermine traditional skills and Pinkerton was forced to work for one of the large enterprises. During the 1880s he became active in the trade union movement, and was elected president of both the shoemakers' union and the Otago Trades and Labour Council. Elected to parliament for Dunedin, he held his seat at the next election in 1893, but lost in 1896 when the Labour Group divided over prohibition. However his skills were recognised by the prime minister and he was appointed to the Upper House, where he became chairman of the labour bills committee.

The Labour Group concentrated mainly on employment legislation and was responsible for the passage of several acts of parliament on working hours and conditions, payment of wages and the establishment of an arbitration system. However, faced with a reaction from disgruntled employers, the Liberal Party buckled under the pressure and drifted from its radical position. By 1904 the trade unions felt alienated by the Liberal leadership and decided to create an Independent Labour Party along the same lines as the British model. They failed to make any headway in the 1905 election but by 1908 Labour polled 20 per cent of the vote and one of the candidates, David McLaren, won Wellington East.

Born in Glasgow around 1870, McLaren emigrated with his parents in the 1880s and worked in various jobs before becoming full-time secretary of the Wellington Wharf Labourers Union in 1899. Although he had left Scotland as a young man, he maintained his Scottish cultural identity and was active in the Wellington Burns Club. He won a seat on Wellington council in 1901, before his success in the 1908 election. But McLaren's parliamentary career was cut short. Although he increased his vote in the 1911 election, he lost by sixty-five votes. However, he retained his seat on Wellington city council and in 1912 became the first Labour mayor of the city. Close friends considered McLaren fairly dull in company, but on a platform he was transformed. His booming voice and use of humour had his listeners engrossed, and he became one of the most influential figures in New Zealand labour circles during this period. His key positions included convener of the Trades and Labour Councils of New Zealand, national organiser of the Labour Party, and Labour Party president.

Many of the radical Liberals started joining the Labour ranks, the most prominent amongst them being another Glaswegian and ex-government minister, Alexander Hogg. A mining surveyor, Hogg had emigrated in 1876 and was a Liberal MP from 1890 to 1911. He was minister of labour in 1909 when he resigned from the government and joined the Labour Party. For the next two years he toured the country addressing trade union gatherings and trades and labour council meetings in the campaign to build the Labour Party. In the 1911 he stood in his own constituency election on a Labour Party ticket, but was defeated. However, four Labour candidates were successful in the 1911 election, including two Scots, William Veitch and John Robertson.

Veitch, who won the Wanganui seat, was born at Port of Menteith in Perthshire in 1870. The son of a schoolmaster, he had a comfortable

David McLaren from Glasgow was secretary of the Wellington Wharf Labourers Union and leader of the New Zealand Labour Party. In 1908 he became an MP and was the first Labour mayor of Wellington in 1912. He lost both positions and became detached from the mainstream labour movement. (Courtesy General Assembly Library Collection, Alexander Turnbull Library, Wellington)

middle-class upbringing and a good education. After school he worked for the post office before emigrating to New Zealand at the age of eighteen. He moved around the country doing any work he could find and took a job as a cleaner in the railway service. He was gradually promoted until he became an engine driver and remained with the railways for the next twenty-two years. His contribution to the Amalgamated Society of Railway Servants followed much the same course. Starting as an active member, he became branch secretary, district chairman and then national president of the union in 1908.

John Robertson was the son of a church minister who was born in Scotland in 1875. He trained as a watchmaker and was a secretary of the Independent Labour Party before he emigrated to New Zealand in 1902. A few years later he was appointed secretary of the Wellington Dairy Workers Union. In the 1911 election he won the Otaki seat but lost the next election in 1914. He did not return to parliament until 1935, when he became MP for Masterton. Between these periods he was editor of the *Commonwealth* newspaper and was involved in the film industry.

The Socialist Party

Another organisation on the left had been established earlier and was recruiting many of the more militant trade unionists. The New Zealand Socialist Party was formed in 1901, and branches had been established in a number of towns, largely as a result of an influx of Socialists from Britain in 1900. They were followers of the English Socialist and humanitarian William Ranstead, who was a founding director of the British left-wing newspaper, the *Clarion*. He came to New Zealand to explore the possibility of creating a utopian Socialist community, and invited others to join him. In response, some two hundred disciples sailed to New Zealand, many of whom bought farms.

By 1903 the Socialist Party had developed into a revolutionary Marxist organisation. Its leader was Robert Hogg, no relation to the above-mentioned Alex Hogg. Robert Hogg was also a Scotsman, and had been a member of the Independent Labour Party and a friend of Keir Hardie. The son of an iron-moulder, he was born in the Blochairn area of Glasgow in 1864. He left Glasgow and started work as a post office engineer in Musselburgh, near Edinburgh. He became owner and editor of a newspaper that was probably financed by William Ranstead, who had married a woman from Musselburgh and often visited the town. Despite being elected to the Musselburgh council, Hogg followed

Robert Hogg was born in the Blochairn area of Glasgow and was member of the Independent Labour Party. In 1910 he became general secretary of the New Zealand Socialist Party, transforming it into a revolutionary Marxist organisation. He edited its journal, the Commonwealth and wrote several books in the Scots dialect, penned under the pseudonym 'Robert Blochairn'.

Ranstead to New Zealand in 1900 along with his wife, three sons and two daughters.

He bought a farm but after a couple of years sold it and found a job in Wellington, where he became leader of the city's Socialist Party. Initially, the party was a loose alliance of autonomous local groups, but by 1908 it had become a more cohesive national organisation with a membership of around three thousand. Around this time Hogg was elected president and in 1910 he became general secretary. He controlled party policy and introduced an uncompromising set of Marxist principles. The Socialist Party attracted many of the more radical and militant trade unionists and was unequivocally opposed to arbitration, which it deemed to be class collaboration. A year later, the labour movement split over the issue, and the Federation of Labour, a new militant trade union centre, was formed (see Chapter 12, page 358). Most of its leaders were members of the Socialist Party, which was now bigger than the Labour Party. David McLaren, Labour Party president, attempted to broker a unity pact between the different factions. He led a reorganisation of the Labour Party, made changes to its constitution, and renamed it the United Labour Party. However, the reforms did not go far enough for the Socialists, who refused to join in any discussions.

Peter Fraser's arrival in Auckland in January 1911 coincided with the political upheaval taking place within the labour movement. Auckland was the biggest city in New Zealand, with 100,000 inhabitants, and Fraser found lodgings in one of the many boarding houses in the central district. The total population of the country was only one million in an area the size of Britain. The principal industry was agriculture, although most of the country's trade unionists worked in transport, food, mining and construction. Fraser did not work at his trade as a carpenter, but instead found a job on the Auckland wharves, and later as a labourer on a building site.

Two Scotsmen were leading the main working-class parties: Robert Hogg was general secretary of the Socialist Party, and David McLaren was the main figure in the United Labour Party. Fraser chose the overtly revolutionary Socialist Party and soon became one of its most active members. The Auckland branch had over three hundred members and owned the Socialist Hall, where it held political and educational activities each night of the week. Many of the bachelors from the boarding houses in the area joined the classes on history, politics and economics. The standard of discussion was high and Michael Savage, a future prime

Socialist Party delegates during its Fourth Annual Conference, 1911 (Robert Hogg is second left, middle row). The Socialist Party attracted many of the more radical and militant trade unionists including Peter Fraser. Michael Savage, a future prime minister, was the Party's Auckland branch chairman. (Courtesy Roth Collection, Alexander Turnbull Library, Wellington)

minister, was branch chairman. Fraser revelled in the branch activities and debates, and within a year was elected vice-chairman.

He joined the Auckland Labourers Union and although he did not have any experience of trade union leadership, was elected president. One of his first tasks was to seek improvements in wages and conditions from the Portland Cement Company. In defiance of the arbitration system, he called a strike, which quickly led to a settlement. He took the union into the Federation of Labour, the new trade union centre, and was made an executive committee member. When a vacancy arose for secretary/treasurer of the Auckland district of the Federation, Fraser was the overwhelming choice. With two union positions, he could now work full time for the labour movement. After only a year in the country, Fraser had become a leading figure in both the trade union movement and the Socialist Party. Few other immigrants had made as much of an impact after such a short period in New Zealand.

However, the following year he was brought back down to earth when he took on a more formidable opponent, the Auckland city council. The council did not recognise the Federation of Labour or any of its affiliates, and when a dispute arose with the Labourers' Union, the city council refused to deal with Fraser. Instead, they encouraged the formation of an alternative union, which half the workforce joined. With the membership divided, Fraser could only watch from the sidelines while a settlement was negotiated over his head. This humiliating defeat forced Fraser's resignation as president. He now focused on his job with the Federation of Labour, but it was not long before he was taught another lesson about the limits of workers' power and solidarity. A strike in the gold-mining town of Waihi coincided with the election of a fiercely anti-union Conservative government, and ended in acrimonious defeat (see Chapter 12, pages 359-361).

Opportunities for unity: the Social Democratic Party

The new government had openly sided with the employers and used the full force of the state to defeat the strike. Even the moderate union leaders were alarmed at the government's harsh response to the dispute. Fraser was dejected at the outcome, but a whole lot wiser. Sensing the opportunities the new hard-line government presented, he arranged meetings with the moderates to discuss ways to bring about unity in the political and trade union movement. Two conferences were held in 1913 based on a set of principles largely drafted by Fraser. Two new organisations emerged from the conferences: a new party and a new trade union centre. But he had to fight against accusations of selling out Socialist principles to achieve the agreements. Responding to attacks from the left, he stated 'I am a revolutionary Socialist. I am an industrial unionist. Socialism is my goal. Industrial unionism plus revolutionary action, in my opinion, provide the most effective and expeditious means of reaching that goal ... Any working-class movement that is not revolutionary is reactionary. It must be either for the perpetuation or the abolition of the capitalist system.' At Fraser's suggestion, the new party was called the Social Democratic Party, and the new trade union centre was named the United Federation of Labour. Fraser decided that his strengths lay on the political wing and he was elected secretary/ treasurer of the Party, a full-time position.

Most Labour Party members joined the new party, including the Scottish MP John Robertson. But David McLaren felt that compromise with the Socialists was impossible and detrimental to the advance of a centre-left party. Shortly before this he had stood for re-election as mayor of Wellington, but lost, blaming the Socialist Party for his defeat. He was not prepared to accept the unity proposals and led a number of delegates out of the conference, including Scots MPs William Veitch and Alex Hogg.

Robert Hogg, the Socialist Party leader, also rejected the compromise proposals at the Unity Conference in 1913. He led the Wellington branch out of the conference, refusing to accept any watering-down of his revolutionary principles. However, most of his membership deserted him and joined the Social Democratic Party. Hogg continued to lead the Socialist Party and to edit its journal, the *Commonwealth*. He was also business manager of the *Maoriland Worker*, a labour-movement newspaper, and wrote for both publications under the pseudonym Robert Blochairn. He was later appointed editor of *New Zealand Truth*, one of a chain of newspapers owned by an Australian. A strong left position was taken on all major issues, particularly labour matters. He used the publication to attack political and commercial scandals until the journal's nervous owner dismissed him in 1922. Throughout this time he was the main cultural figure in the Scottish community. A foundation member of the Wellington Burns Club, Hogg was a fine poet in his own right and an expert on Scottish literature. He composed several volumes in the Scots dialect, again penned under the name Robert Blochairn, and bequeathed his own writings, together with an extensive collection of Scottish literature, to the Alexander Turnbull Library (part of the national library of New Zealand). He was honorary bard of the Glasgow United Burns Club, President of the Scots Social Club, and editor of the *NZ Scotsman*. Although he remained committed to the Socialist Party, it was relegated to the fringes of the left and made no electoral impact.

After the establishment of the Social Democratic Party, Peter Fraser moved to its headquarters in Wellington to take up his position as secretary/treasurer. The new party made an immediate impact by winning two by-elections shortly afterwards. Within a year there were forty-five branches and thirty-four unions affiliated. The future looked bright for both the new party and the new trade union centre until the United Federation of Labour became embroiled in a general strike that collapsed after eleven days. The strike was called against the better judgment of the leadership and once again divided the labour movement (see Chapter 12, pp 361-363). Fraser, who had been charged with incitement during the dispute, began to question his previous views on the efficacy of strike action. His opinion moved more towards political action to achieve change.

An election was due in 1914, but after the strike only sporadic support was forthcoming from the trade unions. The Social Democratic Party managed to hold on to the two seats it had won in the by-elections, but its candidates lost everywhere else, including John Robertson, who was defending his Otaki seat. The United Labour Party, which was now a loose grouping of individuals, won four seats, but David McLaren once again came agonisingly close, losing by only forty-eight votes. This campaign was his last connection with the labour movement. He became more detached from the mainstream labour movement, convinced that it had been taken over by extremists and revolutionaries. He spent much of the rest of his life attacking the organisation he had helped to create. Two Scots candidates were successful. William Veitch held his Wanganui seat and was joined in parliament by Andrew Walker, who won in Dunedin. Walker was a printer and was secretary of the Dunedin Typographical Union as well as president of the Otago Trades and Labour Council. He emigrated from Scotland in 1860 and was sixteen when he arrived in New Zealand.

The Social Democratic Party still had seven thousand members, but its branch organisation was in a poor state and little effort was being made to collect membership subscriptions. Fraser often went unpaid and was forced to find a job on the Wellington wharves to make ends meet. In an attempt to revitalise the party, he spent six months touring the country, addressing meetings in towns and villages. He lived off what he could collect and met with some success in rebuilding the organisation. But the First World War created deep divisions in the labour movement, as it did in every country. Nevertheless, Fraser's nationwide campaign convinced him that a further attempt was needed to bring the left together into one party.

A new Labour Party formed

Only a rump of the United Labour Party was left, but a new constitution was proposed that would bring the moderates and militants together. A conference was arranged in 1916 to form another party, which reverted to the name New Zealand Labour Party. Fraser did not stand for any of the key positions and settled for a place on the national executive. But Andrew Walker and fellow Scot Joseph McKenzie were part of a committee of seven who drafted the constitution. For a short period, Walker became party president, and was secretary of the parliamentary Labour Party until he was defeated in 1919. McKenzie, who was secretary of the Grocers' Union, was elected vice-president.

As the war dragged on, the New Zealand Government was put under pressure from Britain to send more troops to Europe. Volunteers for the armed forces had dwindled to a trickle and, to meet the British demands, the government was forced to introduce conscription. The Labour Party led a widespread campaign in opposition, but the Military Service Act became law in August 1916. Labour's campaign continued, causing divisions within the party. William Veitch, one of the few Labour MPs, supported the government and gradually drifted away from Labour. Under a variety of party labels, he won election after election, and became minister of labour, mines and transport in 1928. He continued in parliament until he was defeated in 1935, after serving twenty-four years as an MP.

Labour continued to campaign against conscription, prompting the authorities to take action against its leaders. Fraser defiantly addressed an anti-war conference in December 1916, stating: 'For the past two years we have been looking at the ruling classes of Europe spreading woe, want and murder over the continent, and it's time that the working classes of different nations were rising up in protest against them. Lloyd George wants to continue hell, and to compel the young life of the dominion into that sweltering hell … It rests with the people to say how long we will stand for it … No longer will we be the dupes of the crowned heads of Europe and their satellites.' When he finished, he was arrested by undercover police officers, and as they marched him out of the conference hall, delegates rose to their feet, singing 'The Red Flag'. Charged with sedition, he was later sentenced to twelve months' imprisonment.

Fraser's year in prison gave him a chance to reflect on the political situation. A voracious reader, he spent his time behind bars immersed in books on politics, economics, history and philosophy. He emerged from prison more focused on the future shape of the labour movement in New Zealand. The next period of his life was the most rewarding and fulfilling he had experienced, from both a political and personal perspective: he was elected to Wellington city council, became the member of parliament for Wellington Central, secretary of the parliamentary party, president of the Labour Party, editor of the *Maoriland Worker* and, at the age of thirty-six, he married Janet Munro.

Janet Munro came from Glasgow and was eighteen months older than Fraser. Her father was an iron-foundry worker and her mother a domestic servant. Janet worked with orphaned children until she married a man who worked in the same foundry as her father. At the age of twenty she gave birth to a son. The family emigrated to New Zealand in 1909 and mixed in Socialist circles. They befriended Peter Fraser when he arrived in 1911. Janet had been a regular reader of the *Clarion* when she lived in Scotland, and had read books by Robert Blatchford and other Socialist authors. She was one of the founding members of the Women's Progressive Society, an organisation established by the Socialist Party in 1913. Her marriage eventually failed and after she divorced her husband in 1918, she married Peter Fraser. She then became president of the Wellington women's branch of the Labour Party and continued a range of other interests mainly connected with women and children. She was very comfortable addressing an audience and her speeches were considered to be witty and intelligent. Her great passion was healthcare and she was elected to the Wellington Hospital Board, topping the poll on one occasion. Her other passion was her husband, whom she felt had the potential to make a major impact on New Zealand politics.

Fraser was almost six feet tall and well built. When he married, his hair was beginning to thin, although he looked younger than his age. He wore thick steel-rimmed spectacles, which made him look rather stern, especially as he seldom smiled. Although he was seen as a committed and talented party worker, he had a reputation for being rather austere and puritanical. Nicknamed 'Pious Peter' by some of his Labour colleagues, he did not smoke or drink and seldom swore. He was seen as rather straight-laced, and became embarrassed at discussions or jokes of a sexual nature. The few clothes he possessed were threadbare and he wore the same tweed suit to every event. However, he had a good sense of humour and away from politics he could be light-hearted. Although normally in control of his emotions, he sometimes became tearful when examples of personal suffering were brought to his attention. Janet did much to bring these human qualities to the surface and helped lift him from the level of a skilful party organiser to become Labour's best all-round politician.

Labour advances to government

Fraser had won a by-election for Wellington Central in 1918, and was comfortably re-elected in the general election of 1919 along with eight other Labour candidates. As he gained experience in parliament, he became the party's most tactically astute politician. Although he was not a great orator, he was a convincing parliamentary debater, conveying authority and commanding attention. His footprints were on every change of policy as the Labour Party gradually dropped its militant Socialist agenda and adopted a more pragmatic set of policies designed to win votes. The arbitration system, which was the cause of divisions within the left when Fraser first came to New Zealand, was now seen as a useful means of protecting the living standards of many workers.

Fraser was one of the party's most influential figures as Labour made steady progress. Its share of the vote rose gradually, polling 23 per cent in 1922 and rising to 27 per cent in 1925. In 1931, it became the official opposition when it won 34 per cent of the vote. Following the death of the party leader Henry Holland in 1933, Michael Savage was elected to replace him, and Fraser was chosen as deputy leader. During this period the country was in the depths of the Great Depression, without any provision for unemployment relief. Hunger and despair followed for many New Zealanders, who were forced to rely on charitable handouts or resort to stealing in order to survive. Work-relief schemes were introduced, with priority given to married men with children but the wages paid were barely enough to survive. Single men were sent to work camps, often in isolated places, where the living conditions were primitive and food substandard. The work was arduous and they were paid a pittance, but the alternative was starvation. Women were offered no support and for many single women the situation was desperate.

As conditions worsened, despair turned to anger. Evictions for non-payment of rent were commonplace but neighbourhood anti-eviction

New Zealand Parliamentary Labour Party in 1922 with nine MPs after winning 23% of the vote. The Party's support rapidly increased and at the 1935 election Labour polled 47%, giving it fifty-three seats out of eighty in the House of Representatives.

committees challenged the bailiffs and the police. Unemployed workers' movements were set up and organised marches that were joined by thousands. A series of riots occurred in 1932 as desperate people demanded food. A procession of the unemployed in Dunedin marched to the Otago Hospital Board pleading for assistance. When it was refused, the enraged crowd stormed a grocery store, where they fought with police. In Auckland, postal workers who were demonstrating against a 10 per cent cut in their wages joined forces with an unemployed workers' march. They clashed with police and, in the aftermath, shop windows were smashed and the goods inside were looted. Sailors with fixed bayonets patrolled the streets in an attempt to maintain order. More looting occurred in Wellington after an unsuccessful attempt to lobby the government.

Labour was increasingly seen as the only alternative to the conservative policies of the government, and there was a growing sense of a major change in the political landscape as the country approached the 1935 election. Expectations were high and the Labour Party was predicted to do well. But the results exceeded all expectations. Labour was swept to power with 47 per cent of the vote, winning fifty-three seats out of eighty in the House of Representatives. As one of the key architects of the victory, Fraser was given his choice of ministerial portfolios, and at fifty-one he became minister of education and health. With additional responsibility for marine issues and police, he set himself a punishing schedule, rising at 6 a.m. and going to bed at 1 a.m. seven days a week. Janet became his research assistant and took an office next to his, where she helped organise his workload and vetted his visitors. But many of his closest colleagues felt that he worked unnecessarily long hours because he became too involved in the minute details of administration and had difficulty in delegating responsibility.

Fraser was passionate about education and was determined to reform New Zealand's system to provide free primary and secondary schooling for all. In his first main speech as minister, he declared 'Every person, whatever his level of academic ability, whether he be rich or poor, whether he live in town or country, has the right, as a citizen, to a free education of the kind to which he is best fitted, and to the fullest extent of his powers.' Legislation was introduced to start primary school education at five years of age and access to secondary education was expanded, especially in rural communities.

These educational reforms were a major advance for the working class and Fraser was deservedly showered with praise for his bold and imaginative policies. But it was his reforms in welfare and health that were probably the greatest political achievement in the country's history. The Social Security Act 1938 was the cornerstone of the Government's welfare programme, and combined the introduction of a free healthcare system with a comprehensive range of welfare benefits. Pensions and family allowance were extended to cover the whole population, financed by a tax increase of 5 per cent. The introduction of the National Health Service ran up against bitter opposition from the New Zealand branch of the British Medical Association, but Fraser eventually negotiated a deal with the doctors and brought them into the new scheme. Janet's expertise in healthcare proved invaluable as her husband steered the Bill through Parliament.

The success of the first Labour government was rewarded with a massive vote of 57 per cent of the electorate in the 1938 election, a figure unsurpassed since. A number of Scots were among the new intake of MPs, but Fraser was particularly pleased at the election of Catherine Stewart, only the second woman to enter parliament. The daughter of an iron-moulder, Stewart was born in 1881, and worked in a Glasgow weaving mill after she left school. She married when she was eighteen and by the time she was twenty-four she had three sons. Determined not to settle for the life of a housewife, she managed to cram in a number of activities to broaden her understanding of politics. She attended evening classes at Glasgow University and economics tutorials given by the famous Marxist John MacLean. One of the founders of the Women's Co-operative Guild in Glasgow, she was a militant feminist and was arrested three times during demonstrations.

After the First World War, with unemployment in Glasgow soaring, the Stewarts decided to emigrate to New Zealand. They arrived in Wellington in 1921, where her husband found a job on the railway. Stewart worked with special needs children and also became active in the Labour Party and the Co-operative Society. In 1938 she became the sole woman in parliament when she won the Wellington South constituency for Labour. In Parliament she concentrated on women and children's issues, but also made significant contributions to economic debates. She was uncompromising in her condemnation of bankers, wealthy businessmen, greedy doctors and the clergy. She called for the abolition of private property and did not hesitate to criticise her own government when they strayed from party principles. In 1943 she lost her seat in a general swing against Labour. Her husband, who had been highly

Peter Fraser, New Zealand prime minister throughout the 1940s, came from Fearn in Ross shire. Initially a radical Liberal, he joined the Independent Labour Party in London in 1908. He was elected to the New Zealand parliament in 1918 and became prime minister in 1940. (Courtesy Library of Congress, USA)

supportive throughout her career, died in 1948, and Stewart decided to return to Glasgow with two of her sons.

Two other Scots had prominent positions in the Labour Party during this period. After the 1935 election, Robert McKeen was appointed Chief Whip, a key figure for maintaining discipline and control of the parliamentary party. McKeen was a miner from Calder in West Lothian, and had been active in the labour movement in Scotland before emigrating in 1909 at the age of twenty-five. He started work in the coalmines on the west coast of New Zealand and became an official with the miners' union. A few years later he moved to Wellington, where he set up a grocery business and served on Wellington city council for eighteen years. He was one of seventeen Labour MPs elected in 1922 and had been a leading backbencher before becoming Chief Whip.

The party's national secretary was David Wilson from Glasgow. Born in 1880 and orphaned at the age of ten, Wilson trained as a tailor. He moved to London for several years and then to Derbyshire, where he was appointed to a leading position in the Amalgamated Society of Tailors. In 1911 he emigrated to Australia and formed the Melbourne Fabian Club, before finally settling in New Zealand in 1916. The Labour Party leadership became aware of his organisational and administrative abilities and appointed him national secretary in 1936. He helped in the drafting of party election documents, and kept discipline at party conference. A trusted friend and ally of the prime minister, he was appointed leader of the legislative council in 1937, and was invited to join the cabinet two years later.

Fraser, the international statesman

The Second World War proved even more momentous for Peter Fraser's career than the First. When war broke out in 1939, deputy party leader Fraser was effectively running the country, as Michael Savage was very ill and unable to fulfil the functions of prime minister. Fraser broadcast to the nation that New Zealand was at war and was summoned to London for a conference of Commonwealth prime ministers to discuss their contribution to the war effort. When Savage resigned, Fraser was elected leader at the next party conference, and officially became prime minister.

As the war progressed, Fraser grew in stature, becoming the most able prime minister New Zealand ever had. He dominated his party and controlled his government in a way no other leader had managed. Confident and resolute in domestic and international affairs, he surprised his party and his civil servants, who had underestimated his abilities. His speeches were also livened up when he employed Robert Riley as his press secretary. Riley came from West Lothian, and had worked for Michael Savage. Although a bit dour, he was a highly talented journalist who helped Fraser's public image considerably.

Despite arguments from some on the left that the war was essentially an imperialist confrontation, Fraser had no doubt that Britain was engaged in a war against Fascism. He intended to maximise New Zealand's contribution to the war effort, raising the issue of military conscription, which was an article of faith in the Labour Party. Fraser and other labour leaders had served prison sentences for opposing compulsory military service during the First World War, but he believed the nature of the Second World War was different. In 1916, Fraser had argued that there should be 'no conscription of men without conscription of wealth'. Therefore, when he addressed the Labour Party conference in 1940 he announced a system of control to place all wealth and property at the disposal of the state. Demanding sacrifices from everyone, Fraser's powerful speech won over the delegates. 'Our duty is plain,' he began. 'We either have to lead the people in this hour of crisis or to give place to others ... The Labour movement is asked to give up, in this hour of danger, certain principles and advantages ... Better that our lives should be sacrificed than we should have to live under the system Hitler would impose on us! If we cannot protect the freedom we have and hand it on to our children, we have no right to live.' He dismissed requests from some delegates for a referendum, stating, 'When a house is on fire no one needs a mandate to fight the fire. When a country's very existence is at stake, no other mandate is necessary to conscript anything and everything.' The conference overwhelmingly supported Fraser's proposals.

In the early military campaigns of the war, New Zealand's forces had almost been decimated in a series of major setbacks. Fraser left New Zealand to visit the troops in Egypt and assure them of his interest in their welfare. The servicemen acknowledged his efforts and appreciated their prime minister's endeavours to boost morale. It had been a successful exercise and a public relations triumph. After he met the forces, Fraser continued his journey to London for briefings with Winston Churchill. During a tour of Britain he collected honours everywhere he went. He was given the Freedom of London, Glasgow and Edinburgh, as well as honorary doctorates from Cambridge and Dublin universities. He then travelled to Fearn for his triumphant homecoming.

When Japan entered the war, Fraser was faced with the agonising decision of whether to leave the New Zealand army divisions in the Middle East and Europe or to bring them home to defend the nation. Britain requested the armies of the Commonwealth nations to remain stationed where they were, but Australia rejected this appeal and its armed forces returned to their home bases. Despite enormous pressure within New Zealand to bring the troops home, Fraser decided to accede to Britain's request. The 1943 election was fought against the background of this unpopular decision. Nevertheless, Labour won, albeit with a reduced majority and 45.5 per cent of the vote. The government was assisted by the votes from the overseas armed forces, who had voted heavily for the prime minister, confirming his popularity amongst the troops and their respect for his decision.

Fraser truly established himself as an eminent world statesman during the course of the Second World War. He forged new relations with Australia and the United States, travelled to Europe and North America, addressed numerous conferences, and met the leaders of the Allies on several occasions. He and his wife became friends of Franklin and Eleanor Roosevelt, staying at their home when visiting the United States. They were given the opportunity to return the hospitality when the American president and the first lady came on a state visit to New Zealand. Fraser had always taken a modest view of his achievements, but as the war progressed he became supremely self-confident in his ability as a politician.

Janet Fraser frequently travelled with her husband and after each trip she gave reports on the way other countries dealt with key issues. Meetings were held to discuss employment and welfare, child health, women's rights, and housing. Aside from politics, she was well read on art and culture and attended the theatre and concerts regularly with her husband. Increases in arts funding and many of the cultural initiatives taken by the Labour government during Fraser's time in office were attributed to her influence. She led the women's war effort and made numerous speeches and broadcasts throughout its duration. But as the war drew to a close, Janet's health deteriorated. She had suffered from tuberculosis for twelve years, and in March 1945, she died.

Janet was Fraser's only close friend and her death was a devastating blow. They had an intimate understanding of each other and there was no other person that Fraser could confide in. But his period of grieving was curtailed when Churchill summoned him to London for a War Cabinet

Janet and Peter Fraser, 1945. Janet came from Glasgow and was a committed socialist before she emigrated to New Zealand. She was an excellent public speaker and was elected to the Wellington Hospital Board. When Fraser became a government minister, she took an office next to his and became his research assistant, using her expertise to advise him on reform of healthcare. (Courtesy N Z Free Lance Collection, Alexander Turnbull Library, Wellington)

meeting at the beginning of April. Churchill also took the opportunity to hold preparatory discussions about a conference to be held in San Francisco at the end of the month. The aim of the conference was to launch the United Nations, and Fraser had an important role to play. On arrival in San Francisco he immediately attracted the attention of the American media, who were impressed by his knowledge of international affairs. He chaired the committee that drafted the chapters of the UN charter dealing with colonial independence. His speech to the plenary session was one of the highlights of the conference for its vision and moral fervour. He received rapturous applause from the three thousand delegates when he outlined New Zealand's commitment to multilateralism and the imperative of achieving world peace and stability. 'I am speaking for a country which, although small in area and population, has made great sacrifices in two world wars. I speak for the New Zealanders who died and are buried thousands of miles from their own land in the cause they believed to be just. I speak for the millions of New Zealanders yet to be born ... It is my deep fear that if this fleeting moment is not captured, the world will again relapse into a period of disillusionment, despair, and doom. This must not happen.' The San Francisco conference was the pinnacle of Fraser's achievements and his contributions boosted his status at home and abroad. It also enhanced the reputation of his country and gave New Zealanders a new sense of pride in their nation.

However, by the time of the 1946 election, New Zealanders were more interested in domestic issues than international policies. Labour's manifesto highlighted proposals for an extension of welfare state provision, including higher unemployment benefit, minimum family income, and the payment of sickness and invalidity benefit. The result was a 51 per cent vote and a clear majority in parliament. The government also introduced a number of measures to assist the arts and established a national orchestra. Women were given an enhanced role in public life with appointments to key positions, and progress was made to settle long-standing Maori grievances.

The post-war years: Fraser's star fades

The stress of leading the nation through the war years began to take its toll on Fraser's health. He now walked with a pronounced stoop, had little hair, and his eyesight was so bad that he had to read documents an inch from his nose. He was getting heavier and looked much older than sixty-two. Many of his old comrades had retired or died and he did not

The Peter Fraser statue at the Government Buildings Historic Reserve, Wellington. Some of his Fraser's former socialist colleagues never forgave him for his post war policies. However, his success as a war leader, and his role in the birth of the UN, mark him as one of the great New Zealand Prime Ministers.

feel comfortable with some of the younger MPs who had replaced them. The young turks conceded that Fraser was a force on the world stage, but found him old fashioned, conservative and suspicious of new ideas. They wanted dialogue about the future while he wanted to preserve the status quo. Fraser was still firmly in charge of the parliamentary Labour Party but, to increasing numbers of New Zealanders, he was out of touch.

His biggest problem was with the trade unions, which had co-operated with the government during wartime, but which were now demanding substantial pay increases. Fraser argued for patience, but the post-war labour shortage put unions in a powerful bargaining position, and a series of disputes arose involving thousands of workers. The government was now at loggerheads with the unions and Labour Party branches were divided over support for the strikes. Many branches ceased functioning as members voted with their feet. Further divisions within Labour ranks were caused by Fraser's decision to place New Zealand firmly alongside Britain and the USA at the start of the Cold War. Not only did he denounce Communism, but he also labelled militant trade unionists as Communists even if they had no association with the Communist Party. Fraser saw the Soviet Union as a military threat to New Zealand's allies and this led to the greatest paradox in Fraser's career: the revolutionary Socialist who was jailed for opposing conscription during the First World War now advocated peacetime conscription. A split Labour Party conference narrowly agreed to hold a referendum on the issue, and the country grudgingly voted in favour.

It was almost inevitable that the long reign of the Labour Party would end at the next election in 1949. The internal disputes had weakened the party organisation and by the time of the election the leadership had run out of ideas, drive, and vision. Both Fraser and the Labour Party seemed exhausted and the dynamism of previous governments was nowhere to be found. With 47 per cent of the vote, it was not an overwhelming defeat, but the National Party won a clear majority. Fraser held on to the leadership of the party after the defeat and for a year he led the opposition to the government.

However, in December 1950, after his fourth heart attack, Fraser died in a Wellington hospital, aged sixty-six. Flags throughout the country were lowered to half-mast for three days. Thousands paid their respects while Fraser's body lay in state in the parliament buildings. Maori ceremonies were held for a man they trusted and supported, and a service was conducted in St John's Presbyterian church, the route from

Funeral procession for Peter Fraser, Wellington. Fraser suffered a forth heart attack in 1950 and died, aged sixty-six. The funeral route was lined with thousands of mourners and messages of sympathy were received from leaders of many countries. (Courtesy Evening Post Collection, Alexander Turnbull Library, Wellington)

parliament to church lined with mourners. Diplomats, politicians and trade union leaders attended the state funeral, and messages of sympathy were received from leaders from all over the world. Fraser was spoken of as a visionary statesman and one of New Zealand's most remarkable leaders.

The two most senior Scots in the party were also nearing the end of their careers. After spending five years as Chief Whip, Robert McKeen was appointed Speaker of the House from 1946 until 1950. He then became mayor of Otaki until his retirement in 1954. After leading the Upper House from 1937 until 1944, David Wilson was appointed New Zealand's High Commissioner to Canada. As one of Fraser's most trusted colleagues, he was needed back home and in 1947, Fraser asked him to return and to once again lead the Upper House. He was appointed to the cabinet and also became New Zealand's delegate to the United Nations. The Upper House was abolished by the national government in 1950.

Walter Nash, who had entered Parliament in 1919, replaced Fraser as leader. Labour lost the next two elections but won back power for three years from 1957 to 1960. To date, the Labour Party has been in government for thirty-four years since its first administration in 1935, roughly 50 per cent of the period since its formation. To many of his former Socialist colleagues and the party faithful, Peter Fraser's final years were a great disappointment. But his success as a war leader and his role in the birth of the UN mark him as one of the great New Zealand prime ministers.

Chapter 12

Angus McLagan, the miners and the New Zealand Federation of Labour

At the height of his popularity during the Second World War, Prime Minister Peter Fraser had received a request for an urgent meeting from the Federation of Labour. Wartime shortages were forcing up the price of basic goods, but pay increases were restricted by the government's incomes policy. Union leaders were coming under increasing pressure from their members to take action. Fraser knew the trade union movement better than any politician and without much thought agreed to what he assumed would be a routine discussion with a compliant trade union leadership. He had not bargained for a four-and-a-half-hour harangue from Angus McLagan, the incensed leader of the Federation of Labour. In the shouting match that followed, McLagan condemned Fraser and called on his government to resign. As the two stern-faced Scotsmen eyeballed each other, colleagues intervened in an attempt to cool tempers. But the outcome of the stormy confrontation was an unequivocal victory for the Federation of Labour. Two weeks later, the arbitration court awarded a substantial pay increase for all workers, and McLagan was invited to join the cabinet.

Angus McLagan was born in Calder, West Lothian in 1891 and started working life as a miner at the age of fourteen. At twenty he was a powerfully built young man who kept himself to himself, rarely smiled and trusted few people. When he decided to emigrate to New Zealand, not many outside his family were particularly interested. A Scottish community was well established in the Grey Valley coalfield on South Island and McLagan settled in the village of Blackball, which was already renowned for its union militancy. He became involved in the local miners' union and was one of a number of activists who were sacked after a strike in 1913. During the strike his colleagues admired his leadership qualities and his excellent organisational skills. His single-mindedness and determination to succeed marked him as a man who was destined for the top. He eventually became one of New Zealand's most influential trade union leaders, following a long and distinguished list of Scots who had made their mark on the New Zealand labour movement.

Many of the early activities of New Zealand unions centred on the fight for reductions in working hours. Immigrants were determined to leave behind the long hours and brutal conditions they had endured in Britain, where the working day could be as long as sixteen hours. The main objective for the small number of trade unionists in the mid-nineteenth century was to campaign for an eight-hour day. Some groups of building workers achieved this target, although the recorded history is patchy. There is more reliable information about the engineers, who established a branch of the British Amalgamated Society of Engineers in New Zealand in 1863. Alexander Bruce, who was a member of the society in Aberdeen, took the charter for the branch to New Zealand when he emigrated. He became New Zealand secretary and, later, vice-president of the Auckland Trades and Labour Council, which he helped found in 1876. The engineers agitated for an eight-hour day as well as pay increases, but Bruce was sacked for leading a strike. He then tried other ways of making a living, including an unsuccessful attempt at digging for gold. However, he returned to Auckland to work as a patternmaker and later became mayor of the borough of Waitemata.

Trades and Labour Councils were formed in the main towns and an annual Trades and Labour Congress was initiated in 1885. The number of trade unionists was very small as a proportion of the working population and consisted mainly of skilled workers. Strikes were frequent during a recession in the 1880s, but were mostly unsuccessful. Then a victory by the Seamen's Union in 1887 transformed the situation. The previous year, the seamen had elected John Millar as their new general secretary, and his dynamic personality revitalised their union.

John Millar and the Maritime Council

Millar's Scottish father was an officer in the British army and was stationed in India when his son was born in 1855. Three years later he returned home to Edinburgh, where young Millar was educated. When he left school Millar decided on a career as a seaman and served his apprenticeship with P. Henderson of Glasgow, agents of the Albion Shipping Company. He had been to New Zealand to visit an uncle and fell in love with the country. He was keen to return at the first opportunity, and by the time he received his Master's Certificate in 1884, he was back in New Zealand sailing coastal steamers. Although ship's officers had their own union, Miller decided to join the much larger Seamen's Union, which already had a sizable number of officers in membership. One of

John Millar was general secretary of the Seamen's Union and leader of the New Zealand Maritime Council, an alliance of the main unions in the country. The alliance collapsed in the wake of a six-week general strike in 1890, but three years later Millar was elected as a Liberal MP and became Minister of Labour. However, he was regarded as a traitor when he tried to have trade unionists imprisoned for taking strike action.

the most educated and committed of the union's one thousand members, he won the election for the full-time position of general secretary a few years later. The first problem he faced was a dispute with the Northern Steam Ship Company. A belligerent management announced a pay reduction and sacked anyone who objected. Instead of calling a strike, Millar tried a different approach. He chartered three ships and ran them in competition against the steamship company. After sixteen months the company agreed to rehire the sacked men at the old rates and to employ only union members. The success of the dispute gave the whole trade union movement an impetus and elevated Millar's status amongst New Zealand seamen. There was an upsurge in trade union membership, which grew from a few thousand to over twenty thousand by 1889.

Millar described himself as a Socialist and believed in the nationalisation of all major companies. He was also a champion of equal opportunities for women and helped organise the Tailoresses' Union in 1889. He firmly believed in solidarity action in support of workers in other industries and looked for ways to build a trade union structure capable of taking on the most powerful of the employers. In Australia, a federation of seamen, miners, railwaymen and dockers had been formed and Millar set up a similar organisation in New Zealand. The alliance was known as the New Zealand Maritime Council, and the unions pledged to assist each other in the event of a dispute by any affiliate. Millar was the obvious choice to lead the new organisation, and he soon took on the mantle of the principal spokesman for the entire New Zealand trade union movement. The Maritime Council insisted on full unionisation of affiliates and instructed its members to refuse to work with non-union labour. Millar achieved several outstanding successes in the council's first year, mainly by boycotts of employers' goods and services. The reputation of the Maritime Council was such that even non-affiliated craft unions handed over their disputes to the Maritime Council for settlement.

By the middle of 1890, the number of trade unionists had multiplied to over sixty thousand and Millar's aim was the unionisation of the whole New Zealand workforce under the direction of the Maritime Council. Everything was pointing in that direction until a general strike broke out in Australia in August 1890 and sucked New Zealand's unions into the dispute (see Chapter 9, pages 256-257). Initially, Millar tried to avoid becoming involved and asked New Zealand shipping companies to cease trading with Australia for the duration of the strike. The request was turned down, and when dockers refused to load Australian ships, non-union labour was drafted in to take their place. Seamen immediately walked off their ships, and before long other Maritime Council affiliates had joined the dispute. It was the first nationwide strike involving more than one union and was a major landmark in New Zealand's industrial history.

Until then, public opinion had been highly supportive of the trade unions and their aims. However, the purpose of the maritime strike was not clearly understood and most people felt that the New Zealand unions should not have become caught up in an internal Australian confrontation. That was the view of the railwaymen, who voted against joining the strike, and their refusal to participate had a significant impact on the outcome. There were other problems facing the unions. Most had only been formed a year or so before and had not yet been tested in terms of the solidarity of their members. Nor had they had time to build sufficient strike funds to sustain a lengthy dispute. In addition, the time of the year was not favourable, as there were adequate coal stocks and ample farm labourers available to do strikers' jobs. The employers saw this as an opportunity to finish off the unions and refused attempts by politicians to conciliate.

The fifty-six day long maritime strike ended in total defeat and the New Zealand trade unions took many years to recover. Even after the Maritime Council called off the strike, the employers refused to accept John Millar as a representative of the workers. They took the opportunity to dismiss union leaders and forced the workforce to sign agreements that they would not join a union. Wages were reduced and hours lengthened, not just for those who had belonged to the Maritime Council unions, but across the board. The Maritime Council collapsed, and although the trades councils managed to survive with a much-reduced membership, the employers were never seriously challenged by any trade union action for years to come. But, paradoxically, the defeat and disintegration of the trade unions led to the introduction of some of the most progressive employment legislation in the world.

The Liberal Party's alliance with the trade unions

Radical Liberal politicians, uncomfortable with the employers' new bargaining strength, began speaking out on behalf of the trade unions. In response, John Millar and others urged trade unionists to vote for the Liberal Party. The Trades and Labour Councils endorsed many of Cthe Liberal candidates, and this working-class support proved crucial in sweeping the Liberals to victory in the general election held at the end of 1890. The new government was keen to reward the unions, and introduced legislation to help redress the balance of industrial power.

A department of labour was set up and James MacKay, from Duns in Berwickshire, was appointed chief clerk. MacKay was born in 1857 and ran away to sea, making several voyages from Britain to New Zealand before he decided to settle in the country, becoming a union organiser for the Knights of Labour when it was established in New Zealand. His department ushered in legislation on a range of industrial issues, the most important of which was the 1894 Industrial Conciliation and Arbitration Act. This statute gave any group of seven or more workers the right to form a union and to take any dispute to the arbitration court. Initially a large proportion of cases found in favour of the unions. Wages improved for most workers and conditions became standardised throughout the country. The unions had to give up the right to strike, but they were so weak at this point that they were delighted to accept the legal protection they were offered. The improved economic conditions for workers were achieved by a sympathetic government rather than by the strength and organisation of the unions.

But the employers were dissatisfied with the change in the balance of forces, and formed an association of their own to lobby the government and to coerce the arbitration courts. Decisions started going against the unions and for several years wages were reduced in real terms. Discontent began to spread, but the unions could do nothing as they were locked into arbitration agreements. By this point the Liberal government had abandoned its radical policies and was uninfluenced by trade union opinion. Criticism of the New Zealand system came from foreign labour leaders, including Ramsay MacDonald of the British Labour Party, who believed that New Zealand's emasculated trade unions only existed for the purpose of litigation, and had become instruments of the state.

It was only a matter of time before breaches of the arbitration court began to occur. A short strike by Auckland tramway workers, the first illegal strike since the introduction of the arbitration system, resulted in the reinstatement of two conductors who had been sacked. A longer strike by slaughterhouse workers in Wellington won an increase in wages. However the minister of labour was determined to make an example of anyone flouting employment law. The strikers were fined £5 each and the slaughterhouse company was charged a substantial amount for agreeing the settlement.

The minister of labour at the time was none other than John Millar, former leader of the Maritime Council, who had been elected

Blackball miners above and below ground in 1908.
A miner's strike in the village of Blackball in 1908 changed the face of New Zealand industrial relations. The illegal strike went on for three months and the government tried desperately to end it by imposing fines on miners and threatening them with imprisonment. The strike gave birth to a militant trade union centre, the New Zealand Federation of Labour, which became known as the 'Red Fed'.

to Parliament in 1893. With his detailed knowledge of arbitration and conciliation, he was appointed chairman of the labour bills committee in 1899 and as minister of labour from 1906 very soon came into conflict with his former comrades in the trade union movement. He pushed through amendments to the arbitration act that increased the penalties for striking, but that did not prevent a growing number of disputes in defiance of the arbitration laws. Then in 1908 a miners' strike changed the face of industrial relations and also gave birth to a new organisation, the New Zealand Federation of Labour. The strike started over the length of the meal break. Instead of the customary half-hour, the miners in the village of Blackball were only given fifteen minutes. When a claim for a half-hour was registered, the local manager sacked five union leaders, which triggered a walk-out. The Employers Association demanded that the government end the strike and Millar's labour department responded by threatening the strikers with imprisonment. The arbitration court ordered the miners back to work and imposed fines on the union and the strikers. However, the strikers ignored the threats and the fines remained unpaid. The strike went on for three months before the company capitulated and conceded the thirty-minute break.

Scots in the new 'Red Fed'

The miners could no longer trust the arbitration court and instead learned to rely on their own strength and organisation. Inspired by the success of the strike, they formed a new union that refused to register with the arbitration court. They then looked beyond their own industry and invited like-minded unions to join them in a new trade union centre, the New Zealand Federation of Labour. The shearers, the carpenters and the waterside workers responded to the call. Within two years, almost a quarter of New Zealand's trade unionists were affiliated to the federation. As some of its key leaders were Marxists and revolutionary Socialists, it became known as the 'Red Fed'.

Many of these leaders were Scottish. John Dowgray, who came from Bothwell, learned his trade and politics in the Lanarkshire coalfields. Born in 1873, Dowgray attended the Coatbridge Mining Academy before following his father down the pit. He joined the Independent Labour Party and became active in the Lanarkshire Miners Union. An avid reader, he accumulated a large collection of Socialist literature, and later recalled that when he first landed in New Zealand he had fifteen shillings in his pocket and two tons of books. His parents and brothers were already in New Zealand when Dowgray joined them in 1907. With his significant trade union experience and commitment, he was a welcome recruit to the Federation of Labour. He was elected treasurer and a member of the six-person management board of its newspaper, the *Labour Leader*.

In 1911 the government set up a royal commission to investigate mounting concerns in the mining industry, and Dowgray was selected to represent the coalminers. His ability to absorb detailed information and to present a case effectively was recognised by his colleagues and by his fellow commissioners. A tough and astute negotiator, he refused to be browbeaten by the more formally educated members of the commission. He rejected the recommendations of the final report and instead produced his own minority report that lambasted the piecework system used in the mines. Dowgray's report became a charter of coalfield grievances. A number of notable victories were won in the federation's first years, mostly without recourse to strike action. But in 1912 it suffered a major setback in the gold-mining town of Waihi when some of the mining mechanics set up a breakaway union. The other miners refused to work with them but the breakaway union had management support. Two months into the dispute a general election was held and the Liberal government was replaced with the anti-union Reform Party. Immediately the new government upped the ante and drafted in extra armed police to the area. At the height of the strike, 10 per cent of the New Zealand police force was stationed in the small town. As the dispute dragged on, scabs were brought to the mines every day under police protection, running the gauntlet of miners and their wives on the picket line.

But it was alleged that the mining company deliberately selected strike-breakers who had police records for violent behaviour. There were reports that some of them were armed and were attacking miners away from the picket lines. On Monday 11 November a crowd of well-organised scabs went on the rampage through the town, attacking anyone who got in their way. They looted the union's general store and when the police commissioner announced he could no longer guarantee public safety, the miners agreed to call off the pickets. But the next day armed strike-breakers, accompanied by police constables, marched on the miners' hall, where pickets normally gathered. Fred Evans, one of only three men present, panicked and drew a gun. The mob continued towards him and he fired, slightly wounding a policeman. Evans was then chased before being felled by a police baton and kicked to death by the scabs. The

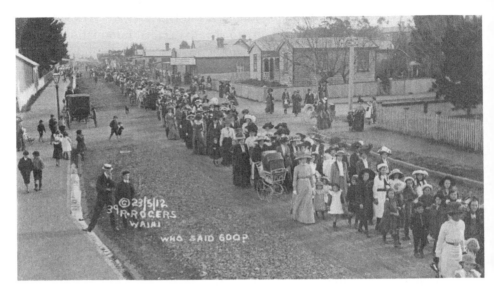

Women and children march during Waihi miners' strike 1912.
The strike in Waihi was a major setback for the Federation of Labour. It was alleged
that the mining company deliberately selected strikebreakers who had police records
for violent behaviour. Miners and their families were beaten, threatened, and chased
out of Waihi. (Courtesy P J O'Farrell Collection, Alexander Turnbull Library,
Wellington)

mob then hunted other strikers and over the next two days miners and their families were beaten, threatened and chased out of Waihi.

Although three thousand mourners attended Fred Evans's funeral in Auckland, the sight of union members being hounded out of their own town by scabs was a humiliating spectacle for the Federation of Labour. But the mining company's tactics alarmed the moderate unions within the Trades and Labour Councils. They were also deeply concerned at the anti-union position the new government had adopted, and this was compounded by the government's announcement of further anti-union legislation. Financial support for strikers was to be made illegal and restrictions were to be placed on picketing during a strike. With the entire trade union movement now under attack from the state, a number of union leaders took the opportunity to call for a united response. In 1913 almost every union in the country attended a conference to establish the United Federation of Labour (UFL). Dowgray was elected vice-president of the new organisation, but within four months its very existence was threatened.

New Zealand's employers and the Reform Party government were concerned that the new unified trade union centre would embark on a campaign of industrial action at the height of the export season, when its bargaining position would be strongest. Evidence suggests that the employers deliberately provoked a confrontation before this could happen and before the new federation was properly organised. Two local disputes happened simultaneously: one in the mines, and one on the docks. At the Huntley mine, which was owned by one of the leaders of the Reform Party, sixteen miners were dismissed for little reason, resulting in all Huntley's miners ceasing work. In the docks, a dispute about overtime payments by a small number of shipwrights led to a mass meeting in working hours by 1,500 members of the Waterside Workers Union. When they returned to work after the meeting they were sent home for violating an agreement and non-union workers were given their jobs.

The two disputes escalated out of the control of the union leadership. Several unions called out their members in sympathy without waiting for instructions from the executive of the federation. Strikers occupied the wharves, but the government enrolled young farmers as 'special' constables to unload the ships. The situation deteriorated into the most violent confrontation in New Zealand's history. The police commissioner told his men to take no prisoners and the local strike leaders responded in kind. The leader of the opposition compared the scene in Wellington

Protest march during 1913 general strike. Two local disputes – one in the mines, and one on the docks – escalated into a general strike. A number of the union leaders were arrested for incitement and after six weeks the strike collapsed. (Courtesy S C Smith Collection, Alexander Turnbull Library, Wellington)

Protest march in Wellington during 1913 General Strike (Courtesy S C Smith Collection, Alexander Turnbull Library, Wellington)

to a Mexican civil war, as daily street fighting took place between strikers and the 'specials'. British Navy frigates visiting New Zealand were put on alert to assist if required, and the marines put on a show of strength to intimidate the strikers.

The UFL felt it had little choice but to issue a call for a general strike. However, the response outside Auckland was not encouraging, with key workers such as the railwaymen declining to participate. The following day a number of the leaders were arrested for incitement, including Tom Young, UFL president and leader of the seamen's union. John Dowgray became acting president for the rest of the strike. In an attempt to extend the struggle he tried to persuade the railwaymen to join in, but was rebuffed by their leaders. An approach to the shearers met with the same response. Realising that there was no way the strike could be won, he then sued for peace, asking the employers and the government to accept arbitration. But it was clear that nothing short of unconditional surrender would be acceptable to the government. After six weeks some of the strikers started drifting back to work. The seamen made a separate deal with the shipping companies, provoking bitterness and derision from the miners and the waterside workers. The UFL was forced to call an end to the strike, but the miners continued for a further three months.

The strike and its aftermath had many similarities with the maritime strike of 1890. Both had been triggered by provocative action by employers, and both were deliberately prolonged to achieve the obliteration of militant trade unionism. They lasted almost the same length of time and ended in divisions between the unions. Both had been difficult strikes to explain to the New Zealand public, who were on the side of the government throughout. The year 1913, which had opened with great hopes of unity within the labour movement, ended in disaster and disappointment. At the UFL conference in 1914, Young and Dowgray resigned and the organisation ceased operating for a period.

The miners, the First World War and its aftermath

Like most of the strike leaders, Dowgray was sacked and blacklisted. Out of work for nine months, he somehow survived and eventually found a job at the Millerhill coalfield. Despite his bitter experience he accepted a nomination for leader of the local union and then became the driving force to rebuild a new national miners' union. Fortunately, this time the miners' bargaining position was much improved by the increase in demand for coal during the First World War. Dowgray returned to centre stage of the United Federation of Labour and was elected president in 1915. The following year, he presided over the UFL conference that agreed to establish the New Zealand Labour Party.

During the war, the coalfields became gripped with anti-war fervour. The Socialists campaigned against New Zealand's involvement and the miners called a strike against the Military Service Act that had introduced conscription. A notable victory was achieved when the government agreed to exempt the miners from the call-up. Women played a prominent role in the anti-war protests, and a number became national figures as a result. One of the best known was Janet McTaggart, who was born in Scotland and had trained as a teacher before emigrating. She had married fellow Scot William McTaggart, and settled in the mining town of Rumanga. She was a committed Socialist and despite raising eleven children, she was still able to devote her energy to the anti-conscription campaigns and the local school board.

There was a general increase in political consciousness during the war. Edward Hunter, from Lanarkshire, who gave classes in Marxism in the mining villages, reported that his attendances had risen four-fold. Hunter, a poet and songwriter, was known throughout the coalfields for his revolutionary views. Under the pen name of 'Billy Banjo', he wrote a column in the *Maoriland Worker*, in which he often condemned the government for its failure to tackle the social problems of the miners. He also used the column to campaign for better planning of mining towns, describing some of them as 'hell-holes'. An active member of the miners' union, he was jailed for sedition during the 1913 strike.

Before the end of the war the miners decided to leave the United Federation of Labour and Dowgray was forced to resign as its president. By the 1920s a new generation of activists began to assert themselves in the coalfields and Dowgray lost much of his authority. A new union, the United Mine Workers was formed, and many of its young radical members owed their political allegiance to the Communist Party. Although it had few members, the Communist Party was beginning to influence key sections of the working class. In 1926, it moved its headquarters from Wellington to New Zealand's coalfield region on South Island, where its leading cadre was Angus McLagan.

After the 1913 strike, McLagan had been blacklisted from the coalmines and was forced to look for work on farms and construction sites. Following the death of his mother in 1919 he went home to Scotland only to find that thousands of miners were emigrating as a result of the post-war depression. Eighteen months later he decided to return to New Zealand and managed to find a job back in mining. During the 1920s he began to be regarded as the mining union's leading figure. Fearless in his condemnation of the mine owners, and renowned for his integrity and strength of character, he was elected general secretary of the United Mine Workers in 1927. Leading the country's miners was a formidable task in itself, but that same year he was also appointed general secretary of the small, but highly active Communist Party of New Zealand.

By the end of the 1920s, the demand for coal fell sharply, affecting the bargaining position of the miners, and consequently the industrial strategy of the union. The changing situation led to a rift between McLagan and members of the Communist Party's executive about the use of strike action. An Australian coal strike became the catalyst for McLagan's departure from the party. The New South Wales coalminers were engaged in a lengthy strike and a union official from Australia came to New Zealand to seek support. The official was a member of the Australian Communist Party and he urged New Zealand miners to refuse to export coal to Australia. McLagan was as militant and as uncompromising in his dealings with employers as any New Zealand trade union leader, but he was also highly pragmatic. On this occasion he felt that the odds were stacked against this type of solidarity action and any involvement in the Australian dispute would invite the union's annihilation. He pointed out that coal was being supplied from other parts of Australia itself and felt the best strategy for the New Zealand miners would be to organise a levy of members to support the New South Wales strikers. However the Communist Party instructed its members to campaign for a ban on the export of coal to Australia, placing its general secretary in an invidious position. But McLagan, known as 'the man of iron', was as unyielding to his comrades as he was to employers. In the knowledge that he would be expelled, he refused to be browbeaten by the party's executive. Most Communist trade unionists supported McLagan's analysis and left along with him, wiping out virtually all the influence the Communist Party had in the trade union movement.

Like most New Zealand unions, the United Mine Workers struggled to survive during the Great Depression and was almost decimated by pit closures and work rationing. Miners were forced to accept a 10 per cent cut in pay in 1931, which was followed by further cuts the next year. The rest of industry fared no better, but political resistance slowly developed and the election of a Labour government in 1935 changed the course of the New Zealand trade union movement. A minimum wage was fixed, a forty-four hour week was established and controversially, compulsory trade union membership was introduced. Under pressure from the government, a new trade union centre was set up in 1937 and given the old title of the Federation of Labour (FOL). Industrial and craft unions joined forces to constitute a formidable organisation with a membership of almost a quarter of a million.

Much of the increase was owing to the law that introduced compulsory union membership, but this could often be a double-edged sword. Many employers supported it because it gave the government a greater degree of control over unions. If a union did not comply with government policy it ran the risk of deregistration, forcing its members to join a government-approved union or lose their job. However, never before had the New Zealand trade union movement achieved such a degree of unity. The militant industrial unions and the moderate craft unions agreed to share the responsibilities of leadership of the FOL.

Angus McLagan was acknowledged leader of the industrial unions and had become a staunch advocate of the Labour government. He had accepted a number of crucial compromises that helped achieve unity at the conference. Although he did not canvass support, the delegates showed their appreciation for McLagan's endeavours by electing him FOL president. Another Scotsman emerged as the champion of the craft unions and was elected secretary/treasurer of the FOL. Fred Cornwell was born in Hamilton, Lanarkshire, and after serving an apprenticeship as a painter and decorator, emigrated to Wellington in 1907. By 1912 he was the full-time secretary of the Wellington Society of Painters and Decorators, and the union's delegate to the trades council. Despite the difficulties the unions faced during the 1920s, the Wellington Trades Council had the funds to build an impressive trades hall, which was opened in 1928 when Cornwell became its secretary. He remained secretary of the trades council until his appointment with the Federation of Labour. Throughout the internal wrangles of the trade union movement, Cornwell was a strong believer in a united trade union movement and his consistent commitment to unity led to his election as secretary/treasurer of the FOL.

Cornwell was described by colleagues as calm and reassuring. He was an extremely popular figure whose management and negotiating skills were essential for the smooth running of the FOL. He had also been one of the key figures in the Labour Party from 1911 and his close contact

Angus McLagan was born in Calder, West Lothian. In 1927 he became general secretary of New Zealand's United Mine Workers. That year he was also appointed general secretary of the Communist Party of New Zealand, but he resigned from the Party in 1929. In 1937 he was elected president of the Federation of Labour and worked alongside fellow Scotsman Fred Cornwell, the secretary/treasurer. (Courtesy S P Andrew Collection, Alexander Turnbull Library, Wellington)

with the Labour Party leadership was a further asset during a period when the relationship with the Labour government was at its most fruitful. Although McLagan generally overshadowed him, the two Scots worked well as a team, bringing different strengths to the movement.

The Second World War, the FOL and a Labour government

The outbreak of the Second World War brought the government and trade unions closer than they had ever believed possible. The wartime economy ended unemployment, but emergency wartime regulations gave the government powers to direct people into essential industries. It also prohibited strike action, although a price-stabilisation programme was supposed to keep wages and prices aligned. Recognising the importance of union co-operation, advisory committees and boards were established involving trade unionists. Fred Cornwall served on a number of these bodies: the industrial emergency council, which regulated conditions of employment; the industrial manpower committee, which administered the direction of labour; and the economic stabilisation committee, which controlled prices and wages. The commitment of the FOL to the government's wartime policies was crucial to their success.

However, there were many clashes between the government and trade unions along the way. Businesses took advantage of wartime shortages and increased the prices of basic goods. This widespread profiteering led to unofficial strike action and trade union leaders were expected to persuade their members to go back to work. However, a ruling by the arbitration court at the end of 1941 threatened to end the FOL's collaboration. The court refused to increase wages in line with price rises. McLagan had just returned from the South Island coalfields, where he had been given a rough time defending the government against a stream of criticism. He called for a showdown meeting with the government and Prime Minister Peter Fraser agreed to his request.

This meeting became famous for McLagan's four-and-a-half-hour tirade against Fraser and his failed price-stabilisation policy. He threatened withdrawal of FOL co-operation and called on the government to resign. No one had dared to address Fraser in this way and as the two Scots locked horns in a fierce row others had to intervene to cool tempers. With neither prepared to give ground, it was agreed to reconsider the issue at a future meeting. However, McLagan was the indisputable victor. Two weeks later the arbitration court reversed their decision and made an acceptable award based on inflation. The government also announced

Angus McLagan addressing a trade union organised anti-facist demonstration outside parliament in Wellington, 1945. During the Second World War McLagan had been appointed to the Upper House and now had several roles: he was general secretary of the United Mine Workers; president of the Federation of Labour; a member of the War Cabinet; and Minister of Manpower. In 1946 he was appointed Minister of Labour. (Courtesy John Pascoe collection, Alexander Turnbull Library, Wellington)

that Angus McLagan was appointed to the Upper House and was the new minister of manpower.

By now McLagan was one of the most powerful figures in the country. He was general secretary of the United Mine Workers, president of the Federation of Labour, member of the War Cabinet, and minister of manpower. Many people, including civil servants, regarded him as the best brain in the cabinet. But he never courted popularity and seemed to have no ambition to climb higher, which was something of an anomaly for a politician. To most people outside his small circle of friends he remained cold and remote. His close colleagues had hoped that his marriage in 1930, at the age of thirty-nine, would have brought out the more tender side of his personality. But they were to be disappointed. Indeed, he seemed happiest when asked to carry out unpopular tasks. Despite this he was easily irritated by hostile or inaccurate reports in the press and would often complain to newspaper editors. Ironically, many of his best speeches went unreported because journalists were scared to misrepresent what he said.

The Cold War and betrayal

The Cold War signalled the start of an anti-Communist hysteria that led to some of the most hostile internal clashes the trade union movement had experienced. The New Zealand Communist Party had lost its trade union core in the late 1920s when most of them followed Angus McLagan out of the party. It made some gains during the Depression, but after the Soviet Union's entry into the war its membership rose. Of the party's one thousand or so activists, a substantial number were highly influential in their unions and trades councils. Alex Drennan, chairman of the Communist Party, was the most high-profile Communist in New Zealand. In 1946 he was president of the Auckland Trades Council, vice-president of the Waterside Workers Union, and a member of the national council of the FOL.

Born in Greenock, Drennan worked as a draughtsman in a local shipyard before he moved to New Zealand in 1925. At the start of the Depression he lost his job and started campaigning for the Unemployed Workers Movement, one of the biggest mass movements in New Zealand. In 1931, he joined the Communist Party and became one of its most active members in Auckland. He was arrested on a number of occasions, the first time for trying to prevent police and bailiffs evicting a mother and her five children from their home. He was sentenced to a month's imprisonment with hard labour, but it did not stop him continuing the anti-eviction work. Along with five others, he was arrested and imprisoned for three months with hard labour for defying a ban on street meetings. He took over the leadership of the Unemployed Workers Movement and organised many of the biggest demonstrations seen in New Zealand. He was arrested again in 1940 for an anti-war speech and given three years' probation, during which he was forbidden to speak in public or take part in any Communist Party activity. He became party chairman in 1946, just in time for the start of the Cold War.

The government continued its wartime policy of stabilisation of prices and wages, or a prices and incomes policy as it was known elsewhere. To profess the Socialist alternative economic strategy was seen as treasonous. The government, along with its allies in the FOL, grew increasingly intolerant of radicals within their own party as well as Communists and others on the left. They began to see the hand of international Communism in any union opposition to government policy, and every strike, regardless of how justified, was blamed on Communist troublemakers.

When Auckland carpenters started industrial action over a pay claim in 1949, the government decided to take a firm stance. The Auckland Carpenters' Union president was a well known Communist and the opportunity presented itself to confront one of the most clearly identified Communist unions in the country. An ultimatum to the carpenters to resume normal working was rejected and the minister of labour de-registered the union. With the assistance of the FOL he then set up a scab union. The carpenters fought on, but in the end lost the dispute and also lost their union. The union-busting minister of labour was none other than Angus McLagan. He had been elected to parliament in 1946 and resigned from his union positions. He was given a portfolio that included labour, mines, employment and immigration, and was one of the key ministers in the cabinet. McLagan was remorseless when he chose to fight, and the former Communist Party general secretary was determined to break Communist control of the carpenters' union. Like John Millar before, his previous union role and left-wing past was no impediment to ruthlessly carrying out government policy.

However, his sharp intellect and single-mindedness often left him isolated in parliament, with few close political allies. His parliamentary colleagues avoided clashing with him and no opposition parliamentarians dared tangle with him in debate. He had taught himself to write accurate shorthand and could quote back verbatim every word used by an opponent.

However, his public speaking style was too cold and belligerent for him to be regarded as a top performer. Despite his talent and determination, he had no ambition to be leader of the Labour Party, or to bother with the political intrigue necessary to achieve the position. When the Labour Party lost the 1949 election and Peter Fraser died the following year, McLagan was content to remain a backbench MP and watch while another epic trade union struggle developed on the waterfront (see Chapter 13, pages 378-381). He held his seat at the 1949 election and remained an MP until his death in 1956. He was never as comfortable in the political field as he was in the trade union movement. For most of his life he was on the militant left of the labour movement, but was never forgiven by his former comrades for his union-busting tactics as minister of labour. He defended his role in destroying the Auckland carpenters' union on the grounds that it threatened the government's stabilisation programme, which, he rationalised, was an essential step to achieve the orderly progress from capitalism to Socialism. But his main legacy was in helping to develop the United Mine Workers and the New Zealand Federation of Labour into powerful trade union organisations, both of which lasted for many years after his death.

Chapter 13

Toby Hill and the post-war New Zealand trade unions

During the Great Depression Christchurch's Cranmer Square was the venue for regular open-air meetings of the unemployed, who were addressed by some of the county's leading politicians and trade union leaders. But on one occasion the official speakers had been held up on their way from the west coast. The crowd became restless and as they began drifting home, a fourteen-year-old boy seized the initiative. He jumped on to the empty platform and started speaking. At first most of the gathering found it amusing to be addressed by a kid in short trousers, but they soon realised that this boy with the slight Scottish accent knew what he was talking about. They stood in admiration as he explained the evils of the capitalist system, and the invidiously unfair position the unemployed were in. They roared their approval as he condemned the government for its inaction and called for a Socialist transformation of society. Their enthusiastic applause at the end of his speech was as much for the conviction he displayed as it was for his delivery. It did not take long for word to spread about the boy's intervention. When Big Jim Roberts, national secretary of the Waterside Workers Union, heard about it, he sent for him and asked him to do small jobs for the union. Perhaps he realised then that he was grooming his successor.

Tobias Hill came from Blantyre in Lanarkshire and was born in 1915. He was the son of an Irishman who had worked in the Belfast shipyards before moving to the Lanarkshire coalmines. His mother was born in Blantyre and had worked in a mill from the age of six. In 1925, when Hill was ten, the close-knit Catholic family emigrated to New Zealand and settled in Christchurch. Even though he was a young boy when he arrived, he never forgot the culture shock of leaving home and settling in a different country. He empathised with others who had gone thorough the same dramatic change, and throughout his life made a point of befriending newly arrived immigrants and their families to give them support. He was a typical football-mad young boy and missed the Scottish passion for the game, which was not New Zealand's most popular sport. But he played football for as long as he could and when he hung up his boots he continued to support his local team. Tobias (Toby) attended St Mary's Primary School and although he was accepted for St Bede's College, his family could not afford the school uniform and books. At the age of fourteen he left school and went to sea as a cabin boy, where he joined the Federated Cooks and Stewards Union. Already a staunch Socialist, he had read *The Ragged Trousered Philanthropists* at age twelve. This, together with his strong Christian beliefs and the grinding poverty of his childhood, moulded his thinking for the remainder of his life.

After two years he had enough of life as a cabin boy and found a job at the Woolsten Tanneries, immediately becoming active in the union and helping lead a strike. But in 1936 he went back to sea as a ship's fireman sailing across the Pacific to California. During this time he made friends with maritime workers on the Pacific coast, particularly Harry Bridges, later to lead the United States Longshoremen's Union. By 1938 he settled down to work as a docker or 'wharfie' at the Lyttleton docks in Christchurch, where he soon became a union delegate. Led by Jim Roberts, the Waterside Workers Union, known simply as the Watersiders, was one of the most powerful and best organised in New Zealand and had developed a highly political cadre of shop stewards. During the Spanish Civil War, they collected over £5,000 for ambulances for the Republicans. In the 1940s the Watersiders continued their support for the Spanish working people by placing a ban on the export of wool to Franco's Spain. Always one of Roberts' favourites, Hill became one of the most prominent leaders of the union and in 1942, when he was only twenty-six, he defeated two other candidates to take over the helm from his mentor.

A year later, the formidable Harold (Jock) Barnes became president. Although born in Auckland, Barnes was nicknamed Jock at school because of assumed Scottish antecedents. Barnes was the more dominant figure, but he was often seen as arrogant and his personality sometimes caused problems with employers, the government, and other union leaders. Hill was neither flamboyant nor theatrical and had the ability and patience to explain complex issues to his members in a way they understood. Although they were never close friends, the pair worked well together and during the 1940s the union became more militant and left wing. In conjunction with the Australian wharfies, they refused to handle any cargo that was going to support the Dutch colonisers trying to resist the Indonesian independence movement, a ban that lasted from 1946 to 1949. They also took a stand in support of Chinese seamen, and achieved equal pay rates for them while they were sailing in New Zealand waters.

Toby Hill and his son Louis, 1948. Tobias (Toby) Hill came from Blantyre in Lanarkshire and went to sea as a cabin boy when he left school. His father was an Irishman who worked in the Lanarkshire coalmines, and his mother had worked in a Blantyre mill from the age of six. He became general secretary of the Waterside Workers Union when he was only twenty-six.

However, problems were developing on the wharves that were leading to a highly confrontational atmosphere. The wharfies were working excessive hours as the amount of cargo going through the main city wharves radically increased. Twelve hour shifts were being worked and a sixty-hour working week was not uncommon. Some of the jobs were dirty, arduous and unsafe. Handling obnoxious substances and rotting food were among the least pleasant tasks, and work in freezer hatches caused the union concern. Accidents were common and injuries of all kinds were reported. Campaigns for bonus payments for handling some of the worst cargos caused disputes and a series of strikes starting in 1947 caused friction between the Labour government and the union. In 1948, Bob Semple, a government minister and former miners' union official, spoke vehemently about the 'Communist wreckers' who were leading the Waterside Workers Union. The press gave the speech extensive coverage and others were encouraged to wade in. Neither Hill nor Barnes was a Communist, and of the leadership only Alex Drennan was a Communist Party member. Drennan, from Greenock (see Chapter 12, pages 370-371) was vice-president of the union from 1943 to 1947 and then after a short break until 1949.

Hill was actually a practising Catholic but it suited the government, the employers and the press to depict any left union leader as a Communist. The campaign took its toll at a personal level, as Hill's daughter Yvonne later recalled. She was soon aware of the increased hostility directed towards her family. Although she was only nine, she was often subjected to verbal abuse by strangers. On one occasion she was approached by a man in the street who poked his fingers in her chest and started a tirade with 'You tell your father ...'. She never did tell her father because she was aware he had plenty to worry about already.

However, within the trade union movement there was also a growing resentment of the Waterside Workers Union, which had sided with the carpenters' union during its dispute in 1949 and had accused the Federation of Labour (FOL) of strike-breaking (see Chapter 12, page 371). The Watersiders' refusal to withdraw this assertion eventually led to its expulsion at the FOL conference in 1950. A large proportion of delegates, representing a third of the FOL membership, joined the Watersiders when they walked out of the conference. A new trade union centre was set up, but most of the other unions that had walked out soon returned to the FOL. This left the Watersiders isolated from the mainstream of the trade union movement. While the union could have

Toby Hill (second from left), along with union president, Jock Barnes (third from left), and two other union officials, inspect a dirty cargo, circa 1949. Some of the warfies' jobs, such as handling obnoxious substances and rotting food, were dirty and unsafe.

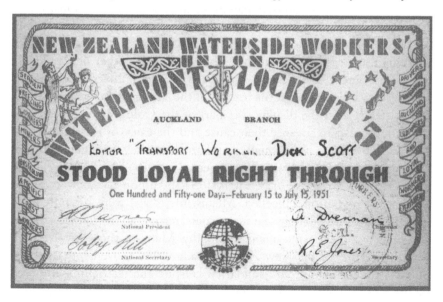

Waterside Workers Union loyalty card. The union prided itself on its excellent organisation and the high level of political awareness of its members. Very few union members broke the five month strike. In the aftermath of the dispute all of Auckland's two thousand union members were sacked.

coped with this under normal circumstances, the conservative National Party had defeated Labour in the 1949 election, and was committed to a hard line against any further waterfront disputes. The inevitable confrontation took place at the beginning of 1951 when the Waterside Workers Union and the government began a vicious battle that was to become one of the defining moments for the New Zealand trade union movement and the most significant class conflict since the strike of 1913.

The Waterfront Lockout

The confrontation started when the arbitration court awarded a 15 per cent increase to all workers covered by the industrial arbitration system. But this did not apply to the wharfies whose employment was controlled by the Waterfront Industry Commission. The stevedoring companies refused to pay the increase to the wharfies and instead offered 9 per cent. The union responded moderately by imposing an overtime ban but then, to the nation's surprise, the employers countered by dismissing the entire workforce and locking them out. Such an immediate hardline reaction was seen as part of a government-inspired plan to break the power of the union. The government called a state of emergency, giving it draconian powers to seize union funds, to ban picketing and demonstrations, and to stop any financial support to the strikers and even any food for the children of strikers. The prime minister made it plain he would not negotiate with the union and was so unequivocal that it was clear that he would use the full resources of the state to defeat the union. The rhetoric of the Cold War was used against the leaders of the Watersiders, the minister of labour stating that the dispute was 'part of the Cold War, engineered by the Communists to advance their cause and the cause of Russia'.

The Watersiders were equally emphatic that they were going to take on the government and win. They rejected an attempt at mediation by the FOL, and at the end of February 1951 the union's assets were seized and their registration cancelled. Meanwhile, scabs were brought in to unload ships. Immediately seamen, miners, refrigeration workers, drivers, and hydro workers came out in sympathy. Many of those involved felt that the destiny of the New Zealand trade union movement depended on their determination and solidarity. Despite the restrictions imposed by the emergency regulations, the Watersiders enjoyed the support of a well-organised relief network.

The union prided itself on its excellent organisation and a high level of political awareness among its members. It had debating clubs, a welfare

Demonstrations during the waterfront lockout in 1951. When the Waterside Workers
Union banned overtime the employers locked-out the workforce and the government
called a state of emergency. Other workers came out in sympathy, but the Federation
of Labour opposed the strikes. The dispute lasted more than five months and ended in
crushing defeat. (Bottom photograph shows Toby Hill in the foreground just before
police attack demonstrators).

structure and its own brass bands. Appeals went out for assistance and farmers donated sheep and cattle. Market gardeners gave vegetables and skilled workers in the towns provided work and services for free. At every port a women's auxiliary was formed to collect money and food.

Agnes Duffy, whose husband was a wharfie, was a member of the Auckland women's branch of the union and during the strike she became well known throughout the country. Agnes was born in the Govan district of Glasgow and emigrated to New Zealand in 1931 when she was nineteen. Arriving alone in the midst of the Depression, and with no New Zealand contacts to receive her, she worked as a domestic servant, sometimes for no more than food and shelter. Afterwards she said that there was little difference between Glasgow and Auckland during the Depression, except in New Zealand the weather was better. Every Hogmanay she cried with homesickness and longed to visit Scotland. During the war she was directed into employment as a cleaner in the main post office in Auckland. She joined the union, but found the officials did not want to know about the problems of women workers. She persevered and forced them to recognise the issues affecting women in the workforce. Her persistence paid off when she was elected to the district executive of the Cleaners and Caretakers Union at the end of the war. She remained on the executive until 1950 when she was elected to Auckland city council on a Labour Party ticket. During the 1951 strike she was the Waterside Workers Union's entertainments organiser and every Sunday actors and musicians volunteered to perform at her fund-raising concerts.

Money poured in from all over the world and some of Toby Hill's contacts proved invaluable. Harry Bridges, the American longshoreman's leader who had been a friend of Hill since his days on the New Zealand to California run, was the first to offer financial support. His union collected $10,000 from its US members within a couple of weeks. The Australian wharfies and British dockers both contributed £50,000, which was the equivalent of £1.25m at 2011 values. But under the emergency regulations it was not possible for strikers to receive the money through the usual legal channels. Instead, union officials made unofficial trips to Australia, travelling in the engine room as a guest of the crew, to collect money contributed by the Australian wharfies. To avoid arousing the suspicion of the police and customs, various methods were tried. On one occasion an eighteen-year-old Maori seaman was handed £2,000 to carry ashore. That seaman was Mat Rata and he later became well known as an MP and cabinet minister.

Toby Hill was responsible for much of the accounting and distribution. As smuggling in money became more difficult, especially after the Seamen's Union joined the strike, he looked for other ways of overcoming the emergency regulations. Then a clever lawyer, who later became a high court judge, gave him the advice he needed. The money was simply deposited in banks in Australia, Britain and America. Hill then arranged for advertisements to be placed in New Zealand newspapers offering foreign currency through a third party at competitive rates. Businessmen exchanged New Zealand dollars for access to the amount they needed. Most hadn't a clue they were dealing with the Waterside Workers Union.

Solidarity action by other key sections of the trade union movement initially strengthened the position of the Watersiders and swung the balance of the dispute in their favour. But nine days after the lock-out began, the Federation of Labour held a special conference that dealt the Watersiders a demoralising blow. In a statement couched in similar Cold War terms to that used by the government, the conference condemned the leadership of the union and accused them of pursuing policies 'that the New Zealand troops were fighting against in Korea'. It called on trade unionists to abandon their Communist leadership and place their dispute in the hands of the Federation of Labour. Soon afterwards some workers began to drift back, but the miners, seamen and refrigeration workers carried on in support of the Watersiders.

By the middle of April, some six weeks into the strike, the Communist Party was urging the Watersiders' leadership to give up, but they rejected the advice. The employers and the government sensed victory and upped the stakes. Instead of simply forcing through the 9 per cent offer, they sought to destroy the Waterside Workers Union. With the assistance of the Federation of Labour, they set up and registered a separate union in each port. The dispute dragged on towards its predictable conclusion. The miners decided to end their strike in July, and very soon the others followed suit. After more than five months, and at enormous expense to the country, New Zealand's longest and most bitterly fought national industrial dispute came to an end.

Repercussions of the waterfront dispute

Militant trade unionism was dealt a crushing blow and the strongest union ever formed in New Zealand was destroyed. It was split into a total of twenty-six port unions, some of which had a membership of fewer than twenty people. All the Waterside Workers Union leaders were banned from ever working in the industry again. In Auckland, where the union was strongest, all two thousand workers at the port were sacked. The refrigeration workers suffered the same fate, with their union deregistered and government-approved unions formed in their place. Shortly after the dispute ended, the government called a snap election and won a resounding victory. Although the Federation of Labour reasserted full control over the trade union movement, those who supported the strike never forgot its betrayal, and the animosity continued for decades afterwards.

Alex Drennan had been under enormous pressure from the start of the Cold War. Before the waterfront dispute he had been defeated as president of the Auckland Trades Council and lost his position on the Federation of Labour national committee. At a Communist Party conference in 1951, he was made a scapegoat for the Watersiders' blunders. He was attacked by delegates for his part in the debacle and was not re-elected to the national committee. He was fifty-two when he was sacked, but he found work in the construction industry. A few years later he was employed as a miller in a distillery and became an executive member of the Brewery Employees' Union. Despite his chastisement by the Communist Party, he accepted the criticism and continued to be an active member. When the New Zealand Communist Party took a pro-China position during the Sino-Soviet split, Drennan and other senior party members left and formed the pro-Soviet Socialist Unity Party in 1966. Most other trade unionists followed him, including Ken Douglas, one of the leaders of the Drivers Union during the waterfront dispute, who went on to become the president of the FOL. Drennan became the inaugural chairman of the Socialist Unity Party and remained its elder statesman until his death in 1971.

Toby Hill was hounded from pillar to post for the next decade, but unlike Jock Barnes, he fought his way back. He worked for a time as a storeman in a print company, but his employer came under pressure from customers to dismiss him. The Cement Workers Union offered him a job as their wages advocate, but the FOL banned his appointment. An outcast for a decade after the dispute, Hill's resilience was strengthened by his support from his wife Florence, whom he married in 1938, and their four sons and a daughter. As a family they were active during the 1950s and 60s in the Campaign for Nuclear Disarmament and the anti-apartheid movement, against the Vietnam War and French nuclear testing in the Pacific.

By 1960 the acrimony in the FOL had subsided, and Hill staged a remarkable recovery. Still only forty-five, his services were coveted by many unions. He was seen as tactically astute and flexible in negotiation. Employers accepted him because of his innate reasonableness and fairness. Many who watched him operate felt that had he been the dominant figure in the 1951 lock-out, events might have taken a different course. He organised the metal workers in Wellington and later agreed to lead negotiations for the firemen, for whom he achieved conditions and wages that they had never dreamed of.

During the 1960s and '70s he was president of the Wellington Trades Council where there were many strong characters and often deep divisions between delegates. Spirited debate and occasional acrimonious exchanges made the chairing of the meetings a constant challenge. But Hill was known for his quick wit and a firm hand that enabled order to be maintained and all points of view to be expressed. During this period, New Zealand's trade unions continued to grow in numbers and in strength. And so did the economy of the country.

From the end of the Second World War until the early 1970s New Zealand experienced a period of sustained economic growth and prosperity. Immigration increased and the population grew from 1.7 million at the end of the war to over three million by 1975. Living standards were high – New Zealand was among the top six countries in the world – and agricultural output doubled. Industrial development in engineering, steel, aluminium, plastics, paper and other timber products contributed to the steady growth of the economy. Labour was in office for only a third of this period, but there was a political consensus between the two main parties around the major economic and social issues. There was agreement on the principle of full employment, an expansion of educational opportunities, support for the national health service, and provision of old-age pensions and other welfare benefits. Governments were prepared to consult with trade unions on the economy in order to ensure industrial peace and stability. In return for steadily growing profits, businesses accepted higher taxation and greater state regulation. Throughout this period, wage differentials remained lower than anywhere else in the world, as did the gap between rich and poor.

When Labour regained office in 1972 under the leadership of Norman Kirk, a highly popular figure, the economic boom initially expanded. The New Zealand dollar was re-valued upwards and the balance of payments was showing a healthy surplus. However, Kirk died in office in 1974, just before a combination of circumstances coincided to bring about an economic collapse. The quadrupling of oil prices in

1973 changed the balance of payments surplus to a deficit, forcing the government to borrow heavily on the overseas markets. In addition, Britain's application to join the European Economic Community was accepted in 1972, closing the main market for New Zealand's agricultural produce. Labour was defeated at the election in 1975, as the country experienced its worst economic problems since the Great Depression of the 1930s. Unemployment and inflation rose to historically high levels and living standards fell. A large proportion of skilled workers began to leave the country and for the first time in the twentieth century, New Zealand's population fell.

The government v. the boilermakers

The National government that took over from Labour was met with growing industrial unrest as wages fell behind price rises. In an attempt to curb inflation, the government introduced a statutory wage freeze and new anti-union legislation. The response from the unions was an increase in militancy, and in the following year the number of working days lost was the highest since the waterfront strike in 1951. In a get-tough policy, the government decided to make an example of the Boilermakers' Union, which it deregistered in 1976. One of the most militant unions in New Zealand, the Boilermakers caused anguish to a stream of ministers of labour. They were blamed for delays in the construction of the BNZ Centre, where members of the Boilermakers' Union did the welding on the thirty-one-storey steel structure. Dominating the Wellington skyline, the headquarters of the Bank of New Zealand was the tallest building in the country. But it was dubbed the 'Boilermakers' Bank' after a series of strikes held up its completion. At one point the prime minister condemned its leaders as 'destructive trade union militants importing their class warfare attitudes from Scotland's Clydeside'.

The prime minister was referring to Con Devitt and John Findlay, both of whom were very proud of their militancy and their antecedents. Despite having been in New Zealand since 1954, Devitt still spoke with a thick Glasgow accent, and was a well-known voice on TV and radio. John Findlay was a Glaswegian who came to New Zealand in the 1940s and was president of the union. Although not as publicly visible as Devitt, he was an astute tactician and a profound influence on union policy. No contract was reached with management unless he gave it the go-ahead. Both men maintained that the Boilermakers' Union never once broke an agreement and in the case of the construction of the BNZ

Toby Hill's daughter Yvonne with Con Devitt. Cornelius Devitt from Dalmuir, West Dumbartonshire led the New Zealand Boilermakers' Union in the 1970s and was a close friend of Toby Hill and his family. Devitt became general secretary of the Manufacturing and Construction Workers Union and led a walk-out of several unions from the New Zealand Council of Trade Unions to form a rival body, the Trade Union Federation.

Centre, claimed they were made scapegoats for an ill-advised contract that caused most of the delays.

Neither Con Devitt nor John Findlay was intimidated by the government and the deregistration announcement only made them more determined. Born in Dalmuir near Clydebank in 1929, Cornelius Devitt started work during the Second World War in Clydeside's shipbuilding industry. He later attributed his knowledge and understanding of politics to the workers' forums that were organised in the shipyards. From these discussions he learned the importance of class solidarity and discipline. When he stood for the leadership of the Boilermakers' Union, he explained to his New Zealand colleagues that these were the principles on which he based his candidacy. Although heavily influenced by the radical Socialists and Communists in the shipyards, he was not a member of any party in Scotland or New Zealand, although it suited the media to describe him as a Communist or fellow traveller, and to portray his militancy as politically motivated.

Devitt was assisted in his rise up the trade union ladder by Toby Hill, who saw him as a young man with great potential. During this period Devitt became a close friend of the Hill family, but they later fell out when Hill's advice on settling some of the Boilermakers' disputes was rejected. The Boilermakers were also involved in the construction of the Mangere Bridge near Auckland airport, which was the scene of New Zealand's longest-running dispute. The union leadership withstood a barrage of criticism from the press and politicians for a strike that started in 1978 and lasted for two-and-a-half years. As a continuing reminder of their defiance, the uncompleted construction was silhouetted against the skyline to every passenger travelling through the airport. The Boilermakers led other major disputes at Marsden Point oil refinery, Kawerau pulp and paper plant and the Kinleith timber mill. However, Devitt contended that no reasonable employer had anything to fear from his union.

Meanwhile in 1974, Toby Hill returned to the first union he had joined as a cabin boy and became general secretary of the Federated Cooks and Stewards Union. Many Scots had played leading roles in the union, which had a history stretching back to the 1880s. Hill took over from another Scotsman, Jock Ramsay, who had emigrated to New Zealand via Canada, where he was also active in the seafaring unions. Shortly after Hill's appointment, Jimmy Savage from Scotland became the national president and Jock Farrell from Dundee was the key representative from South Island on the executive. Farrell, who settled in New Zealand in

Toby Hill, 1972. After the destruction of the Waterside Workers Union, Hill was ostracised by the trade union leadership but fought his way back. During the 1960s and '70s he was president of the Wellington Trades Council, and led negotiations for a number of groups of workers. In 1974, he returned to the first union he had joined as a cabin boy and became general secretary of the Federated Cooks and Stewards Union.

1959, had trained as a tailor but left his trade to work as a ship's steward. He was once asked by a tutor on a union training course what were the qualifications to be a good shop steward. He replied, 'To be a diplomat, a doormat and an acrobat.'

The Boilermakers was not the only militant union during the latter part of the '70s and early '80s when inflation was spiralling. Despite a statutory wage freeze, strike action intensified as unions sought to catch up on lost earnings. Legislation was introduced imposing penalties for illegal strikes, but this only caused more unofficial action. Daily TV and radio news bulletins were dominated by industrial disputes that were taking place in every corner of the country, and trade unions were the subject of numerous current affairs programmes. A large proportion of the prime minister's time and that of the cabinet was occupied trying to deal with strikes.

More strife as import controls are abolished

New Zealand governments had traditionally used import controls to correct deficits in the balance of payments. However, in the mid-1970s they began an industrial restructuring programme focused on industries such as textiles, footwear, cars and electronics, whose domestic prices were much higher than foreign substitutes. The protection granted to these products in the form of import tax was reduced, and in a few years almost 80 per cent of New Zealand's imports were exempt from any licensing. The effect of this policy was devastating for manufacturing industry. The textiles industry was particularly affected by cheap imports of clothing from sweatshops across the globe.

The Canterbury Clothing Workers Union was in the forefront of the fight to protect jobs in the industry. Their leader was Hugh McCrory, from Tollcross in Glasgow. He became secretary of the union in 1972 and led it for seventeen years, building a strong organisation with a number of dedicated organisers and a network of factory floor delegates. McCrory organised a vigorous campaign of resistance to the lifting of import controls, uniting workers in the industry along with sympathetic manufacturers. Street demonstrations attracting thousands of supporters were held and the National Party conference was lobbied. Throughout the early part of the '80s, the union kept up a constant steam of publicity about the effects the abolition of import controls was having, and the threat to 10,000 jobs in the apparel industry on South Island. Despite the best efforts of McCrory and his union, the predictions proved to be

Hugh McCrory from Tollcross, Glasgow was general secretary of the Canterbury Clothing Workers Union and was in the forefront of the fight to protect jobs in the textile industry.

accurate. But the job losses did not stop the union campaigning vigorously for higher pay, and workers in a number of factories took strike action to back up their demands.

McCrory had started working life as a fur cutter but changed trades to become a dental technician with Ronald McLeod Veitch, who had a shop in Peel Street in Glasgow. He joined the Union of Shop Distributive and Allied Workers and was secretary of the dental technicians' branch from 1955–61. In 1963 he emigrated to Australia, but moved to New Zealand when his family found the Sydney climate too severe in summer. He worked in a hospital in Christchurch, and although he enjoyed the job, he left his profession a year later when a full-time union position was advertised for the shop assistants' union. But it was as leader of the clothing workers that he became a well known and highly respected trade union leader.

As a male official in an overwhelmingly female occupation, McCrory naturally fought for women's rights. He was one of the few men in the leadership of the trade union movement to support equal pay for women in the 1960s. McCrory was a quiet and modest man with a good sense of humour, and was fully committed to the members he served. He was also known as an internationalist and was a central figure in the committee that organised the campaign against the war in Vietnam, an issue that caused a huge public debate about New Zealand foreign policy. As a fervent anti-racist, he was also prominent in the anti-apartheid movement. When he retired his union members placed a notice in a Christchurch newspaper that summed up how he was seen by his colleagues and members: 'Your contribution to the struggles of the working class are immeasurable and your willingness to fight oppression and exploitation wherever it occurred characterised a unique and exceptional person. Your loyalty, dedication and commitment in representing the interests of union members will never be forgotten.'

Despite the animosity between unions and the government, Prime Minister Robert Muldoon had a very cordial and constructive relationship with the president of the Federation of Labour (FOL), Tom Skinner. But when Skinner retired in 1979, a more militant president was elected to take his place, and a Communist was appointed general secretary. It was not long before the FOL flexed its muscles. In an attempt to restrain wages, the government refused to allow a 20 per cent pay deal that had been reached in negotiations between the lorry drivers and their employers. This provoked the FOL to call its first nationwide general strike. But a day before it was due to start, the government caved in and the lorry drivers received a full settlement. Two years later, however, a lengthy campaign by the FOL was powerless to prevent a wage and price freeze that lasted from 1982 until 1984.

New Zealand copies Thatcher's policies

Then the government called an early election. One factor that contributed to the decision to go early was a dispute that was taking place at the Marsden Point oil refinery. Three thousand strikers had mounted a picket line to prevent eight scaffolders from working. The scaffolders had broken ranks with their trade union over Saturday working and were being escorted to the site by police in closed vans with windows screened by heavy wire mesh. The nation watched nightly television bulletins as police in full riot gear confronted the pickets. Robert Muldoon thought he could capitalise on the country's anger against the strikers. He had been closely monitoring events in Britain and thought he could learn some lessons from Margaret Thatcher's government.

The British Trades Union Congress had reached a membership of thirteen million when the Tories won the 1979 election. This was the highest level in its history, but it was about to experience an onslaught from the newly elected government. The country had just emerged from the winter of discontent, as the media dubbed the great public sector strikes of 1978. The Labour Prime Minister, James Callaghan, was expected to call a general election in the autumn of 1978, when Labour was well ahead in the opinion polls and before the strikes began. Instead, he made the fatal decision to delay the election until the spring of 1979. The election campaign was then held amidst rapidly rising unemployment and industrial strife. The Tories were able to launch their election campaign with the slogan 'Labour isn't working', accompanied by a highly successful poster showing a dole queue stretching into the distance.

However after the Tories' victory, unemployment rose to levels not seen since the 1930s. Scotland's manufacturing base was devastated and many parts of the country are still living with the legacy today in the form of alcoholism, depression, drug-taking and heart disease. Margaret Thatcher set out to deregulate the markets, privatise state assets and dismantle the welfare state. Her great resolve was to break the power of the state and, starting with British Telecom and British Gas, she launched a fire sale of nationalised industries. She broke the link between earnings and state pensions, guaranteeing the value would become progressively lower over the years. By the end of her time as prime minister, she had unravelled the social, political and economic fabric woven by generations of trade unionists, Socialists, Social Democrats and Communists that had endured in Britain since the Second World War. By a succession of policies she broke the unions, but waited until 1984 until she took on the strongest of them. The mighty National Union of Mineworkers had launched two successful national strikes against the Tory government in 1972 and 1974, the latter bringing about the fall of the government. Determined not to fail again, and perhaps motivated by a desire for revenge, Thatcher authorised the spending of billions of pounds to defeat a strike that lasted over a year. It ended with the NUM destroyed, and the trade union movement seriously weakened.

However, in New Zealand, Robert Muldoon's gamble to play on anti-union sentiment backfired. Labour won the 1984 election and trade unionists breathed a sigh of relief on the assumption they would be spared the carnage experienced in Britain. David Lange, the new Labour prime minister, was seen as a breath of fresh air. He was a charismatic leader and powerful parliamentary performer. But the country was in severe economic trouble, with a massive trade deficit and high inflation. The economy was in danger of imploding, and creditors were severely worried about the low levels of foreign exchange reserves.

Very few people in the Labour Party, or the country at large, had a clear idea of the government's intentions regarding economic policy. Labour had been elected on a platform consistent with the Social Democratic tradition it had supported for decades. However, immediately after the election, the government began to implement policies at variance with its election manifesto. Many union leaders were desperate to believe that Labour would save them after nearly three years of a wage freeze, but any expectations they had of a close relationship with the government were soon dispelled. There were few trade unionists in the new cabinet, which consisted mainly of lawyers like Lange. There was a lack of personal rapport between the leadership of the FOL and the parliamentary Labour Party. For the first time, very few MPs had any association with the trade union movement. Indeed, the Employers Federation leaders said that Robert Muldoon was 'far more sympathetic to the workers than those who replaced him after 1984'.

The following years were bewildering to many New Zealanders, especially Labour Party members. Tight monetary policy was regarded as the key to running the economy. Economic development was to be influenced by market forces, and highly regulated and protected sectors of the economy were exposed to the market. All subsidies and incentives to farmers and business, barriers to entry to the New Zealand market, and all forms of price regulation were abandoned. The financial market was deregulated, the New Zealand dollar was allowed to float and all exchange controls were lifted. These policies sent interest rates and unemployment soaring. This was New Zealand's Thatcherite revolution but, bizarrely, the Labour Party was carrying it out.

The early call of a general election had pre-empted a proper debate on economic policy within the Labour Party. Indeed, the economic policies came, not from the Labour Party itself, but from a think tank in the Treasury. The same advice had been offered to the conservative Muldoon government, but had been rejected. Over the next two years, despite criticism from trade unionists and party activists at branch meetings and at regional conferences, the government continued the momentum to introduce monetary policy. The top rate of tax was reduced from 66 per cent to 33 per cent, and a goods and services tax (VAT) of 10 per cent was introduced. The economic policies were at odds with Labour's traditional approach and the party became locked in an ideological struggle, with many Labour activists feeling betrayed by the government's neo-liberal policies. The dramatic and instant removal of business subsidies wiped out 50 per cent of manufacturing industry and almost 300,000 jobs. The executive of the FOL seemed paralysed in disbelief as Labour embarked on an economic programme that went even further than Thatcher in Britain and Reagan in the USA.

The New Zealand Council of Trade Unions

The reform of the public sector was just as comprehensive as the private sector. State-owned enterprises were set up and in most cases were the first step towards privatisation. Major restructuring, usually associated with large-scale redundancies, preceded the sell-offs. Thirty-eight state-owned assets were sold between 1988 and 1996. New Zealand's employment legislation had historically differentiated the state-sector workers from private industrial employees. Since the formation of trade unions in New Zealand, the public sector, with the exception of the railway unions, had remained separate from the mainstream trade union movement. Civil servants, local government officers, teachers, health workers and other public sector workers were not affiliated to the Federation of Labour. They were organised collectively in their staff associations and had their

Steve Grant, general secretary of the Railway Tradesmen's Association from 1969-92, came from East Wemyss in Fife. He was also secretary of the Federation of Labour's transport unions. When the Combined State Unions and the FOL merged, Grant was elected to the national executive of the New Zealand Council of Trade Unions.

own public sector umbrella group, the Combined State Unions. But many did not regard themselves as trade unionists, and kept their distance from the industrial unions. However, the distinctive system was abolished with the passing of the State Sector Act and the public sector unions were brought within the mainstream of employment law.

One positive outcome of the upheaval was a merger between the FOL and the Combined State Unions. In 1987 the New Zealand Council of Trade Unions (CTU) was established, with a combined membership of 683,000. Ken Douglas, the Marxist leader of the Socialist Unity Party, was elected president. Faced with the merger proposals, many public sector workers were appalled at the idea and threatened to leave. On the other hand, many traditional trade unions dismissed the public sector unions as featherbedded staff associations whose policies would dilute the militancy of the FOL. Public-service unions were larger in size by New Zealand standards, national in their scope, and industry-or service-based. They differed greatly from the small, regional occupational unions, which were suspicious of the predominantly white-collar, middle-class unions wielding too much influence. As a result almost a third of the FOL conference in 1986 opposed the merger, and some of the most militant unions refused to join the CTU.

The Railway Trades Association was one of only two unions that had a foot in both camps before the merger. Railway workers were classified as industrials and had a long association with the FOL. But as their pay and conditions were covered by public sector legislation, they were also part of the Combined State Unions. The general secretary of the railway tradesmen was Steve Grant, who came from East Wemyss in Fife. His father had been a miner at the Michael colliery, but joined the Merchant Navy during the Second World War. In 1946 he sailed on the delivery voyage of a ship to New Zealand, which was built at Henry Robb shipyard in Leith. Like many seamen, he fell in love with New Zealand as soon as he sailed into the harbour in Auckland, and decided that this was the place to bring up a family. Steve Grant joined his father in Auckland in 1947. After he finished his schooling, he then served his apprenticeship as an electrician with the Union Steamship Company. For the next decade he sailed to different parts of the world, including a spell back in Scotland, where he worked at the Henry Robb shipyard in Leith. In 1959 he returned to New Zealand and found a job in the railway workshop in Auckland.

Having been a union activist throughout his time away, Grant soon became Auckland branch secretary of the Railway Trades Association, and in 1969 he was elected general secretary, a full-time job based in Wellington. Grant negotiated the pay and conditions of all railway trades and was appointed vice-chair of the Combined State Unions. He was also secretary of the FOL transport unions. When the Combined State Unions and the FOL merged, Grant was elected to the national executive of the Council of Trade Unions and held his position until he retired in 1992.

Like many trade union leaders, Grant was angry at the economic policies of the Labour government but recognised some of the beneficial social policies the government pursued. Despite its right-wing economic programme, it was committed to the expansion of the health service and the development of the education system. In foreign affairs, New Zealanders were proud of the independent stand taken by their government, especially in relation to nuclear weapons. In July 1985, the Greenpeace vessel *Rainbow Warrior* was on its way to protest against the French nuclear tests in Mururoa, and was blown up in Waitemata harbour. A crewman was killed and world attention was focussed on New Zealand in anticipation of its response. It held the French government responsible for the act of terrorism and two members of the French secret service were arrested and jailed for their roles in the plot.

However, the progressive policies adopted on these issues were not enough to convince the party activists and trade unionists. The tensions created by the Lange government's economic policies tore the Labour Party apart, led to the founding of a breakaway New Labour Party, and forced the resignation of the prime minister in 1989. Not surprisingly, the National Party won the next election and the Labour vote collapsed.

Anti-union legislation

The new National government embraced Labour's economic strategy, but began to change social policy. It embarked on a major transformation of New Zealand's welfare state, education, and healthcare system. And it also had in its sights the one market that had not been deregulated – the labour market. The Employment Contracts Act was introduced shortly after the National Party's return to government, and had a devastating effect on New Zealand's trade unions. The Act prohibited compulsory union membership, greatly restricted union access to workplaces, introduced major obstacles to multi-employer bargaining, and encouraged a shift to individual employment contracts in place of collective bargaining.

The unions mounted a vigorous campaign of opposition and organised some of the biggest protest demonstrations ever seen in New Zealand. A united front was formed of trade unions, church leaders, social action groups and some employers who saw it as a ruinous interference in employment relations. But the action fell short of a national strike and at a special conference of the Council of Trade Unions there was a major split when unions voted narrowly against a twenty-four-hour strike. The rejection of even a one-day strike against the anti-union legislation was too much to bear for some unions. They were angry and felt betrayed by the failure of the CTU to resist the union-busting legislation more forcefully. The dissident unions, led by Con Devitt, walked out of the CTU in 1993 and formed a rival organisation, the Trade Union Federation.

Devitt, by now one of New Zealand's most senior union leaders, was elected president of the new federation. His Boilermakers' Union had formed mergers with other unions and he was now secretary of the Manufacturing and Construction Workers Union. He had argued for strategic strike action against the legislation, using key workers who could have been supported indefinitely by a levy on the rest of the trade union movement. He had been a close colleague of CTU president Ken Douglas in the past, but now criticised him for failing to take the necessary steps to defend the trade union movement.

The Employment Contracts Act savagely exposed the frailty of New Zealand's unions. Their distinct legal status was removed and the practice of union registration was ended. Collective bargaining was replaced by individual contracts between employer and worker. By 1999 almost 75 per cent of the workforce was employed on individual contracts and many workers could see little point in belonging to a union that had no bargaining rights. Union membership plummeted from over 600,000 before the Act to less than half that total within a few years.

The effects of the anti-union legislation were much less marked in the public sector where, historically, membership of unions had been voluntary, and where staff rejected individual contracts. The main problem for them was that the legislation removed the exclusive representation rights enjoyed by registered unions and gave encouragement to the birth of rival organisations. The Public Services Association (PSA), the dominant union in the public sector, found itself vulnerable to breakaways by groups who did not agree with its policies. Sections of staff in the prison service, the inland revenue and customs, as well as members in the utilities, health, and local government, set up their own organisations. The formation of these groups made the task of negotiating more difficult, especially when they undermined industrial action.

Joe Toner and the partnership agreements

The PSA's response to these and other challenges was to espouse a 'partnership' approach in the public sector. Employers were invited to sign up to a partnership with the PSA in the management of their organisation. The adoption of this strategy was extremely controversial both inside the PSA and in the wider trade union movement. Joe Toner, its chief architect, was a Scotsman and one of the union's three national secretaries. But to many of his colleagues, Toner's advocacy of the partnership model came as a shock, given his political history.

One of the leading members of the Socialist Unity Party, and very closely allied with CTU president Ken Douglas, Toner had become convinced of the need for the New Zealand trade union movement to change its confrontational approach to industrial relations. But it was discussions in the Soviet Union during Gorbachev's revolutionary changes that led Toner and others to the conclusion that partnership agreements were the way forward. Soviet Communist Party officials outlined their reasons for embracing *perestroika* to Douglas, Toner and other Socialist Unity Party officials. The Soviet officials felt that there was still much to learn from capitalism and believed that it had a long way to go before it outlived its usefulness. The conclusion reached by the New Zealand Communist leaders was that trade unions in the capitalist countries should engage with employers. They should try to influence the direction of their business to the mutual benefit of workers and owners. This was a complete change in strategy for Communists, and came as a bombshell to many trade unionists in New Zealand.

Joseph Toner was born in Old Kilpatrick in 1950 and attended St Patrick's Primary in Dumbarton and St Columba's High School in Clydebank. He left at fifteen and did various jobs before serving an apprenticeship as a sheet-metalworker at the engineering company D. and J. Tullis in Clydebank. Some of his close friends were Communists and they encouraged him to read Marxist literature. With a wife and two young children to support on an apprentice's wage, Toner could easily relate to Socialism but did not have much time for political or trade union activity. He wanted a better life for his family, and when the General Electric Company advertised for workers in New Zealand, he took the opportunity to emigrate.

Joe Tonner, national secretary of the Public Services Association, was born in Old Kilpatrick, West Dumbartonshire. One of the leading members of the New Zealand Socialist Unity Party, he surprised colleagues by proposing a new strategy for the Public Services Association based on partnership agreements with employers. After the concept was accepted by his union, he surprisingly failed to be re-appointed to his position

After paying £10 each for the flight, Toner and his family had £80 left to start a new life. But they needn't have worried. They were met at Wellington airport by the company's personnel manager, who drove them to their temporary accommodation, a fully furnished three-bedroomed house. He even gave them back the money they paid for the fare. The house was like a palace compared to the room and kitchen they left in Clydebank and they could not believe their luck. The following day Toner was given a lift to work by the manager, and then shown around the factory. He was introduced to his fellow workers and had lunch at the manager's home. The afternoon was spent touring the local pubs. 'I thought I had died and gone to heaven. It seemed like a worker's paradise,' Toner recalls of his first couple of days in New Zealand. 'It was an amazing change of culture for me, as our managers in Scotland only spoke to the foremen and never to us.'

The desperate shortage of skilled labour in New Zealand forced employers to value their best workers. Toner spent the next few years as a quality controller and a supervisor in the plant. But he felt it was time for another challenge and was chosen from hundreds of hopefuls who had applied for a job as a trainee government factory inspector. He loved the job and revelled in the three-year training course, which included modules in employment legislation and regulations. He also became active in the Public Services Association in Wellington, and began to think about working full time for a union. Just after he completed his factory inspector training, the Public Services Association advertised a job for a union field officer based in Waikato. His successful application in 1979 was the start of a twenty-year involvement with the PSA, which took him to the highest position in the union by the time he was forty-six.

Around the same time he applied for the job with PSA, Toner took the plunge politically and joined the Socialist Unity Party. Although he had a lifelong interest in left-wing politics, Toner had never found an organisation he could join. The first book he ever read was *The Ragged Trousered Philanthropists*, which had been recommended reading by his Communist friends in Clydebank. He had gone along to meetings of the New Zealand Labour Party but left unimpressed. He thought of applying to join the Communist Party, but decided against it after reading some of their policies. But the Socialist Unity Party was different and he could relate to its policies and objectives. Although it was a very small organisation, some of New Zealand's key trade unionists were members, and its influence in trade union circles was substantial.

When Toner first started working for the PSA, many of its own members did not acknowledge the organisation as a union, and did not see themselves as trade unionists. Therefore much of the work of the field officers and branch activists was to convince the members of the need for a trade union approach to employment issues.

But by the 1990s the attitude of public-service workers had changed. They were radicalised by the repeal of the legislation differentiating public sector unions, by the introduction of state-owned enterprises, and by privatisation. They were more inclined to take industrial action and gradually the public sector unions became more militant than the rest of the trade union movement. In 1990 around a third of all strikes were in the public sector, but by 1995, 43 per cent of the stoppages involved public sector workers, although they only accounted for 20 per cent of the labour force.

Joe Toner had been climbing the ranks of the Public Services Association, which was the largest union in New Zealand by the mid-1990s. From field officer he became the Auckland regional secretary before taking charge of Wellington, the union's biggest region. A three-year spell as national operations manager was followed by his appointment as national secretary in 1996, part of a triumvirate that led the union. A new union management structure was introduced alongside the collaborative approach to employment relations. But during the next three years the PSA was engulfed in turmoil as the debate on the new strategy tore the union apart. Toner and his supporters believed that the partnership strategy offered a way for the union to consolidate itself as a strong and effective presence in the workplace and that without it, the union's decline would continue. But it was condemned by others who saw it as a betrayal of trade union principles and destined to fail. They argued that it was based on the flawed assumption that employers would be willing to compromise.

Toner's main adversary was another Scotsman, who was one of the most highly respected figures in the union. Alan Millar was a senior member of staff who had come through the ranks of the union from branch secretary to national executive and then to full-time official. He felt that those who were proposing changes to the structure and philosophy of the PSA had not lived through the battles others like him had fought. Although he had no objection to good working relationships or agreements with employers, he bitterly opposed the nature of the partnership agreement. He described the reformers as magical thinkers who were trying to build a pyramid from the top down.

Millar was born in North Berwick in 1940 and attended the local primary and secondary schools. Although an academically gifted pupil, he left school at fifteen after the death of his mother and joined the Merchant Navy as a cabin boy. On his first trip to New Zealand in 1956, he was so overwhelmed by the beauty of Auckland, that he jumped ship. But he was caught a few days later, and since he was only sixteen, was deported back to the UK. But he loved New Zealand so much he paid his own fare to return two years later. He found a job as a steel erector and joined the Boilermakers' Union, making a favourable impression on its leader, Con Devitt. Despite Devitt's encouragement to become more involved in the union, Millar did not see his future in construction. Instead, he left to train as a psychiatric nurse, and achieved the highest marks in the country for the written exams.

But his passion was trade unionism and he soon became one of the most vocal activists in the New Zealand health service. After several years on the national executive of the PSA, he was appointed a full-time official. One of his many achievements was the development of a computer programme for union organisation. The programme was used throughout the PSA and beyond, with Australian unions seeking Millar's assistance to set it up. Over the years he was promoted to become responsible for the overall management and organisation of one of the largest regions.

The divisions in the PSA caused Millar terrible angst and, after carefully weighing up all the options, he decided to resign at the age of fifty-six. The alternative would have meant leading a split in the union and he did not want to destroy the organisation he had helped to build. Nevertheless, he criticised the reformers in the union for believing that agreements would work if everyone was nice to each other, explaining 'It is OK for the lion to lie down with the lamb, but that only works until the lion get hungry. It is inevitable in our political system that politicians get hungry and once that happens the symbiotic relationship goes out the door. Governments control budgets and if there is limited finance they have to fear the trade union action that would be triggered by any attacks they make on workers' conditions.'

Despite the objections, the partnership approach and new structure was accepted as policy. Joe Toner wanted all officials, including those who had opposed the changes, to buy into the new strategy. He proposed that all jobs were declared vacant, including his own. The Executive Board reaffirmed their support for the partnership approach and wanted simply to confirm Toner's position as national secretary. But he insisted they advertised the job. Unfortunately for him, they followed his advice, and then appointed someone else, ending his PSA career in 1999. Alan Millar did not dislike Joe Toner, but he admitted experiencing a sense of *schadenfreude* when Toner lost his job.

Millar was one of the most colourful characters in the PSA, and was well known throughout the New Zealand trade union movement. Indeed, at one stage he was a member of four different unions at the same time. Apart from his job with the PSA, he was the staff representative in the Clerical Union, joined the National Union of Journalists when he worked as a freelance journalist, and did a bit of part-time acting, entitling him to be a member of Equity. He even appeared in a popular soap opera on New Zealand TV. Possessing a fierce intellect and an independent spirit, he considered himself a Marxist, but did not join any political party. In his seventies he was still full of energy and operated an employment relations consultancy whose motto was, 'We comfort the afflicted and afflict the comfortable.'

New government reverses right-wing policies

A few months after Joe Toner lost his job, his partnership strategy took off. A Labour-led coalition government was elected and eagerly embraced the concept. Helen Clark was the first woman to lead the Labour Party and her government signed three partnership agreements with the PSA. The first two laid the groundwork for more productive relationships, and the third agreement was designed to give the employees a stronger voice in the workplace. The partnership model of good workplace practice recognised that union members had an important investment in the success of their organisation. Soon partnership agreements were reached between other unions and employers. The Council of Trade Unions recommended them as the way forward to build decent, productive workplaces and quality jobs. Toner watched these developments from his new role as employee relations adviser with Christchurch city council.

One of the first changes in legislation submitted by the coalition was the repeal of the notorious Employment Contracts Act. On a point of principle Con Devitt's breakaway Trade Union Federation had refused to discuss rejoining the mainstream Council of Trade Unions while the Act was still in place. However, its abolition paved the way for a reunification of the trade union movement and Devitt, by then retired, was delighted by the *rapprochement*. Other legislation in the first term included the creation of the state-owned Kiwibank, and the renationalisation of the struggling Air New Zealand, which had been privatised in the '80s. Labour was re-elected in 2002 and turned its attention to other failed privatisations. New Zealand had been the first country in the world to fully privatise its railways, but for a decade after its sale there were stories of financial scandal, asset-stripping and neglect. The Rail and Maritime Transport Union campaigned to 'Take Back The Track' and won high levels of public support for railway renationalisation. In 2003 Labour renationalised the track, but the system was in such a poor state that it cost the government just $1 to buy it back. At the union's conference following the purchase, Jim Kelly, the union president, symbolically handed over a $1 coin to the minister of finance, Michael Cullin.

Kelly was born in 1946 and was brought up in Govan, Glasgow, where he attended Harmony Row School. His family were moved to Drumchapel under Glasgow's slum-clearance programme and he transferred to Summerhill Road primary and later Waverley secondary school in Knightswood. His father, a Communist Party member, was a shop steward in John Brown's in Clydebank, and secretary of his tenants' association. Although his father was a huge influence on him, Kelly never joined the Communist Party. After leaving school at fifteen he tried various jobs before starting an apprenticeship as a car mechanic at Hunter's garage in Whiteinch. The garage closed after a few years, but he managed to finish his time with the SMT bus company in Finnieston Street. He then joined the Merchant Navy as a ship's engineer until the birth of his first child, when he found a job in the railway workshops at Eastfield depot in Springburn.

The election of the Thatcher government in 1979 was the main reason Kelly emigrated. His parents had moved to New Zealand in 1969, along with his brother and sister, and had been pleading with him to join them. As Thatcher's policies started to cause industrial havoc in Scotland, Kelly could see no future for him or his two children, aged three and nine. In 1982 he arrived in Dunedin and found a job as a fitter at the Hillside railway workshop. Having been a shop steward in Springburn, he was soon active in union affairs. Then in 1985 a vacancy arose for branch secretary of the Railway Trades Association, one of four unions in the railway industry. After five years in that position, he was elected national president of the union. Alongside him was fellow Scotsman and general secretary Steve Grant, from Fife. The railway unions were historically moderate, but the government knew that any strike action could paralyse the country in a short space of time. In 1993, after privatisation, the rail company attempted to renegotiate a deal struck before the introduction of the Employment Contracts Act with a view to changing conditions and pay rates. It only took a one-day strike, which closed the entire rail and ferry network, to force the company to withdraw their proposals.

By 1992, three of the four railway unions had amalgamated and Kelly was elected president of the combined organisation. Then in 1995, the fourth union, the National Union of Railwaymen, joined as well, to form the Rail and Maritime Transport Union, and Kelly was again elected president. The success of the 'Take Back the Track' campaign was continued in order to persuade the public and the government to take the final step and renationalise the whole industry. In 2008 the campaign ended in victory when the entire rail and ferry system was taken back into public ownership and renamed KiwiRail. The Helen Clark government was also responsible for the reform of labour and social legislation. She encouraged members of her cabinet to attend union conferences and was keen to put her views directly to union activists. She brought a number of women into government and others were encouraged to participate in the Labour Party. Patricia Webster, who came from Edinburgh, was senior vice-president of the party from 1993–94 and again from 2000–2006 and contributed significantly to Labour's success.

Born in the city's West Port district before moving to Burdiehouse, Webster attended St John's primary school in Fernieside and Holycross secondary in Trinity. She studied to be a PE teacher and, after leaving teacher-training college, taught at Stirling High School. In 1972 she met and fell in love with a computer programmer from Edinburgh who had been working in Wellington. He gave her a glowing account of life in New Zealand and after they married she was happy to move there. At first she loved the country, but then became homesick, a common emotion felt by many immigrants. The couple returned to Scotland but by 1977 they missed New Zealand so much they went back. As soon as they returned, Webster decided to take a more active part in the Labour Party and the teacher's union at the college where she worked.

At constituency level, work to modernise canvassing techniques was carried out by her husband, John Webster. He developed a computerised system for recording canvassing returns, which was adopted by the party nationally. By the time Labour won the 1984 election, Pat Webster had left teaching and was appointed Wellington organiser of the Labour Party. Two years later she was responsible for trade union liaison and communications. This was during the period of the Lange government's

Pat Webster with Prime Minister Helen Clark. Webster, from Edinburgh, was senior vice-president of the New Zealand Labour Party from 1993–94 and again from 2000–2006. During the latter period, she helped to overhaul the party's organisation, contributing significantly to Labour's success in winning three general elections in a row, the first time this was achieved in its history.

economic policies, and she found the task of persuading the unions to remain loyal to the Labour Party almost impossible. Some key trade unionists left and joined the New Labour Party when it was formed in 1988, and it was hardly surprising that she was burnt out by the time Labour lost the general election in 1990.

Two years later a revitalised Webster joined the Council of Trade Unions as communications officer. The organisation was struggling with the fallout from the split over how to deal with the Employment Contracts Act. That same year she was voted on to the Labour Party's national executive, and a year later she successfully stood as the left candidate for senior vice-chairperson. She played a prominent strategic role during the next decade, and became more involved in the governance and restructuring of the party, which was especially important with the looming introduction of proportional representation. The position of trade union affiliates in party decision-making was under threat from some of the so-called modernisers, and Webster devised a method to maintain a significant trade union role. But then in 1994 a unique opportunity arose to become executive director of the Council for International Development, the umbrella organisation for NGOs in New Zealand. Webster relished the challenge, but was forced to resign her senior Labour Party role due to a perceived conflict of interest.

Party organisation had begun to weaken, and shortly after the election of a Labour-led administration in 1999, she was persuaded by her trade union colleagues to run again for senior vice-president of the party. After an intense battle, she won the election, and remained in the position unopposed until she resigned in 2006. During this period, the party organisation was stabilised and Labour went on to win three general elections in a row, the first time this was achieved in its history. Many people contributed to this period of success, and Pat Webster was credited by the leadership for the part she played.

In 2008 Labour lost the election and the National Party formed a government. One of its first acts was to withdraw from the partnership agreements with the PSA and embark on a series of cuts in public spending. However, the Council of Trade Unions retains its healthy fighting spirit, and although much diminished in size, continues to campaign as vociferously as ever.

Toby Hill died of a heart attack in 1977 at sixty-two years of age. The Cooks and Stewards' Union named a welfare hospital after him. From the moment he took over the leadership of the Waterside Workers

Union, Hill was pilloried by the press and demonised as part of the Red peril threatening New Zealand. His comeback was a tribute to his ability and to his deeply held commitment to the principles of trade unionism. It was said that his untimely death occurred before he had fully achieved a cult status within the New Zealand trade union and labour movement. It is claimed that he would have had a major hand in preventing the betrayals during the Lange government. His son Gerry Hill was elected to the national executive of the Cooks and Stewards Union in the 1980s where Scotsman Eddie Aitkin was the national president and Charlie Lyons from Glasgow was the South Island representative. After an amalgamation with the Seamen's Union in 1988, Gerry Hill served on the national executive of the Seafarers' Union until 2000.

Conclusion

Many of the characters in this book are unknown in Scotland but their contributions are celebrated by the organisations they helped build. Monuments have been erected in their memory and union buildings named after them, as well as streets, districts, university centres, and schools. Those mentioned were selected because of the availability of information about them and because they were prominent in the organisations researched. But as Chapter 3, pp 74-107, on the United Autoworkers mentions, every toolroom in Detroit during the 1930s seemed to have a shop steward who answered to the name Scottie or Jock. This level of Scottish input was replicated in the coal mines, engineering shops, shipyards, and construction sites wherever the Scots settled. These industries were particular sectors of Scottish influence but as trade unionism developed in the public services there were also significant Scottish contributions. Naturally, as the indigenous population gained experience they took over many of the roles once held by immigrants.

Scottish emigration to the United States declined after the 1930s, but Canada, Australia and New Zealand remain attractive destinations for many young Scots. Scottish participation in the labour movements of these countries continues, but it is unlikely to reach the scale of the past. Scots once had the advantage of being amongst the few immigrants who had industrial and trade union experience. They also had a head start politically, but the days are long gone when Scottish shop stewards attended lunch-time meetings or evening classes on Marxism, economics, and politics. Immigrants from other countries are now more likely to be better equipped for the level of dedication and sacrifices made by Scots in the past.

Perhaps that level of commitment is required now if the decline of trade unionism is to be halted. The four countries studied have, like Scotland, suffered a serious drop in trade union membership and influence over the past thirty years. Since the 1980s they have been faced with a number of inter-related problems including the contraction of manufacturing, the privatisation of nationalised industries, and hostile anti-union legislation. The sectors where unions have been traditionally strong have diminished and the weakest area is the newer fast-growing private service sector where trade unionism is often non-existent. There are few of the lengthy strikes of the past and workers are less willing to undergo weeks or months without pay. It is a long time since employers could evict workers from their company-owned property during a strike, but home ownership has added new financial pressure for those on strike. The fear of losing much the capital invested in their houses or even having them repossessed by banks and building societies has often inhibited workers from taking militant action. However, as readers will have noted, the labour movement faced more demanding problems in the past and came back stronger.

The main purpose of this book is to record the determination, sacrifices and unqualified heroism of many Scottish migrants who passionately believed in the cause for which they fought. No attempt was made to compare the Scottish input with that from the English regions, Wales, Ireland or other European countries with large diasporas. But there is ample anecdotal evidence that the Scots exerted an influence that was disproportionate to their numbers. This book acknowledges their contribution and gives them their proper place in Scottish history.

Sources

Chapter 1

Books

Babson, R.W., *William B Wilson and the Department of Labor*, (New York: Bretano's, 1919)

Campbell, Alan, *Lanarkshire Miners: a social history of their trade unions, 1775-1974*, (Edinburgh: John Donald, 1974)

Fink, Gary M., *Biographical Dictionary of American Labor*, (Westport, London: Greenwood, 1984)

Laslett, John H. M., *The United Mineworkers of America, a Model of Industrial Solidarity?* (Pennsylvania USA: Pennsylvania State University Press, 1996)

Laslett, John H. M., *Colliers Across the Sea: a comparative study of class formation in Scotland and the American Midwest, 1830-1924*, (Urbana: University of Illinois Press, 2000)

Roy, Andrew, *History of the Coal Miners of the United States*, (Cornell University, 1907)

Sexton, John L., *History of Tioga County*

Zieger, Robert H., *John L Lewis*, (Boston: Twayne Publishers, 1988)

Online

William Wilson Story: http://www.blossburg.org/wb_wilson/thestory.htm

The Samuel Gompers Papers: http://www.history.umd.edu/Gompers/books.htm

US Dept of Labor: History: http://www.dol.gov/oasam/programs/history/dolchp01.htm

City of Braidwood: www.braidwood.us/braidwood%20history.htm

United Mine Workers of America: History: http://www.umwa.org/index.php?q=content/lattimer-massacre

Chapter 2

Books

Allen, Douglas J., *Industrial Unionism in a Twentieth Century City: The Background and Development of the CIO in Buffalo, NY, 1936-42*, (Unpublished M.A. Thesis: Edinburgh University History Dept, 1973)

Angelo, Pat, *Philip Murray: Union Man*, (Pat Angelo, 2003)

Chaplin, Jenny, *The Blantyre Calamity: the mine explosion of 1877*, (Scots Magazine, Vol. 137, No 7, Oct, 1992)

Clark, Paul F., *Forging a Union of Steel*, (New York: Cornell University, 1987)

Cook, Roy A. P., *Leaders of Labor*, (Philadelphia: Lippincott, 1966)

Fink, Gary M., *Biographical Dictionary of American Labor*, (Westport, London: Greenwood Press, 1974)

Laslett, John M., *The United Mineworkers of America, A Model of Industrial Solidarity*, (Pennsylvania USA: Pennsylvania State University, 1996)

Nasaw, David, *Andrew Carnegie*, (New York: Penguin, 2007)

Palmer, David, *Organising the Shipyards: Union Strategy in Three Northeast Ports, 1933-1945*, (Ithaca, NY: Cornell University Press, 1999)

Senior, Hereward, *Constabulary*, (Toronto: Dundurn Press, 2004)

Tate, J. D., *Philip Murray as a Labor Leader*, (Unpublished PhD Thesis, New York University)

Williamson, John, *Dangerous Scot*, (New York: International Publishers, 1969)

Yellen, Samuel, *American Labor Struggles*, (New York: Hardcourt Brace and Co, 1936)

Zieger, Robert H., *The CIO, 1935-1955* (Carolina USA: University of North Carolina Press, 1995)

Newspaper/Other Sources

Undated letter, probably to John Brophy, University of Maryland

Blantyre Newspaper, Nov 1952.

Daily Mirror, 15/1/1963.

Letter Kramer to John Brophy, Dec 28, 1936, McKeldin Library, Univ of Maryland.
Recorded Interviews

Doyle, Jack, nephew of Charlie Doyle.

Online

Fried, Emmanuel, *Democratic Leaders at a Fork in the Road*, (Emmanuel Friedcenter, 2007), http://www.autodidactproject.org/other/mfried/dems07.html.

http://www.grahamstephenson.me.uk/ Charlie Doyle.

Administrative History Paper, IUMSWA, University of Maryland, http://hdl.handle.net/1903.1/1707

Chapter 3

Books

Aitken, Keith, *The Bairns O' Adam - the Story of the STUC*, (Edinburgh: Polygon, 1997)

Babson, Steve, *Building the Union: skilled workers and the Anglo-Gaelic immigrants in the rise of the UAW*, (New Brunswick: Rutgers University Press, 1991)

Barnard, John, *Walter Reuther and the Rise of the Auto Workers*, (Boston, Toronto: Little Brown and Co, 1983)

Devine, T. M., *Scottish Emigration and Scottish Society*, (Edinburgh: J Donald, 1992)

Foner, Philip S., *US Labor and the Vietnam War*, (New York: International Publishers, 1989)

Greaves, C. Desmond, *The Life and Times of James Connolly*, (London: Lawrence and Wishart, 1972)

Walsh, Pat, *Essay Labor Roots Course-George Campbell*, Wayne State University, L600 class, fall 1985.

Recorded Interviews

Fraser, Douglas, June 1999.

Newspapers/Journals

Detroit Free Press, 3/4/1987

Online

Ford website: http://www.thehenryford.org/rouge/historyofrouge.aspx.
William McAulay family website: http://mcaulay-james.o1913-2002ancestry.home.
sprynet.com/id12.html.

Chapter 4

Books

Benn, Caroline, *Keir Hardie*, (London: Richard Cohen, 1997)
Campbell, Alan, *Scottish Miners 1874-1939. Vol. 2. Trade unions and politics*, (Aldershot: Ashgate, 2000)
Frank, David, *J B McLachlan: a Biography*, (Toronto, Ont: James Lorimer, 1999)
MacEwan, Paul, *Miners and Steelworkers: Labour in Cape Breton*, (Toronto: S. Stevens, 1976)
McIntosh, Robert, *Boys in the Pits: Child Labour in Coal Mines*, (Montreal and Kingston: McGill-Queen's University Press, 2000)
McKay, Ian , *Labour/Le Travail*, (No 18, Fall 1986)

Newspaper/Journal Sources

The Sydney Post, (12/6/1925).

Online Sources

Dictionary of Canadian Biography Online http://www.biographi.ca/index-e.html

Chapter 5

Books

Borden, Robert Laird, *Memoirs*, (Toronto: McMillan, 1938)
Gallagher, William, *Revolt on the Clyde*, (Lawrence and Wishart, 1936).
Heron, Craig, *The Canadian Labour Movement: a Short History*, (Toronto: J Lorimer, 1989)
Lazarus, Morden, *Up From the Ranks*, (Toronto: Co-Operative Press Associates, 1977)
McEwen, Tom, *The Forge Glows Red*, (Toronto: Progress Books, 1974)
Manley, John, *A British Communist MP in Canada*, (University of Lancashire)
Morton, Desmond, *Working People*, (Montreal, London: McGill-Queen's University Press, 1998)
Osborne, Kenneth W., *R B Russell and the Labour Movement*, (Agincourt, Canada: The Book Society of Canada, 1978)
Scott, Jack, *A Communist Life*, (St John's Nfld: Cttee on Canadian Labour History, 1988)

Online

Nationmaster Encyclopaedia. http://www.nationmaster.com/encyclopedia/Springburn
Canadian Museum of Civilisation Online Exibition-Canadian Labour History, 1850-1999, http://www.civilization.ca/cmc/exhibitions/hist/labour/lab01e.shtml
Bennett, Joshua, *Canadian National Security: Legislations vs. Practices 1919-1946*, Royal Military College of Canada,

http://www.cda-cdai.ca/cdai/uploads/cdai/2009/04/bennet03.pdf

Dishaw, Garnet, Encyclopaedia of Saskatchewan, http://esask.uregina.ca/entry/estevan_coal_strike.html

Socialist History Project, *They Fought For Labour, Now Interned*, 1941, http://www.marxistsfr.org/history//canada/socialisthistory/Docs/CPC/WW2/FoughtFor.htm.

Canadian Encyclopaedia-online, *The CCL*, http://www.thecanadianencyclopedia.com/index.cfm?PgNm=TCE&Params=A1ARTA0001273.

A History of the United Steelworkers in Canada, socserv2.socsi.mcmaster.ca/labourstudies.

George Siammandos, *Winnipeg Time Machine Website*, RB Russell. http://www.thecanadianencyclopedia.com/

Bumstead, J. M., Multicultural Canada-Encyclopaedia of Canada's Peoples online-William Cooper. http://www.multiculturalcanada.ca/ecp/

Chapter 6

Books

Avakumovic, Ivan, *The Communist Party of Canada: a history*, (Toronto: McClelland and Stewart, 1975)

McLeod, Thomas H. and McLeod, Ian, *Tommy Douglas: the road to Jerusalem*, (Edmonton: Hurtig, 1987)

Mardiros, Anthony, *William Irvine: the life of a prairie radical*, (Toronto: J Lorimer, 1979)

Margoshes, Dave, *Tommy Douglas: building the new society*, (Series, The Quest Library; 4, 1999)

Palmer, Bryan, *Jack Scott and the Canadian workers movement 1927-1985*, (St John's Nfld: Committee on Canadian History 1988).

Rodney, William, *Soldiers of the International: a history of the Communist party of Canada, 1919-1929*, (Toronto: University of Toronto Press, 1968)

Shackleton, Doris, *Tommy Douglas*, (Toronto: McClelland and Stewart 1975)

Online

Canadian Broadcasting Corporation - The Greatest Canadian, http://www.cbc.ca/greatest/

http://www.falkirkonline.net/For%20Visitors/Heritage/Carron%20Iron%20Works.aspx

George Siamandas, *The Winnipeg Time Machine*, http://winnipegtimemachine.com/wtm/

Jean Larmour, *Saskatchewan Doctors Strike*, Canadian Encyclopaedia, http://www.thecanadianencyclopedia.com/index.cfm?PgNm=TCE&Params=A1ARTA0007155.

Chapter 7

Books

Davidson, J., *Joe Davidson*, (Toronto: James Lorimer & Co, 1978)

Freeman, Bill and Hewitt, Marsha, *Their Town*, (Lorimer, 1979)

Lazarus, Morden, *Up From The Ranks*, (Ontario, Co-op Press Associates, 1977)

Recorded Interviews

Donaldson, John, November 2008.
Gordon, John, November 2008.
Hynd, Harry, October 2008.
Nelson, Eddie, November 2008.

Newspapers/Journals

Donaldson, John, *Our Times*, Sept 1984.
McKetcher, Catherine, *Canadian Journal of Communications*, vol 30, no2, 2005.

Online

A History of the United Steelworkers in Canada website, socserv2.socsi.mcmaster.ca/
labourstudies
Canadian Museum of Civilisation Online Exibition-Canadian Labour History, 1850-
1999, http://www.civilization.ca/cmc/exhibitions/hist/labour/lab01e.shtml
Hamilton history - Found Locally Website, www.foundlocally.com/Hamilton
Ontario Government website, http://www.ontario.ca/en/about_
ontario/004593?openNav=economy

Chapter 8

Books

Buckley, K. D., *The Amalgamated Engineers in Australia, 1852-1920* (Canberra: Dept
Economic History, Australian Nat Univ, 1970)
Devine, T. M., *The Scottish Nation 1700-2000*, (London: Penguin, 1999)
Gollan, Robin, *Radical and working class politics: a study of Eastern Australia, 1850-1910*,
(Carlton, Victoria: Melbourne University Press, 1967)
Hearn, Mark and Knowles, Harry, *One big union : a history of the Australian Workers
Union, 1886-1994*, (Cambridge: Cambridge University Press, 1996)
Jilbert, Allison R., *Transportation and Travelling Conditions for Immigration to Australia
in the 1880s*, (Port Adelaide: S Australia Museum, 1997).
Merritt, John, *The making of the AWU*, (Melbourne: Oxford Oxford University Press,
1986)
Serle, Geoffrey, *The rush to be rich; a history of the colony of Victoria, 1883-1889*,
(Melbourne: Melbourne University Press, 1971)

Newspapers/Journals

Red & Black - an anarchist journal, Summer 1978/79

Australian Dictionary of Biography

Bartlett, Geoffrey, 'Grant, James Macpherson (1822 -1885)', ADB Volume 4,
Melbourne University Press, 1972.
Bartlett, Geoffrey, 'McCulloch, Sir James (1819 -1893)', ADB Volume 5, Melbourne
University Press, 1974.
Beever, Margot 'Gillies, Duncan (1834 -1903)', ADB Volume 4, Melbourne University
Press, 1972
Gollan, Robin 'Fletcher, James (1834 -1891)', ADB Volume 4, Melbourne University
Press, 1972

Guyatt, Joy 'Lane, Ernest Henry (1868 -1954)', ADB Volume 9, Melbourne University Press, 1983.

Lansbury, Coral & Nairn, Bede 'Spence, William Guthrie (1846 -1926)', ADB Volume 6, Melbourne University Press, 1976

Merrifield, S. 'Don, Charles Jardine (1820 -1866)', ADB Volume 4, Melbourne University Press, 1972.

Murphy, D.J. 'Fisher, Andrew (1862 -1928)', ADB Volume 8, Melbourne University Press, 1981

Nairn, Bede 'Cameron, Angus (1847 -1896)', ADB Volume 3, Melbourne University Press, 1969.

Online

Arts Victoria Eight Hour Day Anniversary 2006 http://www.8hourday.org.au/about.asp

Australian Christian lobby, http://www.acl.org.au/national/browse.stw?article_id=14712.

Australian Government: Australian Stories-Eureka Stockade: http://www.cultureandrecreation.gov.au/articles/eurekastockade/.

Harvie, J., Ballarat history, www.ballarat.com/history.htm.

National Library of Australia: http://www.nla.gov.au/epubs/waltzingmatilda/

People in Mining, http://www.mininghall.com/MiningHallOfFame/HallOfFameDatabase/Inductee.php?InducteeID=1213.

Victorian Cultural Collaboration, SBS Gold, http://www.sbs.com.au/gold/.

Chapter 9

Books

Bastian, Peter, *Andrew Fisher: an underestimated man*, (Sydney: UNSW Press, 2009)

Crisp, Leslie Findlay, *The Australian Federal Labor Party, 1901-1951*, (London: Longmans, 1955)

Davidson, Alistair, *The Communist Party of Australia; a Short History*, (Stanford, Calif. : Hoover Institution Press, 1969)

Day, David, *Andrew Fisher: Prime Minister of Australia*, (London: Fourth Estate, 2008)

McKinlay, Brian, *A century of struggle : the A.L.P., a centenary history*, (Blackburn: Collins Dove, 1988)

Macintyre, Stuart, *Reds*, (Sydney: Allen and Unwin, 1998)

Malkin, John, *Andrew Fisher, 1862-1928*, (Ayrshire: S.L. s.n. David Walker & Connell Ltd. Printers, 1980)

Murdoch, John, *A million to one against: a portrait of Andrew Fisher*, (London: Minerva, 1998)

Pelling, Henry, *A Short History of the Labour Party*, (London: McMillan, 1965)

Newspapers/Journals

MacIntyre, Stuart, *Australian Studies*, Vol. 12, No2, Winter 1997

Online

Australian Trade Union archives http://www.atua.org.au/archives/ALE1095a.html

Curthoys, Barbara, *Labour History*, Sydney number 64, May 1993. http://members.optushome.com.au/spainter/Curthoys.html.

Cook, Peter 'Guthrie, Robert Storrie (1857 -1921)', ADB Volume 9, Melbourne University Press, 1983.1

Costar, B.J.'Smith, William Forgan (Bill) (1887 -1953)', ADB Volume 11, Melbourne University Press, 1988

Dingsdag, Don 'Nelson, Charles (1896? -1948)', ADB Volume 10, Melbourne University Press, 1986 3

Dingsdag, Don 'Orr, William (1900 -1954)', ADB, Volume 11, Melbourne University Press, 1988 2

Edgar, Suzanne 'McPherson, John Abel (1860 -1897)', ADB Volume 10, Melbourne University Press, 1986

Edgar, Suzanne 'Hutchison, James (1859 -1909)', ADB Volume 9, Melbourne University Press, 1983.

Farrell, Frank 'Grant, Donald McLennan (1888 -1970)', ADB Volume 9, Melbourne University Press, 1983, pp 75-76.

Fitzhardinge, L. F. 'Hughes, William Morris (Billy) (1862 -1952)', ADB Volume 9, Melbourne University Press, 1983.

Grainger, G. C. 'Newland, Sir John (1864 -1932)', ADB Volume 11, Melbourne University Press, 1988.

Grainger, G. C. 'McGregor, Gregor (1848 -1914)', ADB Volume 10, Melbourne University Press, 1986.

Lee, Andrew 'Fraser, James McIntosh (1889 -1961)', ADB Volume 14, Melbourne University Press, 1996.

Macintyre, Stuart 'Miles, John Bramwell (Jack) (1888 -1969)', ADB Volume 15, Melbourne University Press, 2000.7

Murphy, D. J. 'Kidston, William (1849 -1919)', ADB Volume 9, Melbourne University Press, 1983 3

Murphy, D. J. 'Fisher, Andrew (1862 -1928)', ADB Volume 8, Melbourne University Press, 1981. 5

Nairn, Bede 'Black, George Mure (1854 -1936)', ADB Volume 7, Melbourne University Press, 1979.2

Nairn, Bede 'Garden, John Smith (Jock) (1882 -1968)', ADB Volume 8, Melbourne University Press, 1981 4

Smith, Howard J. 'de Largie, Hugh (1859 -1947)', ADB Volume 8, Melbourne University Press, 1981.

Spaull, Andrew 'Dedman, John Johnstone (1896 -1973)', ADB Volume 13, Melbourne University Press, 1993

Turner, Ann 'Earsman, William Paisley (1884 -1965)', ADB Volume 8, Melbourne University Press, 1981 2

Chapter 10

Books

Aitken, Keith, *The Bairns o' Adam: the story of the STUC,* (Edinburgh: Polygon, 1997)

Buckley, K.D., *The Amalgamated Engineers in Australia, 1852-1920,* (Canberra: Australian National University, 1970)

Hammerton, A. James, and Thomson, Alistair, *Ten pound Poms: Australia's invisible migrants* (Manchester: Manchester University Press, 2005)

Muir, Kathie *Worth Fighting For*, (Sydney: University NSW, 2008)

Sheridan, T., *Mindful militants-the Amalgamated Engineering Union in Australia, 1920-1972* (Cambridge: Cambridge University Press 1975).

Newspapers/Journals

Argus, 1/9/1890.

Robinson, Paul, *The Age*, 26/3/2004

Recorded Interviews

Cameron, Doug, May 2006

Ferguson, Jock February 2007

Correspondence

Davidson, Jim

Fraser, Ian

Gray, David

Oliver, Bill

Parkin, John

Rowland, Doug

Sibbald, Danny

Wilson, George

Online

Australian Socialist Party http://www.socialistpartyaustralia.org/archives/317.

Mac Yourselfathome, political blogger, http://moderatelyleft.blogspot.com/

Green Left http://www.greenleft.org.au/2007/717/37239

Parliament of Australia, Senate - Doug Cameron aph.gov.au/senate/senators/homepages/first_speech/sfs-AI6.htm

Dept Immigration and Citizenship 2007. http://www.immi.gov.au/media/fact-sheets/08abolition.htm

Australian Dictionary of Biography

Ferguson, Audrey 'Dalgleish, Daniel Cameron (1827 -1870)', ADB Volume 4, Melbourne University Press, 1972

Saffin, N.W. 'Bennet, David (1830 -1915)', ADB Volume 3, Melbourne University Press, 1969

Other Sources

John Shields' database 2006:

a) Campbell, William, by Andrew Moore

b) Scott, John Lyden by Allison Murchie

Chapter 11

Books

Bassett, Michael, *Tomorrow comes the song: a life of Peter Fraser*, (Auckland: Penguin Books, 2000)

Binney, Judith, *An Illustrated History of New Zealand 1820-1920*, (Wellington: Allen and Unwin, 1990)

Clark, Margaret, *Peter Fraser*, (Palmerston North: Dunmore Press, 1998)

Gustafson, Barry, *From the Cradle to the Grave: a biography of Michael Joseph Savage*, (Auckland: Penguine Books, 1988)

Gustafson, Barry, *Labour's path to political independence*, (Auckland: Auckland University Press, 1980)

Hobbs, Leslie, *The Thirty Year Wonders*, (Christchurch: Whitcombe and Tombs)

Kelly, Daniel J., *Peter Fraser*, (Wellington: Reed, 1968)

Taylor, Marjorie E., *Peter Fraser: Hill of Fearn*, (Fearn: Fearn Community Council, 2006).

Online

An Encyclopaedia of New Zealand 1966: www.teara.govt.nz/1966

Dictionary of New Zealand Biography, www.dnzb.govt.nz

Chapter 12

Books

Grant, David, *The Big Blue: snapshots of the 1951 waterfront lockout*, (Christchurch: Canterbury University Press and the Trade Union History Project, 2004)

Hobbs, Leslie, *The Thirty Year Wonders*, (Christchurch: Whitcombe and Tombs Ltd, 1967), Chapter McLagan-Man of Iron.

Olssen, Erik, *The Red Feds: revolutionary industrial unionism and the New Zealand Federation of Labour, 1908-14*, (Auckland: Auckland Oxford University Press, 1988)

Richardson, Len, *Coal, class and community: the United Mineworkers of New Zealand, 1880-1960*, (Auckland: Auckland University Press, 1995)

Roth, Herbert, *Trade unions in New Zealand, past and present*, (Wellington: Reed Education, 1973)

Scott, Sid, *Rebel In A Wrong Cause*, (Auckland: Collins Bros. & Co Ltd)

Online

Amalgamated Workers Union NZ-History. URL:www.awunz.org.nz/history

Dictionary of New Zealand Biography, updated 22/6/2007: Bruce, Cornwell, Dowgray, hill, McLagan, Miller - URL:http://www.dnzb.govt.nz.

Correspondence

Correspondence, son of Agnes Duffy.

Chapter 13

Books

Bolger, Jim, *A View From the Top: My Seven Years as Prime Minister*, (Auckland; New York: Viking, 1998).

Brooking, Tom, *The History of New Zealand*, (Westport, Con; London: Greenwood Press, 2004).

Clark, Margaret, *For the Record: Lange and the Forth Labour Government*, (Wellington, NZ: Dunmore Press, 2005).

Clark, Margaret, *Sir Keith Holyoake, Towards a Political Biography*, (Palmerston North, NZ: Dunmore Press).

Fairbrother, Peter and Rainnie, A., *Globalisation, state and labour*, (London and New York: Routledge, 2006)

Franks, Peter, *Print and Politics: A History of Trade Unions In New Zealand Printing Industry, 1865-1995*, (Wellington: Victoria University Press, 2001.

Gustafson, Barry, *His Way: a Biography of Robert Muldoon*, (Auckland: Auckland University Press, 2000)

Gustafson, Barry, *Kiwi Keith*, (Auckland: Auckland University Press, 2007)

Lange, David, *My life/David Lange*, (Auckland; London: Viking, 2005)

Levine, Stephen I., and McRobie, Alan, *From Muldoon to Lange: New Zealand Elections in the 1980s*, (Rangoria, NZ: MC Enterprises, 2002)

Sinclair, Keith and Dalziel, Raewyn, *A History of New Zealand*, (Auckland, London: Penguin, 2000)

Walsh, Pat, *Pioneering New Zealand Labour History: Essays in Honour of Bert Roth*, (Palmerston North, NZ: Dunmore Press, 1994)

Wilson, Margaret A., *Labour in Government 1984-87*, (Wellington, NZ: Allen and Unwin, 1989)

Online

New Zealand Parliament Research Papers - Trade Union Numbers and Membership Trends, 21st March, 2000. http://www.parliament.nz/en-NZ/ParlSupport/ResearchPapers/b/c/4/bc49498b300b4079b860b3101595064f.htm

PSA Website, Partnership Agreements, http://www.psa.org.nz/Campaigns/Partnership_for_Quality.aspx

Correspondence

Devitt, Con
Grant, Steve
McCrory, Hugh

Recorded Interviews

Kelly, Jim
Millar, Allan
Toner, Joe
Webster, Pat

Newspaper/Journals

New Zealand Herald, 24/9/2005-John Findlay.

Index

Y

Lightning Source UK Ltd.
Milton Keynes UK
UKOW07f0647281114

242329UK00006B/81/P

Scotland's Radical Exports

"I am exceptionally proud of all of Scotland's achievements and particularly the different ways in which Scots have helped to shape the modern world. Scotland's contribution to the Trades Union movement and enhancing the rights of workers - at home and around the globe - is hugely significant. It is important that these stories are captured and celebrated."— Alex Salmond, First Minister of Scotland

"Much has been written about Scotland's contribution to the development of the modern world, in science and literature, in trade – good and bad, and of course, in enterprise and philanthropy. This book adds another important chapter to that remarkable history – to the values we shared and the inspirational individuals who spread them far and wide."— Lord Jack McConnell, First Minister of Scotland, 2001-2007

"This excellent book is an opportunity to look at trade unionism and working class politics in the Scottish Diaspora. Wherever they travelled the Scots helped workers organise and build better lives for themselves and their families. This is a story which reflects well on Scotland and one we should be proud of."— Henry McLeish, First Minister of Scotland, 2000-2001

"This book is a fascinating and timely contribution to the history of the Scottish people. Scottish men and women leaving these shores have carried their commitment to organising labour with them, and have left their mark wherever they have settled.

Because of the way history is recorded and leadership defined, it is inevitable that the stories of male leaders are the most accessible when we reach into the past. A more recent history of labour would see ever more women in the forefront of the picture, but we are aware of the hidden women of the past who paved our way for us on so many fronts."— Pat Stuart, chair of the Trades Union Congress Women's Committee

"Pat Kelly's book brings to our attention the stories of people who took trade unionism and working class politics from Scotland to the countries where they settled. We can be justly proud of the achievements of these deeply committed and courageous Scots who helped build crucial democratic institutions. The book is well written and entertaining and I would recommend it to trade unionists and anyone with an interest in the Scottish Diaspora." —Campbell Christie, former general secretary, Scottish Trades Union Congress

Scotland's Radical Exports

The Scots abroad — how they shaped
politics and trade unions

Pat Kelly

FORMERLY SCOTTISH SECRETARY OF THE
PUBLIC AND COMMERCIAL SERVICES UNION
AND
PRESIDENT OF THE
SCOTTISH TRADES UNION CONGRESS

The Grimsay Press

The Grimsay Press
an imprint of
Zeticula
57 St Vincent Crescent
Glasgow
G3 8NQ
Scotland.

http://www.thegrimsaypress.co.uk
admin@thegrimsaypress.co.uk

First published 2011.

ISBN-13 978-1-84530-110-1